Pvt. Ltd.

Innovation and Education

Dr. Virendra K. Goswami
Former Vice Chancellor: Sangam University & Sunrise University
Founder President 'Environment & Peace Foundation'
F-82, Sector-41, Noida – 201 303

&

Dr. Rashmi Jain
Department of Sociology
University of Rajasthan
Jaipur – 302 004

•

Executive Editor
Dr. J N Govil

2018

Studium Press (India) Pvt. Ltd.

Innovation and Education

ISBN: 978-93-85046-04-9

Published by:

Studium Press (India) Pvt. Ltd.
4735/22, 2nd Floor, Prakash Deep Building
(Near Delhi Medical Association),
Ansari Road, Darya Ganj, New Delhi-110 002
Tel.: + 91-11-43240200-15 (15 lines); Fax: 91-11-43240215
E-mail: studiumpress@gmail.com

Printed at India

About the Editors

Dr. V.K. Goswami, Ph.D. Indian Institute of Technology (IIT), Kharagpur, MS from the University of Wisconsin, USA. Post Doctorate Fellow (PDF) at the University of Illinois, Chicago, USA. 'Visiting Scientist' to United Nations Industrial Development Organization (UNIDO), ICTP, Italy. Expert Panelist International Civil Aviation Organization (ICAO), Canada and United Nations. *Dr. Virendra Goswami worked at Space Science Engineering Centre, NASA NOAA (National Oceanic Atmospheric Administration) at University of Wisconsin, USA. Also, Special Invitee by the World Meteorological Organization (WMO) of United Nations, Geneva in 2001. Special Invitee in Apr'15 at NPW: NCAR USA. Expert panelist of Association of Indian Universities (AIU), Vice Chancellor: Sangam & Sunrise Universities. Had been, Director General of Management Institutes & Director of Engineering Institutes as well as Vice-President Havells India Ltd. Ph. D&M. Tech Examiner at Centre of Energy Studies at IIT Delhi. Editor in Chief: Journal of Advanced Research in Alternative Energy, Environment and Ecology, Founder President' Environment & Peace Foundation (EPF) & Hon. Director ICMEI (International Chamber of Media & Entertainment Industry).* Presented Papers in the field of Chemical Technology, Atmospheric Sciences, Space Sciences, Satellite Application, Control of Global Warming & Quality Higher Education at International and National Conferences held in India, USA, UK Latin America, South Africa, Canada and Europe (more than 27 countries of all the Continents). Chaired Sessions/Guest Speaker in *Int. Natl. Conf.* & National Conferences. More than 44 years of teaching, research and administrative experience at Home and Abroad.

Dr Rashmi Jain, Director, Centre for the Study of Social Exclusion and Inclusive policy, and Associate Professor, Department of Sociology, University of Rajasthan, Jaipur has her interest in the area of Development Communication, Gender studies, Sociology of Law, leisure studies and European Studies. She has been regularly taking part in conferences and

seminars both in the country and abroad and has been active in organizing national and international conferences. Her published work includes 'Communicating Rural Development- Strategies and Alternatives' and more than 20 research papers in national and international journals. She is Convener of research committee on Sociology of Law of Indian Sociological Society. Besides being an academician, she has been working for raising voice for destitute women and citizen's issues by collaborating with civil society organizations of Rajasthan. She is also member of Ethics committee for clinical trials at Monilek Hospital and Research Centre and member of several bodies of the University and state government.

Dr. J.N. Govil *(b. 1945)*: Obtained his Master's and Doctorate degrees from Agra University, Agra, India. In his career span of 41 years research experience at the Indian Agricultural Research Institute, New Delhi, Dr. Govil has been involved in the breeding of cross-pollinated, often cross-pollinated, and self-pollinated crops. His research was mainly focused on breeding for better quality, disease resistance, and for higher productivity in *Pennisetum, Sorghum,* maize, chickpea, and pigeonpea. During these years at IARI, he has released nine varieties of early pigeonpea in arhar-wheat rotation. Dr. Govil has been well exposed to the international scientific community through various programmes at UK, Denmark and Thailand. He also participated in various international seminars and conferences. Dr. Govil is credited with more than ninety research papers in various journals of national and international repute in various aspects of genetics, crop breeding, and topics on general agriculture. He has also guided more than a dozen post-graduate students. Dr. Govil is recipient of no. of Awards and Honor presented by ICAR and Agricultural Societies. He has written and edited a number of books on Medicinal Plants and other books with international authors. A new series **"Recent Progress in Medicinal Plants"** has been published by *Studium Press, LLC, USA* in 46 volumes under Dr. Govil's Chief Editorship. Dr. Govil has been the main resource person as Executive Editor in Execution, Co-ordination and Completion of Projects in bringing 12 Vols Set each on ***Nanotechnology, Biotechnology, Energy Science and Technology,*** and ***Environmental Science and Engineering***. Simultaneously, Dr. Govil has brought four volumes set of Chemical Technology Series comprising 2 vols each on ***Advances in Fertilizer Technology*** as well as on ***Petroleum Engineering*** under the capacity of Acquisition Editor of the Series. Dr. Govil retired from ICAR service during the year 2007. Presently, he is working as Publishing Director and Managing Editor with Studium Press LLC, USA (Camped at New Delhi, India) and has brought out nearly 310 scientific books publication during last eight years.

E-mail: jngovil@gmail.com; jngovil@hotmail.com

Preface

Innovation: means (Latin word. innovare: "to change") *i.e.* doing something different or doing in different ways. Innovation refers to the use of a better and, as a result, novel idea or method. What are the best types of innovation that fit the activities of an organization. How to change the education pedagogy, what should be methodology, how can it be standardised, how to import quality into education and be sustained as well. Well, can there be Sustenance of Quality Higher Education through Foreign Direct Investment (FDI) and Innovation or one has to adopt supplementing of traditional teaching through innovative tool of Planning and Facilitating Small Group Learning. How communication skills are important for imparting quality education and can teaching be done without sensitizing the students about the cultural niceties. If so then what kind of tools, activities, and exercises can be administered in the classes to teach effective communication by developing intercultural competence.

Education inculcates a respect and decency to all persons and for the cultural pluralism of our society. It provides themeans and opportunities to enhance the creativity, capacity for innovation and aesthetic appreciation. Education is an effective instrument of qualitative transformation of human beings through acquisition of: Knowledge, Understanding, Internalization, Application, Skills, attitudes and value samalgamated with Peace, Harmony. The system of the values, rules, ethical standards of behavior, accepted in various civilized society have been analyzed.

On the other hand Skill is the endowment or capacity of an individual to do something well with one's mind as well as body and is a supplement to Education. If, so then what are the Silver-linings of Education and Skill Training in Indiaand abroad.

The future of any nation depends on the young minds or aptly said the young force of that particular nation. In order to focus on a global development, it becomes extremely important that the focus is maintained on the quality of higher education and its sustenance throughout the education churning mills.

The quality of higher education requires an excellent galaxy of Professors, Scientists, Inventors, Innovators, dedicated Students and the Entrepreneurs, as well as beyond doubts matching infrastructure of buildings, labs, libraries, workshops and other amenities needed to run higher educational institutions.

To attain the quality in higher education not only the strong base of secondary and primary education is needed with the proper understanding of the problems of students in rural and urban areas but, the Stimulation of Scientific Investigation in the Classroom through Didactic Sequences is potentially a powerful instrument for improving science teaching. As the Reading, Writing, Revision and Understanding analytically are tools to learning so the Organizational Culture is a basis for Implementing Innovation leading to Improved education system.

The second phase of sustenance of quality Education sustenance of its infrastructure *e.g.* buildings, labs through energy consumption behaviour *vis-à-vis* energy management by the qualified facilities managers, through an 'energy culture' framework comprising an amalgam of 'material culture', 'cognitive norms', and 'energy practice'.

To maintain these phases and for increasing the socio-economic condition of society; the innovation by the Researchers and Academicians is the key to the World Production Development of quality professionals in the Millennium through the INNOVATION & EDUCATION.

14 Nov'16 **Dr. Virendra Goswami**

Table of Contents

About the Editors v

Preface vii

1. Qualitative Approach for Sustenance of Quality Higher Education through Foreign Direct Investment (FDI) & Innovation 1
   Virendra Goswami and Himani Goswami Sharma (India)
2. Types of Innovation and its Impact on the Organizational Performance 27
   Martha Paola Alvarado Vera (Ecuador)
3. Standardization of Education 46
   Cdr Alok Mohan (India)
4. Planning and Facilitating Small Group Learning: An Innovative Tool for Supplementing Traditional Teaching 57
   Swagatika Samal and Rabindra Garada (India)
5. Culturally Responsive Pedagogy for Effective Teaching of Communication Skills 71
   Pushp Lata (India)
6. Peace, Harmony and Harmonious Education 86
   Surendra Pathak (India)
7. Education and Skill Training in India Silver-linings *vis-à-vis* Problems, Constraints and Challenges 114
   Lakshmidhar Mishra (India)
8. Development of the Rural School Children's Value Conscious Attitude to Family 145
   Gulfiia Parfilova and Roza Valeeva (Russia)

9. Buildings Are Not Enough: The Importance of Economic Planning in Education Infrastructure 171
ITALO ARBULÚ AND PAOLA LAZARTE (PIRU)

10. The Stimulation of Scientific Investigation in the Classroom through Didactic Unities 197
KENIA NAARA PARRA ABD ANA CLÁUDIA KASSEBOEHMER (BRASIL)

11. Understanding EFL Learners' Revision in Writing: A Comparative Study 224
HAFIDA HAMZAOUI ELACHACHI (ALGERIA)

12. Organizational Culture as a Basis for Implementing Innovation Leading to Improved Business Results 249
YOEL SULLAM (ISRAEL)

13. The Need for Facilities Managers in Adopting Energy Consumption Behavioural Assessment for Malaysian Universities 265
MOHD HAFIZAL B. ISHAK (MALAYSIA)

14. Third World Production Development in the Millennium: The Role of Researchers and Academics 298
KIFORDU ANYIBUOFU ANRHONY, MUHAMMAD ABUBAKAR ABDULLAHI AND CHINEDU ONUEIZUGBE (NIGERIA)

15. Reflection of the Kazakh Culture in Language 317
S.S. ISSAKOVA, A.T. TAGANOVA AND B.SH. BAIMUKHANOV (KAZAKHSTAN)

Subject Index 337

1

Qualitative Approach for Sustenance of Quality Higher Education through Foreign Direct Investment (FDI) and Innovation

VIRENDRA GOSWAMI[1*] AND HIMANI GOSWAMI SHARMA[2]

ABSTRACT

In the present study an effort has been made to analyze the role of Foreign Direct Investment (FDI) and innovation qualitatively for sustenance of Quality in Higher Education in India and all over the Globe. Although, the role of FDI is well discussed in retail business but, hardly studies are available as regards the role of FDI in Higher Education and sustenance of its quality. Globally, the "Hub and Spoke" spatial model focused with production and storage system commonly used by organized retailers; has been incorporated with production of Quality Professionals (QP) and storage by creation of Quality Infrastructure of building and laboratories by the entrepreneurs in the field of Higher Education. Next, based on the multiplicity of FDI; the Gateway / Highway for Sustenance of Quality Higher Education has been laid down. FDI will be an important tool for development quality and its sustenance in the realm of higher education, particularly for the developing and the poor nations

[1] Sangam University & Sunrise University, India
[2] Institute of Science & Technology, India
* *Corresponding author*: E-mail: vk_goswami@rediffmail.com

as well as the developed States all over the Globe. Thus FDI, also brings international cooperation, develop friendship between two nations and in nutshell brings peace to the humanity. After a critical examination, it was noted that since FDI considers relations on a broader platform amongst different countries, it not only would encourage qualitative approach towards sustenance of quality education but also enhance international cooperation, global friendships and tie-ups between two nations and in the long run encouraging peace across boundaries because of commonality of interests and objectives and safeguarding against any confrontations. Next, the Optimization and Sustenance of Quality in Higher Education aims to build up Intellectual Property of the State vis-à-vis India by encouraging the public private partnerships amalgamated with FDI; in the field of Aerospace, Biotechnology, Chemicals, Drugs and Pharmaceuticals, Energy, Food and Food Processing, Information Dissemination, Leather and Metal, Minerals and Manufacturing as well as human resource development. In order to achieve this one has to develop Work Culture, Academics and the 'Education Management Systems (EMS) to impart Innovative Education in Engineering, Pharmaceutical, Legal and Management Sciences.

Keywords: Qualitative Approach , Sustenance of Quality, Hub & Spoke Model, Foreign Direct Investment (FDI), Education Management Systems (EMS), Retail, Highway, Higher Education, AICTE (All India Council of Technical Education), UGC (university Grant Commission), University, Biotechnology, Engineering, Management

---

1. INTRODUCTION

"Only the Person having firm conviction and
Iron volition can attain strength and Energy.
At no stage of karma does he ever hesitate."

.... Rigveda

The quality of higher education is paramount for the development of each and every education imparting institutions *viz.*, Colleges and Universities. *vis-a-vis* the development of each and every nation over the Globe. It's not only important to achieve the higher education but, to sustain the same for longer duration. The quality of higher education can only be improved and sustained by retaining the same. Whereas;

the quality of higher education requires an excellent galaxy of *Professors, Scientist, Inventors, Innovators, dedicated Students and the Entrepreneurs,* as well as beyond doubts *matching infrastructure of buildings,* labs, libraries, workshops and other amenities needed to run higher educational institutions.

Although, the *alum of these two* may be easily resourceful for the few developed nations, but certainly do not for the poor and developing nation. No doubts the few developed nations may have enough resources but, they do require the collaboration of the foreign nationals for the development of the quality and sustenance of these *two important parameters of intellectual property and the infrastructure* for the sustenance of their Higher Education systems.

The future of any nation depends on the young minds or aptly said the young force of that particular nation. In order to focus on a global development, it becomes extremely important that the focus is maintained on the quality of higher education and its sustenance throughout the education churning mills *viz.*, institutions, colleges and universities. *The focus is not only needed on imparting but also retaining quality education.*

United Nations Conference on Trade and Development (*UNCTAD*) defined FDI as:

> *"FDI is an investment involving a long-term relationship and reflecting a lasting interest and control by a resident entity in one economy (foreign direct investor or parent enterprise) in an enterprise resident in an economy other than that of the foreign direct investor (FDI enterprise or affiliate enterprise or foreign affiliate)".*

Moreover, increased investment in higher education through FDI, would lead to increase in number of institutions, opportunity to attain international qualification at cheaper rates (though we really need to fight against the norm that a foreign degree is acceptable regardless of the grade scored), technological advancements and innovations which would further provide an edge against competitors.

Now, this forms a vicious circle which further promotes cut throat competitions for focussing on improvement in quality w.r.t. curricular, research and development, optimum utilisation of available resources, international exposure and a complete check on emigration of students and brain drain.

The Optimization and Sustenance of Quality in Higher Education is much needed to build up 'Model State' through Innovation, Intellectual Property, and Public Private Partnerships (PPP). In order to achieve this one has to develop academics, work culture, *EMS, HEGS* in corporation with *Education-Foreign Direct Investment (Ed.FDI).*

2. FDI CONSISTS OF THREE CORE PARTS *VIZ.*,

Equity Capital

Refer to ownership and a foreign investor's purchase of shares of an enterprise that is in a country other than his own.

Reinvested Earnings

Refer to the investor's share of earnings that are not distributed back to him, *i.e.*, profits that are not given out as dividends but are kept within the firm (or any of its affiliates).

Intra-Company Loans

Refer to debt transactions in the form of short and long-term lending by the foreign parent company to its affiliates If, one examines critically then would definitely agree that *FDI* (Foreign Direct Investment) will be an important tool for the felicitations of the development quality and its sustenance in the realm of higher education, particularly for the developing and the poor nations as well as the developed States all over the globe.

FDI is cross-country investment for sustenance of quality and the governance of higher education.

The FDI not only add in the development of higher education and it sustenance but, also brings *international cooperation, develop friendship between two nations* and in nutshell brings peace to the humanity. One may feel surprised, how the *peace* will get established by the FDI but, the answer is very simple that all FDI investors will safeguard their mutual interests and avoid any kind of confrontation.

India, being the third largest higher education system in the world in terms of enrolments, number of higher Education Institutions after

China and the US, needs more FDI to meet its target of doubling the gross enrolment ratio (GER) by 5050. There are more than *719 Universities, 54,055 Colleges with 18 million students enrolled a regular students* excluding the students enrolled in Open and Distant learning in the session 5015-14.

Thanks to Govt. of India for successfully introducing FDI (Foreign Direct Investment) in organized retail sector and hence the challenge is to leverage the expected FDI inflows.

2(a) Education Foreign Direct Investment (Ed.FDI)

In the same fashion, the FDI should be allowed in Higher Education to get the expected inflows as the organized retail increases efficiencies in trade by removal of intermediaries in the supply chain, so the, FDI in Higher Education would increase the efficiency of academics and Quality of Higher Education as well as reduction in intellectual corruption, due to removal of intermediaries and rising competition.

In my view, FDI–in Sustenance of quality higher education may be summarized as below.

> *"Making FDI in Higher Education initially to upgrade the quality of middle academic and back-end resulting in full utilization of the existing higher academic institutions, academician and academics."*

FDIs, in the form of capital, technology, technical and managerial skills bundled together, have taken an altogether new magnitude and have begun playing an increasing role in the developing countries. They have also proved to be more reliable than other forms of foreign capital during financial crises. FDIs may not only bring new technology and knowledge to the host countries, but also contribute to human capital accumulation by increasing the demand for skilled labour and thus, creating an incentive to participate into higher education.

According to *Deloitte*, estimates by as per the recent National University of Educational Planning and Administration (*NUPEA*), in order to achieve this target, an additional investment of $190 billion which includes capital expenditure and operating expenditure, has to be made in the next eight years.

Therefore, it is important for foreign investment and experience to flow in this sector to transform the domestic higher education institutions into the world's top league.

3. FDI–IN SUSTENANCE OF HIGHER EDUCATION QUALITY (SHE-Q)

Globally, the organized retailers commonly have used the "Hub and Spoke" spatial model focused with production and storage system. *Similarly*, in the field of Higher Education *"Hub and Spoke" spatial model* focused with *production of Quality Professionals (QP) and storage by creation of Quality Infrastructure* of building and labs are to be devised by the organized entrepreneurs. The Educational Entrepreneurs in India; have to be very cautious while developing the "Hub and Spoke" model for Quality in Higher Education (QHE) and they should be more focus on "Hub" and less on "Spoke".

In *India, contrast* to globally "Hub and Spoke" spatial model, the organized *retailers went 180 degree opposite* having primarily focused on the front-end hence landed up into the possibility of disinvestment resulting the make-over, in efficiency in the distribution system due to the loss incurred by the organized retailers. Also, initially the *Educational Entrepreneurs* in India *more focused on* 'Spoke' *and less on "Hub"* and thus result the poor *Quality of Higher Education, poor professionals and spectral fall in admission of the students leading to the closure of Higher Education Institutions in India.*

> *"Making FDI in Higher Education initially to upgrade the quality of middle academic and back-end resulting in full utilization of the existing higher academic institutions, academician and academics".*

Recently, Govt. of India is almost successful in introducing FDI (Foreign Direct Investment) in organized retail sector and hence the challenge is to leverage the expected FDI inflows. *Similarly, the FDI should be allowed in Higher* Education to get the expected inflows as the organized retail increases efficiencies in trade by removal of intermediaries in the supply chain, so the, FDI in Higher Education would increase the efficiency of academics and Quality of Higher Education as well as reduction in intellectual corruption, due to removal of intermediaries and rising competition. Globally, the "Hub and Spoke" spatial model focused with production and storage system is commonly used by organized retailers.

Similarly, "Hub and Spoke" spatial model focused with *production of Quality Professionals (QP) and storage by creation of Quality Infrastructure* of building and labs by the quality and organized entrepreneurs in the field of Higher Education are to be devised. One has to be very cautious while developing the "Hub and Spoke" model for Quality in Higher Education (QHE) by the Educational Entrepreneurs in India. They should more focused on "Hub" and less on "Spoke".

In *India, contrast* to global "Hub and Spoke" spatial model, the organized *retailers* have primarily focused on the front-end hence enhanced the possibility of disinvestment resulting the make-over, in efficiency in the distribution system due to the loss incurred by the organized retailers. Similarly, initially the *Educational Entrepreneurs* in India more focused on "spoke" *and less on* "Hub" and thus result the poor *Quality of Higher Education, poor professionals and spectral fall in admission of the students leading to the closure of Higher Education Institutions in India.*

For example, as per the report (15 May 2014), *AICTE* (All India Council for Technical Education), the AICTE given the approval to shut down 150 private Engineering and Management Colleges – making up for a whopping 15000 seats. These institutions have shown inability to fill up the seats as the reason for closure. The trend of deterioration of quality in Higher Education has been observed in these Engineering and Management Institutions during the last 5–4 years.

Next; as per the HRD Ministry sources, 500 technical institutions have submitted applications for closure of the courses due to various reasons, including poor admission. Of these 145 has been permitted to close their institutions. To elaborate the few state-wise shut down is as below:

Statewise shut down Institutions

State	***No.***	***State***	***No.***
Andhra Pradesh	56	Haryana	06
Tamil Nadu	05	Uttar Pradesh	17
Punjab	06	Bengal	05
Rajasthan	18	Chhattisgarh	04
Uttarakhand	01	Gujarat	15
Karnataka	05	Bihar	01
Maharashtra	07	Madhya Pradesh	05

Against this back-drop the *Govt. of India has put a check* on both of private engineering colleges. For example, the new engineering colleges approved during 2009-10 were 550 and it fell down to 171 in 2010-11. Not only this, the AICTE has *stopped giving the approval to any new colleges till 2014.*

The impact of this is obviously incurred debts on Educational Entrepreneurs, depletion in the national economy (Loss of GNP and GDP) and production of Quality Professionals. As the Indian corporate who invested in the front-end may try to make windfall gains by off-loading their investments leading to manage the thwarting the main objectives of allowing FD in retail.

Similarly, the Educational Entrepreneurs mainly Indians; who had invested in "Spoke may also try to make windfall gains by off-loading their Educational Investments and thus thwarting the main prospective of allowing FDI in Higher Education in future.

4. HIGHWAY TO FDI – IN SUSTENANCE OF HIGHER EDUCATION QUALITY (SHE-Q)

To overcome this one way is to *superimpose* of *"Hub and Spoke"* on the existing built-in environment. Thus, the traditional and present Higher Education System created by average Indian Educational Entrepreneur will perform the role of "Spokes with Hub" being managed by Foreign Educational Entrepreneurs (FEE). The other ways to overcome is to initiate some of the Quality Higher Education (*QHE*) *Awards*.

For example: QUEE-P (Quality Educational Entrepreneurs– Prize), should be initiated in establishing the college institutions of Higher Education and Research (HER) and the sustenance of the Total Quality of Spectrum (TQS).

Create Quality Professionals (*CQP*) a global initiative should be launched by QUEE-P. Awardees to facilitate the imparting of *Quality Higher Education* (*QHE*) to presently, 61 million children world-wide still deprived of their fundamental right to education and who are the prospective higher education students, by bringing High Quality Learning (HQL) to mainly such students affected by poverty, lack of opportunity, prejudice, natural calamities and handicapped.

For the sustenance of Quality in Higher Education (QHP), we have to produce a *Quality Task Force* (*QTF*), with task to rebuild the Higher

Education Management System. (HEMS) in India and export of the – HEMS model, abroad by creating innovating Quality Education Hub (QEH) through the Quality Higher Education Activists (QHEA) at national and international levels.

It would be not out of the way to set up *SHEQZ* (Sustenance of Higher Education Quality Zones) in different geographical areas wherein, quality higher education is promoted and sustained by development tools *e.g.,* setting up and governance of institutions of higher learning and research by using tax and business incentives to attract foreign investment and technology.

These SHEQZ could drastically improve the economic activity in the country, make the country's export competitive in exporting the Knowledge, building up intellectual property and globally noticeable by attracting the overseas students, intellectuals and Educational Entrepreneurs. Thus, be net foreign exchange earner and provide immense employment opportunity.

Relaxed Tax norms, Labor laws and statutory regulations will surely attract foreign investment and major industries to setup Institutions of Higher Education and Research in the SHEQZ's making it profitable and meeting its desired results.

> *It would be nice if, United Nations comes forward to create a fund like UNSHEQ (United Nations Sustenance of Higher Education Quality Zones) for sustenance of quality and governance of higher education.*

As the charity begins at home, so we Indian should take lead in setting up some sort of *council e.g., ICFQHE* (*Indian Council for Quality of Higher Education*) to deal solely to attract FDI in Higher Education sector, to monitor, to formulate standards, devise models for sustenance of Quality and governance of Higher Education.

No doubt the *Private Sector* has to play much *larger role* in *attracting the FDI* in higher Education Sector, as the amount of FDI attracted by this sector since 2000 stood dismally low at just $400 million. Also, the Private Sector in establishment of university (*Approx. 146 Private Univ. and 1546 AICTE approved Technical Colleges.*) level institutions is increasing substantially and the opening of the economy world over has resulted into exposure of Indian higher education system and demanding for the cross country collaboration in higher education.

At the same time the major network of *Public Sector Higher Education Institutes i.e.*, Government owned Institutes of *National Importance* (7%) *viz., IITs, IIMs, AIIMS* and *Universities viz., Central universities* (8% funded 100% by the Central Government), *State Universities* (57% funded by the State Government and marginally by the UGC), *Deemed to be Universities* (57%) and 1% are the *institutions other than universities* established under the State Legislation; do require FDI for their quality expansion and the sustenance of Higher Education.

The other *milestone* on the *Highway to FDI –in Sustenance of Higher Education Quality* (*SHEQ*) be the Public-Private sector Higher Institutes should join hand together in attracting FDI for SHE-Q by establishing a *cell for PP-FDI*. We Indians are the third largest Technical and Scientific Men Power in the World enriched with rich cultural heritage; must contribute generously our efforts to not only attract FDI from the foreign investors but, more so contribute ourselves in form of *Direct FDI* as an *Individual, ALUMNI* (*e.g.*, IITs, IIMs, AIIMS), *Organizations* (Public and Private Sectors), *Entrepreneurs* (Public and Private) acronym as ICAOE

The *strategies* are to be prepared by us; befitting to our needs and to be consulted with State/Central Governments and statutory bodies etc before they draw firm guidelines for the growth of FDI in sustenance of Higher education. *On a macroeconomic level*, Third World Nation and Developing countries particularly SARC Nations must expand their inflows of foreign investment into the Higher Education sector to enhance quality economic production, growth and its sustenance as well; as FDI would provide capital from sources abroad which these countries are unable to supply domestically.

This would facilitate the growth of a number of economic sectors, *e.g.*, industry, manufacturing, infrastructure, energy and Higher Education as well as rise in the availability of jobs and a *fall in the unemployment rate vis-à-vis increase in GDP and per capita income*.

The multiplicity of FDI in Sustenance of Higher Education – Quality (SHE-Q); depicts the Highway for SHE-Q with the following milestones;

(A) *IMPORTED-FDI* from overseas + (B) *P-FDI* (Public FDI) +

(C) *Pr.-FDI* (Private-FDI) + *PP-FDI* (Public–Private FDI) +

(D) *D-FDI* (Donated FDI by means of ICAOE: Individual, ALUMNI, Organizations, Entrepreneurs)

5. OPTIMIZATION AND SUSTENANCE OF QUALITY IN HIGHER EDUCATION

The Optimization and Sustenance of Quality in Higher Education is much needed not only for the development and sustenance of quality of higher education but, to build up the each and every State of the Globe into a Clean and 'Model State' amalgamated with:

—Systems;-—Professionalism enriched with ethics;-—proven Governance;—Happiness—-and a GLOBAL Friendly Super Power by developing:

********the Intellectual Property of the State,

********innovating the qualitative changes in*:

(a) Scientific and Professional Education comprising Engineering, Pharmaceutical, Legal and Management Sciences.

(b) *Education System* in totality by making it:

Application oriented,

Patent oriented in the field of Engineering, Pharmaceutical, Legal and Management Sciences; with the three 'Is' *viz.*, *Improvement, Innovation, Invention*.

In Global perspective to compete at International level.

Optimization and Sustenance of Quality in Higher Education inherits

(a) *The Quality Intellectual Property*

(b) *Quality Input in Respect of Students, Infrastructure of Building, Labs, E-Library etc*

(c) *Quality Product Vis-à-Vis Leaders, Engineers, Scientists, Professionals and Alumni.*

(d) *Work Culture Blended with Ethics and All Round Development of Personality.*

(e) *'Success Mantra'*

(f) *Innovation with Global Perspective*

(g) *'Education Management Systems (EMS)'* to impart Innovative Education in Engineering, Pharmaceutical, Legal and Management Sciences.

(h) *Higher Education Governance Systems* (*HEGS*)

The Optimization and Sustenance of Quality in Higher Education through Innovation aims; to build up Intellectual Property of the State *vis-à-vis* India by encouraging the Public Private Partnerships (PPP) in the field of:

Aerospace; Biotechnology; Chemicals; Drugs and Pharmaceuticals; Energy; Food and Food Processing; Information Dissemination; Leather; Metal, Minerals and Manufacturing as well as

Human Resource Development-cum-Management Sciences

In order to achieve this one has to develop:

1. Academics and Work Culture
2. The 'Education Management Systems (EMS) to impart Innovative Education in Engineering, Pharmaceutical, Legal and Management Sciences.
3. Higher Education Governance Systems (HEGS)
4. *Ed. FDI i.e.*, Educational FDI

5(a) Quality Intellectual Property

Quality Intellectual Property is simply a galaxy of Excellent *Professors, Scientist, Inventors, Innovators, dedicated Students and the Entrepreneurs.*

"The mediocre teacher tells.
The good teacher explains.
The Superior teacher demonstrates.
The great teacher inspires."

William Arthur Ward

The Great teachers make the great Institutions of quality professionals blended with ethical work culture.

In my view; 'these great teachers are ever great students'; embedded with 5 Cs:

- Character
- Conviction
- Courage
- Commitment
- Courtesy

5(b) Quality Inputs

"Quality is never an accident; it's always the result of:

- High intention
- Sincere effort
- Intelligent direction and
- Skillful execution;

It represents the wise choice of many alternatives. Performing at a high level of excellence is always a choice, an act of the will."

William A. Foster

5(c) Quality Product *vis-à-vis* Leaders, Engineers, Scientists, Professionals and Alumni

5(c) i. *Quality leader*

"I always Create, never Destroy
I always Believe, never Doubt
I am a Successful person, not a Victim
I have the Capacity and Knowledge to help People
I am a Leader"

5(c) ii. *Engineers, scientists, professionals and alumni*

The trends of these are pictorially represented below:

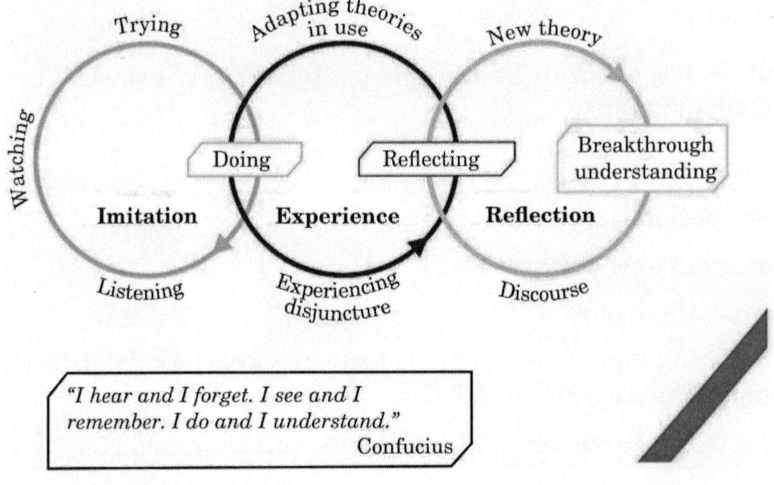

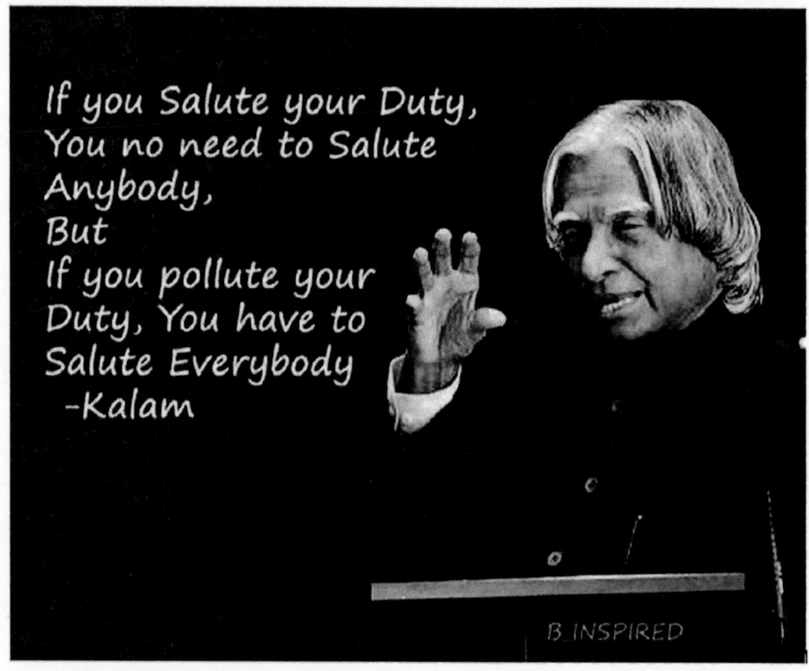

5(d) Work Culture Blended with Ethics and all Round Development of Personality

An ethical, enjoyable, professional and target oriented work culture embedded with positive attitude to be developed in the Universities in order to produce *quality leaders* of cheerful personality in their professional life.

I recall the *Work Culture* as a Graduate Student at Wisconsin*, USA and IITKGPian** w.r.t:

- Home Assignment
- Examination Hall etc.
- Research Paper publication
- Dignity of Labour
- Fabrication and Design of High Pressure Reactors, High Temp. Tubular Furnace and B.E.T
- Hard Work, Persistence, Perseverance and *Never QUIT*

Target Oriented approach is the must to achieve the goals.

5(e) 'Success Mantra' *i.e.*, the Elements of Success are

- WATCH
- Clear purpose
- Team attribute
- Strong relationships
- Communication
- Trust and Confidence
- Accountability
- Leadership

Success Is affected by

- *Competition*
- *Innovation*
- *Globalization*

Einstein success equation

$$S = X + Y + Z$$

S-Success, X-Think (Dream), Y-Hard work and Z-Rest (Quiet)

Success requires

- *Vision i.e.*, DREAM
- *Planning*
- *Execution*

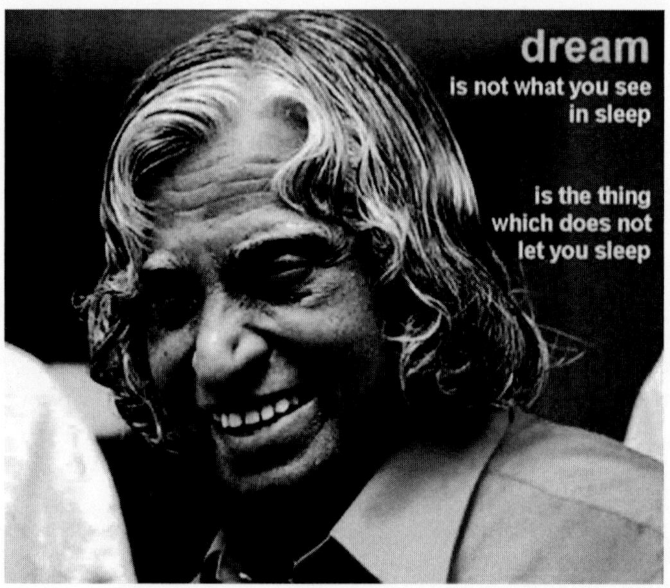

5(f) Innovation with Global Perspective

Innovation: Means (Lat. innovare: "to change") *i.e.*, doing something different or doing in different ways.

5(f) i. *Innovation*, invention, improvement

Innovation, differs from invention *i.e.,*

Innovation refers to the use of a better and, as a result, novel idea or method, whereas

Invention refers more directly to the creation of the idea or method itself and

Improvement refers to doing the same thing better.

Innovation is an important topic in the study of

Economics, business, entrepreneurship, sociology, Law, Management Sciences, design, technology, engineering, Pharmaceuticals

In society, innovation adds in

Comfort, convenience, and efficiency in everyday life.

For example, Innovation in Engineering, Science and Pharmaceutical.

Innovation in Engineering: the benchmarks in railroad equipment and infrastructure added to: greater safety, maintenance, speed, and weight capacity for passenger services.

These innovations included

- Gas lighting to electric lighting,
- Steam–powered to diesel-powered to electric-diesel locomotives.

Innovation in Science, Pharmaceutical includes Radioactive materials, Penicillin etc.

5(f) ii. *Conceptual meaning of invention and innovation*

- Conceptually, Invention is a creative process,
- The application of the process in creative and new manner is Innovation.
- An open and curious mind allows an Inventor /Innovator to see beyond what is known/and what can be known.
- While seeing a new possibility, connection, or relationship can spark an Invention; the
- Innovation may add the new processes of its applications.

Inventive and Innovative thinking

- Frequently involves combining and applying the concepts or elements from different realms that would not normally be put together.
- Sometimes Inventors/Innovators disregard the boundaries between distinctly separate territories or fields.

5(f)(iii) *Concepts about invention/inventor and innovations/ innovator*

Several concepts may be considered when thinking about Invention and Innovations.

Innovation can also be linked with:

> Play lead invention. Childhood curiosity, experimentation, and imagination, can develop one's play instinct—an inner need.

According to Carl Jung, Inventors feel the need to play with things that interest them, and to explore, and this internal drive brings about novel creations.

Thomas Edison said, "I never did a day's work in my life, it was all fun". Inventing and Innovation can also be an obsession.

- To invent is to see a new and to innovate is apply in different way or even invent in different way.
- Inventors often envision a new idea and apply the idea by, seeing it in their mind's eye.
- New ideas can arise:
  - When the conscious mind turns away from the subject or problem,
  - When the inventor's /Innovator's focus is on something else,
  - While relaxing or sleeping.
  - A novel idea may come in a flash—a Eureka! moment.

For example, after years of working to figure out the General Theory of Relativity, the solution came to Einstein suddenly in a dream

"Like a giant die making an indelible impress, a huge map of the universe outlined itself in one clear vision"

5(f) (iv) *Invention vs. innovation*

- Inventions can also be accidental, such as in the case of polytetrafluoroethylene (Teflon) but, the Innovation is rarely accidental perhaps?
- Although, the Invention is often an exploratory process, with an uncertain or unknown outcome but, the Innovation is non exploratory amalgamated with uncertain or unknown outcome.

- There are failures as well as successes. Inspiration can start the process, but no matter how complete the initial idea, Inventions typically have to be developed liked.

Innovations, Inventors and Innovators are often famous for:

- *their confidence,*
- *their perseverance and*
- *their passion.*

Inventors and Innovators are alike as they may, for example, try to improve something by making it more:

- effective, healthier, faster,
- more efficient, easier to use, serve more purposes,
- longer lasting, cheaper, more ecologically friendly, or
- aesthetically different, lighter weight, more ergonomic,
- structurally different, with new light or color properties,

5(f)(v) *The idea for an innovation vis-à-vis invention may be developed*

- on paper or on a computer,
- by writing or drawing,
- by trial and error,
- by making models,
- by experimenting,
- by testing and/or
- by making the invention/innovation in its whole form. Brainstorming
- also can spark new ideas for an invention.
- Collaborative creative processes are frequently used by designers, architects and scientists.
- Co-inventors are frequently named on patents.

5(f) (vi) *VG: Innovation and satisfaction*

In my view, "Innovation (Ivg) is affected by Satisfaction (Svg)."

Mathematically, $Ivg = 1 / Svg$

i.e., (Innovation)vg is inversely proportional to (Satisfaction)vg

OR

Mathematically, Ivg = DSvg

i.e., (Innovation)vg is directly proportional to (Dissatisfaction)vg

5(f)(vii) *Correlation with improvement, innovation and invention*

If, '(Dissatisfaction)vg' is replaced by '(Curiosity)vg' (an essential ingredient of Innovation) *i.e.,*

'(Dissatisfaction)vg ~ '(Curiosity)vg'

i.e., (Innovation)vg is directly proportional to '(Curiosity)vg'

Mathematically, $Ivg = Cvg$ Eqn.(1)

Similarly, *(Invention)vg is directly proportional to '(Creativity)vg'*

Mathematically, $INvg = CRvg$ Eqn.(2)

Similarly, *(Improvement)vg is directly proportional to '(Betterment)vg'*

Mathematically, $IMvg = Bvg$ Eqn.(3)

Adding, Eqn.(2) and Eqn.(3) we get *Correlation with Improvement, Innovation and Invention*:

(Bvg)+(Cvg) =(CRvg). Eqn.(3)'

Or,

$IMvg + Ivg = INvg$ Eqn.(4) *i.e., 'VG Invention Eqn'.*

Simply, $(I1)vg + (I2)vg = (I3)vg$ Eqn.(5) *i.e., 'VG Invention Eqn'*

Where, I1 = Improvement, I2 = Innovation and I3 =Invention

i.e., Betterment +Curiosity = Creativity

i.e., Improvement +Innovation = Invention

In other words, *Improvement leads to Innovation and Innovation leads to Invention*

Again, the other corollary can be devised as:

From Eqn.(1). Ivg = 1/Svg and IMvg = Bvg Eqn.(3)

We can write, Bvg / Svg = (CRvg) Eqn.(6)

0r (IMvg)x(Ivg) = (INvg) *Eqn.(6)'*

Bvg X Cvg = CRvg Eqn.(6)"

"The product of betterment and curiosity is Invention" VG

i.e., (VG Improvement-Innovation –Invention) or 3IvgEqn.

In other words it proves that:

"*Improvement* is directly proportional to Betterment. *Innovation* is inversely proportional to satisfaction and directly proportional to Curiosity. *Invention* is a product of improvement and Innovation"

VG Hypothesis of Invention

I'll like to sing: the 'Innovation Song'

"Life thy name is Innovation,
Innovation thy name is Life,
Where it ends, there strikes
The arrow of Death"

5(g) Virendra Goswami Education Management Systems (VGEMS)

VGEMS is an innovative integrated Education Management Systems for the qualitative and quantitative estimations of imparting quality education as well as its sustenance amalgamated with practical governance of higher education imparting institution developed and experimented by the author based on 44 years of teaching, research and governance of higher education institutions *e.g.*, professional Colleges and Universities at home and abroad. The brief outline of the VGEMS is enlisted below:

As regards the course manuals, planning of lessons, learning activities and examination tasks; I developed an innovative integrated

Education Management Systems) acronym as "VG: EMS" "(Virendra Goswami Education Management Systems)"

"VG: EMS is a system covering the complete spectra of Quality Higher Education Governance (QHEG) at College and University level. It deals widely the following aspects:

5(g) (i) ***Admission of students: Criteria, eligibility, entrance test and 'VG: Three-Tier-admission' i.e.,***

- Admission Test, (Physical or Online)
- Grading of qualifying examination,
- Personal interview (Personal or Video Conferencing)

5(g) (ii) ***Faculty recruitment through 'VG: Three-Tier-system' i.e.,***

Advertisement of faculty position with criteria, eligibility, qualification through print and electronic media

Initial personal interview (Personal or Video Conferencing) based on the objective and subjective techniques by the 5-Member Board of Experts (External and Internal) headed by Head of Department through the designed 'VG 50-Point'

'Faculty Proforma' comprising the following criteria:

- Qualification=10 Marks,
- Experience (Teaching, Industry) = 5+5 Marks,
- Research and Publications = 5+5 Marks,
- Communication and Professional Skills, Personality = 5+5 Marks
- Subject Knowledge and Capability of Imparting Knowledge (To be judged through Demonstrative Lecture on a topic either in the Student Class or to the Interview Board) =10 Marks

Final Interview Personal OR Video Conferencing) by the Head of Institution (Principal/Director/Vice Chancellor)

The ratio of appointment of faculty in case of professional courses should be 30% from industry and 70% from Academician.

5(g) (iii) *VG: Outline of syllabus and feedback proforma (VG: OSFP) on the scale of 10" completion in a 6 months semester in a tabulated form comprising the column viz.*

- Divide the semester syllabi into 10 topics
- Assign Number of hours required to complete the particular lecture/topic assuring that the total hours do not exceed the prescribe hours to the particular subject (Generally, 30-36 hrs)
- After Every two units conduct 'Class Test' of 1 hr and after 1/2 the syllabi Midterm test of 1-3 hrs to be conducted followed by End Semester exams of 1-3
- At least 5 (Home assignments+ Class Assignments) to be given to students after completion of two units on week-ends and to be returned 7 discussed after evaluation of the same by the teacher in the next week.
- The daily meetings to be held by HOD to monitor the completion of Syllabi with the faculty and monthly Fortnightly meeting with of HOD's with Principal/Director /Vice Chancellor.
- Monthly meetings of Class representatives (student), staff, Faculty with Principal/Director /Vice Chancellor.
- FEEDBACK of Completion of the Syllabi consists of ticking/ Writing against the each topic on the above scale of 10 by;

  C = Completed

  R = Revision required if, 50% students have not understood the topic taught by the teacher.

  NC = Not completed with reasons and to be completed by holding extra-classes.

5(g) (iv) *Personality development program for students (PDP)*

5(g) (v) *Faculty development program (FDP)*

5(g) (vi) *'VG academic calendar'*

Comprises the following in the tabulated form having the three columns:

- Date of Class tests, Mid Term and end semester exams with the dates of submission. Examinations and discussion of questions paper with model answers of selective difficult questions.

- Dates of Seminar/Workshops/Conferences with the separate detailed 'VG: Implementation Calendar' mentioning as:
  - Serial Number,
  - date of assigned work,
  - Work assigned to,
  - probable date of completion,
  - date of completion and
  - Remarks if any.
- Guest Lecture/Invited Talks/Visiting Professors Lecture Schedule Calendar in the above fashion comprising
- Similarly, VG: Calendar of Extra-Curricular Activities *e.g.*, Industrial Visits, Blood Donation Camps, Annual day celebration and Convocation etc in the above fashion comprising:

5(g)(vii) ***VG; course/syllabi development cycle***

As a Founder Vice Chancellor of Sangam University and Sunrise University not only I devised Ordinances, Statutes of the University but, also the Courses/Syllabi of all the Courses in Engineering, Science, Arts, Law and Education from Diploma to Doctorate levels, were developed, revised, modified by constituting the expert committee keeping in view that:

- Its Industry Oriented
- Value addition
- Internship in all the professional courses of at least 6 months at par with medical education.
- Practical's
- Foreign Language Courses
- The' VG:5 member Expert committee' comprising:
  - External Subject Expert
  - Internal Subject Expert
  - Industry Expert
  - Alumni
  - HOD / Dean

5(g) (viii) *'VG course scheme' or 'VG teaching methodology'*

For Example: All the four years degree courses of 8 Semester (B. Tech) had the specific layout. The first and second semester syllabi in all the branches is same and it differs as per the branch of engineering from 3rd semester onward.

6. SCOPE OF FDI IN SHE-Q

We Indians firmly believe in "*Vasudev Kutumbakam*" (Global Family). Our epics have taught us to give wealth and to impart Knowledge. We must not forget that we all human beings are *Global Citizens* and a quote: "God has given us two hands, one to receive with it and the other to give." Therefore, after having imported FDI from overseas, we must *export-FDI* in order to sustain our brand equity of SHE-Q but, also to attract more FDI in SHE-Q to maintain the balance of Import-Export FDI in SHE-Q. Then the Scope of our National Highway would lead to International Highway of FDI in SHE-Q; enriching our belief of "*Vasudev Kutumbakam* (Global Family).

7. REFERENCES

This review article entitled as '*Qualitative Approach for Sustenance of Quality Higher Education Through Foreign Direct Investment (FDI) and INNOVATION*' is an original work and personal views of the authors compiled from the addresses/ lectures delivered by them as an invited Speaker/Guest Speaker/Panellist at the International and National conferences in the last 5 years or so.

1. Goswami, V.K. (2015). 'Optimization of World Peace through Spiritual, Innovative, Demographic Education (side)' Presented as Madhya Pradesh Government State Guest speaker at International Seminar on 'Value Based Life', Bhopal, M.P.
2. Goswami, V.K. and Sharma, Himani Goswami (2014). Qualitative Approach of Benchmarking & Ranking for Sustenance of Quality Higher Education – Indian Perspective 'ISBA' (Indian Standard of Benchmarking & Accreditation), appeared in the Proceedings of 10 QS Applle Conf. Tapei, Taiwan.
3. Goswami, V.K. (2014). Global Perspective of Optimization & Sustenance of Quality in Higher Education Through Innovation in Engineering, Pharmaceutical, Legal and Management Sciences.'; Delivered Key Note Address at National Conference on "Innovation in Engineering, Pharmaceutical, Legal and Management Sciences" held at Bahra University, Shimla Hills.

4. Goswami, V.K. (2014). 'Optimization of University Governance & Sustenance of Quality of Higher Education through Human Valued Education Management Systems' presented as an Invited Speaker at 3rd ICHVHE (Int. Natl. Conf. on Human Values & Higher Education, PTU (Punjab Technical University) Jalandhar.
5. Goswami, V.K. (2013). Role of FDI in the Sustenance of Quality in Higher Education', Proceedings of National Conference on Higher Education in India: The Changing Facet (HEI-2013), Organized By: CTIEMT (CT Institute of Engineering & Management Technology), Jalandhar in Association with PTU (Punjab Technical University).
6. *AICTE (All India Council for Technical Education) Report May' 14*
7. *Deloitte, 'National University of Educational Planning and Administration (NUPEA) Report 2013,*

2

Types of Innovation and its Impact on the Organizational Performance

Martha Paola Alvarado Vera[1*]

ABSTRACT

Currently, investment in innovation is in the plans of an organization. However, for some organizations find it difficult to know what the best type of innovation that suits their business. Also, what activities of innovation will direct to an organization to generate competitive advantage. Therefore, this essay aims to identify the types of innovation and the reasons for implementing them in an organization. In addition, it search to demonstrate the benefits obtained when commitment to innovation and check its impact on organizational performance. For this, a descriptive analysis of some organizations that invest in innovation activities in each of its processes, services and products will be developed. In this way, you can identify what are the best types of innovation that fit the activities of an organization.

***Key words*:** Innovation types, Organization, Organizational performance, Investment, Activity

[1] Universidad Espiritu Santo, Ecuador

* *Corresponding author*: E-mail: malvarve@uees.edu.ec; malvar94@hotmail.com

INTRODUCTION

Spending on innovation is more than spending on R&D. To develop new products or processes, firms invest in R&D and in other tangible and intangible assets.

The impacts of innovations on firm performance range from effects on sales and market share to changes and improvements in productivity, efficiency, knowledge and workplace organisation. Currently, markets and industries-domestic and international-introduces innovation on the economic activity of firms in their markets.

To achieve in, there are many activities of innovation will direct to an organization to generate competitive advantage in innovation as: all scientific, technological, organisational, financial and commercial steps. Innovation activities for product and process innovations are R&D, acquisition of capital goods, new process to create new products, introduce market preparations and training. On the other side, innovation activities for marketing and organisational innovations are preparations for marketing and for organisational innovations. In that way, the firms can identify what are the best types of innovation that fit the activities of their organisation.

Therefore, spending on innovation changes the structure of the market, create new markets, or render existing products obsolete. It‘s important to know, variety of innovation types demonstrates that the benefits of innovation are not limited to new product development, because goes way beyond.

INNOVATION

The innovation consists of three (3) essential components: theoretical conception +technical invention +commercial exploitation. About the theoretical conception, many authors focus innovation on new product or process. For example, one of them, Love and Roper (2009) has noted that innovation is a process rather than an occurrence which embraces many activities, starting from the identification of innovative products to their development, production and the ful-fillment of marketing strategy (Love and Roper, 2009). Also, The Organisation for Economic Co-operation and Development (OECD) explains that “An innovation is the implementation of a new or significantly improved product (good or service), or process, a new marketing method, or a new organisational method in business practices, workplace organisation or external relations" (OECD/EUROSTAT, 2005).

Invention involves the discovery of new processes, ideas or tools. Respect to Commercial exploitation is considered as distribution to the public for commercial purposes excludes from the offers to sell or transfer that are not allowed.

So, Innovation depends on invention but inventions need to be harnessed to commercial activities before they can contribute to the growth of an organization.

Investing in Innovation

Expenditure on innovation is in the plans of an organization. Total expenditure incurred by firms are for the following activities: intramural R&D; extramural R&D; acquisition of other external knowledge (*e.g.,* patents, licences, trademarks); and acquisition of machinery, equipment and software. It's important that the organizations don't consider that expenditure on innovation is a waste or only don't need applied it in their process or products. The organisations need to keep in constant evolution. Investment in R&D is an important input factor for innovation performance (Royal Academy of Engineering, 2015).

Table 1: R&D ranking of the top 50 companies in the 2004 and 2013 Scoreboards.

Rank	*Company*	*Country*	*Rank change 2004-2012*
1	Volkswagen	Germany	up 7
2	Samsung Electronics	South Korea	up 31
3	Microsoft	USA	up 10
4	Intel	USA	up 10
5	Toyota motor	Japan	down 1
6	Roche	Switzerland	up 11
7	Novartis	Switzerland	up 13
8	Merck US	USA	up 21
9	Jhonson & Jhonson	USA	up 3
10	Pfizer	USA	down 8
11	Daimler	Germany	down 8
12	General Motors	USA	down 6
13	Google	USA	up > 200
14	Robert Bosh	Germany	up 12

Table 1: (*Contd...*)

Table 1: (*Contd...*)

Rank	*Company*	*Country*	*Rank change 2004-2012*
15	Sanofi	France	up 40
16	Honda Motor	Japan	nil
17	Siemens	Germany	down 13
18	Cisco Systems	USA	up 13
19	Panasonic	Japan	up 128
20	Glaxosmithkline	UK	down 9
21	IBM	USA	down 12
22	Nokia	Finland	down 12
23	Ford Motor	USA	down 22
24	Sony	Japan	down 9
25	Nissan Motor	Japan	up 9
26	Eli Lilly	USA	up 15
27	BMW	Germany	up 1
28	Ericsson	Sweden	down 11
29	Oracle	USA	up 42
30	EADS	Netherlands	up 5
31	Huawei	China	up > 200
32	General Electric	USA	up 5
33	Astrazeneca	UK	down 8
34	Fiat	Italy	up 10
35	Abbot Laboratories	USA	up 17
36	Bayer	Germanydown 4	
37	Hitachi	Japan	down 13
38	Qualcomm	USA	up 99
39	Denso	Japan	up 13
40	Bristol-Myers Squibb	USA	up 2
41	Taked Pharmceutical	Japan	up 31
42	Boehringer Ingelheim	Germany	up 20
43	Toshiba	Japan	down 13
44	Canon	Japan	down 5
45	Hewlett-Packard	USA	down 22
46	Apple	USA	up 109
47	Amgen	USA	up 9
48	Peugeot (PSA)	France	down 10
49	Alcatel-Lucent	France	down 32
50	NTT	Japan	down 29

Source: The EU Industrial R&D Investment Scoreboards 2013 and 2004.

In the Table 1, *R&D ranking of the top 50 companies in the 2004 and 2013 Scoreboards*. Show that most firms in USA apply on R&D. Also, on average, firms tend to invest 1-2% of their sales on various innovation-related activities, but this share exceeds 5% for large firms in some countries, one of them, is Germany, especially in the automotive sector as Volkswagen. In most countries, 5-7% of firms' turnover comes from products that are new to the market (OECD, 2010), for example, Samsung Electronics South Korea (European Commission's Joint Research Centre (JRC)-(IPTS) and Directorate General for Research and, 2013).

Nevertheless, R&D usually accounts for around one-half to two-thirds of all innovation expenditure, but the share varies widely by sector and firm size. Therefore, budget should consider spending between 10 to 25% of sales on R&D. R&D expenditure is frequently expressed as % of sales= (R&D expenditure/total sales income x100%). Setting the R&D budget can influence expenditure volatility and firm performance (Berumen, 2011), Performance fluctuations and Availability of funds. Huawei's R&D expenses totalled CNY30,090 million in 2012, accounting for 13.7% of the company's annual revenue. Of the total R&D expenses, CNY1,300 million was invested in research (Huawei, 2015).

It's important to know what Research and Development (R&D) means. So, it's a "comprise creative work undertaken on a systematic basis in order to increase the stock of knowledge (including knowledge of man, culture and society) and the use of this knowledge to devise new applications" (OECD, 2013). The organisation should apply research, discover new solutions to create new process or products. Through economic history, the United Kingdom (UK), industrial technological innovation has led to substantial economic benefits for the innovating company and the innovating country (Royal Academy of Engineering, 2015).

Besides, for many companies, collaborating with external partners reduces costs and is also a faster route to market. Successful innovators discover they can achieve significant multiples for every dollar invested in innovation by accessing the skill and talent of others. Co-creating with business partners and crowd sourcing with customers and other stakeholders' present opportunities to extracts more value from innovation investments. Companies should therefore aim to become the "partner of choice" in the areas where they need to extend (de Jong, Marston, Roth and van Biljon, 2013).

For example, L'Oréal has organized its Research and Innovation around six regional platforms (Europe, United States, Japan, China,

Brazil and India) (LOREAL, 2015). There are major region of the world, where the activities of research are applied. In Fig. 1. show that L'Oréal increased their Research and Innovation (R&D) Budget of €748 million (2013) to €761million (2014) or 3.4% of sales. There are 3782 researchers in some thirty disciplines from fundamental research to product development (LOREAL, 2015).

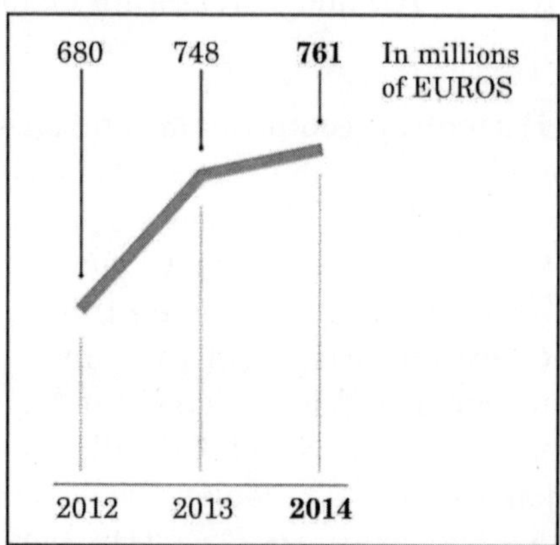

Fig. 1: *L'Oréal's Research and Innovation Budget (2012-2014). Source*: (LOREAL, 2015)

Since its creation, L'Oréal has always invested in research to better understand the secrets of hair and skin. L'Oréal has been applied the observation of beauty rituals around the world, in this way, they can get the scientific knowledge, in which, this platform is the source of all innovation (LOREAL, 2015).

Types of Innovation

The types of innovation are divided in three (3) categories (Benavides, 1998): by its nature or object, for the degree of novelty, and for its economic impact. So, of these three, we will focus only the type of innovation by its nature or object, which are product innovation, process innovation, marketing innovation and organisational innovation. That the reasons for implementing a type of innovation in an organization.

Product innovation of a good or service that is new or significantly improved with respect to its characteristics or intended uses. This includes significant improvements in technical specifications, components and materials, incorporated software, user friendliness or other functional characteristics (UNESCO Institute for Statistics, 2009). The outcomes of product innovations can be measured by the percentage of sales derived from new or improved products. In the category, Innovating Sustainably, period 2014, L'Oréal got 67% of new or renovated products, thanks to, a new formula using renewable raw materials or derived from green chemistry (LOREAL, 2015).

Process innovation consist implementation of a new or significantly improved production or delivery method (UNESCO Institute for Statistics, 2009). In this case, also requires significant changes in techniques, equipment and/or software. Process innovation, which is already found to be significantly correlated to innovative performance, influences it through product innovation. Gunday (2009) defines product and process innovations are closely related to the concept of technological developments.

Marketing innovation leads to introduce of a new marketing method involving significant changes in product design or packaging, product placement, product promotion or pricing (UNESCO Institute for Statistics, 2009). Organisations can apply marketing innovations target at addressing customer needs better, opening up new markets, or newly positioning a firm's product on the market with the intention of increasing firm's sales according to Kloter (1991). Marketing innovations are strongly related to four (4) pricing strategies, which are, product package, design properties, product placement and promotion activities along the lines of four P's of marketing.

L'Oréal is a good example in marketing field, because L'Oréal has a big portfolio of international brands that is unique in the world and covers all the lines of cosmetics.

Organizational innovation involves a new organizational method in the firm's business practices, workplace organisation or external relations (UNESCO Institute for Statistics, 2009). L'Oréal has external relations to promote innovation on their products and process (see Table 2. Global Research and Innovation distribution).

Organizational innovations has a tendency to increase firm performance by reducing administrative and transaction costs, improving workplace satisfaction (and thus labour productivity), gaining access to non-tradable assets (such as non-codified external knowledge) or reducing costs of supplies (OECD/EUROSTAT, 2005).

Table 2: L'Oréal's Portfolio of International Brands. Source: (LOREAL, 2015)

Portfolio of internation brands	***Distribution channels***
L'Oreal	Luxe products are available at department stores, cosmetics stores, travel retail, but also own-brand boutiques and dedicated e-commerce websites.
Consumer products division	The consumer products division brands are distributed in retail channels
Professional products division	The professional products division distributes its products in salons worldwide
Active cosmetics division	The active cosmetics division brands are sold in healthcare outlets worldwide, including, pharmacies, drug stores and medi-spas.
The body shop	The body shop has always believed that business can be a force for good, and now its commitment is stronger than ever.

Table 3: Global Research and Innovation distribution. *Source*: (LOREAL, 2015)

	Organisations
5	hubs (United States, Japan, China, India and Brazil) : and I world center
23	Research centers
16	Evaluation centers
49	Scientific and technico-regulatory departments
More than 30	collaborations with universities, public research centers or start-ups

That is why L'Oréal uses Activities Research and Development (R&D), Science and Technology and Innovation, because it has more than 30 collaborations (see Table 3.) with universities, public research centers or starts-ups around the world and assisted by external actors supporting funding. Thus, organizational innovations are strongly related with all the administrative efforts of renewing the organizational routines, procedures, mechanisms, systems etc. to promote teamwork, information sharing, coordination, collaboration, learning, and innovativeness (Gunday, 2009). Besides, the organizational innovation is observed to be the strongest driver of innovative performance.

ORGANIZATIONAL PERFORMANCE

Organizational performance is an analysis of a company's performance as compared to goals and objectives. Organizational performance encompasses three specific areas of firm outcomes: (1) financial performance (profits, return on assets, return on investment, etc.); (2) market performance (sales, market share, etc.); and (3) shareholder return (total shareholder return, economic value added, etc.) (Devinney and Yip, 2008).

Besides production capacity performance is analyzed by managers. Production capacity is the volume of products in a given period with the available resources. Organizational innovations play a fundamental role for innovative capabilities as it has the greatest regression coefficient with innovative performance.

So, L'Oréal has been innovations on their process and products, in this way, this firm get a good performance in the following areas: financial, market and shareholder. In the Table 4 show a significant increase in their profit and investment, financial ratios period 2013-2014.

Table 4: L'Oréal´s Financial Ratios. *Source*: (LOREAL, 2015)

Financial ratios	*2013*	*2014*
Operation profit / sales (% of sales)	17.0%	17.3%
Net profit excluding non-recurrent items after minority interest / Opening shareholder's equity (% of shareholders' equity)	14.5%	13.8%
Net gearing (% of shareholder's equity)	n/a	3.3%
Cash flow / Investments	3.7x	3.8x

On the other hand, market performance, in 2014, L'Oréal in Active Cosmetics got 22.7% of sales, this is the best division, which, it belongs to the portfolio of international brands. Active Cosmetics represents €1,269 million. "The Active Cosmetics Division's mission is to help everyone improve the quality and health of their skin, whether they are affected by sensitive skin or dermatological conditions (...)" (LOREAL, 2015). So, their results in their sales was demonstrated the mission.

Thank to the strategies and each of the actions implemented by L'Oréal, generated favorable results according to the objectives.

Table 5: L'Oréal´s Operating Profit by division, 2014. *Source*: (LOREAL, 2015)

2014 Operation profit by division	*C millions*	*% of sales*
L'Oreal Luxe	1,269	20.5%
Consumer Products Division	2,186	20.3%
Professional Products Division	609	20.1%
Active Cosmetics Division	379	22.7%
Non-allocated	–615	–2.8%
Divisions total after non-allocated	3,825	17.7%

In Breakdown of Shareholding Structure (Fig. 2.), the best shareholder is the International institutional investors with 28.06%.

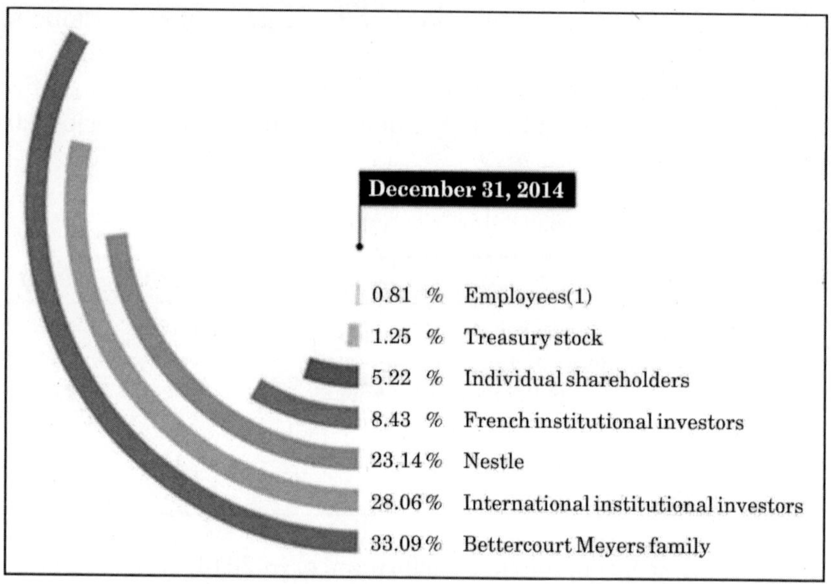

Fig. 2: L'Oréal´s Breakdown of Shareholding Structure (2014). *Source*: (LOREAL, 2015)

L'Oréal applied simultaneously different type's innovation as production innovation, process innovations, marketing innovation and organizational innovation. L'Oréal developed new sources of supply of raw materials and constantly establishes a feasible market structure changes. "The efficiency goes hand in hand with technology, and this depends on research, technology transfer and innovation and financial resources for its proper implementation" (Díaz, 2014).

L'Oréalis a firm that plans, coordinates, design processes, in which each of the strategies and actions to identify activities that will improve the ability of the organization and stakeholders to adopt innovations, and thus obtain results goals and objectives.

Best Type of Innovation that Fit the Activities of an Organization

The aim is how to choose the type of innovation that fit the activities of an organization, in that way, to get to competitive advantage or get a great effects on firm performance. In fact, "the effects of innovations on firm performance differ in a wide spectrum from sales, market share and profitability to productivity and efficiency" (OECD/EUROSTAT, 2005).

Product innovation is applied to New–to-market product innovations are new or significantly improved goods or services introduced to the firm's market before its competitors, while new-to-firm product innovations are goods and services already available on the market. Nevertheless, in dynamic markets, product innovation alone is insufficient. A strong innovation portfolio goes beyond new products to include other factors, including new business models and distinctive business processes that can create advantage (de Jong, Marston, Roth and van Biljon, 2013). Of all innovation types, business-model innovation can create the most significant long-term value. These innovations can include new distribution and production methods; both can disrupt current practices and erect powerful barriers to competition (de Jong, Marston, Roth and van Biljon, 2013). Product innovation provides new products and rapid growth on five (5) industries as: Chemical, Electronics, Automotive and Pharmaceuticals.

Product innovation also appears as a critical driver for innovative performance, which also acts as a bridge carrying positive impacts of process innovations to innovative performance (Gunday, 2009). For example, on Electronic industry, Huawei, this firm invests over 10% of our annual sales revenue into R&D and more than 45% of our 170,000 employees engage in R&D (Huawei, 2015).

Organisation whose activity belongs to the technology sector, are those that are in constant innovation, which in a few days, weeks and months produce a new breakthrough in technology. These organizations develop different market structures in each of the types of innovation (product, process, source of supply of raw materials), which invest large sums of money to stay competitive advantage and satisfy its customers.

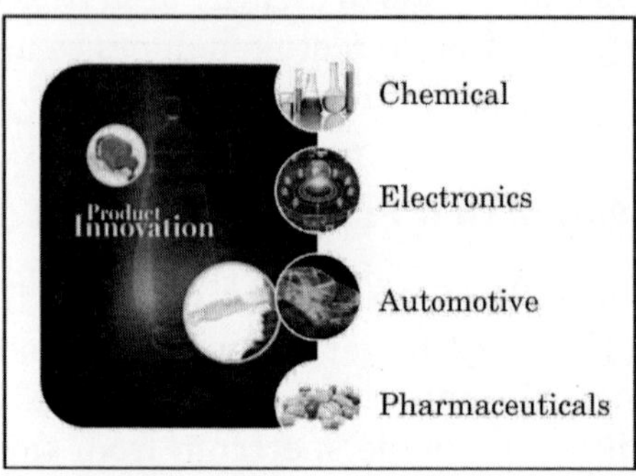

Fig. 3: Product Innovation on five main industries.

"Countries like the United States, Denmark and France generate more than 70% of value added, primarily directed to business and technological innovation (San Gabino, 2012)" (Díaz, 2014).

To produce a quality product, you need to be prepared with quality ingredients, too. But in the field of innovation goes beyond considering the raw material quality , but also consider other points as developing new sources of supply of raw materials or intermediate products so that the product progresses or better in their lightness, cleanliness, aesthetic, functional, performance, cost and price.

Process innovation, in a Germain's study (1999) revealed that organizational structural characteristics might be significant predictors of process innovations in the logistics sector (Gunday, 2009). So, logistics sector is in services category, which, process innovation is more applied by services firms. For example, FedEx and UPS, because they supply chain and logistics innovation. Nevertheless, *Organizational innovation* is applied in services firm too. Other point, study on Chinese firms showed us that process and product innovations were significantly correlated to each other (Gunday, 2009).

Besides, Walker (2008) announced that organizational, marketing and service (or product) innovations were found to be interrelated in a study on public organizations (Gunday, 2009).

On the other hand, is very relevant that organisations reply the following questions before introduce one type of innovation or invest on R&D. Because, each decision must be align with their missions, objectives, visions and their operational activities. It is therefore important for organizations to share, communicate goals to carry out, which itself is the essence of inspiration for all those who are part of the company and all are directed towards achieving that goal. "With respect to group processes, clear objectives and standards encourage innovation" (da Costa, Páez, Sánchez, Gondim and Rodríguez, 2014). In this case, for example, R&D investment, the relevant questions are:

- Which projects and technology to invest on?
- When to stop pouring money into a project that look likely to fail but could yet deliver enormous profits?

For example, a clear answer to these questions, large organization with more resources can clearly afford to invest more in R&D than their smaller counterparts. Huawei localize their operations and building a global value chain, with the purpose to help local innovators maximize their global value and share win-win outcomes (Huawei, 2015).

So, the firms must analyse this questions to obtain the following aspects below and finally take a right decision on how to invest on R&D in their activities.

- To make comparisons to be made between small and large firms.
- R&D intensity within the organizations.
- R&D expenditure across different industry sectors.

In this case, generally some industries are technology intensive with relatively high levels of R&D expenditure. But, the qualified expenditure may include ways as materials, machinery, equipment and some overheads. Huawei works closely with partners from the industry, academia, and research institutes. They have set up 16 R&D centers in countries that include Germany, Sweden, the US, France, Italy, Russia, India, and China. Huawei has also set up 28 joint innovation centers with leading carriers to translate leading technologies into a competitive edge and business success for customers (Huawei, 2015).

So, the organization on how to get money to invest on R&D, they need to answers this questions:

- How much money should companies invest in R&D?
- How much should be used for applied research and how much for pure research?

Huawei's R&D expenses totaled CNY30,090 million in 2012, accounting for 13.7% of the company's annual revenue. Of the total R&D expenses, CNY1,300 million was invested in research. Huawei has cumulatively spent more than CNY130,000 million on R&D over the last decade (Huawei, 2015).

Requirement investment R&D is defined by three aspects, so, it depends on business status. There are:

- Existing business
- New business
- Exploratory research

To Development of business strategy, the questions are:

- What might the company do?
- What can the company do?
- What should the company do?

Huawei is as an advocate of socioeconomic sustainability, in which, their business strategy is support secure and stable network operations, and help customers and industries improve efficiency to drive low-carbon economic growth (Huawei, 2015).

In conclusion, is not more important to get Firms' share price, but rather focusing in R&D intensive firm is increasing.

In addition, the market will be different, there is no market in the country, because in this way would be innovative. That is a radical change of approach, for example, opening a new market for low-cost insurance products to the community, among others. However, the opening of new markets in a foreign country involves taking into consideration the following: market research, regulations, identify potential customers, partners and distributors, marketing strategy, introduction costs, foreign trade procedures, trade agreements, freight and insurance, etc. (Cuesta Valiño, 2006).

The aim is to increase the participation of the company's commercial distribution in the markets in which it operates and current products.

In the case of Nokia's global presence it has been boosted because he has taken advantage of the commercial opportunities beyond small local markets in Finland.

INNOVATION ECUADORIAN COMPANIES

Innovation in Ecuadorian companies, depends on the sector where it performs its operational and commercial activities. For example, companies that belong to the service sector are more innovative than the manufacturing sector, with a gap of 7.39% difference (see Fig. 4).

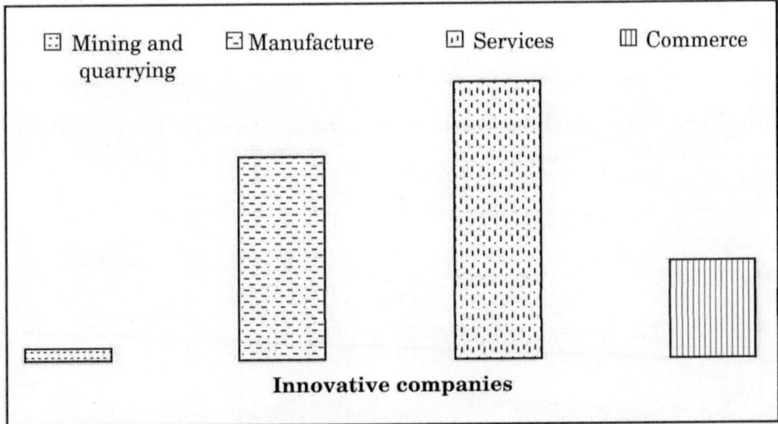

Fig. 4: Innovative companies according to their economic activity. *Source*: (INEC y SENESCYT, 2013)

In addition, the service sector focuses on organizational innovation reaching the highest percentage (51.6%) in this type of innovation (see Fig. 5). Therefore, the services sector is more likely to innovate in the country's economic activity.

On the other hand, the type of innovation most applied by Ecuadorian companies is innovation in process with a 36.88%, followed by product innovation a 36.21% implementation.

Impact of Innovation on the Organizational Performance

Innovation has a considerable impact on corporate performance by producing an improved market position that conveys competitive advantage and superior performance (Walker, 2004).

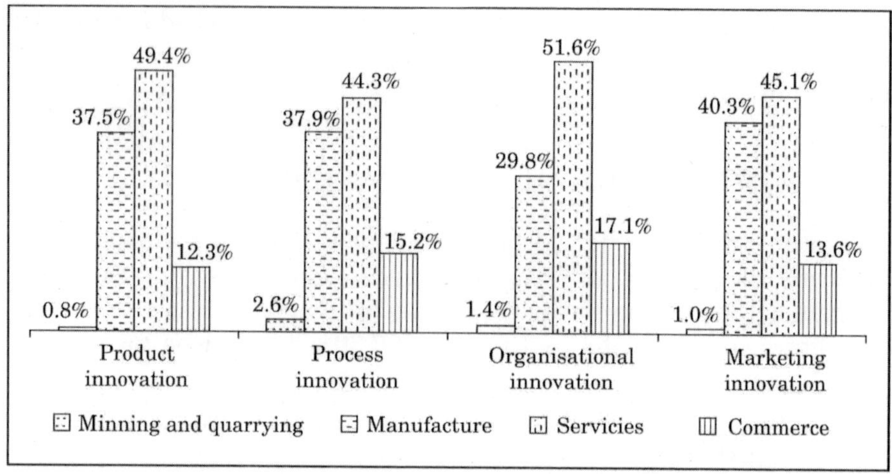

Fig. 5: Type unbundled innovation by economic activity. *Source*: (INEC y SENESCYT, 2013)

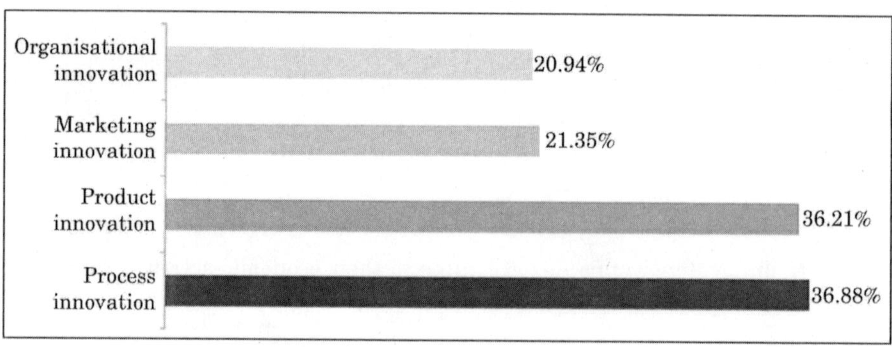

Fig. 6: Percentage of firms by type of innovation. *Source*: (INEC y SENESCYT, 2013)

Process innovation, which is already found to be significantly correlated to innovative performance, influences it through product innovation production and innovative performances have indirect positive impact on financial performance *via* market performance, which is the main contributor to it.

Also, higher product innovation is correlated with higher market share. Innovative firms especially those with a higher innovativeness score for product, process, and organizational innovations have significantly higher total sales and exports.

Innovation plays a significant role not only at the markets or industrial level, because it‘s very important at country and continental level, so it developed countries economic policy debate, and various international organizations and institutions documents emphasize that innovation is a key engine for economic growth (OECD/EUROSTAT, 2005).

CONCLUSION

Investment in innovation is essential implement in any organization regardless of business or sector develops. What is required is that every organization is clear about its values, mission, vision and strategic objectives for implementing innovation, so it makes sense and motivation for employees that make up the organization and its stakeholders to meet targets established and favorable results. Otherwise, no vision, no clear objectives, the organization would not use resources efficiently involving money, time and overall organizational performance is affected.

Another important point when choosing a type of innovation is necessary to verify if it meets economic activity or sector in which the organization develops. Each of these types of innovation have a purpose, but the purpose is the same, to introduce something new, something that impacts , generating value to its customers, and does not exist in the existing market. It is here where the basis for innovation lies.

Ultimately, value is created in the decisions made for the business. A decision framework provides the complete environment for innovation. It simultaneously identifies the type of innovation, along with the context to evaluate the potential value, impact and scope needed to make an effective investment choice. We observed that innovative firms have higher market share, also total sales and exports as L'Oréal and Huawei firm.

Activities that would direct an organization innovation to generate competitive advantage are: Activities in Research and Development (R&D), Science and Technology and Innovation. Undoubtedly, large sums of money required to invest in R&D activities to encourage innovation, but these companies (L'Oréal and Huawei firm) as well as others, have the support of external actors who support the financing of investment such as NGOs, Higher Education, Government or strategic alliances with institutions abroad. The important thing is not to limit innovation by cultural, demographic and economic factors. "The control of uncertainty may hinder innovation" (Armenteros Acosta, Guerrero Ramos, Noyola del Río and Molina Morejón, 2012). But, rather take advantage of both the opportunities and the crisis, because that's where the best ideas and innovative and momentous creations are obtained.

So, market demand, technological advances and speed of trade relations worldwide involve organizations remain vigilant, offering a new product, implementing new strategies and make timely decisions. These activities involve investments, expenses and time, but the result is uncertainty, because they do not necessarily when an investment is made a better result will be obtained. This will depend on who is investing your money and time. And also, what are the resources that are sacrificing the company to obtain or fulfill a goal. It is there, where innovation plays an important role in the objectives of the organizations.

Therefore, the organization must be clear that you want to achieve, that will determine what kind of innovation will fit your company.

BIBLIOGRAPHY

Armenteros, Acosta M., Guerrero, Ramos L., Noyola del, Río F.G. and Molina, Morejón V.M. (2012). Cultura organizacional y organización que aprende un análisis desde la perspectiva de la innovación. (spanish). Obtenido de Revista Internacional Administración & Finanzas: *http://web.b.ebscohost.com/ehost/detail/detail?sid=ef360610-86e5-444e-bc5d-ae48529d9c0c%40sessionmgr111&vid=0&hid=1m05&bdata=Jmxhbmc9ZXMmc2l0ZT1laG9zdC1saXZl#db=fua&AN=67092268*

Benavides, C. (1998). Tecnología, Innovación y Empresa. Obtenido de Ediciones Pirámide.

Berumen, S.A. (2011). *Innovation Systems of Europe.* Madrid: ESIC.

da Costa, S., Páez, D., Sánchez, F., Gondim, S. and Rodríguez, M. (1 de Agosto de 2014). Factores favorables a la innovación en las organizaciones: Una integración de meta-análisis. (Spanish). Obtenido de Revista de Psicologia del Trabajo y de Las Organizaciones: *http://web.b.ebscohost.com/ehost/detail/detail?sid=0ccf9f5b-efc5-46a0-9a59-4a80bd807db4%40sessionmgr111&vid=0&hid=105&bdata=Jmxhbmc9ZXMmc2l0ZT1laG9zdC1saXZl#db=fua&AN=97293671*

de Jong, M., Marston, N., Roth, E. and Van Biljon, P. (2013). The eight essentials of innovation performance. Retrieved from McKinsey & Company.

Devinney, T. and Yip, G. (2008). Measuring organizational performance as a dependent variable: Towards methodological best practice. Retrieved from research gate.

Díaz, J.A. (2014). Comercialización de los productos y servicios de la ciencia: Retos y perspectivas. Obtenido de Revista Cubana de Ciencia Agrícola: *http://www.redalyc.org/articulo.oa?id=193030122007*

European Commission's Joint Research Centre (JRC)-(IPTS) and Directorate General for Research and (2013). 2013 EU Industrial R&D Investment Scoreboard. Obtenido de European Union: *http://ipts.jrc.ec.europa.eu*

Gunday, G. (2009). Effects of innovation types on firm performance. Retrieved from Sabanci University.

Huawei (2015). *Research & Development.* Obtenido de Huawei.

Kloter, P. (1991). *Principles of Marketing.* NJ: Prentice Hall.

LOREAL (2015). *Research and Innovation in key figures.* Obtenido de loreal.com.

Love, J.H. and Roper, S. (2009). Organizing the innovation process: Complementarities in innovation networking. Obtenido de Industry and Innovation.

OECD (2010). Innovation microdata project.

OECD (2013). OECD factbook: Economic, environmental and social statistics. Obtenido de OECDi Library.

OECD/EUROSTAT (2005). Oslo manual: Guidelines for collecting and interpreting innovation data. (3rd Edition), 162. Paris: The measurement of scientific and technological activities. Retrieved from *http://www.sourceoecd.org/scienceIT/9264013083*

OECD/EUROSTAT (2005). Oslo manual: Guidelines for 40(Third ed.). Paris: OECD Publications. doi: *http://www.sourceoecd.org/scienceIT/9264013083*

Royal Academy of Engineering (2015). Investing in innovation. Retrieved from royal academy of engineering: *www.raeng.org.uk*

UNESCO Institute for Statistics (2009). Measuring innovation. Obtenido de training workshop on science, technology and innovation indicators.

Walker, R.M. (2004). Innovation and organizational performance: Evidence and a research agneda. WP: Advanced institute of management research working paper.

3

Standardization of Education

Cdr Alok Mohan[1*]

1. SCOPE

a) To strengthen and enhance the quality of students
b) To sustain an environment in which excellence in learning and teaching in university campus as well as surroundings
c) To encourage everyone involved in teaching and supporting learning to play their part in enhancing as well as ensuring quality criteria
d) To allow members of public especially immediate neighborhood to check the learning systems in university campus for better transparency

Keywords: Standardization , Sustenance of Quality, AICTE (All India Council of Technical Education), UGC (University Grant Commission), Engineering, Management, Strengthen, Enhance, Quality of students, Underpinning principles, Institutional strategic objectives, Anti national event, JNU, Sanskar', Optimizing business services, Organizational effectiveness, Protecting learners rights.

[1] C/o Sangam University & Sunrise University, India
* *Corresponding author*: E-mail: mohanalok@gmail.com

2. UNDERPINNING PRINCIPLES

Learning and Teaching Enhancement Strategy of any educational institute should be underpinned by the following principles:

a) It should be well-aligned to the University's strategic goals, mission and ethos
b) It must complement the learning and teaching strategies
c) It should be forward-looking, engaging with evolving needs and circumstances and addressing prospective challenges and opportunities
d) It must be inclusive, encompassing the full range of levels of study
e) It must continue to value initiatives by individuals, course teams and subject groups to enhance local practices

3. INSTITUTIONAL STRATEGIC OBJECTIVES

To stimulate in students a lifelong thirst for knowledge, learning and to encourage a pioneering, innovative and independent attitude and an aspiration to achieve success within and beyond campus.

The main aim of this exercise is that the educational institutes must aim to achieve the highest quality of educational experience for all students on the basis of identified best practices, rigorous feedbacks and evaluation from students, staff and employers and a policy of proactively enhancing the educational environment for both students and all staff with responsibilities in learning and teaching. For enhancing the comparability and transparency services the educational institutes must aim to preserve and enhance the enthusiasm of students by avoiding overload of factual information and assessment, providing clear learning outcomes and goals and ensuring a supportive learning environment.

The learning institutes must prepare students for lifelong learning by developing generic skills such as time management, the ability to manage their own learning, study skills, the ability to critically appraise, writing skills, data collection and management etc. A variety of teaching methods may also be developed and utilized within the College to support a range of learning styles and to ensure that students are prepared to the highest standard for entry to the professions. Identifying training needs of teaching Staff, the educational institutes must be committed to evaluate expertise of staff periodically.

There is also a requirement to stress on competence level of faculty so as to enhancing service quality in the field of learning. If organizations maintain a competence matrix of individuals and identify the competency needs of the faculty and provide them necessary training to sharpen their teaching skills, I am sure new mile stones can be achieved. As far as evaluation of the teachers is concerned, necessary feedbacks may be obtained for example inputs like previous pass percentage of students, Feedback from students, Placement of students consequent to graduation etc. are some factors which may define the capabilities of teachers and therefore fare comparison can be made to build career profile of the teaching staff. The education institutes may build strategies which align their plans keeping a focus on following main objectives:-

a) Self-control by management
b) Character building of students *i.e.,* inculcating sanskar
c) Social cohesiveness
d) Personality development
e) Physical, mental and spiritual well- being of the disciple
f) Preservation of knowledge and culture.

4. NATURE OF EDUCATION IN INDIA

Nature of education in India, stress more on bookish knowledge while all round development of a child's personality should have been the primary aim of our education system. Overall physical and intellectual development of the wards should be given maximum attention in our educational institutes. From time immemorial, India has explicitly recognized that the supreme goal of life is self-realization and hence the aim of education has always been the attainment of such a fullness of being. But at the same time, it was also recognized that different individuals have different inclinations and capacities. Hence not only the highest philosophy, but also ordinary subjects like literature and science as also vocational training find a place in the ancient education systems of ancient India. Ancient education system of India had always been a source of inspiration for one and all, as it aimed at infusion of sanskar and personality development, which used to result in formation of character building and inculcating civil and social sense among wards. The primary aim of ancient education in India, was to instill into the minds, of pupils a spirit of being pious and religious. The pursuit of knowledge was a pursuit of religious values. The life of the pupil was full of ritual acts. Stress was always laid on character building of students in the ancient gurukul system of education, which was based on ancient vedic system of education. The teacher and the taught were ideals of morality as both practiced it all through their lives. The inculcation of civic virtues and social values was an equally important objective of education in India. Students were required to become brahmacharis. The Brahmachari after his education in the Gurukulas went back to the society to serve the rich and the poor, to relieve the diseased and the distressed. He was required to be hospitable to the guests and charitable to the needy. After a certain period of studies, he was required to become a householder and to perpetuate his race and transmit his culture to his own off springs. The Guru in the ancient times realized that the development of personality is the sole aim of education. Human personality was regarded as the supreme work of God. The qualities of self-esteem, self confidence, self restraint and self respect were the personality traits that the educator tried to inculcate in his pupils through example. Today also Vedic culture, which has been transmitted to our present generation through the word of mouth, has been a prime motivator, and which binds us as a united nation.

5. ABOUT RECENT ANTI NATIONAL EVENT AT JNU CAMPUS

Recently there was a furious debate among our political leadership, on different TV channels, consequent to a recent anti national event at JNU campus by a few students *i.e.,* An event which was organized to criticize the supreme court verdict of hanging of Parliament attack convict Afzal Guru, a terrorist, who had masterminded terror attack on our most important institute of our democracy *i.e.,* the Parliament. I understand the JNU student organisers, had pasted posters across the campus inviting students to gather for a protest march against "judicial killing of Afzal Guru and Maqbool Bhatt. They tried to honor the terrorists as martyrs. Some of these student leaders, also made damaging statements against the interests of our nation. They shouted anti India slogans. This event coincided with another event at a nearby place *i.e.,* RR Hospital wherein a brave soldier from Indian Army, had taken his last breath consequent to his last battle in life (for close to a week) Nine of his brother soldiers were earlier buried alive in a snow storm, while protecting our borders at Siachen. This anti national act had definitely a potential to disturb socio, legal environment in the immediate surrounding of the university campus.

During this unfortunate event at JNU, some student's leaders, had expressed their intentions to destroy our nation. In the brain storming session at various TV channels, some participants, tried to sell an idea that JNU being a premier institute of India, gives freedom to its students to discuss any issue (including venting anti national sentiments). They stated that the purpose of this system is to enhance their thought process and reasoning ability.

Some of the participants considered that we must permit students with a freedom of expression for their overall development and towards achievement of next higher level for quality education. This was definitely an anti-national event and should not have been permitted by JNU management as this was meant to disturb social environment of our nation and no civilised society can permit such nuisance in its neighborhood. I understand that this was not the first time that JNU students had organised this kind of anti national such event.

This is pertinent to mention here that the individual Afjal Guru had masterminded 2001 parliament terror attack, which had led to loss of several innocent lives. Several people were injured during this attack. Trying to brand him as a martyr by some of JNU students was definitely an injustice to the victims of the terror attack *i.e.,* the departed innocent souls. The centre of discussion on the TV channels was revolving around this incident and the age old sick secular/communal political ideologies of some political leaders. Some of the participants of this debate openly sided with anti national elements. They criticized high handedness of police at JNU campus, while others considered it as part of quality education, being given to JNU students for their overall development. I am of a considered opinion that right to quality education does not mean right of freedom of expression, a right if misused, may break the social fabrics of our society. Education must be available and accessible, but should also be acceptable and adaptable within the socio- legal environment and should be adequate, safe and non-violent. This incident had definitely created insecurity in the minds of large population of India as all social fabrics of a peaceful society of India, was attacked in the heart of our nation by a very few anti social elements.

I wish to add that all political ideologies have only two dimensions and the most important dimension is to adopt a most appropriate way to organize society. A political ideology comprise some ethics and ideals and need to be distanced from such events *i.e.,* antinational acts as events of such nature are generally planned by enemy nations to promote anarchism and are being planned with an aim to destroy socio-economic fabric of our nation.

6. HIGHER QUALITY EDUCATION

Being a quality professional, I strongly feel that the goal of our educational institutes should have been to enable students with knowledge skill and competencies, as well as to infuse sanskar *i.e.,* infuse deep sense of nationalism.

Sanskar' is a process, which transforms a person into an ideal and outstanding personality by eradicating/diminishing the negative mental tendencies existing in him and by inculcating human values and qualities to make him more dynamic, discreet, duty conscious and responsible towards himself as well as the society.

To achieve, our education institutes should have a thorough system of internal quality system, which should be frequently assessed by "Quality Assurance Professionals" to make it more transparent to society. This system of external checks of the organizations shall prevent reoccurrence of these unfortunate events. The educational institutes must establish a corrective and preventive system to avoid recurrence of such incidents. Therefore, there is a pressing need to have a flexible innovative learning approach to improve quality and relevance and to take our education system to next higher level by providing a corrective and preventive system. This system shall help us in reinventing our education model and continual improvement of this model.

Therefore, there exists a requirement of reforms and modernization of our existing education system. I understand there are millions of education and skill development institutes in India which provide formal and non formal education to students. Thus there is a need to standardize education in such a manner that there is no scope for anti national acts by any student. Thus there is a need to redesign education system in such a manner that it is open for public scrutiny. I understand a lot of work has already been done in this field of standardization of education system *i.e.,* an international standard ISO 29990 has already been prepared by a committee ISO/TCS 232 with following main objectives of

Enhancing service quality in the field of learning

Enhancing the comparability and transparency services

Optimizing business services

Organizational effectiveness

Protecting learners rights

Reducing possibility of discrimination in learning services using national standards

Although this standard enables change of focus from training to learning to meet the undefined need of learners and focus on the outcome of the training with respect to the needs of students, but it is limited to non formal education institutes only.

I feel if formal education institutes of India like universities and colleges, implement this management standard, we may prevent reoccurrence of such unfortunate events. The system caters to every event and every educational activity of students inside or outside of institute campus.

Basic aim of this international management standard is to identify appropriate training needs of students, design a training model and thereafter monitor and evaluate it and review it periodically for allocation of adequate resources...

This standard also facilitates a provision for internal and external audits so that all non conformances are addressed in time and in a systematic manner.

There is also a provision of feedback system from public as well as interested parties in this international management standard. The standard is intended to assist students for development of their competency and capabilities. However at present it is limited to non formal education systems only. I strongly feel that the standard can be used for redesigning education model of our formal institutes with an aim to improve the existing education system so that there is no room for anti national activities taking place on our lands. Retired defence personnel of India, can be effectively employed as external Auditors/ Assessors, consequent to implementation of the management standard requirements by formal educational institutes, being audited as they possess education expertise and experience in this field. It is pertinent to mention here that the main aim of education is to provide good training to young men and women in the performance of their social, economic and religious duties. Also preservation and enrichment of culture, character and personality development and cultivation of noble ideals were the other aims of education in ancient India.

7. METHODS OF LEARNING

In ancient India, a close relationship existed between the pupil and the teacher. The teacher used to pay individual attention on his students and used to teach them according to their aptitude and capability. Knowledge was imparted orally and the different methods of learning were-

a) ***Memorization:*** The preliminary stage of learning was learning by heart the sacred text through indefinite repletion and rehearsal by both the teacher and the taught.

b) ***Critical analysis:*** This was another method in which knowledge was comprehended. It was through critical analysis Teachers were open to new ideas and views articulated by their students.

c) ***Introspection:*** Sravana (listening), Manana (contemplation) and Nididhyasana (concentrated contemplation) of the truth so as to realize it was another method to study Brahma Vidya.

d) ***Story telling:*** The teacher used stories and parables to explain.

e) ***Question and answer method:*** In this method the pupils used to ask questions and the teacher used to discuss at length on the topics and clear their doubts.

f) ***Hands-on method:*** For professional courses including medical science, students/apprentices used to learn by observation and through practical method.

g) ***Seminars:*** The students also gained knowledge thought debates and discussions which were held at frequent intervals.

The quality of education imparted in ancient India was therefore unparalleled. Hence in spite of various hardship and hurdles students from different parts of the world flocked to Indian universities. With the invasion of Muslim conquerors nearly all the centers of higher learning of the Hindus and Buddhists were destroyed. Nalanda was burnt to the ground in 1197 A.D. and all its monks were slaughtered. Kanauj and Kashi were looted and plundered. Temples and educationals institutions and libraries were put to destruction and they were replaced by mosques. In spite of such merciless and extensive destruction, Hindu educational institutions remained a living reality. They sustained strength from its inherent vitality and vigour and maintained the Hindu education system. Even during the reigns of terror and turmoil, merciless persecution and wanton destruction, the Hindu culture and scholarship continued to survive, though it had to migrate to more congenial regions within the country.

8. APPLICATION OF QMS CONCEPT IN OUR EDUCATION SYSTEMS

Education system is just like a factory, which is manufacturing quality products. Product of education system is a student. As we are aware that each manufacturing activity leads to interaction with the environment. Factory management frequently identifies the most significant activity which may have harmful consequences to the environment *i.e.,* the process may lead to pollution in air soil or water. Similarly there may be some significant activities in education systems, which may have harmful effects on social environment. Therefore there is a need to implement checks and balances in our education system *i.e.,* through rigorous internal and external auditing system.

To produce a quality product a manufacturer prepares a quality assurance plan considering all statutory and legal requirements and get it approved from his clients similarly there is a need to prepare a quality assurance plan for educational institutes which should be approved by all stake holders. Different stages of education to students should be identified. During each stage of manufacturing product there is an independent inspection by a qualified QC expert similarly for producing a quality student there is a need to check the quality plan at each stage by an assessor.

Purpose of quality plan is to make a quality product right the first time and to critically examine each activity so that there is no harmful effect on environment. Similarly while producing quality student, each activity needs to be examined critically so that any activity may not disturb socio legal environment. All non conformances need to examine and corrective preventive action is required to be carried out for continual improvement of the system.

To sum up it is opined that our education system should have deep impact in the uplift and advancement of our society as well as over all development of students, so that they become responsible citizens of India. Following objectives should therefore be ascribed while preparing quality assurance plan for our education system to produce quality citizens for future generations of India.

a) Self-control
b) Development of character
c) Generation of sociability or social awareness
d) Integral development of personality
e) Propagation of purity
f) Preservation of knowledge and culture

9. BUSINESS STRATEGIES FOR EDUCATION INSTITUTES

Developing right business culture is key to success and for this organization have to define their mission as people don't just buy products and services only but they do also look for the results. Purpose for being in education business should be to turn the unfulfilled desires of students into reality, you can feel justifiably proud of your contributions. Taking an ethical approach to the business, performing as promised, and operating in a sound manner are the keys to success in any education business ventures. The growth of business is the aggregate of the growth of individual team members. By constantly training everyone in education business to perform at higher levels than competitors, is a good strategy. Periodically motivation levels of staff as well as students also need to be measured by internal and external assessors. Various Other Strategies Include:

1. Articulating core values
2. Coaching for performance
3. Doing everything with passion
4. Doing whatever it takes to serve or add value to the system
5. Systematize every aspect of business

10. ORGANIZATIONAL EFFECTIVENESS

Organisational effectiveness is basically about the ability of the organisation to meet its set goals and objectives given the resources at its disposal. The main measure of organizational effectiveness for a business will generally be expressed in terms of how well it's net profitability as compared with its target profitability. Additional measures might include growth data and the results of customer satisfaction surveys. Highly effective organizations exhibit strengths across five areas: leadership, decision making and structure, people, work processes and systems, and culture. For an organization to achieve and sustain success, it needs to adapt to its dynamic environment. Evaluating and improving organizational effectiveness and efficiency is one strategy used to help insure the continued growth and development of an organization.

In many cases, a business' success or failure cannot be measured by financial performance as well. Even a company that is currently making a profit may be ineffective if it is failing to meet the core values of its mission statement, attract and retain talented workers, and plan for the next generation of projects. Since organizational effectiveness is difficult to express in a concrete formula as far as educational institutes are concerned the organization may choose to state the results of an assessment carried out by external assessors through specific goals achieved or desired. Organizational resources, namely, Human, Financial and Technological resources may be assessed by external auditors/assessors.

The organizational effectiveness also calls for creating sustainable growth and development by taking care of not only the share holders' expectations but also the expectations of other stake holders. It is pertinent to mention here that immediate stake holders to any education institute are the people residing in immediate neighborhood of educational institutes *i.e.,* public and the activities of any educational institutes have to care for these important stake holders. It also means that management must take the right ethical decisions in the interest of all the stake holders including general public.

11. CONCLUSION

Consequent to critical examination of recent anti national incidents and the dangerous trends in some universities campuses it is opined that no university or educational institute should be given total autonomy or Independence and the working of education systems of all universities be made more transparent and presented for external assessment for the interest of its all stakeholders.

4

Planning and Facilitating Small Group Learning: An Innovation Tool for Supplementing Traditional Teaching

SWAGATIKA SAMAL[1*] AND RABINDRA GARADA[2]

ABSTRACT

Small group learning is the dynamic way to enhance teaching and learning performance. Across the globe today different innovative teaching methods are in use with emphasis on what the students are actually doing in the class. Small group learning method has been found to be effective at raising the level of learning for all students formed into smaller groups as a part of the larger group. It is quite beneficial to achieve the ultimate goal of teaching i.e., raising level of learning. One of the advantages of such practices is flexibility. This tool can be adapted, and not just adopted, in a wide variety of disciplines, institution types and cultural / political / economic environments. Faculty members in India have very little flexibility with the course syllabus on an average. But within that constraint, there are opportunities for teaching the material differently so that students learn more, without sacrificing content coverage. Small group learning facilitates adopting more student-

[1] Department of Anthropology, Sambalpur University, Jyoti-Vihar, Burla, Sambalpur - 768019, Odisha, India.

[2] Department of Sociology, Utkal University, Vani Vihar, Bhubaneswar, Odisha, India

* *Corresponding author*: E-mail: swagatikasamal70@gmail.com

interactive practices which can significantly increase student learning. So, keeping in view the suitability of small group learning method, this chapter provides rationale and benefits of small group learning, attempts to differentiate it from the traditional teaching, describes features of effective small group learning, discusses steps to planning for effective small group learning by considering essential factors and finally it describes the facilitation strategies for effective small group learning, common challenges and strategies to address the challenges.

Key words: Small group learning, Pedagogic innovation, Active learning, Supportive environment, Teacher-facilitator, Engaged learner

---

INTRODUCTION

Education and innovation has become the need of the hour today for a country like India to find its suitable place in the global community on the grounds of its education system. It is vital to emphasize on the pedagogic innovation to effect raising level of learning for all the students in any discipline. Across the globe today different innovative teaching methods are in use with emphasis on what the students are actually doing in the class. These are lecture, interactive lecture and discussion, student-peer feedback, small group work, writing/speaking exercises, case method, problem-based learning, project-based learning, simulations, fieldwork/clinical experience etc. Small group learning is one among them. It is a dynamic way to enhance teaching and learning performance. Small group learning method has been found to be effective at raising the level of learning for all students formed into smaller groups as a part of the larger group. In a small group learning situation, the learner learns to create, evaluate, apply, understand and remember more effectively and collaboratively. In small group learning, learners feel engaged, motivated to participate and learn actively. This can be well supplemented to the traditional lecture course for effective learning.

The chapter discusses about small group learning, provides rationale and benefits of small group learning. It attempts to recognize how and why teaching in small groups differs from teaching in other settings. It also introduces the role of teachers in small group learning and describes four features of effective small group learning. It presents the unique opportunities and challenges in small group learning. Further the chapter discusses how to plan for effective small group learning by considering essential factors such as planning goals and objectives, considering learners, developing educational activities and determining assessment tools. It also describes the facilitation strategies for effective small group learning, common challenges and strategies to address the challenges.

SMALL GROUP LEARNING: WHAT IS IT?

Small group learning can supplement or companion to a traditional lecture course. It may be a main organizational unit of learning for a course. It is important to understand first what the small group is. A typical view of a 'small group' is around eight to twelve learners facilitated by a teacher. The purist view of small group teaching is that it must be learner-centred, with all students joining in free discussion of a particular topic (McCrorie, 2006: p. 5). In some contexts, however, groups may be smaller than this, sometimes even a pair of students or trainees. Small group teaching is necessarily more demanding of staff and room resources and time than lectures. However, well-designed small group teaching has clear benefits for student learning in terms of retention of information, critical thinking and consolidation of learning from different parts of a programme (McCrorie, 2006). What characterize a 'small group' is not so much its size, but the teaching and learning context and the way in which the teacher works with and facilitates the learning process.

Small groups provide opportunities for learning that are difficult to establish in large group settings. They are particularly useful to enable learners to take part in discussion, active participation, feedback and reflection, and to consolidate learning, clarify understanding, and explore ideas and concepts. Depending on the purpose and nature of the group, small group teaching can also help to develop 'transferable' skills, such as study skills, communication skills, teamwork, problem solving and personal development. One of the characteristics that differentiate small group teaching from large group teaching is that there is a greater attention to group processes as well as to achievement of tasks.

The size and composition of the group are important but may vary based on course content, the learner's needs and goals and sometimes more importantly the availability of resources such as space and facilities. However it is important to understand that the exact size is much less critical than what happens in a small group in terms of teaching and learning.

In an incredibly effective small group learning situation, what we can imagine that a group of learners together discuss ideas, compare and contrast opinions, test hypotheses, practice skills, receive real time feedback, reflect on their learning needs and goals. In traditional lecture sessions, learning is mostly passive, unidirectional and instructor driven which is just opposite to the learning in the small group teaching-learning situation. The small group learning provides opportunities for more open and active learning.

Benefits of Small Group Learning

The unique features of small group learning allow for the application of theoretical learning to real life contexts. It allows for opportunities to master higher order skills and creates opportunities for deeper and longer lasting learning. All these benefits can be achieved when educators plan and implement effective small group learning sessions that are characterized by learning that is active, collaborative, and self-directed and that emphasizes a supportive and open learning environment. These are the four very important features of small group learning.

Features of Small Group Learning

The Fig. 1 depicts the basic features of the small group learning and here we can discuss each of these components of small group learning individually.

a) ***Active learning***: It is any process in which learners regularly reflect on content (often in an experiential context), and reassess their understanding of the content and its real world applications. This results in deeper and longer lasting levels of learning in which learners demonstrate the ability to analyze, evaluate, and create using content in a real life context (Fig. 2).

Now question arises here is that how we can promote active learning? This must be accompanied with adoption of many strategies called active learning strategies. The learning strategies that can be used to promote active learning that engage learning in the process.

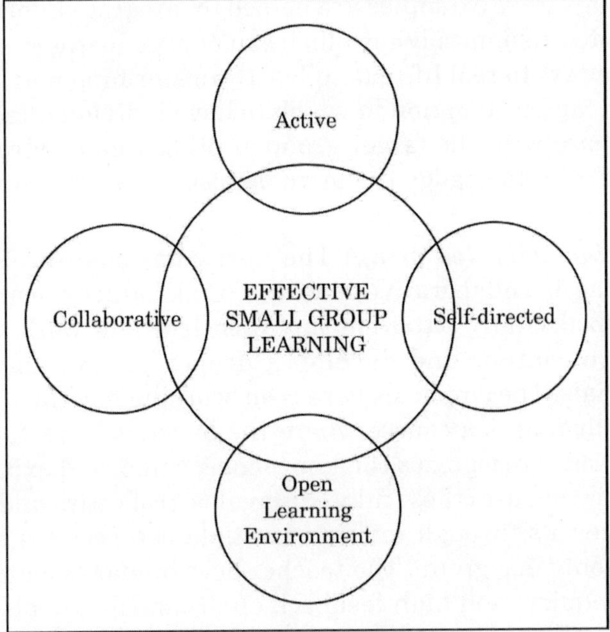

Fig. 1: Characteristics of small group learning

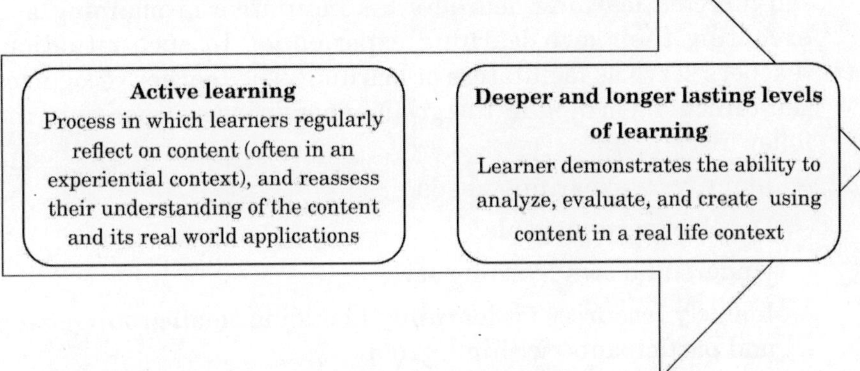

Fig. 2: Active learning

The strategies which can be used for effective active learning can be to develop discussion between learners or discussion between learners and teachers. Questioning techniques can help learners explore the context and issues in a much deeper level. Cycles of reflection and action can be used *e.g.*, simulation and role play. Case examples are helped to integrate information and promote problem solving which can engage learners and connect the context to real life examples. Brainstorming and Think/Pair/ Share can be an option in which to have individual talks in pairs and share with the larger group or other related strategies also can be used to engage the more introspective learners into small group.

b) ***Collaborative learning*:** The next component of small group learning is collaborative learning. Collaborative learning to be described is any situation in which learners work together to explore content and develop a deeper understanding of the materials. The emphasis here is on 'working together'. Collaborative learning is a course where the learners work together and the teacher recognizes the knowledge, skills, and expertise of all learners and uses these fully. He creates a collective understanding of materials through inviting multiple perspectives that can be found only in a group. The teacher here promotes a high support, high inquiry, and high feedback environment. He also creates a system of interdependent, shared leadership and accountability that sustains a small group over time.

c) ***Self-directed learning*:** The next component in small group learning that is critical to exercise is self-directed learning. In self-directed learning, learners take initiative in planning and executing their own learning experiences. In such situation, teachers serve as facilitators of learning. The teacher recognizes self-directed learning in the group when learners engage in the following:

   - Identify own learning needs
   - Develop learning goals
   - Understand own learning style
   - Identify resources for learning (including small group setting and participants) within a group
   - Reflect on action (what they are doing in a group) and revise in changed behavior and learned format.

d) ***Supportive learning environment*:** Creating a safe and supportive learning environment is critical to promoting effective small group learning. Learners require a balance of challenge and support to take risks in their learning. This actually takes effort and planning. Educators or facilitators use a variety of techniques to create a supportive learning environment. The educators monitor and guide group process, develop group norms for questioning and peer feedback, facilitate trust, respect, and full participation of small group participants. The facilitator may also role model reflective practice or learning message that we include in small group. They may also use self-disclosure of their own personal success and challenges to model a supportive learning environment where learners are willing to take risks in their learning.

ROLE OF THE TEACHER IN SMALL GROUP LEARNING

There are three main activities that small group teachers have to manage simultaneously:

1. Managing the group
2. Managing activities
3. Managing the learning

In many small group teaching situations, the role of the teacher is that of a facilitator of learning: leading discussions, asking open-ended questions, guiding process and task, and enabling active participation of learners and engagement with ideas. In small group learning the role of the teacher can be as listed below:-

- Facilitator of learning *vs.* Transmitter of knowledge
- Creating a supportive and open learning environment
- Planning sessions and activities to meet learning goals
- Monitoring and facilitating group process to enhance learning goals and
- Role modeling active, self-directed, collaborative learning.

Planning for Effective Small Group Learning

To plan effective educational activities, begin with asking yourself certain questions such as

- What is it I want to teach?
- Who are my learners?
- How will I teach the material?
- How will I know that my learners have mastered the material?

If you can address these questions you can plan effective small group learning. Translating these questions in to specific action items would be as like, identifying goals and objectives, considering your learners and group factors, developing educational activities and determining assessment tools. These action items are the possible factors needed to be considered as you plan your small group learning sessions. Let's discuss these factors.

- ***Planning goals and objectives*:** To begin with planning goals and objectives you need to identify clear, specific and measurable goals and objectives for small group learning session. Remember to consider the entire curriculum of the course while you consider objectives and goals for your small group. Also remember that one of the benefits of small group learning is that you can address 'content' as well as 'process' goals. For example, if you are facilitating a small group session that supplements an undergraduate level course on research methods, the content goal of the small group is to learn about different research designs and the appropriate use of each whereas, the process *goal* is to improve learners' collaboration, communication, and presentation skills during the course.
- ***Understanding the learners*:** While understanding your learners, you need to consider each learner individually and attempt to learn about what is their level of experience and expertise, what are their learning needs and goals, their learning styles, what are their prior norms for learning- was it more active and collaborative or passive learning? Do they have prior relationships with other small group members and what impact might that have on them? While considering individual learners you need to consider them within the context of learning group or community and how all they function together. In this way you learn to consider the composition of the group in terms of variety of factors such as gender, experience level, communication and participation style. You identify others as you get to know your learners. Then you ask yourself the following questions –

  How might these factors influence the group in terms of learning?

  How might group size effect small group learning?

  What physical setting is best for effective group learning?

  Where there is no absolute correct answer to these questions, careful consideration of size and composition may help to anticipate and prevent potential challenges into small group learning and improve learning significantly.

- ***Planning educational activities***: In this case you have to identify educational activities that promote individual accountability and a high level of collaboration amongst your learners. You have to promote an exchange of diverse perspectives and critical thinking and problem solving in the small group experience. Your all activities should address differences in learning style (use a range of educational activities) and hopefully promote perspective transformation in which learners are challenged to question existing assumptions and beliefs and trying to use it in their learning.

  Consider for a moment how the following activities might promote small group learning. Taking example of teaching the learners about research methods, ask yourself how can I facilitate discussion of pre-assigned questions for more learning, what about sharing of personal real life experiences and challenges related to course content by the participants of your group.

- ***Planning assessment***: Finally, you need to think about assessment. You have to base your assessment on course goals and objectives. If you find you have done jobs of writing clear, specific and measurable goals, planning appropriate educational activities by meeting these goals and facilitating a supportive environment, you have no trouble planning your assessment. Remember that you can choose from two types of assessment *i.e.*, formative, and summative.

  The two types of assessment are discussed below. A teacher can choose any of the two or both to assess the achievement.

  – Formative assessment helps to monitor learning by providing ongoing feedback to improve learning. The assessment starts from small group sharing where we can often practice skills, be observed and get feedback in the moment and practice the skills again.

  – Summative assessment uses to evaluate learning often by using some standard or benchmark at the end of a course.

While planning for assessment, you need to consider your understanding and need of the course design and decide which type or both types of assessment you would like to use.

FACILITATION STRATEGIES FOR EFFECTIVE SMALL GROUP LEARNING

For a teacher, it is important to understand the group dynamics to use it as a means of teaching and learning. Remember that the teacher has to use the whole group as a means to satisfy the group's purpose. Here we can put some light on the processes through which a group goes and the role of the teacher facilitating small group learning based on Tuckman's (1965) framework of stages of group development. These are forming, storming, norming, and performing.

- ***Forming*:** This is the initial or beginning stage where, a group comes together for the first time. In this stage, most team members are positive and polite. Some are anxious even, as they haven't fully understood what work the team will do. Others are simply excited about the task ahead. The teacher can help by facilitating introductions, using ice-breaking tasks, and explaining the tasks and purpose of the group.
- ***Storming*:** Next, the team moves into the storming phase, where group members start to push against the boundaries established in the forming stage. Storming often starts where there is a conflict between team members' natural working styles. Or, if you haven't defined clearly how the team will work, people may feel overwhelmed by their workload, or they could be uncomfortable with the approach you're using. In this stage there may be conflict between one or more group members as the group sorts itself out and becomes more functional. This is the stage where many teams fail. The teacher can help by clarifying and reflecting ideas, smoothing over and moderating conflicts and acting as a bridge between the members.
- ***Norming*:** Gradually, the team moves into the norming stage. This is when people start to resolve their differences, appreciate other members' strengths, and work together. This is the stage where the members of the small group know one another better, they may socialize together, and they are able to ask one another for help and provide constructive feedback. The teacher can find the members in the group having developed a stronger commitment to the team goal and can start to see good progress towards it. In this stage the group begins to share ideas, thoughts and beliefs, and to develop shared norms (group rules). The teacher can help by clarifying ideas and ground rules, encouraging more

reticent people to participate and moving the group towards its purpose.

- ***Performing*:** This is when the group focuses on the activity and starts to work together as a team to perform the set tasks. It feels easy to be part of the team at this stage, and people who join or leave won't disrupt performance. The teacher's role is to keep the group focused and to encourage and facilitate it as necessary.

In small group learning, we might also add some final stages, such as 'adjourning' or, in the case of a group that has successfully worked together, 'mourning'. 'A good group will look back over its achievements and reflect on each others' contribution, on lessons learnt, on what worked well and what could have been done better' (McCrorie, 2006).

To assume effective small group learning, the facilitator has to promote active, self-directed, and collaborative learning and create a supportive learning environment. In small group learning the "teacher's" role differs from other teaching settings. The teacher becomes a facilitator of learning as opposed to a transmitter of knowledge in the traditional learning formats.

As the facilitator in small group learning, the teacher performs the following activities. He

- Fosters a supportive and open learning environment
- Coaches learners to identify learning styles, needs and goals
- Plans sessions and activities to meet learning goals
- Monitors and facilitates group process
- Role models active, self-directed, collaborative learning

The teacher as a facilitator for effective small group learning must be flexible, non-judgmental in attitude, supportive, enthusiastic, time and task focused, group process oriented, and shares power and leadership in the group experience. The facilitator what he does in a small group learning is that of

- Setting a precedent for group participation
- Assessing what experiences and expertise each group member brings to the collective experience
- Role modeling reflective questioning
- Inviting learners to self assess and state goals in the context of real life educational and career needs

- Promoting active learning through a paired discussion among group members
- Keeping the group on time and task

The other behaviors and skills of an effective facilitator in small group learning are listed below. The facilitator

- Bridges discussion to conceptual framework as well as "real world" inferences or implications
- Uses reflective open ended questioning, active listening and silence
- Summarizes at close of session (or invites group members to do so, this serves an added purpose of assessing what the learners have learned from the session)
- Elicits next steps for learning
- Periodically checks in around group process. Asks the group to consider how they are functioning, what is working well and not so well.

COMMON CHALLENGES IN FACILITATING SMALL GROUPS

Leading small groups can be challenging and the facilitator must monitor group process and intervene when the group gets derailed. In the small group learning, the common challenges include:

i. The "quiet" student
ii. The "domineering" student and
iii. The emergence of strong or negative emotions

These challenges, when handled well may build group trust and collaboration and enhance deeper learning. Jacques (2000) says 'If you haven't got problems in your group, then something is wrong'. So, it is natural that the group does have problems. With regard to resolution of issues in the group, McCrorie suggests that the best strategy is to let the group sort out its own problems. Here we discuss the issues in details.

- ***Low participation***: Sometimes in small group learning, a participant may be more introspective and requires/prefers time to process ideas or it may be that others do not provide space for a balance of participation in a group. Some participants are quite for different reasons (may be they are not prepared or shy or not feeling safe in the group etc.) In such a situation, it is the responsibility of the facilitator to create specific activities for reflection/processing and group sharing (examples are Think/Pair/Share or Think/Write/Share). The facilitator also may invite input from all participants in a nonthreatening way and in a way that provides advance warning and time for low participators to prepare to speak.

- ***The domineering participant*:** This participant may monopolize small group discussions to promote a specific agenda. This may be motivated by passion for the subject, competitiveness, or a desire for validation. In this case, the facilitator needs to be very tricky to handle it and may support and invite minority opinions and encourage clarification and discussion or refer back to group guidelines that encourage balanced participation and valuing of all perspectives and respectfully and non-judgmentally point out the issue.
- ***Group climate and emotion*:** It can have a profound impact on group function and learning. When challenges arise and they are not addressed this can negatively impact group function moving forward. So, the facilitator has always to be alert about the challenges arising in small group learning experience and handle it, and must keep an eye on the group processes. The facilitator in this case may recognize and acknowledge changes/tensions in group climate, name the issue, reinforce and support desirable behavior, model non judgmental language, directly address maladaptive conflict, competition, avoidance to better the experience. Moreover, the facilitator needs to be careful about what is going on with the learners in the group, attentive to individual learners, anticipate natural psychological group dynamics and to be ready to settle it timely to provide the learners much richer learning experience.

CONCLUSION

At any time, the core objective of teaching is passing on the information or knowledge to the minds of the students. Any teaching method without destroying the objective could be considered as innovative methods of teaching. There are a number of ways that teachers can offer students the tools, techniques and experiences that spur an innovative mindset. To conclude, it can be said that small group learning or students working in groups in today's context can be a boon to effect quality in the students' learning.

REFERENCES

Center for Teaching and Learning (1999). Cooperative learning; students working in small groups. Speaking of teaching. Standford University Newsletter on teaching. *Winter*, 10: 2.

De Villers, M., Bresick, G. and Mash, B. (2003). The value of small group learning: An evaluation of an innovative CPD programme for primary care medical practitioners. *Medical Education*, 37: 81521

Jacques, D. (2000). The tutor's job. Learning in groups (3e), London: Kogan Page, p. 15580.

Jacques, D. (2003). Teaching small groups. Cantillon, P., Hutchinson, L. and Wood, D. (*eds.*), BMJ ABC of learning and teaching in medicine, London: BMJ Publishing Group, p. 1921.

McCrorie, P. (2006). Teaching and leading small groups. Association for the study of medical education, Edinburgh.

Michaelsen, L., Fink, D. and Knight, A. (1997). Designing effective group activities: Lessons for classroom teaching and faculty development, DeZure, D. (*ed.*), to improve the academy. Stillwater. OK: POD Network.

Richmond, D.E. (1984). Improving the effectiveness of small-group learning with strategic intervention. *Medical Teacher*, 6: 13845.

Tiberius, R. (1990). Small group teaching: A trouble-shooting guide. Ontario: OISE.

Tuckman, B. (1965). Developmental sequence in small groups. *Psychological Bulletin*, 63(6): 384–399. available at *http://psycnet.apa.org/journals/bul/63/6/384*.

Westberg, J. and Jason, H. (1996). Fostering learning in small groups: A practical guide. New York: Springer.

5

Culturally Responsive Pedagogy for Effective Teaching of Communication Skills

PUSHP LATA[1*]

ABSTRACT

Communicative Language Teaching, the most acknowledged framework of second language teaching, is increasingly facing a major question as to whether L2 teaching can be done without sensitizing the students about the cultural niceties. As the framework of communicative competence aims at developing discourse competence for communicative purposes, the present paper reflects our conceptualization of communicative language teaching in brief but the need of Socio cultural awareness among teachers at large for effective teaching. It means it considers the intercultural component as the point of departure for teaching communication skills to learners. This paper also outlines how information about intercultural communication if that is integrated into teaching methodology can foster greater awareness of sociocultural relativity and facilitate teacher's reflection on their preconceived notions of target learner groups as they require to make their methodological decisions. Finally, the paper highlights what kind of tools, activities, and exercises can be administered in the classes to teach effective communication by developing intercultural competence.

[1] Department of Humanities and Social Sciences, BITS, Pilani Rajasthan

* *Corresponding author*: E-mail: pushplatabits@gmail.com

Keywords: Communicative Language Teaching; Inter cultural awareness; cross cultural competence; CRP Motivational Framework; student - teacher relationship

---

INTRODUCTION

Language is inseparably intertwined with both the tangible and intangible aspects of culture. Before globalization a strong need was not felt to know the culture of the taught as the classroom was dominated by the learners from the culture of the place. Lately, language teachers have realized the interdependence and inextricability of language and culture which has brought a paradigm shift in focus for Language teaching and learning. This change has become the key feature of today's classroom due to the multicultural setting. Language and culture interact with each other in a way that culture associates to all levels of language use and structures. None of the levels of language is independent of culture. In fact, Bennett *et al.*, have strongly supported the need for intercultural awareness (IA) in language teaching and have stated, "The relationship between language and culture is made meaningful in language learning as "the person who learns language without learning culture risks becoming a fluent fool" (Bennett, Bennett and Allen, 2003, p. 237). Discussing the intrinsic relation between the two Cui and Awa (1992) and McAllister and Irvine (2000) have aptly defined intercultural competence (IC) as something typically related to cognitive, affective, and behavioral components. Cultural competence therefore, is not considered innate; it is something that can be learnt and developed. It offers a lens through which beliefs, values, customs and issues of a culture can be understood better. The question arises how IA helps the language teachers in bringing effectiveness in their pedagogy. Before answering this question, it is essential to know that merely having an awareness about the cultural differences or niceties does not mean that a person has the competence to use the knowledge appropriately. Therefore, in the ensuing part of the paper an attempt has been made so as to define the term Intercultural competence also known as cross cultural competence (CCS). Finally, it aids us to understand how IA among teachers helps in enhancing IC and thereby, bring pedagogy effectiveness.

Intercultural competence helps in managing multiplicity and diversity in ways that craft an environment in which the possible advantages of diversity are capitalized while the impending disadvantages are curtailed. It is "a complex of abilities needed to perform *effectively* and *appropriately* when interacting with others who are linguistically and culturally different from oneself" (Fantini, 2006: p. 12). Fantini here emphasizes on the pragmatic aspect of competence. LoCastro (2003) in his paper entitled *an introduction to pragmatics: Social action for language teachers* defines the pragmatic competence as 'the ability to use language to carry out everyday functions in culturally appropriate ways' (p. vii). Gumperz (1999) views pragmatic misunderstandings as more serious than lexical or grammatical mistakes because the latter will be attributed by listeners to the speaker's attempt to learn the language, whereas the former creates subconscious negative impressions about the speaker. He further discusses how in case of non-native speakers' (NNSs'), culturally different ways of speaking and understanding are judged as indicators of character or overall competence in the workplace. To perform well in today's Cosmo cultural business environment, students need to possess a high degree of cross-cultural competence, which may be defined as "the process of acquiring the culture-specific and culture general knowledge, skills, and attitudes required for effective communication and interaction with individuals from other cultures" (Paige, Jorstad, Siaya, Klein and Colby, 2003: p. 177).

Researches have shown that for inculcating an intercultural awareness and developing a competence for using the knowledge appropriately, students need to be trained during their graduation studies. For this teacher also need training to deal with a class, with the cross cultural setting. Most of the teachers lack basic knowledge about the differences that exist between cultures. A lack of cultural knowledge spoils the relationships between the teachers and their taught which results into inadequate learning outcome and lack of cultural sociability in their professional life. Thus, in order to develop linguistic competence in a cross cultural setting, it necessitates the teachers to learn and then create an awareness and understanding of the cultural differences among their learners. This awareness will equip them enough against any kind of linguistic and cultural barriers that crop up in communication. The question that needs to be addressed is whether cultural diversity always poses a threat to the teaching learning environment. No cultural diversity, which poses major professional challenges to the language teachers, also adds value to the learning environment.

Teaching from an intercultural perspective involves critical cultural awareness which shapes the teachers' own views, values, and behaviors. Besides, IC includes the skills and attitudes to understand and successfully interact with people from other cultures, that is, to become interculturally as well as linguistically competent" (Ho, 2009: p. 63). In recent years, there is a change in focus as *culture is treated as content* in language pedagogy. In fact, the intercultural understanding has become the DNA of multicultural classroom pedagogy and successful businesses. Barkhuizen and others too have emphasized upon the fact that language pedagogy essentially encompasses the cultural appropriateness especially as they deal with cross cultural contexts (Barkhuizen, 1998; Coleman, 1996). Holliday has made an extensive research and has pointed out how a lack of consideration of variations in cultures of learning can lead to frustration and subsequent failure in language classrooms (Holliday, 1994). Teachers' lack of sensitivity about the respective cultural norms fructifies a lack of fit among students due to wrong type of communication exposure. Research has also revealed how "behavior in language classrooms is set within taken-for granted frameworks of expectations, attitudes, values, and beliefs about what constitutes good learning, about how to teach or learn, whether and how to ask questions, what textbooks are for, and how language teaching relates to broader issues of the nature and purpose of education" (Seran Dogancay-Aktuna: 99). EFL teachers, therefore, need to change their gear from a traditional stance to one to develop both linguistic and intercultural competences of their learners. For discussing this change in depth let us first deal briefly with Communicative Approach to Teaching which has been the basic precept behind ESL and EFL teaching for past few decades.

CRITICAL REVIEW OF COMMUNICATIVE APPROACH TO LANGUAGE TEACHING

In response to the limitations of grammar translation method, audio lingual, aural oral approach and situational approaches, the educators and researchers felt that L2 learners do not learn the language in a natural and realistic manner. Since communication is a vital point in language learning, the practitioners, require an understanding of the complex and integrated nature of the theoretical concept of communicative competence (Celce-Murcia and Olshtain, 2005). A British linguist, Wilkins (1972) proposed a functional or communicative definition of language that could serve as a basis for developing communicative syllabuses for language teaching. Wilkins's contribution was an analysis of the communicative meanings that a language learner needs to understand and express rather than emphasizing the core of language through traditional grammar and vocabulary. Though this brought a change in the focus of language teaching from language skills to communication skills, yet the researchers and educationists felt that learners still fail to communicate with others using appropriate social language, gestures, or expressions as they are not aptly sensitized about the culture of the language studied and respecting the others' cultural nuances. For example, Hu (2002) reports that communicative language teaching (CLT) has failed to have the expected impact on ELT in China because assumptions underlying CLT conflict with the Chinese culture of learning. His argument is supported by others who have shown how Chinese teachers and students view explicit grammar analysis as crucial to foreign language learning, and believes that the teacher should dominate the classroom. Moreover, Chinese students face problems in accepting group work, debates, and other interactive activities as meaningful or relevant to their learning. Instead, they value mastery through memorization because they perceive it as knowledge that will bring them confidence and a feeling of success (Cortazzi and Jin 1996). Both Dewey and Vygotsky also emphasized the role of cultural forms and meanings in perpetuating higher forms of human thought. Both of them underscored a notion of cultural progress within the concrete realities of shared human purposes and social means (Susan J. Mayer, 2008 p. 7). Interactional sociolinguistics (Campbell and Roberts, 2007; Kerekes, 2007; Li, 2000) have also examined how pragmatic competence which involves knowing what is culturally and contextually appropriate to say in a given situation, relates to a second language (L2) learner's success in communicating with people from other cultures. Crandall and Basturkmen (2004) and Bardovi-Harlig (2001) emphasize that it is necessary for learners to notice these pragmatic factors before they can begin to improve their competence.

Why to Build Cultural Awareness and Sensitivity among Teachers

Globalization has been furthered by the invariable growth in telecommunication, technology, and transportation, and the influence of media; all have made the world increasingly small and interconnected. Thus, people across the globe are exposed to each other's cultures like never before. In addition, increase in international business, and surge in the number of international joint ventures and mergers and acquisitions have forced managers of Multinational companies to frequently interact with people from different cultures. Academicians, researchers and scientists also need to address this issue in their curriculum and pedagogy so that their students, the would be professionals and businessmen get some training during their studies. Today they require to be competent enough to collaborate and communicate with their counterparts from other nationals. If the teachers themselves are proficient in dealing with cultural diversity, this will facilitate constructive learning outcomes as they will be the role models for their students for embracing different cultures which involves learning how to accept, adapt and interact with others in an ethnically culturally racially diverse environment. Gay holds the view that classroom teachers, administrators, and policymakers carry their cultural experiences and perspectives into their everyday decisions and actions– educational and personal– and so do students from various ethnic and cultural backgrounds (Gay, 2000). As is well known the academic success squarely depends on how they communicate with each other without creating discomfort or hurt. Teachers require to devise and use effective instructional strategies which are culturally responsive for all students. Many authors have argued that teachers with a high level of cross cultural competence have better ability to deal with the challenges and issues of culturally-diverse classes. Cross-culturally competent teachers operate simultaneously and effectively with students from multiple cultures (Korhonen, 2002: p. 32). Educators and teachers in management discipline strongly believe that to perform well in today's cross-cultural business environment management graduates should develop a high degree of cross-cultural competence, which may be defined as "the process of acquiring the culture-specific and cultural general knowledge, skills, and attitudes required for effective communication and interaction with individuals from other cultures" (Paige, Jorstad, Siaya, Klein and Colby, 2003: p. 177). Cross-culturally competent teachers operate effectively with students from multiple cultures. Rothstein-Fisch and Trumbull (2008) emphasized that teachers be trained in techniques of classroom management from a cultural perspective in that "cultural values and beliefs are at the core of all classroom organization and management decisions" (p. xiii). They are unique as they are able to overcome the differences in cultural backgrounds, expectations, educational needs, and academic traditions. However, there is a lack of empirical research on the relationship between the cross-cultural competence of faculty and their performance in terms of effectiveness of their teaching. However, Byram who has done extensive research and has refocused the goal of language education with culture integrated into language study, calls it *intercultural communicative competence*" (Byram, 1997).

In response to the changing needs and limitation of much adopted communicative approach to language teaching, Grant (1991a) came up with the concept of *culturally responsive pedagogy* (CRP). He believed that knowledge has no intrinsic power unless it is disseminated through communication with the interests, aspirations, desires, needs, and purposes of the students.Thus, student relevance and participations are the upmost concerns in *culturally responsive pedagogy* whereby indigenous pupils should not be seen as merely "consumers" but should be given the responsibility to co-design (along with the teachers) the trajectory of their education. This pedagogy actually offers equitable and unbiased access to education for students from all cultures.

Moreover, while formulating teacher education programs it is essential to make the teachers understand learn how to consider students' sociocultural backgrounds while designing and implementing lessons. As acquiring cultural competence is a gradual process, it is achieved by observations, experiences, and interactions in the classroom and playground, and other recreational activities with parents, teachers and peers. However, the process can begin with the knowledge and understanding of the basic cultural differences that teachers are likely to encounter in the culturally diverse classroom. Familiarity with these differences will begin to aid teachers in understanding the complexity of teaching heterogeneous groups of students. Culturally Responsive Teaching is a pedagogy that recognizes the importance of including students' cultural references in all aspects of learning (Ladson-Billings, 1994). In this pedagogy student differences are studied as a basis for planning and designing the curriculum and pedagogy.

Considering the above emphasized need for changes in teaching learning environment, given below are some of the important characteristics of *culturally responsive pedagogy:*

Positive viewpoints on parents and communities

If carefully observed the students even before they come to school family and other community people use certain strategies to teach them life skills and basic notions like greetings, dining etiquette and most importantly the social conversational tips. CRP leverages the brain's memory systems and information processing structures. For example, in case of students who come from oral cultural traditions, their primary ways of knowledge transfer and meaning-making are oral and active. These very strategies can be used to make the students inclusive in the teaching learning process.

Communication of high expectations

In the CRP environment, Students help other students and the teacher solve problems. Students work with the teacher to establish both whole-class and individual goals.

Learning within the context of culture

One of the desired features of this pedagogy is making lessons more culturally relevant in order to accelerate student learning. According to Beauboeuf-Lafontant culturally responsive classrooms can create a space where harmful images can be deconstructed and positive self and cultural affirmations can be portrayed. Diverse students can learn the content more effectively if they can to create a coherent narrative about the topic or process presented.

Student-centered learning environment

Besides instruction, there is a provision of continuous evaluation system. In CRP assessment is an ongoing process and problem-solving approach can be used for making instruction more responsive to the learners. Furniture is arranged to promote group work and flexible grouping and pairing are used for desired learning outcome. Games are other powerful strategy for culturally-grounded learning because they get the attention of brain easily for active information processing. Most of the games employ a lot of the cultural tools repetition, solving a puzzle, making connections between things that do not seem to be related.

Traits of a quality teacher

Though desired in any type of classroom pedagogy, yet in CRP the teacher has a strong belief in students' ability to learn. He/she has the desire and capacity to differentiate curriculum and instruction, and also understands diversity and thinks about students' growth and development.

AN INTRINSIC CRP MOTIVATIONAL FRAMEWORK

Intrinsic method of motivation can readily accommodate the cultural differences. Wlodkowski and Ginsberg (1995) have emphasized upon four conditions which are necessary for Culturally Responsive Teaching.

Within this pedagogical framework, the synchronization of approaches to teaching ensures maximizing the benefits of cultural diversity and minimizing the conflicts that thwart the environment. It is the key precept of this model because harmony, communication and mutual respect lead to an environment where students are likely to feel encouraged and intrinsically motivated.

The framework names four motivational conditions that the teacher and students continuously create or enhance. They are:

1. ***Establishing inclusion*****:** In this teacher creates a learning atmosphere in which both students and teachers feel respected and valued by each other. They feel connected to one another.
2. ***Developing attitude*****:** As part of the framework teacher always aims at creating a favorable disposition toward the learning experience by making the teaching, assignments and evaluation personally relevant and meaningful to students.
3. ***Enhancing meaning*****:** Besides making the pedagogy relevant teachers also need to create challenging and thoughtful learning experiences that include student perspectives and values.
4. ***Engendering competence*****:** Finally, Wlodkowski and Ginsberg stress upon creating an understanding that students are effective in learning something they themselves value.

Besides student's voice and personal experience and inquiry Gay (2000) identifies the six important attributes of a culturally responsive teacher and classroom (Fig. 1). These conditions are vital to developing intrinsic motivation as they are sensitive to cultural differences.

CHANGE IN THE TEACHER'S ROLE

Teachers have to adapt to the changes occurring in the society, business and particularly educational settings. They need to reflect on the fears, stereotypes and biases which they hold about other people who are different from them. Only then they can start investigating and appreciating the traditions and values of other cultures. They aim to provide students with opportunities to connect their learning experiences to their own lives. Given below are some of the efforts that teachers need to make in order to implement CRP effectively:

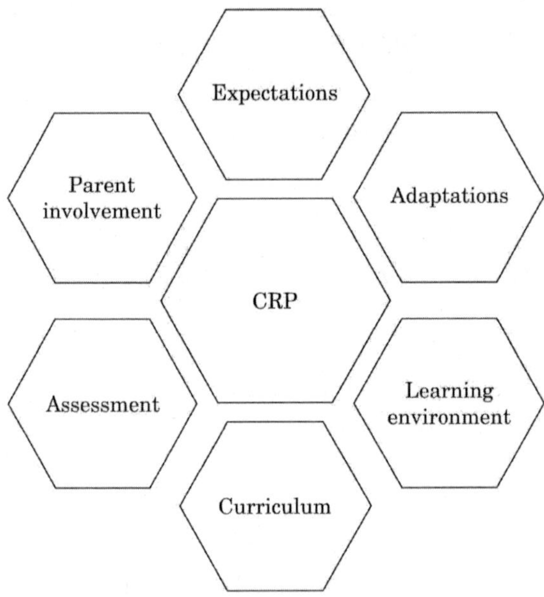

Fig. 1: Six Important attributes of CRP by Gay (2000)

- Teachers should reflect upon their own pre-existing biases so that they can overcome them by making conscious efforts. Teachers should have an open mind to the emerging changes, new ways, varied beliefs and differences of perceptions.
- In the multicultural classroom, teachers must shed the old practices, modify their stance and ask open-ended questions.
- Teachers must play a lead role for bringing a positive change in classroom environment with regard to cultural tolerance, cultural awareness and sensitivity so as to instill respect for diversity.
- Teachers must encourage students to respect multiplicity of cultures, opinions and show sensitivity for cultures different from theirs.
- They should acknowledge the medley of background experiences students bring to the classroom and ensure the materials and

methods are representative of this ever-growing diversity. So they should include multicultural activities in classroom as these will enable the students to play a more active role in the learning process.

- Teachers need to employ structured instructional techniques such as group work, pair work, field work etc as the diverse learning groups will encourage each student.

TEACHING MATERIALS AND STRATEGIES TO ENHANCE CROSS CULTURAL SENSITIVITY

To develop intercultural competency in communication, English teachers need to devise teaching materials which focus on the use of online collaborative learning technologies. According to O'Brien and Ericksson it will enable the teacher to have "globalised- distributed teams." Teachers can administer the assignment online where students would require wrestling with different interpretations or unveiling the layers of text involving cultural tinge. Through the globalized– distributed teams, teachers can help their students explore the multiple perspectives through cross cultural connections and widen their spectrum for greater intercultural competencies and bring about improved global relations and help developing global citizens. For example, I have used various *case study discussions* such as Euro Disney Failure, Walmart Debacle, Mercedes Benz conflict or Coco Cola Issue in Kerala for discussion where cultural insensitivity had been the main reason for their failure in foreign land. Lot of case studies are available on net related to mergers, acquisitions and take overs which fail due to cultural conflicts besides financial and legal complexities contributing to major fiascoes. These case study discussions enhance the cultural awareness about varied cultures on one hand and the other elements of communication skills such as argumentative skills, body language, voice modulation, accuracy, fluency and knowledge about the subject under discussion on the other hand. These types of assignments foster respect among the students for other cultures. I have also used various *advertisements, poems,* songs and novels and speeches in my classes for *rhetorical analysis* which enable me to draw the attention of my students to the cultural niceties with grammatical nuances, phrases, parallelism and figure of speech. Ho has rightly remarked that with a critical eye, learners can increase their awareness of observable features of the target culture for reflections and language production (Ho, 2009). For example, a video clip about a Chinese family having dinner with some guests can help learners identify Chinese people's cultural norms in dining manners. This gives an opportunity for self-reflection in their own culture and discusses cultural similarities and differences. By observing cultural behaviors of people from the target culture, learners "become aware of the ways in which their own cultural back-ground influences their own behavior, and develop a tolerance for behavior patterns that are different from their own" (Tomalin and Stempleski, 1993: p. 82). Even after the school or college hours students can be encouraged to interact with each other in a meaningful way. For example, students can be divided into group or pairs and can be asked to work on a project. For this Synchronous *online video conference using Skype* can be held for brainstorming and collaboration. This activity may increase motivation for learning from others, expressing one's own views, discussing the issues without any hesitation and collaborating for accomplishment. Similarly, in a 30 minute conference the students may be asked questions related to common interests such as their favourite movie, stars, books, personality, place, player or songs. Each student can be asked to *develop a one-minute video using the free Microsoft Photo Story software or personal Digi camcorder* to introduce himself or herself. During the self-introduction speech, they should be encouraged to include something related to their own cultural heritage in addition to their family, habits, and friends. These videos can then be uploaded on a *YouTube* channel created for this project and ask other students to comment on them. Similarly, as one of the pedagogical activity teachers can ask the students to take up one novel and one movie which reflect one culture and should be asked to make a *15 minute presentation* in the classroom. Students should be encouraged to use *clippings from movie and excerpts from novels* to illustrate their points. There are other assignments such as term papers, language games, profile making, cultural prop presentations, documentary selection and discussion. This pedagogy offers an opportunity for students to develop a shared world of interaction and experience through discovering the meaning of text within its context with keenness to construct own learning. In this process of discovering meanings and practices, students negotiate and create a new reality by using their own frames of reference (Cortazzi and Jin, 1999; Holliday, 1999), deriving basically from their life world experience and socio-cultural background. Thus teachers can develop intercultural sensitivity with new networking technologies and help in creating and widening global citizenship education.

CONCLUSION

Since learners still fail to communicate with others using appropriate social language, gestures, or expressions when taught through much used communicative language teaching approach, as they are not aptly sensitized about the culture of the language studied and respecting the idiosyncrasies and nuances of others' culture. The study serves as a good start to explore better teaching strategies for both online cross-cultural collaboration and explore many a face to face teaching materials and strategies. For culturally different students, engagement in learning is most likely to occur when they are intrinsically motivated to learn. Talking from the perspectives of grouping and assignment design, the study explored several issues and identified some possible suggestions. Future studies can investigate the appropriate strategies of regulating the interaction among students from different cultures, as well as the strategies to evaluate their performances. Additionally, it will be helpful to explore the teacher-student relationship, online behaviors, and privacy issues on *Facebook* as well as other Web 2.0 applications in cross-cultural context in order to design a better learning community. Developing new strategies and evaluation methods to integrate multimedia into the design of cross-cultural assignments will also be useful. This CRP framework provides a holistic and culturally responsive way to teachers so as to increase the learning motivation among their students by creating, planning, devising and enhancing their teaching activities, lessons, and assessment practices based on cross cultural understanding and competence.

REFERENCES

Aktuna, Seran Dogancay (2005). Intercultural communication in English language teacher education. *ELT Journal,* 59(2). Oxford University Press 99.

Bardovi-Harlig, K. and Griffin, R. (2005). L2 pragmatic awareness: Evidence from the ESL classroom. *System*, 33: 401–415.

Barkhuizen, G.P. (1998). Discovering learners' perceptions of ESL classroom teaching/learning activities in a South African context'. *TESOL Quarterly* 32(1): 85–108.

Beauboeuf-Lafontant, T. (1999). A movement against and beyond boundaries: "Politically relevant teaching" among African American teachers. *Teachers College Record*, 100(4): 702–23.

Byram, M. (1997). Teaching and assessing intercultural communicative competence. Clevedon: Multilingual matters.

Bennett, J., Bennett, M. and Allen, W. (2003). Developing intercultural competence in the language classroom. *In*: Culture as the core: Perspectives in second language learning. USA: Information Age Publishing.

Campbell, S. and Roberts, C. (2007). Migration, ethnicity and competing discourses in the job interview: Synthesizing the institutional and personal. *Discourse and Society*, 18: 243–271.

Celce-Murcia, Marianne and Olshain, Elite (2000). Discourse and context in language teaching. A guide for language teachers. Cambridge: Cambridge University Press.

Coleman, H. (*ed.*) (1996). Society and the language classroom. New York: Cambridge University Press.

Cortazzi, M. and Jin, L. (1996). Cultures of learning: Language classrooms in China. *In:* Coleman, H. (*ed.*), Society and the language classroom Cambridge: Cambridge University Press, pp. 169–206.

Crandall, E. and Basturkmen, H. (2004). Evaluating pragmatics focused materials. *ELT Journal,* 58(1): 38–49.

Cui, G. and Awa, N.E. (1992). Measuring intercultural effectiveness: An integrative approach. *International Journal of Intercultural Relations,* 16: 311–328.

Fantini, A.E. (2000). A central concern: Developing intercultural competence. *SIT Occasional*

Papers Series, 1. Retrieved August 18, 2013, *http://www.sit.edu/publications/docs/competence.pdf*

Gay, G. (2000). Culturally responsive teaching: Theory, research and practice. *Multicultural Education Series*, Banks, J.A. (*ed.),* New York: Teachers College Press.

Grant, C.A. (1991). Mapping terrains of power: Student cultural knowledge versus classroom knowledge. *Empowerment through Multicultural Education*, 49. *http://research commons. Waikato.ac.nz/bitsream/10289/3228/Franken,m.pdf*

Gumperz, J. (1999). On interactional *sociolinguistic* method. *In:* Roberts, C. and Sarangi, A. (*eds.*), Talk, work and institutional order: Discourse in medical, mediation and management settings, pp. 453–471. Berlin: Mouton de Gruyter.

Ho Si, Thang Kiet (2009). "Addressing culture in EFL classrooms: The challenge of shifting from a traditional to an intercultural stance". *Electronic Journal of Foreign Language Teaching,* 6(1): 63–76. Centre for language studies: National University of Singapore.

Holliday, A. (1994). Appropriate methodology and social context. Cambridge: Cambridge University Press.

Hu, G. (2002). Potential cultural resistance to pedagogical imports: The case of communicative language teaching in China. *Language, Culture and Curriculum*, 15(2): 93–105.

Kerekes, J. (2007). The co-construction of a gate keeping encounter: An inventory of verbal actions. *Journal of Pragmatics*, 39: 1942–1973.

Koester, A. (2006). Investigating workplace discourse. Milton Park, UK: Routledge.

Korhonen, K. (2002). Intercultural competence as part of professional qualifications: A training experiment with bachelor and engineering students (Unpublished doctoral dissertation). University of Jyväskylä, Jyväskylä, Finland.

Ladson-Billings, G. (1997). The dream keepers: Successful teachers of African American. San Francisco: Jossey-Bass.

Li, D. (2000). The pragmatics of making requests in the L2 workplace: A case study of language socialization. *The Canadian Modern Language Review*, 57: 58–87.

Liddicoat, A.J., Papademetre, L., Scarino, A. and Kohler, M. (2003). Report on intercultural language learning. Canberra ACT: Commonwealth of Australia.

LoCastro, V. (2003). An introduction to pragmatics: Social action for language teachers. Ann Arbor: University of Michigan Press.

Mayer, Susan J. (2008). "Dewey's dynamic integration of Vygotsky and Piaget". *Education and Culture,* 24(2): 6–24. Accessed 22 September 2013. *http://muse.jhu.edu/results#type=ajax&startYear=&stopYear=&limits=subscription:Y&terms=content:Vygotsky:AND&m=1*

McAllister, G. and Irvine, J.J. (2000). Cross cultural competency and multicultural teacher education. *Review of Educational Research*, 70: 3–24.

O'Brien, Alyssa J. and Eriksson, Anders (2008). Cross-cultural connections: Intercultural learning for global citizenship, *In*: *Intercultural Communication Competence: Educating the World Citizen (eds.*), Alagic, Mara and Glyn, Remington. Accessed *http://ccr.stanford.edu/archive/articles/Cross_cultural_connections.pdf, 20 June 2016.*

Olshtain, Elite and Cohen, Andrew (1991). Teaching speech act behavior to non-native speakers. *In*: Celce-Murcia, M. (*ed*.). Teaching English as a second or foreign language. Boston, MA: Newbury House, pp. 154–165.

Paige, R.M., Jorstad, J., Siaya, L., Klein, F. and Colby, J. (2003). Culture learning in language education: A review of the literature. *In*: Lange, D. and Paige, R.M. (*eds.*), *Culture as the core: Integrating culture into language education,* Greenwich, CT: Information Age Publishing. pp. 173–236.

Rothstein-Fisch, C. and Trumbull, E. (2008). Managing diverse classrooms. Alexandria, VA: Association for supervision and curriculum development.

Tomalin, B. and Stempleski, S. (1993). Cultural awareness. Hong Kong: Oxford University Press.

Wlodkowski, R.J. and Ginsberg, M.B. (1995). Diversity and motivation: Culturally responsive teaching. San Francisco: Jossey-Bass.

6

Peace Harmony and Harmonious Education

SURENDRA PATHAK[1]*

We are living in extremely explosive times when the context of human life is changing every moment. Our society is crumbling; the waves of destruction are so strong that they are breaking up the moral fabric of our life. The world is facing many challenges like pollution of air, water and soil. Natural resources are fast depleting. Population growth-rate is outstripping resources worldwide. There is an uneven distribution of sources of livelihood. Multinational corporations are putting undue pressure on governments and twisting their policies. Nuclear weapons pose an imminent threat to the survival of mankind. Confrontationist policies and use of military power to resolve economic and political interests are on the rise. Genocide, racism, fundamentalism and terrorism have wrought havoc worldwide. Issues relating to personal life like rising divorce rate, depression, stress and lifestyle diseases etc., are causing an unbearable tension in the society. Therefore, a holistic approach is needed to grapple with the current unhealthy syndrome. The ecological crisis, population explosion with increasing poverty, hunger and violence, economically imbalanced world, and arms race are all pulling us away from the real purpose of our life. Instead they are challenging us to think how to reverse this man-made

[1] Value Education and Project Director-Existential Harmony Projects, IASE Deemed University, Sardarshahar, Rajasthan, 331401
* *Corresponding author*: E-mail: pathak06@gmail.com

destructive path or face our own extinction. The crisis of humanity is not a political crisis, it is not an economic crisis, and it is not a military crisis – yet we continue to find only political and military solutions. The crisis in fact is an educational crisis, which can only be resolved by peace and harmony and human values education, *i.e.,* Harmonious Education.[1]

One way to build world peace is on the solid foundation of co-existential harmony.[2] To accomplish this goal, it is important that process of globalization of education and the reorientation of education come together to accomplish a common goal for harmonious and peaceful civilization. This can be achieved if we gain a better understanding of the reality of the existential and natural orders, and the interrelationship between the various systems, *i.e.*, ecological, environmental as well as social, economic and legal. To reorient the education and include the peace and harmony and human values based educational content (teachings and trainings) we may change the scenario on earth.

"Peace and harmony have been the universal and eternal human aspirations. In fact, all material or physical development is also finally targeted to enable all human beings to live in peace and harmony with certain values-adequately fulfilling their physical needs and inculcating skills, values and attitudes which are conducive to live in peace and harmony at the individual level, live in peace and harmony with other human beings and finally, be in harmonious co-existence with rest of nature. In the final analysis, all developmental goals must cater to this universal aspiration only.

Research studies, right from the earliest literature down to recent times are focused on the essential cosmic harmony-interrelatedness and Interdependence of all planets, all units and all beings. There is divine unity in the phenomenal harmonious diversity. There is continuity in the process of evolution in the four stages of the natural orders-material order, respiratory order, animal order and knowledge/ human order. Every unit in the Nature is coherent from within and correlated to the cosmic order from without. All existing living and non-living objects are self-controlled and inherently balanced by the Laws of Nature.[3]

---

1. *http://www.globalissues.org*
   http://www.un.org/en/globalissues/index.shtml
2. *http://www.madhyasth-darshan.info/introduction/* (A. Nagraj)
3. *http://www.peacefromharmony.org/?cat=en_c&key=605* (Dr. Surendra Pathak)

To study the harmonious orders, the earth planet is an important part of the whole cosmos. It is essentially governed by the laws of nature and it functions in a harmonious manner. It serves as the most important natural source to the survival of a number of material bodies. On the Earth planet, there are billions of objects, comprising human beings, flora and fauna, the atmosphere, hydrosphere and geo-sphere, which are interdependent and interrelated in a harmonious existential order. This order has its own intrinsic laws, which regulate its functioning, articulating physical, chemical, biological and ecological aspects as well as human activities.

In order to live in harmony with nature, human beings must recognize and respect its intrinsic laws and its vital cycles. In such a system, all the objects, being and non-beings have to live within their limits as determined by the laws of nature. The deviants of the laws of nature are bound to impinge upon the rights of others and disturb the system of eternal harmony. Therefore, it is irrational and immoral to recognize any kind of extraordinary privileges for human beings at the cost of several other components/units/lives of the Earth planet. *Human beings have to understand their essential obligation and function in coherence with the larger context of existence. The human existence has to function and sustain itself within this system. Accordingly, we need to create political, economic, religious and educational institutions in consonance with the spirit of the laws of existential harmony.*

MICROCOSMIC AND MACROCOSMIC HARMONY

To understand the harmonious nature of the existence it is said that Microcosm means Mankind viewed as the epitome of whole Universe and Macrocosm is the Cosmos which is the whole complex structure of the Universe. Charaka, says "*Purushyo'yam loka sannidah*"[4] (Man is a miniature universe) and Yajurveda says "*Yatha pinde tatha brahmande, yatha brahmande tatha pinde*"[5] (As is the individual, so is the universe, as is the universe, so is the individual" or "As is the atom, so is the Universe" or "As is the human body, so is the cosmic body). It means the governing eternal laws are cause of internal codes, evolutionary processes, motions, and all natural phenomena which create the harmony relation and coexistence between Microcosms to Macrocosm.

4. Charak Samhita, Volume 4, P.V. Sharma (2008), Pub: Chaukhambha Orientalia
5. Yajurveda 224

Sankhya Darshana[6] describe the human body as a mini universe and whatever elements or entities exist in the universe they exist in the human body also *i.e.,* five fundamental elements (ether, air, fire, water and earth) of the universe. The human body cannot exist or cannot be properly identified without appropriate combination of the above. Every entity is constituted and coexists in harmonious relationship of all the fundamental elements, which create the bodies with eternal order (plants, animal/bio-bodies, human bodies). Even in natural process these bodies and its components exist in harmonious relationship with each other.

The basic premise of Ayurveda is that the entire cosmos (or universe) is part of one singular absolute. Therefore, everything that exists in the external universe (macrocosm) also appears in the internal cosmos of the human body (microcosm). The human body, when healthy, is in harmony, self-perpetuating and self-correcting just as the universe.[7] It means that harmony, coexistence, microcosm, macrocosms, eternal order, Oneness etc. are not new terms for Indian philosophy and literature. If we compare perceptions and views of ancient Indian Vedic wisdom with modern science, metaphysics and recent trends on consciousness studies, we will find a definite holistic view of harmony and coexistence.

EXISTENCE IS COEXISTENCE

Philosopher and propounder of *Madhyasth-Darshan Sah-astitva-vad* (existence-rooted human-centric studies) A. Nagraj (2003) elucidates the existential order (Existence as coexistence) as an alternative to instability-uncertainty based matter centric Materialism / Science and mystics Idealism. He says *'Existence is in the form of coexistence'*[8,9] as

6. Cowell, E. B.; Gough, A. E. (2001), *The Sarva-Darsana-Samgraha or Review of the Different Systems of Hindu Philosophy: Trubner's Oriental Series*, Taylor & Francis, ISBN 978-0-415-24517-3 (p.222)
7. Basis for Ayurvedic Philosophy, *http://www.ayushmedica.com/basis.php*
8. Nagraj A., Samadhnatmak Bhotikvad, (2003) p.7
9. अस्तित्व ही सह-अस्तित्वः सत्ता मे समपृक्त प्रकृति अनन्त इकाईयों के रूप में है। सत्ता व्यापक रूपी किसी लंबाई चौड़ाई में सीमित नहीं है, इसका कोई मापदण्ड न ही बन पाता, इसलिए सत्ता व्यापक है। प्रकृति रूप में जितना भी इकाईयाँ है उन सबकी गणना नहीं हो पाती इसलिए वे अनंत है इस प्रकार अस्तित्व स्वयं व्यापक और अनन्त है। सत्ता अरूपात्मक और सत्ता में प्रकृति रूपात्मक अस्तित्व है। अस्तित्व का तात्पर्य होने से और अविनाशिता से है। सत्ता गति और दबाव विहीन स्थिति में है। जबकि सत्ता में ही सम्पूर्ण प्रकृति गति और दबाव सहित विद्यमान है। दबाव अर्थात् वातावरणवश (परस्परतावश) आकर्षण विकर्षण के लिए बाध्यता। सत्ता अरूपात्मक होने के कारण आयामों में सीमित नहीं है जबकि सत्ता में सम्पृक्त प्रकृति अनन्त इकाईयों का समूह है। साथ ही प्रत्येक इकाई आयामों सहित छः ओर से सीमित है।

units (*anant prakriti*) submerged in absolute (zero) energy/space/ consciousness (*Satta*). "Energy is with distinction of absolute and relative. It is recognized and understood in the form of absolute-energy (zero-energy) and relative-energy. Work-energy is relative (among units of Nature) and absolute-energy is eternal-present as omnipresence (pervasive Spirit)."[10] He further says "Consciousness (absolute energy) is omnipresence. Consciousness is permeating and transparent and it is a non-activity (devoid of pulse or pressure). Consciousness does not prove to be a unit due to its being all pervasive (endless/boundary-less). Consciousness does not prove to be the root-cause of cosmic-order. Coexistence (units submerged in absolute energy) alone is the root-cause of cosmic-order (existential harmony)."[11]

Existence is not just material (physical-chemical matter)–but all physical-chemical-entities and conscious-entities are inseparably and eternally actively-present in all-pervasive space. Existence is *stable*. There is no increase or decrease in existence. Existence has *definitiveness* for *progress* and *awakening*. All principles in existence are *natural*. There is harmony, orderliness in existence. Each unit is organized within itself and participates harmoniously with the overall orderliness. Existence is limitless, eternal. There is no 'limit' to existence. Wherever existence is deemed to be 'upto', there is always space 'after' that. There is no 'cause' for existence, existence is eternally-present as coexistence. No cause for matter or space is evidenced. Existence has always been 'this way', and will always be 'this way': as units saturated in space.[12]

Since long time, human-beings have remained unaware about the source of energy required for continuous activity of atoms and its particles; philosophy of coexistence explains that absolute-energy (zero energy) is everywhere known as 'all pervasive energy'. It is found everywhere homogeneously. There is no activity which is devoid (*rikt*) of and without (*mukt*) omnipresence space/consciousness. Space itself is absolute-energy, space itself is omnipotence."[13] (Nagraj, 2012) "The state (reality) of non-activity is known as space, and knowledge while not doing any activity or while not being in an activity is the basis and

---

10. Nagraj A., Manav vyavhar Darshan (mathaysth darshan-part-1), Pub. By IASE Deemed university, Rajasthan (2012) p. 14
11. Ibid., p.70
12. *http://www.madhyasth-darshan.info/postulations/existence-reality-truth/sequential-progression/*
13. Nagraj A., p. 16

source-of-inspiration/source of entire activities. Therefore, knowledge (*Gyan*) and space/absolute energy prove to be one and the same – and it is only from being situated in it, inspiration for activity always remains available. There is no unit which is devoid of or liberated from this zero energy."[14] Because of the presence of this absolute energy each unit is self-organized within itself (*niyam, niyantran, santulan sahit nishchit aacharan ke sath)* and fulfils its harmonious relationship with all other units/orders. Vedas say that "Everything is essentially consciousness, purity and joy."[15] And, "the Universal Laws are laws of truth,[16] truth is knowledge (*Gyan*).

HARMONIOUS RELATIONSHIP AMONG FOUR ORDERS

The Human centric philosophy *'Madhyasth Darshan Sahastitvavad'*[17] elucidates Coexistence, *i.e.*, existential/ natural order among material-mineral order (*padarth avastha*), plants order (*pranav astha*) and animal order (*jivavastha*). The relationships among the material-mineral order, cells/plants order and animal orders are mutually fulfilling and mutually enriching and this process is cyclic (*avartansheel*) in nature as shown in diagram-I. Right understanding between Human being (*gyanavastha*) and Nature will be necessary to fulfill the relationship with all these orders. Ultimate desire of human being is also to live in the harmony with rest of the nature/cosmos /existence.

It means that no one has to create the harmony; it is already available, it exists in the form of co-existential harmony with mutual fulfillment. One only needs to understand existence and align oneself with it. By understanding these internal activities/ phenomenon and processes of manifestation in nature, human being can survive and flourish easily. All the three orders *i.e.,* (material-minerals, plants, animal orders) are fulfilling their relationship with human being.

---

14. Ibid., p. 70
15. Shankara – Viveka-Chuda-mani (Hindu mystic - 9th century)
16. Edgar Cayce (1877-1945), Quotation in Bruce McArthur, Your Life: Understanding the Universal Laws, 1993, p. 119.
17. मध्यस्थ दर्शन, सह-अस्तित्व-वाद : आदर्शवादी शास्त्रों एवं रसस्य मूलक ईश्वर केंद्रित चिंतन ज्ञान तथा परंपरा के अनुसार - ज्ञान अव्यक्त अनिर्वचनीय, मध्यस्थ दर्शन के अनुसार - ज्ञान व्यक्त, वचनीय, अध्ययन विधि से बोध गम्य, व्यवहार विधि से प्रमाण सर्व सुलभ होने के रूप में स्पष्ट हुआ। अस्थिरता, अनिश्चयता मूलक भौतिकवाद के अनुसार वस्तु केंद्रित विचार में विज्ञान को ज्ञान माना। इसके विकल्प में सह-अस्तित्व रूपी अस्तित्व मूलक मानव केंद्रित चिंतन ज्ञान के अनुसार अस्तित्व स्थिर, विकास और जागृति निश्चित, सम्पूर्ण नियम प्राकृतिक होना-रहना प्रतिपादित है। अस्तित्व केवल भौतिक-रासायनिक न होकर भौतिक रासायनिक एवं जीवन वस्तुएं व्यापक-वस्तु में अविभाज्य वर्तमान हैं।

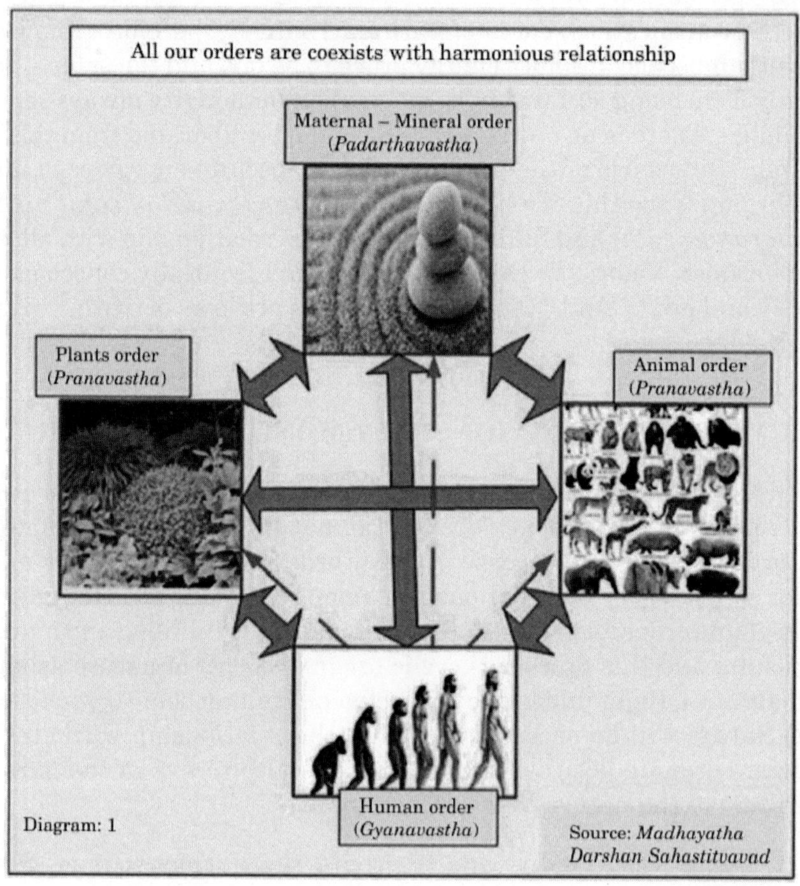

Diagram: 1

Source: *Madhayatha Darshan Sahastitvavad*

Subsequently human being must organize their life style to fulfill other three orders so that civilization can move towards this path. Harmony in the individual and harmony in human-human relationships (from family to world family) is only possible by understanding the relationship between humans and the rest of nature/cosmos.

The Earth planet is an important part of the whole cosmos. It is essentially governed by the Laws of Nature and it functions in a harmonious manner. It serves as the most important natural resource for the survival of a number of material bodies. On the planet earth, there are billions of objects, comprising human being, flora and fauna, the atmosphere, hydrosphere and geo-sphere, which are interdependent, interconnected and interrelated in a harmonious existential order. This order has its own intrinsic laws, which regulate its functioning, articulating physical, chemical, biological, and ecological aspects, as well as human activities. In order to live in harmony with Nature, human being must recognize and respect its intrinsic laws and its vital cycles. In such a System, all the objects, being and non-being must live within their limits as determined by the laws of nature digress.

Anybody who digresses with the laws of nature is bound to impinge upon the rights of others and consequently disturb the system harmony. Therefore, it is irrational and immoral to recognize any kind of extraordinary privileges for human being at the cost of several other bodies/units of the earth planet. Human beings have to understand their essential obligations and functions in coherence with the larger interest of existence. The human existence has to function and sustain itself within this system. Accordingly, we need to create political, economic, and educational institutions in consonance with the spirit of the laws of existential harmony.

We can conclude here that (Universal) Existential Harmony[i] is the supreme potential of all natural balance and control. The purpose of activities of nature is to attain harmony. If one throws a stone into a pond it would disturb the harmony of the pond by creating ripples but after some time ripples flow out and back until harmony is restored, it is the same in natural patterns. This means disharmonious/conflicting action/activities in nature are temporary and this existential harmony is perpetual and perennial as shown in the diagram II.

NATURAL PATTERNS INDICATE INHERENT HARMONY

In modern scientific studies of the patterns in nature, (visible regularities of form) are found in the natural world this supports the logic of perpetual and perennial existential harmony. These patterns recur in different contexts and can sometimes are modeled mathematically. Natural patterns include symmetries, trees, spirals, meanders, waves, foams, arrays, cracks and stripes.[18] Early Greek philosophers Plato, Pythagoras and Empedocles studied pattern; attempting to explain order in nature. The modern understanding of visible patterns developed gradually over time. "The long-sought "grand theory of everything" must begin where there is no beginning and end

---

18. Stevens, Peter. Patterns in Nature, 1974. p. 3

(i) *Existential harmony*: Every unit in the existence is self-organized, harmoniously ordered and in a definite system.

where there is no ending: patterns which repeat themselves in nature and which give rise to infinite symmetry. Similar patterns are repeated from the micro-atomic/quantum to the macro-atomic/galaxy, from snail shells to spiral galaxies. There is no reason to suspect these patterns end with individual galaxies. This does not stop with individual Galaxies, but characterise collectively all Galaxies and the Cosmos. Patterns repeat and this is the key for understanding the ultimate nature of the universe."[19]

We can conclude that this order and harmony transit/percolates/ penetrates and innately exists from microcosm to macrocosm, as show in diagram II. Donald L. Hamilton, in his work 'The Nature of Universal Space' explains that "The 'Laws of Nature' contain all the physical laws in the universe. They are inseparable and invariant - all intertwined and working in perfect harmony. Each law has its specific duties. They create and guide the matter and energy of the universe."[20] He further says the "Laws of Nature" are the Foundation of the Universe, without these "Laws" the Universe would not exist. John Adam (his book Mathematics in Nature, 2002) is an enthusiastic and clear writer, and manages to explain "symbiosis that exists between the basic scientific principles involved in natural phenomena and their mathematical description". He presents the various phenomena at different levels of description, from the fundamental power of estimation or the effects of scale, to more sophisticated concepts, such as the connection between the Fibonacci sequence and the branching patterns of trees. It means that nature has its own mathematics and harmonious rhythms.

All tradition of wisdom speak of the existence of such universal laws. At first sight, each wisdom tradition seems to describe the details of these underlying ordering patterns in a different way. This is not surprising when we realize that every attempt to describe something so vast and all-encompassing will always be different to some degree and in a sense incomplete. Moreover, the different universal laws do not operate in isolation from each other, but simultaneously and intertwined, like parts of a gigantic dynamic network. Consequently, it is effectively not possible to totally separate one from the other and

---

19. Rhawn Joseph, Infinity, Patterned Symmetry, Pythagoras, and the Black Hole at the Edge of the Universe, Journal of Cosmology, Vol. 13, In press (journalofcos mology.com) 2011

20. Donald L. Hamilton. The Nature of Universal Space, A New Cosmology for the 21st Century! 1999

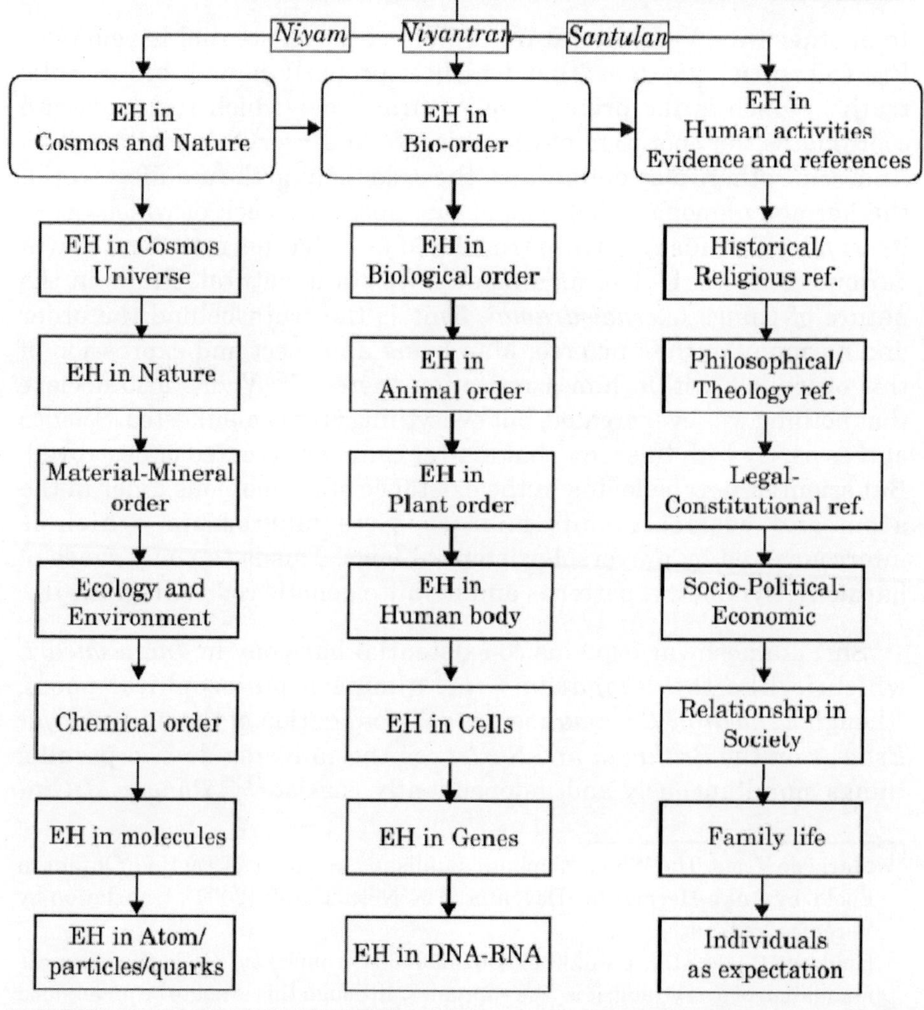

every attempt to describe this dynamics as a whole, in the form of the operation of a number of universal principles, will be done from each individual perspective or orientation. We may compare the differences in the descriptions of these patterns with the attempts of the blind people to describe the elephant in the Sufi story.[21]

HARMONY PREVALENT UNIVERSALLY

In another way, Vedic literature explained the existential harmony as Rta (*Sanskrit*: ऋतं, *rtam* "that which is properly joined; order, rule; truth"), which is the principle of natural order which regulates and coordinates the operation of the universe and everything within it.[22] And, some others may define it as "the order behind the manifest world, the harmony among all aspects of manifestation each of which obeys its own level. Thus rta is also translated as order, harmony and law in various contexts. Unlike man-made laws rta is natural. Rta is in the nature of things (*eternal drama*). This is the truth behind the order and harmony in the universe. Man being an aspect and expression of this order has within him a reflection thereof."[23] Vedas also declare that nothing was ever created, but everything is only manifested. Science agrees partly with this view that matter cannot be created or destroyed. But scientist now believing in the existence of harmonious order in the atom and cosmos means microcosm to macrocosm, which is interconnected by universal/existential laws. This is the only cause of harmony, symmetry, patterns and definite genetic code (Diagram-II).

Shri Jnaneshwar explains co-existential harmony in *Jnaneshwari,* which is like the *Bhagavad Gita*, a superb philosophical poem, "though *Eshwar* or *Brahman* is the sole foundation of the universe yet *Eshwar* or the *Brahman* and *Shristi* or the universe do two parallel things simultaneously and independently coexist.[24,25] *Bhagavad Gita*

---

21. Marja de Vries, The Whole Elephant' published in Dutch as 'De Hele Olifant in Beeld' by Ankh-Hermes bv, Deventer, The Netherlands (2007), translation by Veronica Verkaik

22. Holdrege (2004:215). Panikkar (2001:350–351) remarks: "*Zta* is the ultimate foundation of everything; it is "the supreme", although this is not to be understood in a static sense. [...] It is the expression of the primordial dynamism that is inherent in everything ...

23. Dr. Satya Prakash Choudhary, The hidden orders of life: An introduction to the ancient Indian world-view, *http://www.karmicrhythms.com/k2.htm*

24. Jnaneshwari, 3/71

25. (Jnaneshwari has become a treatise equally charming and attracting the philosophers, the scientists and the religious people alike over seven hundred years and the passage of time has only revealed its growing strength. And this

explain this "Know that prakriti and purusha are both beginningless, and know also that the modifications and the gunas arise from prakriti" (13:19). We can say *Brahman* and *Prakriti*, in other way explains the coexistence of consciousness/spirit (*purusha*) and Creation (*kriyasheel prakriti*).

Hazrat Inayat Khan (1923) explains this harmonious relation as "the existence of land and water, the land for the water, and the water for the land; the attraction between the heavens and the earth, all demonstrate the universal harmony. The attraction of the sun and moon to each other, the cosmic order of the stars and the planets, all connected and related with each other, moving and working under a certain law (universal harmony)."[26] If the material content of the universe is supposed to be sustained by the energy of light from stars and gravitational forces between the planets, the material content of the human body is supposed to be sustained primarily by the energy of 'life' (*Pran)* and vibration forces of heart and brain. We are told that in the Macrocosm, energy can be converted into matter and *vice versa*. So also in the Microcosm we see that a thought process generates neuro-peptides, some sort of chemical substances for various types of body reactions"[27] (Sekhar, 2003).

Philosophy of Ayurveda indicates "Human life is seen as a note in the cosmic harmony. The individual, who is a 'one-off', a once-only, unrepeatable event, exists as a microcosm in the being of macrocosm. The two systems, human and cosmic, are linked permanently, since both are built from the same basic elements. All the elements contained in the macrocosm are also present in the microcosm. The five human senses correspond to the five fundamental elements out of which everything that exist is constructed."[28] This also defines the importance of balance and order in most of its concepts and theories, even *Sushruta*

---

is so because his heart expanded to include not only the human but the birds, beasts and plants and his total concern for ecology, and the orderly existence of all the Cosmic Objects aims at establishing and ensuring Universal Harmony.)

26. Hazrat Inayat Khan, (1923)Volume II - The Mysticism of Music, Sound and Word, Part I: The Mysticism of Sound, Chapter III- Harmony *http://wahiduddin.net/mv2/II/II_3.htm*

27. Sekhar A.C., Microcosm and Macrocosm, (2003), *http://www.cincinnatitemple.com/articles.html*

28. Birgit Heya, Ayurveda, the Indian Art of natural Medicine & Life extension (1990); Healing arts press, ISBN 0-89281-333-4 Page No. 34

Samhita defines of health as a balance when all three doshas (bioenergy) and agni (metabolic process) are in balance, and excretions are in proper order. When atman (soul), senses, manah (intellect) are in harmony with internal peace, then the svastha (optimal health) is achieved. (Sam dosha, samagni, samdhatu malakriyah, Prasannatma, indriyas manah swath abhidayate - Sushruta stru 24/41— Adopted by the World Health Organization)[ii] which also support the reality of prevalent harmony, innate balance, interconnectivity and coexistence of microcosm to macrocosm.

Ancient Greek philosophers describe human being and their place in the universe. They viewed the individual human being as a little world (*mikros kosmos*) whose composition and structure correspond to that of the universe, or great world (*makros kosmos,* or *megas kosmos*). Greek word '*Kosmos*' meant "order" in a general sense and implied a harmonious, and therefore beautiful, arrangement of parts in any organic system; hence it also referred to order in human societies, reflected in good government. Comparisons between society and the human being, as well as society and the universe, were varieties of microcosmic theory. These analogies enjoyed a long life, first in the Mediterranean region during antiquity and later throughout Europe during the middle Ages. The ideas were commonplace during the Renaissance and early modern times but lost their plausibility when a mechanistic model of the universe became dominant in the seventeenth and eighteenth centuries.[29] (Bernardus Silvestris, 1973)

Thus, we can say that Ancient mystical, esoteric and secret teachings from Ancient Egypt, Ancient Greece, Indian Vedic tradition, Chinese Tao and Buddhism and Japanese esoteric teachings found and tried to explain the perfect harmony in the universe and nature. There is almost common understanding between all these faiths regarding Harmony.

[ii] The correct bibliographic citation for the definition is: Preamble to the Constitution of the World Health Organization as adopted by the International Health Conference, New York, 19-22 June, 1946; signed on 22 July 1946 by the representatives of 61 States (Official Records of the World Health Organization, no. 2, p. 100) and entered into force on 7 April 1948.The Definition has not been amended since 1948.

29. Ziomkowski, Robert, Microcosm and Macrocosm, New Dictionary of the History of Ideas (2005) *http: / /www.encyclopedia.com / doc / 1G2-3424300477.html*

The concept that everything that exists is connected with everything else in accordance with the Law of Oneness[iii] encountered in science as the concept of quantum Entanglement[iv] and was first revealed in sub-atomic particles at quantum level.[30] Harmonious coexistence is the source of manifestation (evolution), the cause of its existence, eternal harmony is the harmony of coexistence. Consciousnes itself eternal, all things and beings live and move in it; yet it remains stable, undisturbed and totally peaceful.

Recent perceptions of some of the scientific researchers suggest that the whole universe in fact appears to be an intrinsically and instantaneously interconnected whole[v], in which everything (large and

---

[iii] The Law of Divine Oneness provides the fundamental understanding that we are all connected to each other, and that we are all connected to the same Divine Higher Entity (God, the Universe, Source, etc.). We coexist equally and collectively in the spiritual world as we are all composed of the same energetic foundation. In physical form, we also coexist with the earth as a reflection of our collective Oneness. The earth then reflects back to us our human and biological evolution.

[iv] Quantum entanglement is a physical phenomenon that occurs when pairs or groups of particles are generated or interact in ways such that the quantum state of each particle cannot be described independently- instead, a quantum state may be given for the system as a whole.

[v] Everything is a part of one whole that makes up something that is, in itself, still small by comparison to the entire being (cells compared to a tissue, tissues compared to an organ, organs compared to an organ system, an organ system compared to the being). As far as I know, our entire galaxy could be the cell... or it could simply be a part of the cell. I would not think that we could call it the tissue (and it's certainly not the organ). Obviously we are much, much smaller than our galaxy is... and given that they're not entirely sure if it's a "universe" or a "multiverse"

30. Quantum entanglement was predicted by the Irish physicist John S. Bell and subsequently the French physicist Alain Aspect (1982) confirmed by experiment the phenomenon that, under certain circumstances, sub-atomic particles prove to be able to affect each other immediately - meaning without any time loss - even if they are at a great distance from each other. These findings have far-reaching consequences, because they are in conflict with the thesis of Albert Einstein that nothing is able to go faster than light. This shows that there is indeed a plane of reality that exists 'beyond space and time'. In 1998 and 2004, the same phenomenon was once again confirmed by Nicholas Gisin of the University in Geneva.

small) and everyone is interconnected *via* the zero-point energy field.[vi] zero-point energy field appears to be heaving sea of energy in the background of our existence. Most recent perceptions in this context by Nicola Tesla, David Bohm and Harold Puthoff have come to the following conclusion: "Interactions in the domains of nature as well as of consciousness operate *via* a fundamental field that retains energy and information and forms the heart of the universe."[31] "What physics calls the vacuum or void is actually filled with incomprehensibly complex dynamic networks of highly organized - and organizing - fields of force. Though physicists do not understand the origin and organization of these invisible force fields, they are convinced that they definitely exist and play a regulating or guiding role in all physical systems."(Gary E. Schwartz, 2006)[32]

EVERYTHING IS INTERCONNECTED WHOLE

Marja de Vries while explaining Underlying organizing principles in book 'The Whole Elephant' (2007) (Chapter 2 - What is the essence of Universal Truth) that "Everything is revealed as a vast interconnected whole, permeated by the same patterns. This marvellous order in the universe is illustrated by the Greek word kosmos, which means 'order' and 'decoration' as well as 'universe'. The common golden thread of universal truth woven through all the wisdom traditions is therefore also about an understanding of these underlying, ordering principles of the universe, by which the universe organizes itself and keeps itself in balance. These ordering principles are patterns that operate at all levels of reality that is to say not only at the physical level of the visible world around us, but also at all the levels of non-physical reality. Because these are the same ordering principles operating at all levels, these Omni applicable patterns are known as universal principles or universal laws." This shows that these universal laws are the main cause of the harmonious patterns and symmetries in all natural phenomena and processes.

[vi] Zero-point energy field appears to be heaving sea of energy in the background of our existence

31. Ervin Laszlo, Cosmic Vision, The Dawn of the Integral Theory of Everything, 2004

32. Gary E. Schwartz, 'Intelligent Evolution', in Shift, June-Aug. 2006, No. 11, p. 10-14

In his autographical note Einstein shows faith that some (inherent) laws exist to predict the events in the atom, the craving for universal harmony (meaning orderliness established by laws) of the macrocosm must be predicated upon a similar harmony within the microcosm of the atom. Further, the harmony of the two cosmos must be joined in a grand harmonious scheme for the entire universe. He was convinced that it is "logically possible to establish such rigorous laws that they demand uniquely determined constants, whose numerical values could not be changed without destroying the theory."[33]

We may conclude that the on-going research and explorations in the domains of natural and social sciences can establish a link between inherent synergy in atoms, cells, chemical and physical processes and human activities, we should understand the elegance of this coherent Order. The principles of harmonious existence will serve as a beacon light in all human endeavours. Otherwise, human beings shall pay the price for their negligence of the law of nature. It will also help the humanity to escape from conflicts and wars. To destruct world peace and natural harmony is a crime against humanity and peaceful coexistence. The foregoing analysis of the current understanding of existence form microcosm to macrocosm shows a definite order in the material, bio (*Pranic*), animal and knowledge orders. Human beings have evolved from the above order possessing the characteristics of these orders. However they are disillusioned to recognize this inherent characteristic with proper understanding of the prevalent orders of the existence, they may begin to realize this order and design education and socio-politico-economic orders to bring harmony based on the natural order. The given in illustration indicates clearly.

In the field of physical and social sciences, research and explorations are being conducted to establish this inherent synergy at the atomic and cellular level of human beings in their chemical & physical and social activities. We should understand the elegance of this coherent order. The principles of harmonious existence will serve as a beacon light in all human endeavors. *We have to understand the meaning of spiritual ecology i.e., living in harmony with everything that nature has created. Man must utilize the sources of nature as per his natural needs and give up his wanton desire for exploiting and overpowering nature.* It may help humanity to escape from conflicts and wars.

---

33. Einstein, "Autographical Notes" p 63 For Extended discussion on harmony in Einstein's Connection of the universe

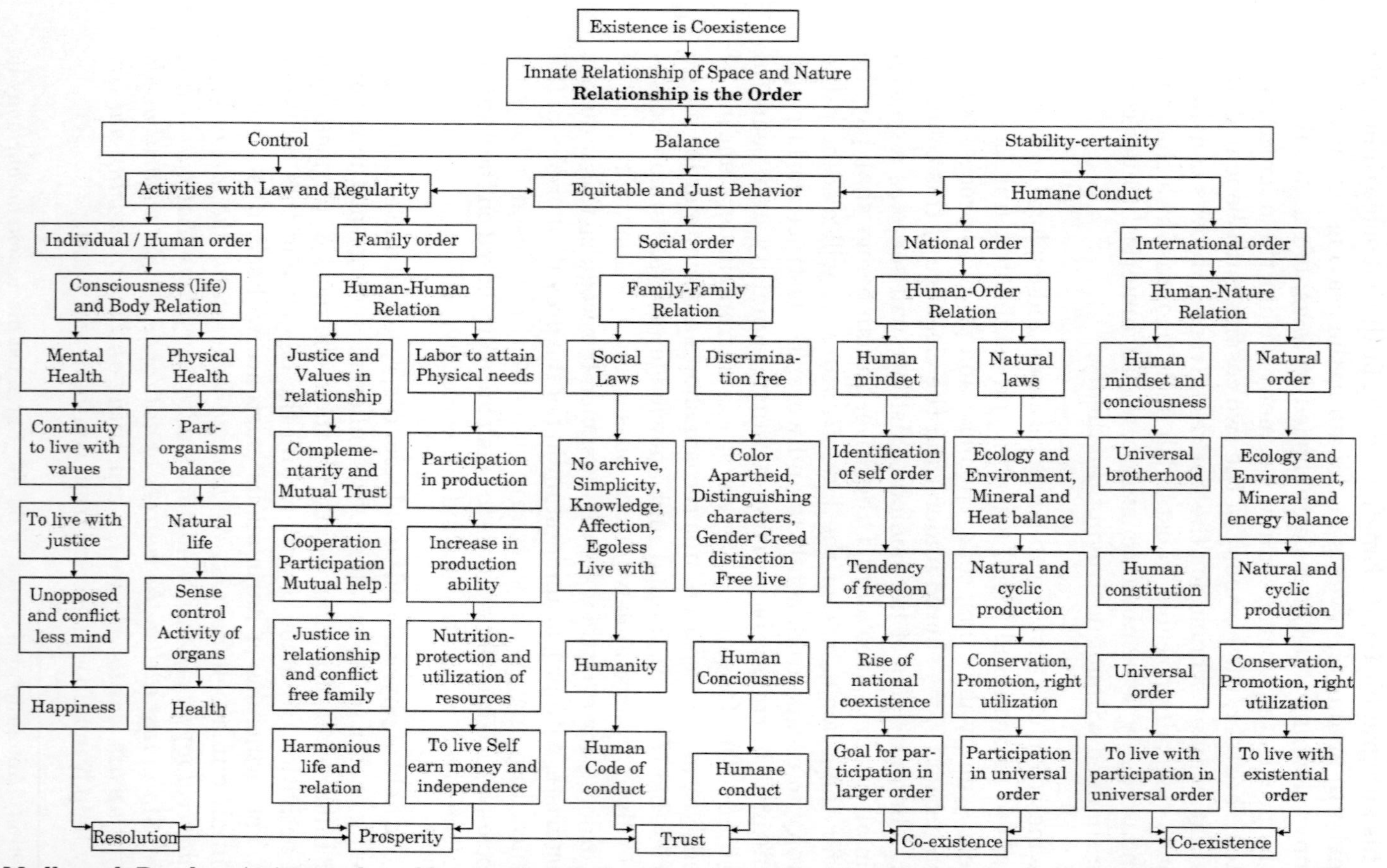

Madhyasth Darshan (existence based human focussed contemplation), or 'Coexistentialism' - Manav Vyvahar Darshan by Nagraj A (2003) Jeevan Vidya Prakashan, Amarkantak, India

Violation of world peace and natural harmony disrupts coexistence, an intrinsic character of existence. To our great satisfaction, the spiritual scriptures of the world and constitutional documents have always espoused the cause of peace and coexistence. We should not retard our ability to think and reason in solving our problems. Solutions are possible and they are waiting to be discovered only by unbiased and objective research. Individuals and organizations all over the world are striving to rectify human errors and restore global peace. Let's explore new possibilities and alternatives to realize the harmony on the planet Earth. Every individual has some responsibility to contribute to the process of global peace.

RE-STRUCTURING EDUCATION

The re-structuring of the curricula and the content of the education necessitate identification and understanding of the existential order of everything from atom to earth; human to human society in a natural context, natural laws to constitutional laws and the philosophies therein. Research studies from the earliest literature down to recent times are focused on the essential cosmic harmony - interrelatedness and interdependence of all planets and all beings. There is a harmonious unity in the phenomenal diversity. In the words of Philosopher Nagraj, (A Nagraj, 2003), there is continuity in the process of evolution in the four stages of the natural order: material order, respiratory order, animal order, and knowledge order. Every unit in the Nature is coherent from within and correlated to the cosmic order from without. All existing living and non-living objects are self-controlled and inherently balanced by the Laws of Nature.

The philosophy of peace and harmony and values education is fundamentally a theoretical exercise, although it may yet serve as an exercise in applied philosophy. A formal philosophy of peace and harmony values education can assist to undergird individual, institutional, societal and governmental commitment to peace and harmony education, in all levels of education. Such education may be thought of as encouraging a commitment to peace-harmony as a settled disposition and enhancing the confidence of the individual as an *shantidoot*; as informing the student on the consequences of wars, exploitation of natural resources, social and economic injustice; as informing the student on the value of harmonious-peaceful and just social structures and working to uphold or develop such social structures;

as encouraging the student to love the civilization and its prosperous future; and as caring for the student and encouraging the student to care for others.

Madhaystha Darshan by A. Nagraj elucidates and explains the Existence as Co-existence. In the light of the above, the restructuring of the education should be on the basis of perfect combination of knowledge (*Gyan*), Wisdom (*vivek*) and Science (*vigyaan*).[34] In Madhaystha Darshan Knowledge may be explained as following three categories:

Knowledge of Existential Philosophy (अस्तित्व दर्शन ज्ञान)

Existence is Coexistence, nature saturated in all-expansive space. Nature manifested as the four 'natural-orders': knowledge order, animal order, bio order, material order. Nature = collection of units = physiochemical and conscious units. Existence is in the form of co-existence, as "nature saturated in all-pervasive-entity or space". There are only two kinds of realities in Existence:

- Units, or Nature (Matter, Mass, Substance, Material)
- All-pervasive space (Omnipresence)

Units are "saturated" *(samprikt)* in the all-pervasive-entity *(vyaapak vastu)*, currently called *space*. Saturated means to be Soaked (*bheega*) by which every unit is energized (उर्जित) –, Encircled (*ghira*) by which every unit is restrained (नियन्त्रित), Submerged (*dooba*): By which every unit is active– *kriyasheel* (क्रियाशील),

'Space' has following attributes:

- All-pervasive – *vyaapak* (व्यापक) (There is no 'place' where space absent. Every 'place' itself is 'space')
- Transparent – *paardarshee* (पारदर्शी) (Reflecting, every unit is able to recognize the other unit by being in it)
- Permeating – *paargaami* (पारगामी) (Space exists 'where' there is a unit, units are soaked in space)
- Omnipotence : *satta* (सत्ता) (Energy in equilibrium: that neither increases, nor decreases)

---

34. *http://www.madhyasth-darshan.info/postulations/*

- Has no activity: *kriyashunya* (क्रियाशून्य) (Inactive, not a 'unit', unchanging)

Knowledge of Conscious Unit - Self (जीवन ज्ञान)

10 Activities in the Self (Conscious) and the 5 Potentials and 5 Forces.

Potential *(बल)*	***Activity in state*** *(स्तिथि क्रिया)*	***Activity in expression*** *(गति क्रिया)*	***Force*** *(शक्ति)*	***'Stage / Degree' of understanding***	
Atma (Soul)	Realization (*anubhav*)	Evidentiality (*pramanikta*)	*Evidence (pramaanikta)*		*Realization (anubhuti)*
Buddhi (Intellect)	Comprehension (*bodh*)	Determination (*sankalp*)	*Truthfulness (ritambhara)*	*Certitude (prateeti)*	
Chitta	Contemplation (*chintan*)	Imaging (*chitran*)	*Desire (ichchha)*		
Vritti (Disposition)	Weighing (*tulan*)	Analyzing (*vishleshan*)	*Thought (vichar)*		*Semblance (abhaas)*
Man (Mind)	Tasting (*aaswadan*)	Selecting (*chayan*)	*Expectation (asha)*	*Glimpse (bhaas)*	

Knowledge of Humane Conduct (मानवीयता पूर्ण आचरण ज्ञान)

Living in human-human relationships and human-nature relationships with values, character and ethics. Values are our participation in the larger orderliness. There are 4 Values in the Self, or Jeevan, 6 Human Values, 18 Values in Human-Human relationship and 2 Values in Human-Nature relationship; totaling 30 values in all. Put together, these are 'human values'. Humane-character is the same for every human. Humane-character is in the form of *righteous-wealth, morality in husband-wife relationship* and *work-behavior filled with kindness.* (चरित्र - स्वधन, स्वनरी/स्वपुरूष, दया पूर्ण कार्य व्यवहार) We realize ethics when we rightly-use and protect our resources (body, mind, and wealth). (तन, मन, धन का सुरक्षा, सदुपयोग) In this way, complete- humane-conduct gets explained as a combination of values, character, and ethics. These are the three pillars for our living in orderliness.

Wisdom (vivek)

- Knowledge of Immortality of Jeevan (Conscious Self) and Mortality of Body

- Knowledge of 'laws of living': intellectual, social and natural laws. (boudhik niyam, samajik niyam, prakritik niyam), Identify the human-goal, the human target

Science (vigyaan)

- Knowledge of activity, time and decision making.
- Sets the direction for human-goals identified in wisdom.

We may reorient and develop the content and curricula of education for the Peace and Harmony. This will be conflict less and conflict free approach.

Based on this the following universal tenets have been understood that should be the content of education:

- Knowledge, Wisdom and Science;
- Reality, Actuality and Truth;
- Justice, Religion and Education;
- Basic Structure of Human Society, and
- World Organization of Nation States.

ANCIENT ROOTS: SANATANA DHARMA

The universal principles of the Sanatana Dharma are the most effective means to fight the ills of wars and religious fanaticism that affect the humanity today; causing untold suffering, meaningless bloodshed and it's a thread of extinction of civilization on earth. The world needs today the solace of the Vedic dictum, *"Vasudhaiva Kutumbakam"*[35] ("vasudhâ", the earth; "eva", indeed is; and "kutumbakam", family) is a Vedic phrase that is often cited to assert that the whole world is one single family. Ultimately, the world is so deeply interconnected that *we simply can't ignore* this fact. Universal human society has to work towards social, political, and environmental change if we are to save ourselves and leave a better world for future civilization.

The modern world has to imbibe the Vedic model that recognizes and accepts the plurality of religious approaches. It is the perfect scientific approach of the Vedantic wisdom to human development, that

35. "The most common Sanskrit phrase quoted in this regard, often repeated at popular gatherings is Vasudhaiva Kutumbakam, which means 'the world is one family'", (Malhotra 2014) "अयं बन्धुरयं नेति गणना लघुचेतसाम्। उदारचरितानां तु वसुधैव कुटुम्बकम् ॥"

is highlighted in the motto of Sanatana Dharma, "*bahujana hithaya, bahujana sukhaaya*"[36] (for the happiness of the many, for the welfare of the many)", which aspires for the welfare and happiness of all people. Brihadaranyaka Upanishad says "Om Sarve Bhavantu Sukhinah, Sarve Santu Nir-Aamayaah, Sarve Bhadraanni Pashyantu, Maa Kashcid-Duhkha-Bhaag-Bhavet, Om Shaantih Shaantih Shaantih.[37] (**Meaning:** Om, May All become Happy, May All be Free from Illness. May All See what is Auspicious, May no one Suffer. Om Peace, Peace, Peace.) Vedic wisdom tradition advocates and aims at the human expansion to universality, universal peace, harmony and Unity. Never indulging in parochialism or pessimism, it always has a universal outlook with optimistic thoughts and presents a noble worldview for the advancement of mankind.

Sixty-sixth session of UN, Item 19 (h) of the provisional agenda, on "Sustainable development: Harmony with Nature" Report of the Secretary-General says that "The evolving relationship of humankind with nature varies greatly in Eastern and Western intellectual traditions. Its roots are originally found in philosophy and religion. Although Eastern intellectual traditions are historically distinct from Western ones, the basic questions the great thinkers of Asia tried to answer are similar to those that have occupied philosophers and religious leaders in Europe and The Americas– how can we give our life meaning? How can we find happiness? The insight and wisdom offered by Eastern and Western traditions provide opportunities for dialogue among civilizations and a deeper understanding of our relationship with nature. The following sections describe the evolving relationship of humankind with nature and how thinking about this relationship has influenced the development of environmental legislation in the twenty-first century. Lessons for achieving harmony with nature today are also considered."[38]

This highest objective of the any wisdom traditions and the purpose of human civilization, *Brihadaranyaka Upanishads*[39] declares the

---

36. Coleman, Bennett (1973). The Illustrated Weekly of India. Published for the proprietors, Bennett, Coleman & Company, Limited, at the Times of India Press. P. 27

37. Brihadaranyaka Upanishad 1.4.14

38. UN, Sixty-sixth session, Item 19 (h) of the provisional agenda, Sustainable development: Harmony with Nature, Report of the Secretary-General (2011)

39. Brihadaranyaka Upanishad (1.3.28)

highest goal of humanity as "*asato maa sadgamaya*" (lead me from untruth to Reality), "*tamaso maa jyotirgamaya*" (lead me from darkness to Light), "*mrityor maa amritangamaya*" (lead me from death to immortality). It looks forward for a world free from wars and degrading religious conflicts.

Swami Jyotirmayananda says in his book "The Relevance of Hindu Dharma for the Modern World and it's Renaissance in the New Millennium" that It is this universality of Hinduism (India ancient wisdom tradition) that inspired the Western thinker, Lord Morley, to observe: "What is found in the Vedas cannot be found anywhere else", and Manning to emphatically highlight the fact that "the philosophy of the Hindus is another proof of their superiority in civilization and intellect to the moderns. The Hindus had the widest range of mind of which man is capable."[40] This means Sanatana Dharma is always promoting everywhere the concept of universality and unity of all mankind as a human family, which has its eternal foundation on the supreme truth and inherent existential harmony. Sanatana Dharma feels the responsibility to help, unify and maintain the concepts of the Dharma present in diverse human cultures and thus spread the gospel of World Peace and harmony and the welfare of all. This will be based on the universal approach of Indian environment and ecological friendly Vedic culture which ensures universal global peace and harmony with unity and human security.

PEACE, HARMONY AND HARMONIOUS EDUCATION

The concepts of peace, harmony and human values have connotations in different contexts. Both words are used quite commonly and are in fact inseparable. While separately, both of the words convey different meanings, together they provide safe conditions for individuals and nations to go ahead with their pursuits of interest. In general this refers to relatively stable social, economic, and political conditions. Social stability implies a state free of conflicts which generate threat and fear. Human rights are protected under stable and harmonious economic and political conditions. The conditions: that support absence of conflicts and protect human values, human rights are important for both peace

---

40. Swami Jyotirmayananda (2006). The relevance of Hindu Dharma for the Modern World & it's Renaissance in the New Millennium. *http://www. vivekanand agospel.org/ RelevanceofHinduDharma.pdf P.6*

as well as harmony. The new notion of peace and harmony is much broader and includes a wide range of dangers and threats to human existence. Among others, these threats may be from terrorism, insurgency, and genocide, denial of human values and human rights, health epidemics, narcotics trade and irrational use of natural resources. This notion is primarily addressed to individuals. It includes freedom of individuals from hunger, freedom from wants, diseases and epidemics, environmental degradation, exploitation and sub-human treatment. In fact, peace and security is to be seen as the precondition to socio-economic development and to the maintenance of human dignity. Literature is replete with views, opinions, philosophies, and rigorous academic work accomplished in peace and harmony studies depending upon the contexts of specific development, democracy, humaneness and humanitarian assistance with regard to socio-economic and political situation considered in the investigation.

As mention above the Indian ancient wisdom tradition there are thousands of references are available with support and motivate the basic principles of peace and harmony. However, Peace can be viewed both as a state of mind, and a socio-political-economic condition. An individual is concerned with peace of mind or tranquility. In such a state of mind, an individual can be at peace irrespective of external disturbances. It is a common observation that we can think about the peace of other people only when we are at peace. Therefore, before promoting peace, we must begin with individual peace first and, this can be achieved by spiritual path available in wisdom tradition of India. Peace is also seen as concord or harmony. So, in relation to a family or a community, peace refers to a state of cordial relationship. On the other hand, peace does not mean a condition of complete absence of disturbances or conflicts. In fact, complete absence of disturbances or conflicts in the society or among nations is not possible. So, our peace must also be understood at the level of societies, nations, and the world.

Peace is a social and political condition for economic growth as well as for the harmonious world that fosters development of individuals, societies, and nations. Perhaps the most popular view is as an absence of hostility, violence, or war but it is not enough. It is possible when justice prevails, *i.e.,* there is a rule of law and there is a rule of law, when order prevails. Under a working political order, there is existence of healthy interpersonal relationships, prosperity in the matters of social or economic welfare, and the establishment of equality that serves the true interests of all. This is the necessity for the peaceful co-existence.

Consistent with this approach, Reardon (1988)[41] places global justice as the central concept of peace and asserts that "justice, in the sense of the full enjoyment of the entire range of human rights by all people, is what constitutes positive peace." In that sense, peace suggests the existence of healthy relationships among nations, and a balance of powers. Peace in national or international relationships is generally considered as the absence of hostility, and lack of conflict or violence. In this context, peace suggests sincere attempts at reconciliation and the existence of healthy international relationships.

Peace has always been among humanity's highest values. It may be just as elusive to define as are other virtues characterized by truth, beauty, trust, love, and justice. In this state, we can celebrate our diversity, and search for the good in each other without the concern for personal pain and sacrifice. It provides us a chance to look at ourselves and others as part of one human family. This state is possible, when all people behave according to prescribed codes of conduct. Correspondingly, we need to create an environment of peace that must begin at homes and in schools.

Kennedy (1963)[42] took a narrow view of the human value of love in international relationships, "World peace, like community peace, does not require that each man love his neighbor–it requires only that they live together in mutual tolerance, submitting their disputes to a just and peaceful settlement." However, he proposed that it was well within the realm of human achievement, "Peace need not be impracticable, and war need not be inevitable. By defining our goal more clearly, by making it seem more manageable and less remote, we can help all peoples to see it, to draw hope from it, and to move irresistibly toward it." He further said, "Let us examine our attitude toward peace itself. Too many of us think it is impossible. Too many think it's unreal. But that is a dangerous, defeatist belief. It leads to the conclusion that war is inevitable–that mankind is doomed–that we are gripped by forces we cannot control. We need not accept that view. Our problems are man-made–therefore, they can be solved by man. And man can be as big as he wants. No problem of human destiny is beyond human beings."

41. B.A., Reardon, Comprehensive Peace Education. New York: Teachers College Press, 1988

42. John F. Kennedy, A Strategy of Peace speech, 1963

Dr. Leo Semashko, President, Global Harmony Association (GHA) says that Global harmonious education is the basic generating mechanism of a harmonious civilization at least in four moments. First, only it is capable to transform the spheral classes of the population from spontaneous in conscious actors of social harmony or harmonious civilization. Secondly, only it provides these classes with scientific knowledge of building this civilization at all levels: global, regional, national and local. Thirdly, only it creates the person adequate to this civilization: homo harmonious. Fourthly, creating the harmonious (multidimensional instead of one-dimensional) human resource, which uniquely makes all resources, harmonious education harmonizes all other social resources through the person: information, including culture and religion; organisation, including finance (money) and democracy; and economy, including markets, property, competition, incomes and environment. Harmonious education provides conscious, peaceful and nonviolent evolution of a harmonious civilization.

This education is harmonious in four aspects: on the purpose, content, way and executors, educators who together will prepare the corresponding Academies of Harmony (above). Only similar education is capable to teach us and our children to become the good citizens of global village, providing it an everlasting peace, prosperity, fraternity and happiness to all nations. Therefore, this education demands the priority development and financing in the process of conscious building of harmonious civilization at all levels and from all sources, including unprecedented, harmonious in essences, philanthropy of 40 billionaires from the USA. If all previous civilizations in history were established spontaneously and violently in continuous wars, the harmonious civilization, the first and unique, can and is established only knowingly, that is why peacefully and non-violently, thanks to global harmonious education. Formation of this education is the most essential requirement of modern humankind without which the harmonious solution of all global problems is impossible and, finally, survival of humankind.[43]

Strictly speaking, peace and harmony is very subjective with certain objectivity and we can't hope for peace and harmony in the world until we all have peace in our own mind and hearts and then in activities. When we are at peace and harmony, we emanate peace and harmony from our personality and thus motivate others to seek peace and

---

43. *http://www.peacefromharmony.org/?cat=en_c&key=440*

harmony. In the state of peace and harmony we have good will toward all people and the thought of hate or violence wouldn't enter our minds and activities. Hence, harmonious education may play a very positive role.

According to Gandhi nonviolence is precondition to the existence of peace. His understanding of nonviolence was *ahimsa*, which is the absence of harm or injury to all beings in thought, speech and action. Practice of *ahimsa* is so powerful that it creates a moral force that has potential to transform all negative thoughts of causing harm, injury, or violence on others with positive thoughts of love, brotherhood and understanding. *Ahimsa* is a universal value that must be cultivated at all levels: personal, social, national, and international so that all conflicts can be resolved through dialog and understanding alone (Rai).[44] Gandhi's thinking was that there is no dividing line between private and public life, so he recommends that moral principles should be followed in politics. World peace is possible if nations willingly cooperate to prevent warfare. But the question is this how to transform the system according to the way of nonviolence.

War and violence result in the systemic and sweeping denial of civil and political rights, along with wrong economic, social, and cultural policies as scarce resources are expended on weapons and preparation for war. Human rights are the crucial connection between peace and security and the rule of law for harmonious society. Some says that enduring peace will be attained only when all human rights are fulfilled. The United Nations Universal Declaration of Human Rights recognizes that if "man is not to be compelled to have resource, as a last resort, to rebellion against tyranny and oppression," human rights should be protected by the rule of law and universal common harmonious education to all.

Anybody who digresses with the Laws of Nature is bound to impinge upon the rights of others and consequently disturb the system harmony. Therefore, it is irrational and immoral to recognize any kind of extraordinary privileges for human beings at the cost of several other bodies/units of the earth planet. Human beings have to understand their essential obligations and functions in coherence with the larger interest of existence. The human existence has to function and sustain

44. Chhaya Rai, Gandhi's Role And Relevance In Conflict Resolution, *http://www.mkgandhi.org/articles/ChhayaRai.htm*

itself within this system. Accordingly, we need to create political, economic, and educational institutions in consonance with the spirit of the laws of existential harmony. Grant Hardy says "Eastern traditions are often interpreted as presenting no sharp divide between creator and created animals, between humans and gods. In Hinduism, for example, there is a focus on metaphysics, including the concepts of samsara (reincarnation), karma (cosmic justice), moksha (liberation from the cycle of existence) and atman (inner ultimate reality)."[45]

[45] Grant Hardy, "Great Minds of the Eastern Intellectual Tradition", The Teaching Company, 2011

7

Education and Skill Training in India Silver-linings *vis-à-vis* Problems, Constraints and Challenges

LAKSHMIDHAR MISHRA[1*]

I

It may be appropriate to begin with the definitional and conceptual aspects relating to education, skill, skill training and employability/employment and establish the complementarity amongst the four thereafter.

Keywords: Education, Skill Training, Silver-linings, Challenges, Constraints, conceptual, Skills, Attitudes and values, Internalization, Attitude, Understanding, Standardization, Communication/interaction; Sustenance of Quality, UGC (university Grant Commission), Strengthen, Quality of students, Understanding principles, Institutional strategic objectives, Anti national event, JNU, Sanskar', Optimizing business services, Organizational effectiveness, Protecting learners rights.

[1] Former Union Labour & Parliamentary Affairs Secretary, C69, Anupam Apartments, B-13, Vasundhara Enclave, Delhi – 110096

* *Corresponding author*: E-mail:

First: What is Education?

Education enables those who receive it to make a sense of their lives, to define and pursue a purpose, to fully develop their potential and recognize the right of others to do the same. It makes the learners sensitive to the environment and need for its protection. It enables the learners to live in harmony within oneself and with one's natural and social environment. It inculcates among the learners a respect for the dignity and decency of all persons regardless of their faiths and beliefs which is a respect for the cultural pluralism of our society. It provides the means and opportunities to enhance the creativity, capacity for innovation and aesthetic appreciation.

As human beings cross the portals of childhood and enter adolescence and later adulthood, education becomes an effective instrument of qualitative transformation through acquisition of:

- Knowledge;
- Understanding;
- Internalization;
- Application;
- Skills, attitudes and values.

Second: What is Skill?

Skill is the endowment or capacity of an individual to do something well with one's mind as well as body. That something could be a:

- Job or task;
- Communication/interaction;
- Transaction at multiple points.

Multiple skills are involved at multiple points for smooth and efficient transaction of business. To illustrate:

- Technical skills are needed for particular trades (garment making, engineering, automobile, electronic, fabrication and services);
- Transaction of business in shop skills (body language characterised by civility and courtesy, social communication, capacity to adjust to a changing environment);
- Computer literacy skills (these are needed in all modern white collar avocations);

- Quality management skills relate to (conservation of energy, avoidance of leakage and wastage of scarce resources observance of work place safety by pre-empting accidents, the extent by which the quality of the product conforms to the norms of standardisation, precision and quality control);
- Entrepreneurial skills relate to the ability to bring about a meaningful coordination between land, labour and capital for creating a new enterprise, ability to face teething problems at the infancy thereof and eventually overcoming them to kick off the enterprise;
- Managerial skills *i.e.,* ability to manage the day-to-day affairs of an enterprise encompassing management of human, material and financial resources to ensure that there are no cost and time over-runs and that activities concerned with production and productivity are carried to their logical close in less time and cost;
- Supervisory skills relate to the ability to oversee the affairs of an enterprise including exercise of continuous vigilance to ensure economies of scale, timeliness in delivery, post-sales services including professionalism in meeting customers' satisfaction.

A worker in addition to being an employee (both wage-employed and self-employed) is also a human being, a citizen, a producer and consumer. The skills required for being a productive human being, a responsible and law abiding citizen, an efficient producer and a meaningful consumer are:

- Life skills;
- Cognitive, affective and psycho-motor skills;
- Communication skills;
- Attitudinal and behavioural skill resting on respect for the dignity and decency of co-workers, supervisors, managers, etc. and conforming to the norms of corporate enterprise discipline;
- Survival skills;
- Leadership skills.

Third: What is Skill Training?

While endowment and capacity of a job seeker to get a job of his/her choice in the labour market is skill, the process of development of such skills or particular skills for particular occupations is known as skill training. It includes acquisition of new skills as well as refinement and sharpening of the existing skills with a view to up-grading them. Skill training boosts employability of a person intending to enter the job/ labour market. Employability gets converted to employment when certain internal and external prerequisites are fulfilled. Skill training is multi-faceted; it takes place at home, school, community, on the job at the workplace as also a training centre. It unleashes new energies, promotes creativity, innovation, adventurism and enhances labour participation and productivity.

Four: What is Employment?

Employment is gainful engagement of an individual in an economic activity. Employment includes wage employment and self-employment. ILO Convention No.122 of 1964 which India has ratified (17.11.1998) speaks of a full, freely chosen and productive employment. Full employment means that any able bodied person offering himself/herself for work should be given an opportunity to work even as an unskilled worker on payment of notified minimum wage or market wage where no such minimum wage has been notified. Freely chosen employment implies that every individual should have the option or discretion to choose a particular avenue of employment according to his/her endowment, preference, aptitude and interest.

Productive employment implies that every employment results in production of certain goods and commodities which are essential to the life of the individual and the community.

The most desirable thing for every worker as a human being, as a citizen, producer as well as consumer should be:

- Stability and durability of employment in a regular job as opposed to contract, casual, part-time or temporary employment;
- Treatment with respect for dignity and decency of every human being;
- Safety, health and freedom from occupational diseases;
- Skills and competencies which can be productively applied;
- Remunerative wage;
- Guaranteed income on a regular basis;
- Protection against various competencies like accidents (either man made or machine made) invalidity and death.

How are the four Complementary?

- There is a clear synergy between the four components as listed above.
- They involve a learning process.
- They involve productive application of knowledge, information and skills which are learnt.
- Making all members in a family literate and educated facilitates an outreach with the labour market and the outer world.
- Functional literacy and education in that sense promote decent livelihood.
- Decent livelihood is an autonomous existence resting on respect for human dignity and decency.

II

Employability and employment is not automatically coterminous. They become coterminous when certain internal and external prerequisites are fulfilled.

The Internal Prerequisites are

- A high level of functional and sustainable literacy and numeracy;
- Ability to use reading, writing and calculation skills effectively in daily life;
- A high level of awareness, agility and alertness of human mind;
- Technical/vocational skills essential for specific trades;
- Ability to handle a situation as it comes with ease;
- Ability to grapple with crisis situations with strength, courage and self-confidence and overcome the same.

The External Prerequisites are

- A comprehensive plan for lifelong education and skill training and modalities for establishing an effective link between the two;
- Complementarity between human, physical and financial capital;
- Policy, structure and mechanisms for creation of a healthy, stable, contented and motivated workforce;

- Plan to harness the findings of scientific and technological research for the benefit of all but in particular, for the deprived section of the society who are also unorganised and un-protected for higher production and productivity;
- A plan for boosting individual and collective savings as a pre-cursor to high rate of investment;
- A hassle free supportive and conducive investment climate contributing to high GDP rate of economic growth.

III

A Few Silver-linings as far as India is Concerned

A.

- India has the single largest young population in the whole world in as much as 35 PC of Indians are below 15 years of age while 18 PC fall within the age group of 15-24 years with a median age of 24 years.
- This is a favourable demographic dividend which according to a projection made by the World Bank is likely to continue till 2040 and will be an important instrument for harnessing India's economic potential.
- If this trend continues and if skill training programmes are successfully implemented as envisioned in the new national skill development policy launched by PM on 15.07.2015, India might emerge as a hub for supply of knowledge workers and skilled professionals to the western economies which are estimated to face a shortage of 39 million skilled workforce by 2020 and who also have a demographic disadvantage in as much as the elderly in those economies far outweighs the young (like Japan where it is 5:1 in a population of 130 million).

B.

- In India, UPE, UEE and AE (including CE) have always been viewed holistically, one complementing, supplementing and reinforcing the other.

- The 86th amendment of the Constitution in 2002 and insertion of Art. 21A provided for free and compulsory education to all children in 6-14 age groups.
- This was in the wake of a judgement of the apex court (JP Unnikrishnan *vs*. State of AP, 1993) in which certain positive and pro-active directions were issued by the apex Court.
- In 2009, a law on the rights of all children in 6-14 age group to free and compulsory education was enacted enforceable from 01.04.2010.
- In 2002 itself, Sarva Shiksha Abhiyan, a national programme for universal education of all children in 6-14 age group had been put in place.
- Substantial progress has been achieved in provision of school infrastructure, enrolment, retention and participation of children.

C.

- Following the call for EFA at the Jomtien Conference in March, 1990, Bharat Gyan Vigyan Jatha (BGVJ) or a countrywide caravan of teachers, students, women and youth was taken out between 02.10.1990 to 14.11.1990 to create a massive ground-swell in favour of functional adult literacy.
- Under the auspices of National Literacy Mission Authority (NLMA), a campaign for total literacy was launched at Ernakulam in Kerala.
- TLC, Ernakulam or 'Lead Kindly Light" became an important pace and trend setter of functional adult literacy for the whole of Kerala followed by Goa, Puducherry and over 200 districts (out of 460 districts in 1990-91).
- The approach which was adopted under TLC *i.e.*, area specific, time bound, volunteer based, result oriented and cost effective was sound and sensible.
- Over 100 million adult learners were enrolled in the campaign over a period of 20 years (1988-2008) and were certified to be functionally literate.
- Life skills, communication skills, vocational skills, survival skills, leadership skills etc. were sought to be integrated with literacy and numeracy skills.

- TLCs also became campaigns for health, nutrition, immunisation, women's equality and empowerment, protection and conservation of environment, adoption of small family norm.

D.

- Considering that skill development is crucial to employability which precedes employment, a new ministry of skill development and entrepreneurship has been formed in 2014-15 with an Independent Minister-in-charge (Sri Rajib Pratap Rudy).
- A new national skill development policy has been announced on 15.07.2015.
- Institutional mechanisms like national skill development board, Corporation and Fund have been put in place.
- To make motivation of the adult learner to go in for skill training which is self-propelled and self-driven, PM's skill development programme (PMKVY) has been launched to act as an external stimulant.
- This makes skill development more demand driven.
- Skill development missions have been launched in each State.
- Sector specific and industry driven skill development councils have been formed.
- In each parliamentary constituency, a calendar of skill development festivals has been drawn up to ensure mass involvement.
- A standardised advertisement campaign has been launched in the regional languages to focus target groups.
- Information in skill development which is being disseminated relates to various training options, possible career paths and income generation potential of each skill.
- Live demonstration of such skills is being organised in mobile vans/buses/centres.
- The PMKVY also envisages:
  - Radio jingles;
  - Print and TV advertisements;
  - Posters;
  - Brochures;

  - Soft copies of poster templates and messaging have been made available on the PMKVY website for usage by training providers.
- NSDC has the overall responsibility to conduct national level campaigns in radio, print and TV advertisements.
- Trainees with prior experience or skills and competencies will be assessed. They will be given monetary rewards for undergoing assessment.
- This is an important step towards recognising the skills already possessed by workers in the informal sector.
- The reward amount which will be fixed after taking into account:
  - Cost of training;
  - Willingness of trainees;
  - Other relevant considerations.
- This is expected to generate and sustain motivation and prevent drop-out of trainees.
- Higher incentives have been fixed for training in:
  - Manufacturing;
  - Construction;
  - Plumbing.
- GoI has introduced a unique identification system through issue of Aadhaar Cards linked to the bank account of every trainee; this will facilitate transfer of the reward amount directly to the trainee's account.
- A modest target of imparting vocational skill training to 24 million in 2015-16 and to 102 million over the next five years has been fixed.
- The post-training phase is meant for supporting and guiding trainees which includes:
  - Career guidance and counselling;
  - Connecting the trainees to employment opportunities;
  - Tracking trainees in the post-training phase.

E.

- On 12.01.2016, at National Industry Conclave on Skills organised by MOS & E, it was announced that skill development projects will now be considered as Corporate Social Responsibility (CSR).

- GoI has also announced an 'India Aspiration Fund' in August, 2015.
- The corpus of this Fund will be used to invest in various start-up projects.
- The start-up policy along with an action plan was launched by PM on 16.01.2016.
- Start-up campaign is a drive to boost innovation, creativity and risk taking in business.
- This is an initiative to unleash and harness the unlimited youth energy to find easy solutions to mind-boggling problems.
- This will undoubtedly boost quality self-employment for the young and budding entrepreneurs.
- A package of concessions for those who take up start-up projects such as:
  - Self-certification for compliance with laws;
  - No inspection (either central excise or customs or income tax or labour) for three years;
  - Complete task holiday for three years;
  - 80 PC exemption from fees payable for filing a patent application;
  - Intellectual property rights become co-terminous with youth property rights;
  - Facilitating exit options.

IV

Grey Areas – Problems, Constraints and Challenges

A. Global

- EFA global monitoring report 'Youth and Skills' –putting education to work (2012) has the following disquieting features in education, skill training and employment scenario:
  - Total number of young persons in 15-24 years in 2010 – one billion;
  - One out of eight of them is unemployed;

- The unemployed are disproportionately concentrated in poorest countries;
- Around 200 million in the same age group in 123 low and middle income countries did not complete primary schooling;
- Over 50 PC are in India, Bangladesh, Pakistan, Ethiopia and Nigeria, 60 PC being girls;
- EFA report has listed three types of skills essential for the employability of the young; these are:
  - # Foundation skills;
  - # Transferable skills;
  - # Technical and vocational skills.

- Foundation skills include a high level of functional literacy and numeracy necessary for entry to the world of work.
- Transferable skills include:
  - Ability to solve problems;
  - Ability to communicate ideas and information effectively;
  - Being creative and demonstrating leadership qualities;
  - Demonstrating entrepreneurial, managerial and supervisory qualities.
- The young need these skills to:
  - Adapt to different work environments;
  - Improve chances of staying in gainful employment.
- Technical and vocational skills involve knowledge, information and endowment relevant for specific occupations.
- The EFA Report bemoans that:
  - Most of the young people are born poor;
  - They grow up in poverty and exclusion;
  - They have limited opportunities to develop the much needed skills for decent jobs;
  - The access to skills for the poor is, therefore, unequal.
- The EFA Report has identified further contributory factors contributing to exclusion, denial of human resource development, denial of access to labour market and denial of participation in labour market as knowledgeable, well-endowed and skilled human resources such as:
  - Around 60 PC of the young have never been to school;

- Those who make it drop-out before completing primary school;
- Large number of young people are still at the primary school at an advanced age (15-17);
- Many children and adolescents are out-of-school and are working;
- An estimated 115 million in 5-17 age group were in hazardous work;
- Without the ability to acquire skills, they are trapped in low paid and insecure jobs throughout life;
- There is no modicum of social protection for such low skilled and under-employed people with under-utilised potential.

- The consequences of such a global phenomenon according to the EFA Report are:
  - 152 Million young people are paid less than US $1.25 per day;
  - In low income countries less educated and low skilled young people cannot afford to wait for the right kind of a job;
  - Poverty, low level of education and skills force young people to be in low paid jobs;
  - Young people in rural areas in low income countries are both school leavers, working children and victims of low paid insecure jobs;
  - Thus poverty, educational deprivation, child labour, insecurity and poor quality of life go together.

B. National

- 23 Million of the world's under five mortality in India every year.
- 40 Million children under five are stunted and 17 million in the same age group are wasted;
- 50 PC of the children under three are under-weight.
- 75 PC children under five are anaemic.
- 30 PC (of the total number of global deaths of children) children die in India due to lack of access to potable water and environmental sanitation.
- National average IMR is around 40 per 1000 live births while national average MMR is around 212 per 100,000 pregnant mothers/women.

- Despite the Right to Food Security Act, 2013 over 30-35 million Indians (global eight million +) go to bed hungry every day.
- About 20 million households in 100,000 villages (out of total number of 700,000 villages) do not have access to potable water.
- Due to consumption of polluted/contaminated water, incidence of fluorosis is high in Gujarat, Maharashtra and Odisha.
- 2.5 Million children are threatened by blindness in early childhood; over one million children suffer from acute vitamin 'A' deficiency.
- Around 12000 to 14000 children go blind every year on account of vitamin 'A' deficiency.
- Anaemia in young children (79 PC) is associated with impaired cognitive performance, psychomotor development and scholastic achievement.
- Thirty PC of the school going children in 5-14 age group are reported to be suffering from:
  - Intestinal infection;
  - Respiratory complaints;
  - Nutritional disorders.
- According to a report captioned, 'Social Inclusion of Internal Migrants in India' (2013) published by UNESCO, the seasonal migrant children are estimated to be around 15 million in India.
- These children are largely invisible since migration sites are located in isolated areas, away from habitation and public view.
- In the absence of early child care services and initiatives for pre-school and formal education, migrant children miss critical inputs absolutely essential in early years for their physical, psycho-motor, cognitive, linguistic and psycho-social development.
- These children are the worst victims of educational deprivation.
- Additionally, of the total estimated number of Indian children in 6-13 age group *i.e.,* 204.01 million, 60.41 lakh children are estimated to be out of school (National Sample Survey conducted in September, 2014 by the Social and Rural Research Institute, a specialist unit of IMRB International).
- These children may be divided into the following categories:
  - Children who have never been enrolled in any school recognised under the RTE, 2009;

- Children have been enrolled, their names are in the school register but they have not been attending the school;
- Children who have dropped out after completing some studies, have crossed childhood, have grown to be adolescents and adults and have remained illiterate.

- Regardless of the factors which may have contributed to the out-of-school children phenomenon, this represents a colossal waste of precious human resource.
- They are not only an accretion year after year to the growing ranks of the unlettered (in the vicinity of 400 million which is the single largest number of unlettered persons in the whole world) but will sadly remain cut off from the world of information, communication, modernisation, innovation and competition.
- To make matters worse, many of the out-of-school children are forced to enter the informal sector where employment is low skill, low wage, low social protection and is neither full nor freely chosen nor productive.
- The overall scenario may be summed up as one of poor quality of education, irrelevant curriculum, poor quality of teacher's training, low level of parental and learner motivation, high levels of drop-outs, low retention, poor participation in curricular, co-curricular and extra-curricular activities and low levels of achievement of proficiency in mother tongue, arithmetic, sciences and environment studies.

C. These have their debilitating effect on the coverage, quality and overall impact of technical education in India. The 61st round of NSSO Survey has brought out some of the disquieting features of the arena of technical education as under:

- Despite a wide network of technical educational institutions in the country, PC of population with technical education is very low.
- Only 1.5 PC of the total population and 2.5 PC of population of 15 years and above is reported to have received any kind of worthwhile formal technical education.
- The PC of women to have received technical education is even lower than 1.5 PC.

- The growth rate of diploma/certificate level education compared to the degree level technical education has declined by 1.3 PC between 1999-2000 and 2004-05.
- The rate of unemployment among educated youth in the last couple of decades has been constantly on the rise.
- Out of 33 million (approximately) youth who received some modicum of vocational training, more than 18 million possess low levels of skills as their general educational achievement levels are below middle level.
- More than 75 million youth with secondary or even higher levels of general education (which includes 13 million graduate youth) are not reported to have received any vocational training.
- It is regrettable but true that the levels of vocational skills in the labour force in India compare poorly with the position obtaining in other countries. Only 5 PC of the Indian labour force in 20-24 age group has got some vocational skills and mostly it is skill in relation to two bare hands which is grossly inadequate. The PC of population (who are skilled and highly skilled) in industrially developed countries of the West and the East is much higher varying between 60 PC to 80 PC except for Italy where it is 44 PC. The PC for South Korea which has recently been categorised as an industrialised country is exceptionally high at 96 PC.
- This author as a member of a high level tripartite ILO delegation led by Mr. Kari Tapiola, former Executive Director, ILO to Seoul in 1997-98 had seen in his own eyes how the highly educated and skilled workforce in that country could erect structures which represented a marvellous combination of physical safety of structures with remarkable aesthetics or sense of beauty and functional utility.
- It may be pertinent to analyse the factors behind South Korea's emergence as such a highly skilled industrialised country.
- The EFA report cited earlier has also cited the example of South Korea from being poor to healthy and wealthy in just 20 years largely through a balanced combination of universal literacy and skill training.
- It has recommended a few conceivable measures to replicate the South Korean experiment such as:
  - Correct identification of demand in the labour market through continuous interaction with employers of enterprises;

- A complete census of skills/trades which are market relevant and demand driven to be undertaken;
- Obsolescent skills to be replaced by new and relevant skills;
- Allocating a higher PC of GDP for raising physical infrastructure, qualified and trained manpower, machinery and equipment;
- Due attention to be paid to the training of vocational skill training providers;
- Revising curriculum, course content and textual materials to make them market relevant;
- Undertaking continuous evaluation of the content, quality and impact of skill training programmes;
- Prior learning and skills acquired in the informal sector to be validated for transition of workers from informal to formal;
- Convergence between lifelong learning and skill training institutions.

V

A.

- The Incheon Declaration, 2015 towards a new vision for education is a timely, appropriate and splendid initiative. It has emphasized amongst other components:
  - Quality education;
  - Lifelong learning opportunities.
- Defined in the simplest terms, quality education ensures acquisition of the following:
  - Functional literacy and numeracy skills;
  - Analytical, problem solving and other high level cognitive skills;
  - Interpersonal communication skills;
  - Constructive social skills.
- Social skills basically relate to skills of tolerance or adjustment which is an important attribute of a learning society which is expected to be tolerant, catholic and egalitarian.
- The concept of lifelong learning removes time horizons and limitations of our current educational heritage. It implies that

learning is a continuum which occurs every day, week, month and year. It begins with birth and goes from the cradle to the grave. It is a gradual and sequential process in which every person learns albeit step-by-step.

- Lifelong learning opportunities include the following:
  - Equitable and increased access to quality technical and vocational education and training;
  - Advanced education and research.
- They also imply the following:
  - Recognition, validation and accreditation of knowledge, skills and competencies;
  - Acquisition of life skills;
  - Acquiring and maintaining desired levels of proficiency in mother tongue, arithmetic, science and environmental studies;
  - Harnessing the findings of scientific and technological research to strengthen primary, elementary, secondary, senior secondary, university and adult education.
- A learning and progressive society is like a pyramid. Two primary attributes for creation of such a society are:

  The first at the base of the pyramid
  - Early childhood education and care for all children in 3-6 age group;
  - All children in 6-14 age group are to be enrolled in an age appropriate class in the formal school system;
  - The children to continue in the formal school system and participate in all school activities – curricular, co-curricular and extra-curricular;
  - Smooth transition from primary to elementary and secondary (lower and upper) after completion of the eight year cycle of learning and acquisition of the minimum levels of proficiency in all subjects taught;
  - Special training to be imparted to all out-of-school children (both non-enrolled and school drop-outs);
  - A complete action plan encompassing special learning materials, selection and training of teachers, venue (both residential and non-residential) and duration of training on

the basis of prior assessment of skills and competencies to be in place;
- Such training to enable them to integrate with the rest of the class – academically and emotionally;
- Skill training to be integrated with school curriculum at primary, elementary and secondary levels.

The second at the top of the pyramid
- All adults (15-35) in their most productive and reproductive age group to be made functionally literate and numerate;
- Basic functional literacy to be supplemented by post-literacy and continuing education to sustain and consolidate the gains of the former;
- Skill training for imparting new and market relevant skills and up-gradation of existing skills of the preferred choice of the trainee to be integrated with literacy programmes;
- A common strategy to make the base as well as the top of the pyramid strong and sustainable through continuous monitoring and evaluation.

B.

- There are three seminal implications of lifelong learning. These are:
  - Span;
  - Space;
  - Pace.
- Span implies learning as a continuum.
- Space implies learning taking place at all conceivable locations (home, school, community, workplace and training centre).
- Pace implies recognising:
  - All learners are not uniformly endowed;
  - Some are slow and some fast learners;
  - Different strategies are needed for differently endowed learners;
  - The teacher imparting the instructional lessons needs to be patient and empathetic in dealing with slow learners so that the latter do not get discouraged by their slow pace of learning.

- Variations notwithstanding, lifelong learning opportunities are relevant for anyone and everyone keen on learning such as:
  - School going and school leaving children;
  - Youth/adults;
  - House wives;
  - Agricultural and industrial workers;
  - Workers in the formal as well as informal sectors.
- Such learning is meant for promoting:
  - Purposeful reading and writing;
  - Perceptive observation;
  - Patient listening;
  - Verbal and non-verbal communication;
  - Understanding, comprehension and internalisation.
- All these are pre-requisites of skill training, employability and quality employment.
- This is how lifelong learning, skill training, employability and eventual goal of full, freely chosen and productive employment are inextricably intertwined.

VI

- Put in a capsule form:
  - Life skills impart safety, security, dignity and decency to the life of every individual; they enable the latter to cope with stress and strain, promote critical and creative thinking, decision making and problem solving;
  - Cognitive skills which represent the basic capacity to learn, promote rational and scientific thinking, reflecting, questioning, interpretation and analysis;
  - Affective skills which are behaviour and emotion related help to establish a correct relationship between self, peers, elders and all members of the family and civil society;
  - Psycho-motor skills promote psychomotor coordination;
  - Inter-personal communication skills help to build the bridge between the sender and the receiver;

- Survival skills impart the capacity to survive in the midst of a difficult terrain, climate, weather, diverse and difficult situations and human beings;
- Leadership skill is a cumulative product of a number of other skills which provide the direction and insight for leading an organisation, a movement as also a group of individuals;
- Right attitudes hold the key to right behaviour and right behaviour holds the key to the success of any programme. This is how on the first anniversary of Swachh Bharat Abhiyan, the PM emphasised the importance of attitudinal and behavioural skills. By implication, if by our attitude, we want to go in for a clean India, this will be reflected in our behaviour and clean India will become a distinct possibility.

• It may be pertinent to ask as to how lifelong learning is considered crucial to the success of skill training programmes. A combination of lifelong learning and skill training would undoubtedly unleash a new energy and create a workforce which will be an asset to the enterprise and the nation. Such a combination or integration will have several built in advantages such as:

I. Skill training programmes envisage preparation of a number of pamphlets, handbooks, advisories etc. covering:
   - The nitty-gritty of the manufacturing process;
   - Description of tools, equipments and spare parts of a machine;
   - Standardisation, precision and quality control devices;
   - How to attend a crisis situation when a machinery has broken down or there is leakage of deadly gas (as it happened on 02.12.1984 at the pesticide plant of Union Carbide Corporation at Bhopal) with possibility of an impending disaster.

• Those who are functionally literate will be able to go through these materials, comprehend and act on them; they will be able to grapple with and overcome the crisis situation much better.

II. Skill training programmes involve a number of drawings with numerical dimensions (length, breadth, height, tensile strength, permeability etc.). Those who are functionally literate and numerate will be able to understand and internalise the shape, size colour and code of various objects which form part of training; they will be able to do mathematical calculations accurately and apply them with equal accuracy.

III.Skill training programmes have both the components of employability as well as actual placement in a job. For the latter, a strong level of general and social awareness, understanding the peculiarities and complexities of certain operations and strength, courage and self-confidence to face these situations or deal with these complexities will be necessary. It may be difficult to acquire the desired level of awareness, understanding, maturity and sensibility without being functionally literate and without pursuing lifelong learning.

- Lifelong learning, it is needless to affirm and re-affirm, will provide an open sesame to a wider world of knowledge, information and skills of interest and relevance to the lives of learners-cum-citizens-cum-workers.
- The PM's Shram Awards Yojana in vogue for quite some time bears testimony to the fact that functionally literate and numerate workers are also reservoirs of knowledge, information and skill, are intensely aware, agile, alert, have saved human lives by pre-empting accidents through preventive maintenance and have saved precious foreign exchange through import substitution measures.
- Workers' Education Programme which is in vogue since 1958 has also facilitated this to a large extent.

VII

- To bring lifelong learning, skill training, education and employment together, we need a number of strategies such as:

  First: Convergence

  - Convergence could be partly on an individual plane, partly on an institutional plane but largely on an emotional plane. As far as institutional convergence is concerned, we have a set of lifelong learning and skill training institutions at the national, state and district levels. Convergence among them can be promoted when the functionaries meet, get to know and understand each other and share ideas, information and experiences which are of interest and relevance to each other.

By necessary implication, opportunities for such meeting and interface will have to be put in place.

Second: Integration with the Curriculum

- Skill training and multiple nuances thereof should be integrated into the curriculum of training of teachers of lifelong learning institutions.
- Such integration will enable the teachers to keep on motivating their students on the importance of acquisition of various skills with which they can contribute their very best to the enterprise where they are employed.

VIII

- In the ultimate analysis, employment is placement of manpower in various activities of an enterprise whereby the manpower converts unfinished materials into finish products.
- It is pertinent to remember that there is a direct correspondency between skills and requirement of the placement.
- The correspondency is not between a piece of paper called a diploma or a certificate or a degree and the placement.
- The certificate may or may not be conclusive evidence of the possession of skills stated therein although it would have been the culmination of an entry point.
- Conversely, non-possession of the certificate is not an evidence of non-possession of the skills.
- For each such skill, there are two important components namely:
  - Natural talent without any formal training;
  - Development of a particular skill through training.
- Skill training performs certain important functions such as:
  - It evokes the latent talents of those who have the basic knowledge of a standard adequate for imparting to them further specialised knowledge;
  - It refines, sharpens and upgrades existing skills.
- Such training may be pre-service or in-service or special job-oriented or acquired informally at home in practical on-the-job experience.
- There is a direct link between training and skill of a particular type.

- There is, however, no such direct link between education and a specific skill and between skill and employment.
- To illustrate, training in pedagogy makes a formally educated person fit for teaching, not merely acquisition of a university degree in science or humanities.
- Any such degree equips a person only to the extent of taking advantage of training to be acquired later for becoming a teacher.
- Education gets enlivened with acquisition of the capacity for training for a specific assignment in a set of disciplines.
- Such an education has a direct association with the training to be received thereafter.
- In other words, active education through training has a co-relation with specific jobs while textbook centred formal education has empirically a weak link with specific jobs for the following reason:
  - It is not imparted for the purpose of equipping a person for a specific job.
- Even in case of active education, it is not the degree but the knowledge acquired through instruction which has a co-relation with jobs.

IX

Education and Manpower Planning

- The principles which have been laid down in S.29(2) of RTE Act for designing an appropriate curriculum for elementary education are:
  - Conformity with the values enshrined in the Constitution;
  - All-round development of the child;
  - Building up child's knowledge, potential and talent;
  - Development of physical and mental abilities of the child;
  - Promoting inquisitiveness, a sense of wonder and exploration;
  - Making the child free of fear, trauma and anxiety;
  - Comprehensive and continuous evaluation of the child's understanding of knowledge;
  - Mother tongue to be the primary medium for imparting instructional lessons.

- Observance of these principles is crucial to the making of a complete adult woman or man out of a girl or a boy who has:
  - The biological energy to work;
  - Who can anticipate the trends in employment;
  - Who can face a situation with strength, courage and self-confidence as it comes;
  - Who can withstand the stresses and strains of work;
  - Who has developed the maturity and wisdom to take decisions appropriate to a particular occasion?
- RTE is only an entry point which is to be carried forward to a logical close – secondary or senior secondary or university level according to personal aspiration social need and economic necessity.
- This being the case, education needs to be structured to suit manpower requirements.
- The requirement up to the middle level of education may be governed by manpower needs for functional occupations such as:
  - Farmers;
  - Labourers;
  - Persons performing other menial jobs.
    # The manpower requirement and the need for imparting skill training to make the manpower productive and competitive should be uppermost in the mind of every planner.
    # He/she has to bear in mind two important objectives of manpower planning:

The First

- Shortages of qualified and trained manpower should not hinder realisation of the goal of development;
- Education and especially higher (including technical) should not develop at a rate faster than what could be absorbed by the economy on the other.

The Second

- The second contingency as above would have a number of negative fall-outs such as:
  # The number of educated unemployed will increase at a rapid pace;

There will be underutilisation of educated persons;

There will be resultant frustration, unwanted mobility and loss of productivity.

X

A Successful Model of Linking Education with Skill Training

- UIE, Hamburg has taken a lead in connecting education to employment.
- The first case study captioned 'Integrating vocational and general education' was brought out by UIE in 1979. The latest one brought out in 1988 relates to seven country studies in five continents.
- The Tanzanian study, one of the seven is a model of comprehensive integration.
- Integrating education with work for self-reliance was emphasised in:
  - Education Act, 1969;
  - Musoma Resolution, 1974.
- The concept of self-reliance has the following connotations:
  - Students who complete primary or secondary education should be able to contribute directly to development of communities;
  - Education should be rooted in production;
  - Linking education to work would contribute to self-sufficiency of schools;
  - It would integrate schools to the local community.
- The strategy adopted to achieve the desired objectives of self-reliance was as under:
  - School terms and time table changed to make full use of agricultural seasons;
  - Teachers given orientation to participate in production activities;
  - School entry age was raised to seven years; this would enable young school leavers to participate in agricultural operations after seven years of schooling;
  - Production units opened in schools to provide work experience; these were open to public.

- Employability became the central focus of Tanzanian experience after graduation from the basic and secondary schooling.
- Six major innovations in the Tanzanian model are:
  - Universal compulsory primary education had a natural and logical link with adult literacy campaigns;
  - Boys and girls were trained through subjects like crafts and home economics to manage Tanzanian Homes skilfully;
  - School education inculcated in students:
    # Manual and creative skills;
    # Respect for dignity of labour;
    # Excitement and joy of creativity;
    # Self-reliance in later life.
  - Establishment of post-primary technical centres (PPTCs) provided a spurt to vocational skills for graduates from basic schools;
  - Skill training to adult neo-literates imparted self-reliance in different occupations;
  - Multi-purpose folk development colleges (MFDC) widened the scope of training of adult neo-literates in village crafts;
  - Pre-vocational and vocational skills in agriculture, commerce and home economics through secondary education boosted employability.
  - In addition to assessment of students' performance in examination, assessment of commitment to and experience of work imparted a new fillip to education.

XI

In Retrospect and Prospect–An Assessment of what has been said so far–Suggestions, Conclusions and Recommendations in a Holistic Perspective

A. Except in case of a few professions, there is no clear, precise and scientific relationship between occupations and educational background.

- In all such cases, the analyst in-charge of manpower planning will have to rely on the present education, employment flow and its trend over the past few years.

- It is worth noting that the demand for manpower in certain occupations is determined by its supply too.
- An economically advanced country does absorb many more highly educated persons or persons with higher educational qualifications in similar activities than a less developed country does.
- The other limitations are:
  - In any specific job, multiplicity of skills are required;
  - Not all of them are acquired by following the curriculum of an educational institution on a vocational institute.
- Similarly tasks and education do not correspond with each other.
- Sometimes there is a lot of improper placement of technical personnel in non-technical posts on account of:
  - They are likely to be paid more as executives in foreign commercial banks;

    or

  - They take up managerial work as caretakers of buildings.
- When work is taken from technical personnel (like engineers qualified to design and construct bridges), which is of non-technical or administrative type; it is bound to be a cause for a lot of dissatisfaction.

B.

- The skills for placement in a particular job are best learnt at the job itself.
- It is futile to think that certificates of competence for a particular job can be given either by the university or the training institute prior to recruitment.
- There is an inherent imbalance between the correspondency of specific requirement of employers with the multiplicity of skills possessed by each prospective candidate.
- Conversely, there is similar lack of correspondency between the specific qualifications which a candidate has as against manifold skills required for a job.
- The answer to this imbalance lies in acquiring the expertise for a specific job by working on it only and in a particular organisation.
- The emphasis should, therefore, shift from recruitment to probation or on-the-job training.

- The recruitment is only a screening process to permit the selected candidates being given a chance to learn the skills required for placement.
- The appointment letter should not be viewed as a certificate to establish a link between skills and jobs.
- The degree or diploma issued by an educational institution has only a remote link with placement.
- An objective, dispassionate and professional evaluation of academic ability *vis-à-vis* the requirements of the job could provide a basis of a proper need based selection.
- This is required to be refined, sharpened and made job oriented as the candidate selected for a particular job acquires the much needed skills on-the-job itself.

C.

- Today's economy is being increasingly characterised by labour markets which are ruthlessly aggressive and aggressively acquisitive.
- The labour market will tend to repulse those who are entering it for the first time if they do not constitute a quality human resource judged by the parameters of education and skill training.
- The workforce to survive the onslaughts of the market forces will have to be productive and competitive.
- They cannot be productive and competitive without being functionally literate, skilled, agile, alert, aware and present minded.
- If the educational levels are low or below the expected minimum the skill levels will be correspondingly low and will not contribute to high production and productivity.
- It has been universally acknowledged that high labour productivity is a necessary pre-condition for raising living standards of both wage and non-wage workers.
- There is a spin-off effect of higher wages and incomes as a result of increase in labour productivity.
- Higher the wages and income, better will be the scope for saving.
- Higher the rate of saving, better will be the scope for investment.
- Higher the rate of investment, better will be the GDP rate of growth.

- Higher the GDP rate of growth, higher will be the allocable surplus to be spent in the following areas of human resource development such as:
  - Child survival, protection and development;
  - Early childhood education and care;
  - Primary, elementary, secondary, higher secondary and university education;
  - Health and medical care;
  - Skill training programmes for better employability;
  - Adult functional literacy, post-literacy and continuing education programmes.
- From the above analysis, it is abundantly clear that:
  - There is a synergetic link between education, lifelong learning, skill training, high productivity and employability;
  - Educational standards of population in general and that of working class population in particular will have to be substantially enhanced if they are to reap the fruits and benefits of the globalised economy;
  - Simultaneous with general education, a big push will have to be given to vocational/technical education up to the degree level;
  - The levels of skills–both social, economic and technical will have to be substantially stepped up while raising the educational levels.
- The million dollar question which remains to be answered is this:
  - How do we integrate vocational skills with programmes for general educational development?
- The scenario is diverse across the globe.
- The Tanzanian model presented in the earlier chapter provides an answer.
- In Tanzania, pre-vocational and vocational education stands incorporated in the curriculum of the basic school.
- Besides, for graduates from basic schools, the scope for receiving further vocational training through PPTCs and DVTCs exists.
- Similar institutional mechanism for adult neo-literates exists through multi-purpose folk development colleges.

- The secondary diversified/vocationalised programme extends over a period of six years after completion of seven years of basic education.
- That creation of a band of productive citizenry is the central vocational goal of education for self-reliance stands embedded in the curriculum at the basic and secondary level and for adult neo-literates.
- This is also the central focus in Tanzanian vocational awareness generation programme.
- Employability in the Tanzanian model is to be seen in the context of a self-reliant economy at the national level and linking the school with the village and students with management of homes at the grass-root level.
- Replicability apart, a number of useful lessons could be drawn from the model for adoption with appropriate changes to suit local conditions.
- It needs to be emphasised that conditions vary widely across a continent, between continents and countries and even within countries and region.
- No single model can, therefore, be identified and prescribed as suitable for the entire globe regardless of these differences.
- Two important dimensions of the problem of linking lifelong learning with skill training will have to be kept in mind.
- One is the special problems of out-of-school children and the other is the special problems at the level of secondary education.
- The fact that we have over 100 million out-of-school children globally is an index of colossal waste of precious human resource.
- A problem of such magnitude will end only when:
  - We have good quality general education which is attractive, exciting, interesting, relevant and worthwhile;
  - Curriculum attuned to the day-to-day needs of life and environment of the learner;
  - A manageable teacher pupil ratio which is sound from the point of social communication;
  - A conducive teaching learning environment;
  - A good quality teaching learning materials backed by a good quality teachers' training;

- Professional development of teachers;
- A high level of parental and learner motivation;
- Institutional arrangement to look after children of migrant parents (through seasonal hostels) if left behind at the originating point;
- Similar institutional arrangement for schooling, skill training and human resource development of these children at the destination point.

* For revitalising secondary education *vis-à-vis* skill training, the following strategies will have to be thought:
  - Formal secondary schooling is the most effective way to develop skills needed for life;
  - The knowledge and skills acquired through eight years of schooling are reinforced through secondary education;
  - The demand for secondary schooling has considerably increased with advancement in science and technology (including revolution in information technology);
  - Regretfully 71 million adolescents at lower secondary school age globally were out-of-school in 2010.
  - The GER for lower secondary schools is 52 PC in low income countries (including countries of SE Asia);
  - It is imperative that all the loopholes which ail the management of secondary education are plugged in terms of access, equity, gender parity, teacher pupil ratio, teachers' training, continuous and comprehensive evaluation of teaching outcome etc.
  - The institutional framework for technical and vocational education in the school and outside is revamped and strengthened.

8

Development of the Rural School Children's Value-Conscious Attitude to Family

Gulfiia Parfilova[1] and Roza Valeeva[1*]

ABSTRACT

The development of the rural schoolchildren's value-conscious attitude to family is caused by a number of factors that are essential to the modern society. Family is one of the most important human values; it plays an important role in the normal functioning of society, forming future generations. Formation of the younger generation's value attitude to the family is the task of education. The article investigates the problems of the rural schoolchildren's value-conscious attitude to family formation. It updates the main objectives and results of this process: development of the unity of knowledge, feelings, volitional and intellectual qualities, skills and abilities as well as three inter-related components of value-conscious attitude to the family: cognitive, emotional and behavioral. Special attention is paid to the concept of value attitude and the basic approaches to its study. The article also describes family as an object of person's value relations. Age features of the adolescents' valuable attitude to the family formation are revealed. The authors consider rural school as the factor of the adolescents' valuable relation of the family formation

[1] Kazan (Volga region) federal university, 18 Kremlevskaya, Kazan, 420021, Russia.
* *Corresponding author*: E-mail: valeykin@yandex.ru

and describe the developed program of the rural schoolchildren's value-conscious attitude to family formation.

***Key words*:** Value-conscious attitude, Values, Family, Rural school, Rural schoolchildren

INTRODUCTION

Family is one of the most important human values. It plays an important role in the normal functioning of the society, forming future generations. Therefore the younger generations' valuable attitude to the family formation is an important aspect of education. It is due to the knowledge of its essence, the corresponding emotional attitude to it, the awareness of the family as personally and socially important value, as well as the implementation of the adolescents' valuable relation to the family.

Relevance of the topic is also caused by the existence of some negative trends in the development of the family institution today. Education of children in rural areas is compounded by the critical state of the village, which contributes to the formation of a special relationship of the child to the rural world, the desire of many children to leave the village and their family. In addition, most rural schools do not sufficiently use achievements of psychological and pedagogical science and advanced pedagogical experience in family education. Today, education in rural areas lags behind the needs of contemporary life.

Some researchers (Antonov and Borisov, 1990; Gozman and Ghilyagina, 1985; Golod, 1984; Druzhinin, 1996) reveal the importance of the family in the formation of personality. Asmolov (1996), Karakovsky, Novikova and Selivanova (1996) show in their works the ideas, approaches, mechanisms and technology of the students' valuable relationships formation. Significant features of education in the rural schools are disclosed in the works of Bayborodova (2008), Plotkin (2003). However, the issues of valuable relation to the family have not yet received a fairly complete coverage.

The analysis of the psychological and educational literature showed the presence of certain contradictions between existing in the psychological and pedagogical science prerequisites for the systematic study of the problem of the valuable relation to a family formation at school and insufficient knowledge of the content, forms and methods of teenagers' valuable attitude to a family in a rural school formation.

THE CONCEPT OF VALUE ATTITUDE AND THE BASIC APPROACHES TO ITS STUDY

The content of modern personality life makes up its current attitude to unfolding around life. In these relationships, the inner autonomous world of the individual is born. Therefore, an objective necessity for the teacher becomes bringing up a child in the context of contemporary culture.

To determine the nature and content of the concept of value attitude, we consider first the categories "value", "value orientation", "attitudes", as well as the characteristic features of their relationship.

The theory of values was originally developed by axiology– the science of values. According to Philosophical Dictionary (Gubskoy, 1997) value is the thing people recognize standing above all and what one can strive for, behold, treat with respect and recognition. Value is not a property of a thing, but the spirit and at the same time the condition of the object's full-fledged being.

Value orientation – is a reflection of values in the human mind, their recognition as strategic life goals and general worldview landmark (Petrovsky, 1990). The concept of value orientation is an analogue of the philosophical concept of values, but a clear conceptual distinction between them is missing. The system of value orientations determines the content side of the personality orientation and is the basis of his views on the world, to others, to himself, the basis of ideology, the core of motivation and the "philosophy of life".

One of the founders of the theory of values was Aristotle, who created his famous ethics of values. Later, the great German philosopher Kant contrasted his formal ethics of values. Friedrich Nietzsche introduced great contribution to the development of axiology in the late XIX century. He proved that the values and value judgments are of great importance for the person's worldview.

In the first half of the XX century, axiology was developed in the works of Agazzi (1985) and Weber (1990). Since the second half of the XX century, the theory of values is gaining increasing recognition in Russian science. In Russia as well as abroad, axiology was developed mainly by the representatives of philosophy, psychology and sociology. The largest contribution to the development of the theory of values was made by Vyzhletsov (1996), Kagan (1997), Stolovich (1994), Tugarinov

(1960). In the field of pedagogy and psychology, the problems of axiology of a man and his vital functions were researched by Abulhanova-Slavskaya (1980), Ananiev (1976), Asmolov (1976), Bozhovich (2001), Vygotsky, A. (1972), Zdravomyslov (1986), Leontiev (1981).

Despite the rich history of axiology, there are still controversies on the nature, conditions of realization and classification of values. In psychological and educational literature, this problem is considered from the perspective of the different schools of thought, which give different notion of values and offer different classifications.

Kagan (1997) described value as a force that determines the behavior of any person. On its basis, people build their relationship, determine their own criteria and priorities, and put forward the goals of their activity.

Tugarinov (1960) believes that values are the subjects, the phenomena of nature and the features that are necessary (observable, helpful, pleasant, etc.) for people of a particular society or a particular class as a means to meet their needs and interests, as well as ideas and as a norm, or ideal goal.

Gavrilova (2002) points out that value are the senses of objects that acquire a positive meaning for a person after their assimilation. This definition does not contradict the previous one, but emphasizes the subjective and social nature of values.

Rokich (1973) defines values as a firm conviction that a certain mode of behavior or the ultimate goal of existence is preferable to personal or social point of view than the opposite or reverse mode of behavior, or the ultimate goal of existence. According to him, values are characterized by the following features: the total number of values that are the heritage of a man, is relatively small, all people have the same values, although to varying degrees, values are organized in a system, the origins of values can be traced to the culture, society and its institutions. Rokich (1973) identifies two main groups of values: values-goals (terminal values) and values-means (instrumental values).

According to the concept of Leontiev (1999), values are associated to some extent with the concept of significance, the alleged connection of an individual representation of values with emotional and motivational sphere. However, specific value only occurs when the subject interacts with the object, drawing it into the material and the spiritual world of human activity, so that value gets its actual existence.

According to Zdravomyslov (1986), values are a generalized representation of people about the purpose and standards of their behavior, embodying historical experience and in a concentrated way expressing the meaning of the epoch culture of a particular society or the whole of humanity. In addition, it is in the consciousness of every human targets with which individuals and social groups coordinate their actions.

The central point of Maslow's theory of a person is self-actualization - the desire of man to a fuller identification and development of their personal capacities, which is the highest level in the hierarchy of needs (Maslow, 2006). Maslow (2006) distinguishes two groups of values: B-values (values of life) - the higher values inherent to self-actualizing people; D-values (deficient values) - the lower values designed to meet dissatisfied or frustrated needs.

The central notion of the Frankl's concept of a person (1990), established in the framework of existential psychology, was the meaning of life. According to Frankl (1990), the meaning of life can be found in three ways: making a deal (feat); experiencing values; and suffering. On this basis, there are three groups of values: the values of creativity, values of experiences, values of relationships.

According to Schwartz (2008), there are two levels of the person's values: the level of normative ideals and the level of individual priorities. Schwartz (2008) considers values not as inherent properties of the object, but the criterion according to which a person acts, assesses his actions, and builds his relationship in the world.

Having studied different authors' theories of values, we found out that the problem is considered from the perspective of the different schools of thought. In our work, we adhere to the definition of Seriy and Yanitskiy (1999), who consider values as a social phenomenon that exists in dialectical relation to the subject-object, which is an important link between personality, his inner world and surrounding reality. We stopped at this definition, as the educational process in the school is based on the system subject relations.

It is important to note that in the process of identifying valuable orientations of students as an indicator of a certain level of development of their personality, the following parameters should be considered:

1. The degree of formation of the hierarchical structure of value orientations.
2. The maintenance of value orientations (their focus).

Scientists note the close relationship of the concept of value attitude to the concept of "evaluation". In the process of establishing the significance of objects and phenomena of reality, a person exposes himself, assessing value, *i.e.,* is aware of the degree of compliance of the subject to his needs, and establishes the ability to meet those needs in a particular situation. The assessment may change, which leads to the process of re-evaluation of human values.

Thus, the value is mobile and volatile, due to the continuous socio-cultural processes taking place in the society and in the life of each individual. Values serve as a kind of "filter" through which only those evaluations pass that are close to the subject.

According Dubrovinoy (1999), values are a guide to human activity and behavior only if the formation of his valuable relation is done.

Valuable relationships - is a subjective reflection of objective reality. The subjects of valuable relationships are important for human objects and phenomena (Mizherikov, 1998).Value attitude is the relationship between subject and object, and one or another property of the object is not just significant, but meets the needs of the subject. Thus, the value of it is a property of the object corresponding to the subject's interests or its goal.

The nature of the valuable relation is of emotional character, as it reflects the subjective and personal relationship experienced by a person with the surrounding objects, events, and people. The values themselves exist independently of the individual and personal attitude of man to them. This is this attitude that creates subjective meaning or personal sense of objective values.

One of the founders of the Russian theory of the relationship Myasischev (2003) identified the following types of valuable relations:

1. To the world of things, natural phenomena;

2. To the people, the phenomena of society;
3. To himself.

Considering the dynamics of value relations, Myasischev (2003) identified some levels of development:

1. The conditioned reflex, characterized by the presence of the original (positive or negative) reactions to various stimuli;
2. Concrete and emotional, where reactions are caused by conditionally and expressed attitude of love, affection, hatred, fear, etc.;
3. Concrete personal, arising out of activities and reflecting the selective attitude to the world;
4. Self-spiritual, in which social norms, moral laws become internal regulative of the person's behavior.

Bodalev (1983) identified three major components of relations:

1. Cognitive (gnostic or informational) component acts as a system of internalized by the individual social beliefs - the concepts, rules, norms, values, assessments;
2. Affective (emotional) component - the personal meaning that is given to the relation;
3. Operational-activity (behavioral, practical) component.

It follows that the concept of "value relation" in psychological science is defined as the mental phenomenon, integrating the result of man's knowledge of any object of reality, all the emotional responses to the object, as well as forms of behavioral responses in contact with the object (Kurland, 2004).

FAMILY AS AN OBJECT OF PERSON'S VALUE RELATIONS

The ongoing economic and socio-cultural changes in the modern world, have led to transformation of marriage and family relations. On the one hand, there is a search for new forms of family life, adequate to the modern state of society (Osipova, 2007), on the other– there is a devaluation of family values, resulting in the weakening of family relationships, loss of continuity and tradition, the increasing number of divorces, and the growth of unregistered marriages. With the re-interpretation of values in the society, there are related changes in the value orientations of children.

Family - is a historically specific system of relationships between spouses, parents and children. It is small group, whose members are linked by marriage or kinship, common life and mutual moral responsibility, social need for which is due to society's need for physical and spiritual reproduction of the population and labor force (Biktagirova *et al.,* 2009).

Analysis of the psychological and pedagogical literature makes it possible to identify the following elements in the value attitude to the family:

1. The subject (person), *i.e.*, one who shows values preference in action;
2. The object (the family) - what has value to the subject (Mizherikov, 1998).

In different historical epochs, value attitude to the family is understood in different ways. Questions of family and family upbringing, undoubtedly, always worried thinkers. In antiquity, in Western as well as in Russian philosophy, the problem of significance for human society of the family and family relations was studied.

Ancient philosophical thought endorse traditional forms of the family, when the main purpose and meaning of marriage is the birth of children. However, there is no common understanding of the values of the birth and upbringing of children among Greek thinkers. According to Aristotle, the value of child-bearing is self-preservation of a man as a biological individual. Xenophon pointed out that children are first of all the breadwinners and assistants of parents in their old age. The philosophical concepts of ancient Greek thinkers first posed an important problem of the valuable attitude to the family - namely, the involvement of family values in the sphere of human interests, fulfilling the role of their daily targets.

Rethinking the ancient philosophical heritage and developing the ethical aspects of a responsible attitude to family, Western philosophers named loyalty to the spouses and productive sacrificial love and respect as essential features of this concept.

For the Russian philosophical thought, which has absorbed on the one hand, Western concept, and on the other - traditional Russian culture, spiritual and moral values, is typical the attitude to the family as a "sanctity " (Stolovich, 1994).

Since ancient times, family had a special significance for the individual and for society, and this is its firm, enduring value. It is possible to highlight the main features of the valuable relation to the family, based on the given philosophical concepts: understanding the importance of the birth and upbringing of children; awareness of belonging to a family, expressed through the respect of parents; the importance of love, friendship and loyalty as a guarantee of family happiness; the willingness of the spouses to mutual aid and support.

Substantially category of the valuable relation to the family is due to both socially and historically conditions. The process of the formation of human character changed people's attitude to the world around them, to themselves, to others, to the family as a mediator between the individual and society, supporting the balance of family and social interests by means of natural control. The vectors of relations that determine the public consciousness values have changed. However, no doubt that value priorities have always been associated with a person, the meaning of his life, family relationships, which take place in a specific cultural context (Uhrbanovich, 2008).

Currently in philosophy, it is generally accepted that the family is value and value attitude to the family is a complex structural phenomenon including not only relevant, manifested in activity attitude of the individual to the family, but also the potential (internal) needs, and interests, by which assessment takes place, *i.e.,* revealing the importance of the family for the individual or society.

The student's value relation to family has its own specifics. It is folding and developing; has not yet formed as property. That's why the problem of the adolescent's value relation to family formation should be considered in the genesis.

Ushinskiy (1988) considered important in the formation of conscious relationship to the family the transfer to the young generation of national and cultural heritage of people through the preservation of family traditions and customs. Demkov (1891) drew attention to the fact that in particular importance in the formation of the future family man has a family microclimate (family atmosphere), which develops children's moral feelings. Sikorsky (1884) believed that the awareness of the importance of birth of the child in the family is the moral challenge of the future parents.

During the Soviet period the attitude towards family was ambiguous. This period is characterized by polar views on family and family upbringing. On the one hand, there were statements by Kollontay (1920) and her supporters that children, husband and the house area relic of the past. Family is "cell" of capitalist private property, therefore it is necessary to overthrow the family as overthrown capitalism.

On the other hand, there have been conflicting judgments on this issue. Makarenko (1988) was one of the first to realize the need to educate young people to form a family and fulfill family functions. The educator noticed that no one is engaged in the upbringing of the younger generation, focusing on family values. The social and production values came to dominate the minds of people, and family boundaries were blurred. He paid special attention to raising of the future family man qualities, to his aesthetic, moral, labor, gender role and economic education. The famous educator insisted that it is not enough to form a correct idea of the future family man qualities, it is important to cultivate the habit of correct attitude to the family, which subsequently will control behavior.

Sukhomlinsky (1990) singled out such important aspects of readiness to the future family life, as the culture of feelings, mutual responsibility of future spouses for each other. He reminded schoolboys that they should be responsible for both the material well-being, and moral atmosphere in the family. Girls are taught that their femininity is an important educational tool. He considered the preparing young people for marriage and family relations as raising conscious attitude to family values and a priority in school education (Sukhomlinsky, 1988).

In the 80s - 90s of XX century, in high schools, students studied the subject "Ethics and psychology of family life", focused on teaching the concepts of masculinity and femininity, the social role of men and women in family and domestic and work areas, the formation of ideas about the future family life and the family itself.

The problems of education of the future family man in the course of practical work with families are considered in social and parenting pedagogy (Ganicheva and Zvereva, 2009; Kulikova, 1999; Mudrik, 2009). Researchers identify such important values of family life as a high level of empathy, mutual respect and acceptance, complete intimacy, a "good parenting", hard work, responsibility, honesty, integrity, tactfulness, politeness, culture, communication, ability to behave in society, hygiene skills, habits to a healthy lifestyle, the ability to organize and spend their leisure time, the ability to raise their children, willingness to enter into marriage and family responsibilities, respect for parents and the elderly.

At the turn of the twentieth century, due to the rapid development of the educational axiology, works have appeared in the Russian pedagogy considering value attitude to native land, labor, family, individual, etc.

Value relation to the family of a teenager is an integral property of the individual, including awareness of the importance of family and family relations, respect between spouses, parents and children, preservation of family traditions; emotional responsiveness to the feelings, experiences and concerns of the family, moral satisfaction from the recognition and love of parents; commitment to hard work, honesty, integrity, tactfulness, politeness, ability to behave in society, the habit of an active lifestyle, the ability to organize and spend their leisure time, the manifestation of culture in marriage and family relations.

AGE FEATURES OF THE ADOLESCENTS' VALUABLE RELATION TO THE FAMILY FORMATION

The search for effective ways of the adolescents' valuable relation to the family formation cannot be carried out without considering the age characteristics of children. Adolescence is the period of childhood's end, the transition from childhood to adulthood. Usually it is related to the chronological age from 10-11 to 14-15 years (Shapovalenko, 2005).

Adolescence is a period when the teenager begins to evaluate anew is relationship with the family (Mukhina, 1999). For a teenager, there are shifts in the scale of values. The desire to find himself as a person gives rise to the need for disposal of all those who usually, from year to year have been influencing him, and first of all, it refers to the parental home. The teenager feels the need for isolation of his "I" from the family "We"; therefore the teen turns his critical eye to family traditions, values and fetishes. The family itself occupies the former position towards the teenager. Usually the family refers to the teen in accordance with the established family traditions (Mukhina, 1999):

1. Family with high reflection and responsibility understands that the child is growing up, and that this must be considered by changing the style of relationships.

2. In alienated family the teenager feels superfluous.
3. In the authoritarian family, the teenager is lonely and unhappy and not sure of himself as a child.
4. The family of a permissive attitude continues to promote the principle of permissiveness.
5. In hyper-occupation family the teenage is still not left alone, the parents watch over him, not only from the outside, but tend to take over him and his spiritual experiences. Here the teenager acts as a child, and is unsure of himself.

Mukhina (1999) also notes that there can be a wide variety of communication styles in the family, arising from different cultural level of its members. However, of great importance in this period, are the uniform requirements for the teenager in the family, as the teens painfully react to real or perceived infringement of their rights; try to limit the adults' claims in relation to them.

A particular problem in the modern Russian family is relationships over goods and financial dependence of a teenager. Until recently, adolescents in the majority of cases were totally dependent on the financial situation of the family and of the pedagogical views of parents regarding pocket money for the grown child. Adults often used this "lever" in an effort to bring their child into submission. Today, the economic situation is different; teens can honestly earn money themselves. However, the opportunity to earn on their own can promote a certain tension in the family relationships.

In addition, money as a sign of well-being, acts at the same time as the equivalent of goods. Teenager evaluates goods belonging to the family as prestigious or as having no value (Mukhina, 1999). Advertising, television, the media, to some extent form the adolescents' needs.

Teen alienation in relation to the family is outwardly expressed in negativism - an effort to oppose any proposals, judgments, feelings of those on alienation. Negativism is the primary form of alienation mechanism, and it is also the beginning of an active search for a teenager's own unique essence, his own "I". However, the teenager is not yet able to stand alone in front of the human world as a unique individual, which he aspires to become. His lost "I" seeks to "We." But this time this "We" make peers, communication with who is the leading activity in adolescence (Khil'ko and Tkachev, 2010). In communicating with peers, teenagers expand the boundaries of their knowledge, develop mentally, sharing their knowledge and demonstrating mastered methods of mental activity (Mukhina, 1999).

According to Mukhina (1999), the teen's "I" longs to connect with the "I" of the other child. This usually occurs after school. Twilight and the upcoming night not only deliver emotional feelings, but also confirm the maturity of the lad, who looked up from his childhood, and now can afford not to go to sleep, but stay with his friends.

Links with parents, that were so emotional in childhood, are not so immediate. In his works, plans, and secrets, he no longer trusts his parents but his newfound friends. In this discussion of another person in any manner, even in the form of praise, it is perceived as an encroachment on his right to choose his freedom and be with his friends (Mukhina, 1999).

Teenage psychological reactions, according to Shapovalenko (2005), arise in the interaction with the environment, and often form the characteristic behavior in this periods:

a. The reaction of emancipation. It reflects the desire of a teenager for independence, for liberation from under adult guardianship.
b. The reaction of "the negative imitation." It manifests itself in the behavior, contrasting with respect to the adverse behavior of family members and reflects the emergence of the emancipation of the reaction, the struggle for independence.
c. Reaction of clustering.
d. The reaction of hobbies (hobby-reaction).
e. The reactions caused by emerging sexual desire.

Adolescence is usually characterized as a watershed, a transition, and a critical period. Teens are usually in crisis between the ages of 12-14 years. At length, it is more than all the other times of crisis. If adults are sensitive to the needs of the child as well as rebuild their relationship with their children with the first negative manifestations, then the transition takes place rapidly and is not painful for both sides.

Formation of the value relation to the family is particularly important in adolescence when the teenager is first awakened to interest in his inner world, which manifests itself in contemplation and reflection on their own experiences, thoughts, former crisis, children's relationship to themselves and to the world, negativism, uncertainty, and crash of authorities. No matter what are the living conditions in adolescence, focus on the family and the need for it at this time requires an extraordinary attention.

In spite of the external opposition in relation to an adult, the teenager feels the need to be supported as well as the need to share his feelings, to talk about the events of his life, but it is difficult for him to start such a close communication. Particularly favorable is when an adult is acting as a friend. In this case, an adult can greatly facilitate the adolescent's search for his place in the system of new emerging interactions, can help to assess his skills and abilities and to understand himself.

Despite all the difficulties of adolescents' relationships with their parents, they cannot lose this age period in the formation of the valuable relation to the family. Adolescence is favorable for formation of such features of the valuable relation to the family like: respect for parents, caring for younger family members, the preservation of family traditions, the establishment of friendly relations, emotional responsiveness to the feelings, emotions and care of family members, assistance with housekeeping, awareness of the importance of family and family relations, understanding of family ownership and family.

Accustomed to the total dependence of their child, parents did not at first agree to release him. However, normal, mentally healthy, loving parents still tend to solve problems with the grown children. They are doing their utmost efforts to ensure the adolescent's sense of security and to create conditions for normal life and development. At the same time, the young man in search of his "I" alienated from their parents and at the same time loving them still learns to take into account the very different plans for human feelings and actions. He learns to rebuild a new relationship with his family. He begins to gain experience and learn to understand and compromise (Mukhina, 1999).

The process of the adolescents' valuable relation to the family formation should be carried out purposefully and systematically. School and the parents of teenagers should take part in it. Especially effective is the use of the media, advertising, collaboration of peers and parents with children.

RURAL SCHOOL AS THE FACTOR OF THE ADOLESCENTS' VALUABLE RELATION OF THE FAMILY FORMATION

Nowadays, there have been negative trends in the development of the family institution, which adversely affect the personal and social value of the family and lead to violations of the relationship between parents and children. These trends include the stability of marriages, early break of ties between generations, the loss of traditions and moral norms. Demographers and sociologists unanimously argue that the cause of fertility decline is the crisis of the family values and family life form. This applies to a certain extent to rural families. According to Plotkin (2003), large multigenerational rural families are left in the past, although in the countryside their number is still higher than in the city. Single-out bachelor existence and "the convenience of independence" become a frequent phenomenon. The situation is worsened by the crisis of the village state, the decline of its economy, the destruction of its infrastructure, the usual way of rural residents' life. This contributes to the formation of a special attitude of the rural child to the world, their desire to leave the village being separated from the family.

It is therefore an important aspect of the younger generations' up bringing is the formation of their valuable attitude to the family. It includes the knowledge of its essence, the corresponding emotional attitude to it, awareness of the family as a personally and socially important value, as well as the implementation of the behavioral aspects of the valuable relation to the family.

Socio-economic changes taking place in the country is caused by significant changes in the activity of rural school. It is today is a major factor in maintaining the viability and development of the village and rural areas.

The specifics of the rural school are determined by a set of conditions that impede the improvement of educational and educational process in it:

1. The economic difficulties of the agriculture development, the impossibility of providing substantial assistance to the school by the enterprises, organizations working in rural areas, as well as by sponsors (Orlov, 2004);

2. Reduction of the rural population living standard, the increasing limitations of the village in the conduction of public leisure, due to the closure of palaces of culture, sports complexes, clubs. The rural school is increasingly transformed into the educational and cultural center, not only for children and teenagers, but also for the rural youth, and even adults (Zaykin, 2004);
3. The prospect of reducing the number of students in the rural educational institutions, because of the decrease in birth rates and the outflow of rural population (Bayborodova, 2008);
4. Insufficiently developed scientific-methodical, organizational, legal and financial framework of the rural schools. The rural school graduates are often unable to compete with their urban peers in enrolling in higher educational institutions) (Bocharovà, 2005);
5. The small number of classes; difficulties with the development of collectivism, moral qualities of students, of their organizational and communication skills (Sidorov, 2003);
6. Limited profiles in high school (actually one or two specialties), the inability to meet even the minimum needs and interests of students in professional self-determination (Frolov, 2004);
7. Rural school teachers often experience shortage of professional and personal communication, limitation of professional development, obtaining new pedagogical information, literature, etc. (Sidorov, 2003).

Despite all the difficulties of the educational activities in rural areas, a number of advantages can be identified, namely:

1. Teachers have broad enough information about children, their living conditions, family relationships, peer relationships, which allows the individual approach to each student, to organize training activities according to their peculiarities ;
2. The closeness to nature, folk customs and traditions, the authority of teachers;
3. A lower crime rate, limited negative impact of the films and video promoting the violence;
4. The majority of parents belonging to on elabor collective, their residence in a small village, the constant communication with colleagues outside the school;
5. The optimal conditions for preparing students for independence in solving economic and vital problems (Bayborodova, 2008).

From the above, it can be concluded that the rural school has quality characteristics that, on the one hand, define its stability and uniqueness, and on the other– are responsible for its internal contradictions and explain its intractable problems.

Today, the rural school as an important link in village life support system forms the intellectual and labor potential of rural society. It is designed to train and educate their children, so that many of them could successfully live and work in rural areas. Before you expect present day students to have "lift-off village" desire, it is necessary to invest a lot of effort into their training, education, health, and cultural development.

Underlying all this depends on strong moral family. To form a strong moral family, we need to bring up a new generation of young people who will be able to create such a family, and it is easier to do this in the village. It is the village and the new village school that can create the moral climate and the educational process, which is necessary for the education of a new generation, as people in rural areas are less susceptible to the temptations that are present in the city.

This unity allows the concentration of all the best cultural and educational force in the overall educational process, to maintain and develop it in the tradition of the Russian school, to maintain the continuity of generations.

Rural family is a special institution, having the following characteristic features: the predominant form of agricultural labor, directly dependent on climatic conditions; a close relationship between work and life; lack of free time; low population density, weakly expressed formalization of social roles, adherence to traditions and customs; behavior under scrutiny with each other; less stressful compared to city life rhythm; simpler forms of communication; a smaller proportion of mental and psychological stress. In addition, it should be stated that the prospects for the modern family development in rural areas are directly dependent on the socio-economic situation in the country, population policies, the process of improving the regulatory framework in the social sphere, implementation of the state policy of the federal target programs to help the family.

In these conditions it is necessary to provide socio-pedagogical support for the family in order to perform its basic functions. Social-pedagogical support is not a list of activities, or the imposition of certain values, but the assistance to the family in the formation of children and young people which should be available to their age, in the development of the capacity to the choice of moral guidelines. To provide social and educational support means to help the child to see and choose the ideal, to realize its value essence.

Due to the nature of interpersonal relations in the village, there is need to pay great attention to the interaction of the school and the family, and also try to make every family ally of schools in the education of children. The efficiency of the teenagers' valuable relation to the family formation in the conditions of rural school largely depends on coordination and coherence on the part of teachers and parents. It is the family's responsibility from early childhood to lay the child in moral values and orientations. The cooperation between home and school, partnership with the family of each pupil, create an atmosphere of mutual support and common interests, which will promote the students' valuable relation to the family formation. There are many possibilities in the knowledge of family history, especially in the rural family, his peasant roots, and in an opportunity to relate their lives with the lives of their ancestors. Parents of a child act as the guardians of ancestral memory, passing on the moral family setup, such as kindness, diligence, and generosity.

According to Plotkin (2003), partnership "family - school" should work in the interests of the child as a whole, sharing the responsibility for his upbringing, education and development. A rural family and the school can contribute to the success of the children: the school and teachers can become teachers of their parents, the school and the teachers have to communicate with their parents all the time, the school and the family should be partners, school can help parents to become qualified home teachers.

The main forms of valuable relation to the family formation in interaction of the family and the school are: parent-teacher conferences, methodical parent committees, parent community meetings with the school administration, with a psychologist, social worker, parent lectures, studios, workshops, group and individual interviews, psychological trainings, conferences that promote parents' pedagogical culture (Uhrbanovich, 2008).

Formation of the teenagers' valuable relation to the family is carried out mainly in the framework of extra-curricular activities, including model situations, psychological workshops, situational role play, contributing to successful implementation and consolidation of the valuable relation to the family, the ability to make a decision in an irregular situation.

In order to achieve efficiency in the formation of adolescents' valuable relation to the family, it is important to have the right choice of methods. In this case, it is better to use such methods as the method of persuasion, discussion, exchange of views, dialogue, motivation methods, the method of raising situations, the example method.

DEVELOPMENT OF THE PROGRAM OF ADOLESCENTS' VALUABLE RELATION TO THE FAMILY IN RURAL SCHOOLS FORMATION

The main purpose of the program "The moral foundations of the family and marriage" is to form a cognitive criterion of valuable relation to the family.

Objectives of the program: to raise the level of children's theoretical knowledge of the family, its functions, relationships in the family, the role of father and mother, housework, family farm, its budget.

The program is based on the concept of Urbanovich (2008) aimed at the formation of adolescents' valuable relation to the family in a rural school. According to it the effectiveness of the adolescents' valuable relation to the family formation depends on a combination of different forms of extracurricular activities organization.

The following forms of work are used in the program: class hours (promoting the accumulation of knowledge about family, family values, role and functional responsibilities of spouses' behavior in the family) may be supplemented by conducting educational workshops (creating conditions for learning and accepting value and practical attitude to marriage and parenthood), interviews (contributing to the consolidation of students' knowledge about the nature of the valuable relation to the family and the development of its components, taking into account the students' interests, needs and level of these features formation), round tables discussions.

The presented program includes 18 sessions, lasting one and a half hours. Classes are held twice a week for nine weeks.

We used different exercises discussing the moral foundations of the family and marriage: "Association", "Pedigree", "Family Happiness", "Responsibilities in the Family", "Conflicts", "What is your family?" Here are some of the training exercises.

Exercise "Association". Students are divided into two groups and give their associations with word "family", for example, happiness, strength, caring, love, focus, warmth, joy, responsibility, comfort. There may be answers: problems, pain, etc.

Exercise "Conflicts". The children discuss why most people are experiencing family conflicts. Conflicts are bound to arise, and will arise - such is human nature. It is important to know how to manage conflicts, to choose the most productive form of behavior in conflict situations. The teenagers are given different conflict situations to solve conflicts from the perspective of parents and children.

Situation 1: Parents insist on the style of clothing that you think, old-fashioned. And the fact that you're wearing, it seems inappropriate, vulgar. How to find out?

Situation 2: Parents are not allowed to be friends with the person, which is interesting to you, citing concern about you (It is bad! "). How to get out of this situation?

The teacher helps children come to the conclusion that aggressive saying, ban, protest are not productive. The teacher reads the legend. In ancient China, there lived an amazing family of 100 people. Love and respect reigned in it. The fame of the family came to the emperor, and he visited the family. Making sure that the rumors didn't exaggerate anything, the Emperor asked the family elders, "How you manage to live in peace and harmony, without quarreling, and without hurting each other" In response to an elder named only one word. What?

The children are invited to guess the word. (Patience)

Conclusion: Learn to control your emotions, and it will help you to adjust the relationship with his family.

Educational workshop "The House I Live In" has the goal of forming the idea about the house of family happiness through understanding the importance of a supportive family atmosphere. Each group develops a "component" of family happiness, from what it is and what it depends on. On the "parts of home" (foundation, roof, walls, etc.), the participants write the most significant sign of marital happiness, and a "component" is attached to a model home on board.

The class hour "Who's in charge?" is aimed at forming a correct understanding of the role of the "head" of the family.

The competition program with parents "Family is seven times me "promotes the formation of moral culture of students, respect for parents, understanding and tolerance of adults and children. One of the contests is "Skillful hands". In this competition only the Dads, the team captains, are involved. As we know not only the mother is caring and looking after children, but also dad. And the fathers demonstrate how they cope with these duties.

Parent Conference "The role of family traditions in the formation of the children's valuable relation to the family" shows parents that family traditions contribute to the development of a common culture of youth, moral self-improvement, actively participate in the spiritual family development. Parents and students introduce the tradition of joint daily family dinners or afternoon tea, during which they exchange impressions, events, news of the day.

Business game "Family Budget "familiarizes participants with the structure of the rational consumer budget of a family. The game simulates the distribution of incomes of the family on the main items of the budget, information balance of revenue and expenditure of the–?

Thus, close cooperation of teachers and parents is an important direction in the formation of the adolescents' valuable relation to the family. It is advisable to organize work with parents through information and methodological assistance, psychological and pedagogical education, drawing on the educational potential of families, taking into account the family structure, lifestyles and traditions; through continuous and systematic monitoring of the development of valuable relationships in the students' families, the study of factors affecting the teenagers' value perception of the family; through the activating parents in joint extra-curricular activities with children.

CONCLUSIONS

Having analyzed philosophical, psychological and pedagogical literature on main aspects of the study of the problem of values and value relationships, as well as the main aspects of the family as an object of an individual's value relations, age characteristics of adolescents, the main aspects of the adolescents' valuable relation to the family in rural school formation, we made the following conclusions.

1. Values are a social phenomenon that exists in dialectical relation to the subject-object, which is an important link between personality, his inner world and the surrounding reality.
2. Value orientation is reflected in the consciousness of human values, which are recognized as strategic goals in life and general philosophical orientation. The concept of value orientation is an analog value of the concept; however, a clear conceptual distinction between them is missing.
3. Values exist independently of the individual, personal attitude of man to them, and only the appearance of relations generates subjective meaning or personal sense of objective values. Valuable relationships are a subjective reflection of objective reality. The object of value relations is important for human objects and phenomena.
4. The science of psychology is accepted to allocate conditional reflex, concrete emotional, concrete, personal and spiritual levels of the individual's valuable relation development. At the same time, the valuable relation structure consists of three major components: cognitive, affective and operational-activity.
5. Family is a historically specific system of relationships between spouses, parents and children; small group, whose members are linked by marriage or kinship, common life and mutual moral responsibility. The social need of it is due to society's need for physical and spiritual reproduction of the population and labor force.
6. In different historical epochs, value attitude to the family is comprehended and understood in different ways. Integrating the data on the essential characteristics of valuable relation to the family, the most common should be noted: awareness of the importance of family and family relations, respect between spouses, parents and children, preservation of family traditions; emotional responsiveness to feelings, experiences and concerns of the family, moral satisfaction from the recognition and love of parents; commitment to hard work, honesty, integrity, tactfulness, politeness, ability to behave well in the society, the habit of an

active lifestyle, the ability to organize and spend their leisure time, the manifestation of culture in marriage and family relations.

7. As a complex purposeful expression of personality, value attitude to the family acts as a manifestation of the unity of knowledge, feelings, volitional and intellectual qualities, skills and abilities. There are three inter-related components of value attitude to the family: cognitive, emotional and behavioral. Formation of valuable relation to a family in adolescents is carried out simultaneously with the development of its three components.
8. Social situation of human development in adolescence is the transition from childhood to independent and responsible adult life. Adolescence involves physiological and psychological changes that lead to changes in the behavior of children. For a teenager, there are shifts in the scale of values. Communication with peers is a leading activity in adolescence. The group creates a sense of "we", which supports and strengthens the teenager's internal position.

   Neoplasm's of adolescence are: sense of maturity, self-development, the formation of the ideal personality, a tendency to introspection (self) interest in the opposite sex, puberty, irritability, frequent changes of mood, the development of volitional qualities, the need for self-affirmation and self-improvement in activity, having personal meaning.

   The problem of formation of valuable relation to the family is especially relevant in the adolescent years. In spite of the external opposition, manifested in relation to an adult, the teenager feels the need to be supported.
9. The process of formation of the adolescents' valuable relation to the family should be carried out purposefully and systematically. It should take place at a school and in the family by the parents of teenagers.

   The family is one of the most important human values, as it plays an important role in the normal functioning of society, shaping future generations. But there are negative trends in the development of the institution of the family, including the rural areas, which negatively impact on the personal and social value of the family and lead to violations of the relationship between parents and children.

   Therefore, an important aspect of the education of the younger generations is the formation of their valuable relation to the family, which is due to the knowledge of its essence, the corresponding emotional attitude to it, awareness of the family as personally and socially important values, as well as the implementation of the behavioral aspects of the valuable relation to the family.

10. The future of the village depends on the goals and values that guide the younger generation today. It is the village and the new village school that can create the moral climate and the educational process, which is necessary for the education of a new generation, as people in rural areas are less susceptible to the temptations that are present in the city.
11. The main forms of education of valuable relation to the family in the process of interaction between the family and the school are: parent-teacher conferences, methodical parent committees, and parent community meeting with the school administration, with a psychologist, social worker, parent lectures, studios, workshops, group and individual interviews, psychological trainings, workshops, conferences that promote pedagogical culture of parents.

The effectiveness of the formation of the valuable relation of teenagers to a family in the conditions of rural school depends on a combination of different forms of organization of extracurricular activities, and their relationship.

REFERENCES

Abulkhanova-Slavskaya, K.A. (1980). Activities and personality psychology. Moscow: Science.

Agazzi, E. (1985). Commensurability, incommensurability and cumulativity in scientific knowledge. *Erkenntnis,* 22: 1–3.

Antonov, A.I. and Borisov, V.A. (1990). Crisis of the family and ways of its overcoming. Moscow: Publishing house of Moscow State University.

Ananyev, B.G. (1976). Problems of modern anthropology. Moscow: Progress.

Asmolov, A.G. (1996). Rendering assistance to a child – personality development. *In*: Krylova, N.B. (*ed.*), Care - support – consultation Moscow: Innovator, pp. 39–44.

Bayborodova, L.V. (2008). Forwarding of rural schoolchildren educational activity. Moscow: Research center of specialists' training quality problems.

Bodalev, A.A. (1983). Personality and communication. Moscow: Pedagogika

Bozhovich, L.I. (2001). Problems of personality development. Selected psychological works. Moscow: Moscow psychology-social institute; Voronezh: MODEK.

Bocharovà, V.G. (2005). Strategy of modernization of rural educational society. *Pedagogika*, 8: 32.

Demkov, M.I. (1891). About Russian family upbringing. *Education Bulletin*, 3–4: 42–46.

Druzhinin, V.N. (1996). Psychology of a family. Moscow: KSP.

Dubrovin, I.V. *et al.* (1999). Psychology. Moscow: Publishing Center "Academy".

Family values in the context of ethnopedagogics (2009). Valeeva, R.A. (*ed.*). Kazan: TSHPU

Frankl, V. (1990). Man's Search for Meaning. Moscow: Progress.

Frolov, I.V. (2004). Profile rural school with a level differentiation. *Rural School*, 1: 91–100.

Gavrilova, T.P. (2002). Family Psychology. Moscow: Vlados.

Golod, S.I. (1984). Stability of a family: Social and demographic aspects. Leningrad: Nauka.

Gozman, L. Ya and Ghilyaghina, E.I. (1985). Psychological problems of a family. *Psychology Issues*, 2: 186–189.

Gubskoy, E.F. (1997). Philosophical Encyclopedic Dictionary. Moscow.

Kagan, M.S. (1997). Philosophical theory of value. Saint-Petersburg: Petropolis.

Karakovsky, VA., Novikova, L.I. and Selivanova, N.L. (1996). Upbringing? Upbringing. Upbringing! Theory and practice of school up-bringing systems. Moscow: Novaya shkola.

Kollontai, A. (1920). The problems of female communist movement. Family and communism. *Communist*, 7: 17.

Kurland, Z.N. (2004). Personality-oriented teacher education as the factor of formation of valuable orientations of the future teachers. *Narodnoe Obrazovanie*, 4: 86–97.

Khil'ko, M. and Tkachev, M. (2010). Age psychology. Moscow: Yurayt.

Kulikova, T.A. (1999). Family pedagogy and home education. Moscow: Publishing Center "Academy".

Leontyev, A.N. (1981). Problems of mental development. Moscow: Publishing House of Moscow University.

Makarenko, A.S. (1988). On education. Moscow: Politizdat.

Maslow, À. (2006). Motivation and personality. St. Petersburg: Peter.

Mizherikov, V.A. (1998). Psycho-pedagogical dictionary. Rostov-on-Don: Phoenix

Mukhina, V.S. (1999). Age psychology: Phenomenology of development, childhood, adolescence. Moscow: Publishing Center "Academy".

Mudrik A.B. (2009). Social pedagogy. Moscow: Publishing house «Academia».

Myasishchev, V.N. (2003). Psychology of relationship. Moscow: Publishing house of Moscow Psychology-Social Institute; Voronezh: Modek.

Osipova, O.S. (2007). Marriage and family relations in the globalization trends: Pluralism, individualism, tolerance. *Family in Russia*, 4: 22–33.

Orlov, V.I. (2004). Restructuring of the network of rural schools: Economic and pedagogical aspects. *Narodnoe Obrazovanie,* 10: 90–101.

Petrovsky, A.V. (1990). Psychology dictionary. Moscow: Politizdat.

Plotkin, M.M. (2007). Prospects for the development of modern rural family as the subject of education and training. Moscow: ISPS RAO.

Rokeach M. (1973). The nature of human values. N.Y.: Free Press.

Seriy, A.B. and Janicki, M.S. (1999). Value-semantic sphere of personality. Kemerovo: Kemerovo State University.

Sikorsky, I.A. (1884). Education in the age of first childhood. St. Petersburg.

Shapovalenko, I.V. (2005). Age Psychology (Developmental Psychology and Age Psychology). Moscow: Gardariki.

Stolovich, L.N. (1994). Beauty. Kindness. Esthetic axiology history. Moscow: Republic.

Sukhomlinsky.V.A. (1990). How to bring up a perfect man. Pedagogical heritage. Moscow: Pedagogika.

Sukhomlinsky, V.A. (1988). Wisdom of parental love. Moscow: Molodaya Gvardiya.

Schwartz, S. (2008). The cultural value orientations: The nature and effect of national differences. Psychology. *Journal of Higher School of Economics*, 5(2): 37–67.

Tugarinov, V.P. (1960). The value of life and culture. Moscow: Publishing House of Leningrad University.

Uhrbanovich, L.N. (2008). Upbringing of high school children's value-conscious attitude to a family during extra-curricular activity (Doctoral dissertation). Smolensk: Smolensk State University.

Vygotsky, L.S. (1972). Problems of children's development age periodization. Moscow: Pedagogika.

Vyzhletsov, G.P. (1996). Axiology: Formation and main stages of the development. *Socio-Political Journal,* 1: 86–99.

Weber, M. (1990).Selected works. Moscow: Progress.

Zaykin, M.I. (2004). Rural school: Modernization of educational content. *Rural School*, 2: 3–6.

Zvereva, O.L. and Ganicheva, A.N. (2009). Family pedagogy and home education of early and preschool age children. Moscow: Sfera.

Zdravomyslov, A.G. (1986). Needs. Interests. Values. Moscow: Mysl'.

9

Buildings Are Not Enough: The Importance of Economic Planning in Education Infrastructure

Italo Arbulú[1]* and Paola Lazarte[2]*

ABSTRACT

Traditionally, infrastructure planning has been approached from an architectural perspective. Although important for the development of functional facilities, by doing so, we neglect several important elements that avoid the best use of economic resources.

This chapter analyses the role that economic and institutional planning within the adequate provision of educational infrastructure and attempts to assess which are the relevant elements that should be considered in order to optimize the use of resources in the provision of a public service such as education, which is considered among the economic literature as a source of positive externalities to society.

In this chapter the authors focus on several aspects of economic planning such as the need to design and implement responsive

[1] Department of Economics, Universidad del Pacífico. 2020 Salaverry Ave. Jesús María, Lima, Perú.

[2] GIZ - Deutsche Gesellschaft für Internationale Zusammenarbeit. Av. Los incas 174, San Isidro. Lima 27, Peru

* *Corresponding author*: E-mail: paola.lazarte@giz.de /paolalzrt@gmail.com; arbulu_ira@up.edu.pe

institutional arrangements that allow effective and opportune gaps reduction, enhance operational schemes to optimize resources from a Public Management analysis. To do so, first we explore how school facilities planning actually is, taking five case studies from five different countries: United Kingdom, South Africa, Colombia, Chile and Peru.

From these analyses authors do not only reinforce the importance of economic planning in decisions for public infrastructure investment, but also find evidence on how operative infrastructure implementation could be actually improved by developing a context-based planning approach that relies in a proper economic planning. This approach is what authors call Integral sustainable infrastructure planning (ISP), for which this chapter develops key concepts.

***Keywords*:** Infrastructure, Education, Public investment, Sustainable planning.

INTRODUCTION

It is undeniable to argue against the idea that infrastructure represents a key component for human capital formation leading to economic development. Many authors argued that inequality is harmful to economic development (Alesina and Rodrik 1994; Persson and Tabellini, 1994; Benabou, 1996; Barro, 1999; Sylwester, 2002) and political environments (Saint-Paul and Verdier, 1992; Alesina and Perotti; 1996).

A commonly expressed suggestion to reduce the undesirable effects of income inequality is through improvements in education (Schultz, 1963; Sylwester, 2002). Education improves human capital, which is considered by economic literature as a way of capital formation. Furthermore, according to some authors income inequality unambiguously declines over time under a public education system (Glomm and Ravikumar, 1992; Saint-Paul and Verdier, 1992; Eckstein and Zilcha, 1994; Zhang, 1996).

On the other hand, some authors argued that many experiences regarding to public education expenditures that do not reduce income inequality since there are no benefits provided to poor people (Fields, 1980; Jimenez, 1986; Ram, 1989). Therefore, the main solution to improve education in poor countries does not involve just more resources to public education but to an improvement in its management and allocation (Devarajan *et al.*, 1996; Hulten, 1996).

Government spending in these studies is divided into aggregate public consumption and aggregate public investment (Gong and Zou, 2002). Furthermore, for many researchers in social science, there is no doubt that investment in infrastructure for public education is a necessary condition for the success of public education (Aschauer, 1989; Cadot *et al.,* 1999).

Traditionally, infrastructure planning has been considered as a task for engineers and architects; however, since governments must allocate resources among several different priorities, it is important to analyse and understand positive experiences regarding to public investment in education in order to promote them and get the best outcomes from such allocation. This chapter analyses the role of economic planning within the adequate provision of educational infrastructure and attempts to assess which are the relevant elements that should be considered in order to optimize the use of resources in the provision of this public service.

I. UNDERSTANDING INVESTMENT IN EDUCATION INFRASTRUCTURE

Investment in infrastructure is a core responsibility of governments for which private sector engagement is important. Infrastructure and capital assets allow for the delivery of key public services. Infrastructure facilities tend to be congestible public goods (Hulten, 1996) and the efficiency of these facilities depends on the size and configuration of the network in which it works. Public schools are a unique kind of infrastructure—both physical and social. They consist of great amounts of land and physical building stock within cities, this is the reason why the planning of infrastructure in education has been traditionally embarked by architects and engineers.

Thus, investment in education–and therefore, in its facilities– has taken an important presence in the economic analysis literature. From Gary Becker's research on human capital formation and its impact on economic growth (Becker, 1975), to the studies exploring the impact of infrastructure investment on learning and school performance (Hanushek, 1971; Berner, 1993; Cash, 1993; Earthman *et al.*, 1996; Hines, 1996), as well as studies that show how some specific features of buildings related to human comfort, can influence student achievement (Schneider, 2002).

It can be said then that there are mixed results regarding the impact that investment in educational infrastructure has on student learning, because the educational infrastructure is a variable that interacts with other social, economic and territorial aspects. Card and Kruger (1996), Parcel and Dufur (2001) show that attending a school with better facilities has positive and significant on student performance results, it is further accentuated when this investment is related to access to public services electricity and telephone, drinking water, drainage and more equipment for classrooms. Thus, the importance infrastructure has in education development.

Yet, the mere existence of infrastructure does not ensure excellent or effective education; that depends on how well the infrastructure is designed and used. Design deals with the scope, content, and organization of curricula; the nature of assessments; the organization and content of teacher education; and the links between these elements. The design of the infrastructure also influences its use, both through the extent to which the instruments are made intelligible and accessible to practitioners and by the existence of agencies and procedures that monitor and improve use (Cohen and Bhatt, 2012).

The United Kingdom represents a leading example on relevant education reforms (Wilkinson, 2002) in particular, the UK has gone through a period of significant change as the government seeks dramatic improvements in educational standards. Not only the policies approached by the British government included the increase of capital investment in school buildings (from £0.7 billion a year in 1996-97 to over £3.5 billion in 2003-04), but also the improvement of local processes for making investment decisions, and the development of prioritization strategies.

As education is a public good (service), the delivery of infrastructure facilities work within the logic of states organization in particular institutional arrangements. These institutional arrangements include constitutional systems, laws, sectorial policies, organizational structures, and institutional bodies; all of them interacting in a particular context (Andrews, 2013). According to some scholars, these contexts affect many institutional reforms.

The analysis of educational facilities provision needs to consider this element in order to understand investment in education. In many countries–particularly developing countries–investment in infrastructure work within National Investment Systems that represent a system of norms, regulatory and operational institutions and tools that shape and oversee the investment of public resources in public infrastructure.

Five aspects are relevant to deconstruct context for policy analysis: (i) constitutional systems that set the institutional basis for the organization of all levels of government and public administration limits; (ii) public administration rules, which are concerned with the immediate set of institutions and norms that establish restrictions, checks and balances to public agencies; (iii) distribution of competences that relates to the type of decentralisation a country exhibits; (iv) investment schemes that consists in sources of income for financing of infrastructure works in education (v) planning systems that refers to the logic of institutions, tools and governance that allows planning to integrate infrastructure needs in all levels of government.

To understand investment in educational infrastructure, Table 1 summarizes the key aspects of the institutional arrangements regarding investment in infrastructure of education in four different countries. In policy practices, these aspects are thought to shape the procurement systems and infrastructure delivery of education facilities. This premise is part of what we call an Integrated Approach for Sustainable Infrastructure Planning; an approach that seeks to explain why planning is needed to be conceived as an economic matter, as a necessary condition to achieve the infrastructure goals. Institutional arrangement is crucial for the understanding of successful schemes of infrastructure planning, rather than just the definition of norms, guides and indexes of functionality, to mention some.

The four countries chosen are different from each other. The United Kingdom has a particular constitutional system where the strong Parliament and a process of devolved administration in Scotland, Wales and Northern Ireland, which are responsible for domestic policy issues such as health, education, culture, environment and transportation. Each administration has their Parliaments / Assemblies that are the law-making bodies for those areas.

The local administration of schools also varies across the UK. For example, England, Scotland and Wales schools are managed by local authorities, whilst schools in Northern Ireland are managed by other boards. The role of the local authority varies between countries, in

Table 1: Investment in education infrastructure in context: Institutional arrangements

Systems / countries	***United Kingdom***	***South Africa***	***Peru***	***Colombia***
Constitutional systems	Unitary fusion of powers, unwritten Constitution. Executive power recruited from Parliament. Legislature driven through party voting.	Unitary state with elements of federalism. Parliamentary representative democracy with a three-tier system of government. Local governance: provincial governments with their own legislature, which are in line with National Constitution.	Unitary State with a constitutional system. Written constitution. Executive power appointed by democratic elections.	Unitary State with a constitutional system. Written constitution. Executive power appointed by democratic elections.
Public administration rules	Administrative law shapes scope of public agencies actions.	Public management guided by written set of norms and a general norm: Public Administration Management Act.	Organic Law of Executive Power embodies core principles of public administration. Constraints and shape of actions of public agencies given by 11 *Administrative Systems*.	National functions organised in Administrative sectors (*i.e.,* defence, culture, education, etc.) System of Administrative Development integrates inter-sectorial procedures.
Distribution of competences	Transference of power to the constituent countries, with a unitary state being replaced by a quasi-federal one Local administration of schools varies across the UK, according to de-	Three tier system of government: central government, provincial government and municipalities. Infrastructure and service provision competences rely in the municipal level.	Political deconcentration of competences. Subnational governments highly dependent on central transfers of central government. Education infrastructure fully and unconditionally decen-	Decentralisation by specialization or services provision. Autonomous territorial organisation. Budgetary intergovernmental relations shaped by the General Systems of Shares. Compe-

Table 1: (*Contd...*)

Table 1: (Contd...)

Systems / countries	***United Kingdom***	***South Africa***	***Peru***	***Colombia***
	volution process. Different types of school owner-ships.		tralised, with exception of Metropolitan Area of Lima.	tences in education conditional to certification of territorial entities.
Investment scheme	Highly developed private participation mechanism such as Private Financial Initiatives (PFI) in investment. New organisation regarding infrastructure: Infrastructure and Projects Authority which is the fusion of 2 existing governmental bodies: Infrastructure UK and the Major Projects Authority.	Grant system for financing of infrastructure and school's improvement. Public Private Partnerships in education originally started for green field projects (2009: building of 6 new state owned schools), also quite successful Corporate Social Investment in schools.	Public Private Partnerships (PPP) in education allowed since 2014 only for central government. Strong limits on internal debt for subnational levels. Transfer from central government builds up the biggest part of infrastructure budget.	Budget allocated throughout Certified Territorial Entities (CTE) upon compliance of goals. Private Private Partnerships mechanisms allowed by law.
Planning systems	Outlined by main national instrument: National Plan of Infrastructure 2013; and National Infrastructure Delivery Plan 2016 to 2021. Autonomous devolved planning guided by both previous instruments.	Autonomous subnational planning aligned with national laws. The first document is a 2013 policy Statement based on the South African Schools Act of 1996. It sets standards for infrastructu re and maintenance. There are nine documents that was created by provinces with their implementation plans; all these plans are approved as of January, 2016.	Currently guided by general prioritisation guidelines set by the Ministry of Education, but in practice, planning of infrastructure relies autonomously in subnational governments.	Policy Counsel "*Consejo Nacional de Política Económica y Social – CONPES*" as main planning authority regarding economic and social policies. Colombia has designed a new institutional arrangement given the infrastructure needs of its National Plan of Infrastructure in Education.

Own elaboration.

Sources: West *et al.*, 2010; Reyes, 2010; Hauss and Haussman, 2012;

particular Scottish local authorities have more power and responsibilities than those in England, which can be explained by neo-liberal reforms embarked in England (West *et al.,* 2010).

The state-maintained school systems in the UK also show differences in service delivery. England and Wales have a similar legislative framework than for Northern Ireland, whilst that for Scotland is completely separate. Nonetheless, across the UK, primary schools cater for children of all abilities. At secondary level, systems and structures differ. In Scotland and Wales there is a comprehensive (all ability) system regarding academic selection, minorities' admissions, and state-funds for schools.

Infrastructure holds a unique institutional arrangement inherited from Thatcher's public management reforms. The Infrastructure Projects Authority a new institution resulting from the fusion of UK Infrastructure and Major Projects Authority. The UK has a simple but comprehensive infrastructure policy that strongly relies in general national planning instruments and private investment engagement (public private partnerships and public finance initiatives); devolution of powers to local authorities and financing per pupil, subject to compliance of standards and regulation that are provided from the Department of Education; and prioritization coming from national planning instruments.

Alike Peru and Colombia, South Africa is overcoming substantial inequalities in educational infrastructure, and is working aggressively to correct these problems. The South African government has a comprehensive plan for improving infrastructure, and these materials are published on the website of its Department of Basic Education (Department of Basic Education, 2013).

Many public schools are in poor condition, lacking a safe building, potable water, sanitation, operations equipment, and learning materials. A set of Minimum Norms and Standards for school infrastructure has been implemented throughout South Africa. The nine provinces are required to develop their own implementation plans. All plans are approved as of January, 2016. Two years after the end of Apartheid, the South African Schools Act of 1996 was approved. This law sought to correct educational inequalities. The goals for improvement were finalized in 2013, when the Department of Basic Education issued the Regulations Relating to Minimum Uniform Norms and Standards for

Public School Infrastructure (DBE, 2013). These norms and standards are minimum requirements that all public schools must meet in South Africa.

The norms and standards have the following priorities: 1.) Basic Services and Structures, 2.) Basic Functionality, 3.) Optimal Functionality, and 4.) Maintenance. “Basic Services and inappropriate Structures” refers to the most severely inadequate structures, such as those constructed of weak or toxic materials. These materials include mud, wood, metal, and asbestos.

The lack of basic services includes water supply, power supply, and sanitation which must be corrected by the end of 2016. “Basic Functionality” refers to having adequate electrical, sanitation, electronic connectivity, security, and space per student. These functionality standards must be met by the end of 2020. “Optimum Functionality” refers to the requirement that all schools must have libraries and separate laboratories for science, technology, and life sciences.

The South African educational system is organized from the top-down. At the top is the Department of Basic Education, or DBE, responsible for the national level. Below this department there are provincial education departments. Beneath the provincial departments are municipalities and schools. The nine provinces of South Africa are the Eastern Cape, the Free State, Gauteng, KwaZulu-Natal, Limpopo, Mpumalanga, North West, Northern Cape, and the Western Cape.

The South African government has a grant system for funding these improvements. These are prioritized by timeline, with some being designated solely for use in a certain task. The most urgent issues are funded by Accelerated Schools Infrastructure Delivery Initiative, or ASIDI, grants (North West Department of Education and Sport Development, 2014). Many provinces lack the administrative personnel necessary to oversee the projects.

With a different institutional architecture, South Africa shows interesting an experiences regarding private sector engagement in school buildings, either by private public partnerships or by corporate social investment funds as the Overseas Development Institute (ODI) appoints (Besharati, 2015). This success factor relies on past practices given the political processes experienced by the country since early 1990’s.

The United Kingdom has a remarkable feature: it does not have a written Constitution. Law systems, and by consequence, public administration laws and procedures follow a different logic from countries like Peru or Colombia, also chosen in the sample analysis. South Africa is another country that alike the United Kingdom, has gone through an interesting process of private investment engagement in school facilities, in particular related to Corporate Social Investment from private companies in the sector, with a different institutional arrangement than the British one, though. In contrast, Peru and Colombia seem to have very similar idiosyncratic variables, but the institutional arrangements and ways to approach the problem of infrastructure deficit are key different nowadays.

In particular, Colombia holds a decentralisation model with a strong emphasis in territorial planning. This way, local authorities called "*Entidades Territoriales*" are administrative and budgetary units of government that hold competences of services and investment infrastructure. Competences, rather than just budget, are devolved to local administrations upon compliance of features and performance that are related to administration management and processes (Schenone and Wiesner, 1994). This constitutes a key factor that allows Colombia to have a relatively developed decentralised system, where fiscal policy and national planning of investment have a solid basis for success.

Similar to the Peruvian case, in Colombia, public infrastructure investment is conducted within the norms and procedures of the National System of Public Investment (SNIP[3]), acquisitions and building contracts regulated by law. School equipment acquired through Central Acquisition Unit "*Colombia Compra*"; in particular, equipment of public schools in Colombia are conducted through *Colombia Compra*.

Peru on the other side, shares very similar features than the Colombian case: public infrastructure projects are also running within the logic and procedures of SNIP, have also embarked in the creation of a Central Acquisition Unit ("*Peru Compras*") that is still under implementation. PPP and PFI are also allowed in education, and Peru has also embarked a process of decentralisation, where education services and infrastructure are the competences of subnational governments. In contrast, rather than a decentralisation with features of fiscal federalism, Peru shows a gradual decentralisation process

[3] Acronym for "National Public Investment System" in Spanish.

responsive to political demands, rather than institutional and management capacity building. This way, subnational authorities (municipalities and regional governments) are responsible for planning and execution of projects regarding education, a competence that is shared with the National Government through the Ministry of Education.

II. BIG GAPS, BETTER PLANNING: AN INTEGRATED APPROACH

From the previous section we would be able to see that investment in educational infrastructure happens in an institutional framework that varies from country to country. With the development of technologies and advice of international policy networks such as the World Bank, IADB, among others (Andrews, 2013); it can be said there is not a unique solution to provide infrastructure. Peru and Colombia, two comparable countries in terms of economic performance, have both embarked the task of bridging up the gap with similar tools, but different processes at the moment. Thus, the need of approaching the problem as a whole.

Over recent years, many researchers have realized that in order to achieve efficient results, it is necessary to design an integrated system rather than selecting individual component subsystems that may not work well together (Fobila *et al.,* 2008; Joos *et al.,* 1999).

Educational infrastructure planning has become a complex task for public authorities not only because of the growing number of students, but also because of the increasing resources needed to operate an effective public education provision. An integrated system requests from public authorities a rational planning approach that involves a global analysis of the several drivers of public education demand (Dennison *et al.,* 1996; Shekdar, 2009). Therefore, an integrated sustainable system may deal with other factors such as socioeconomic conditions, environmental impacts, social support and institutional coordination at different government levels (see Fig. 1) Own elaboration.

The interrelationships among these factors are usually complex (Al-Khatib *et al.,* 2010). Given these characteristics, there is no unique parameter with which to assess the effectiveness of the system; therefore, the performance of the economic planning should consider different measures in each part of the process in order to assess its performance and sustainability.

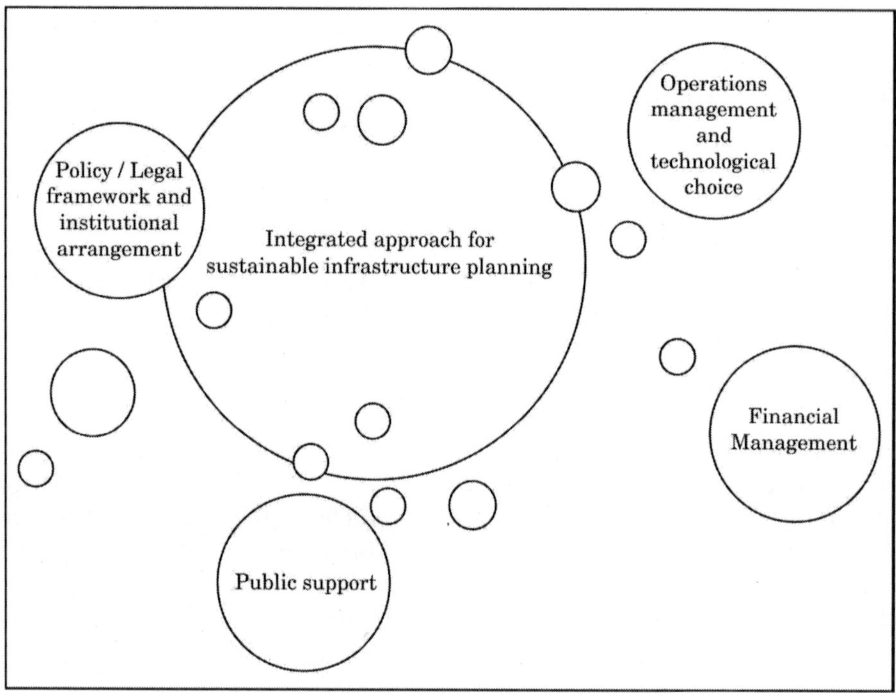

Fig. 1: Integrated sustainable infrastructure planning approach

New Public Management (NPM) became a popular approach while the Margaret Thatcher's regime in the United Kingdom setting as a core idea that best practices from the private sector can be implemented by public agencies (Gruening, 2001). Although the Integrated Sustainable Infrastructure Planning approach (ISP) does not explicitly rely on theories of New Public Management, it does join the stream of *policy entrepreneurs* that allow taking practices from the private sector to be effectively implemented in public management. This way, ISP takes the key concepts from Supply Chain Management that reinforces the importance of functional areas in the final provision of outputs, processes of inputs transformation and service delivery components. Thus, from an ISP perspective, infrastructure planning has more to do than the compliance of design standards and architectural planning; ISP argues that four components are vital for an infrastructure planning oriented to results: (i) responsive institutional arrangements to address problems, (ii) context based financial management, (iii) problem-solved based operations management, (iv) public support.

From case studies selected in previous section, it was seen that even countries with similar economic indicators, population size and similar education policies may exhibit substantial (or not) institutional arrangements. To explain, institutional arrangements are shaped by political system features, mechanism of accountability and audit, decentralisation structure and devolution processes, public administration laws, and sector legal framework, to mention some.

According to ISP, institutional arrangements constitute the basis for which success of policies and its implementation can be measured. It represents a key component of this approach. In terms of general infrastructure, the institutional arrangement refers to the following:

- Institutional structure, which consists of laws governing public agencies' actions and management. This dimension does not refer exclusively to audit mechanisms; it refers to set of institutions, formal laws, procedures and policies that shape public administration management.
- Available systems for infrastructure execution. This refers in Colombia and Peru, for example, to the National System of Public Investment (SNIP); this is to the particular institutional framework in which investment develops and procurement takes place.
- Planning framework: either top down or bottom up structures[4], planning framework refers to how planning takes place in a context of devolved competences to subnational levels.

The ISP approach defends the hypothesis that before fancy fads on facilities planning that obey to trends of functionality and architecture design; in order to provide an effective solution for the infrastructure deficit of infrastructure in education, an assessment of the institutional arrangement is needed, if policy practice aims to be successful. However, institutional arrangement by itself do not explain the success of policies, other aspects related to day to day practices, informal institutions and management systems are also at interplay. Therefore, the second component of ISP is related to financial management, including traditional budgeting, domestic debt in forms of public private partnerships, foreign debt and others. Financial management refers to the best use and allocation of resources at disposal. From a public

[4] See Pissourios (2014).

financial management perspective, it refers to the best institutional design to reach the most efficient and effective outcome regarding policy success.

In this area, traditional public procurement can be either financed by domestic resources or foreign debt. ISP does not focus on the effectiveness of sources of financing, but rather on the best practices that allow best results and final outcomes. There are already suggested practices by international organisations such as Budget-Based on Results, the use of Systems of Information in order to dispose of indicators that allow measurement of policies and budget efficiency, private engagement; among others. ISP joins this stream of networks, reinforcing the idea that budget based on the results as well as the need for multiannual budget programming. For example, Colombia represents a good example on how a programming of budget that does not correlate immediately with short or medium term periods, generated beneficial and solid basis for building complex and responsive institutional arrangement to overcome the deficits and problems of infrastructure.

Traditionally in economic literature, the responsibility, provision and management of public schools should exclusively rest with the public authorities (Sawell *et al.,* 1996; Shekdar, 2009); however, several scholars have suggested recently that cooperation between the public and private sectors would increase efficiency by allowing the former to participate in building, operation and maintenance of public infrastructure, while the public sector keeps its responsibilities for public education policy and planning (Bartone, 1990; Bartone *et al.,* 1991; Rotich, 2006).

During the last decades, many national and regional governments have increased cooperation with the private sector through public-private partnerships (PPPs) in which the private sector investment in public projects, whereby investors receive a return on their investment within a specific legal framework (Chang *et al.,* 2003). Public-Private Partnerships can be found in many countries all over the world and are based on the idea that extra value can be obtained by combining knowledge and co-production; therefore, a PPP implies cooperation between public and private actors to develop products or services sharing risks, costs and benefits (Osborne, 2000; Sullivan and Skelcher, 2002; Klijn *et al.,* 2008).

Most of PPP projects are related to urban reconstruction or renewal of public infrastructure (Iosa *et al.*, 2013). PPPs are long term contracts between the public and private sector in which the private sector has responsibility for significant aspects of the building and operation of an infrastructure for the delivery of public services that the government should provide while both sectors share risks, costs and benefits (Iosa *et al.*, 2013).

These kind of contracts seemed to be an effective means to attract funds from the private sector to provide public infrastructure and services, while improving resource efficiency (shorter construction time, lower construction, operation and maintenance costs, etc.); however, the analysis of experiences regarding to PPPs performance in many sectors suggests that there is no a uniform principle to design PPP contracts (Chong *et al.*, 2004; Iosa *et al.*, 2013). There are many factors that can impact in the likelihood of success or failure in PPP agreements. Therefore, the analysis of the contract design in PPPs is significantly relevant to understand PPP outcomes (Iosa *et al.*, 2013).

Under PPPs public authorities play a key role as regulators that set the main goals that public education should reach, while private sector brings financial resources, technical capability, and entrepreneurship to provide the public service. Therefore, for successful PPPs in the public education provision, there is the need for a strategic vision from public authorities. As argued above, institution building and the possibility to set clear and stable policies would reduce risks from the public side and encourage PPP projects by reducing possible negative impacts on their financial stability (Chang *et al.*, 2003; Iosa *et al.*, 2013). Furthermore, PPPs not only requires of a legal framework and policies that set goals, but also need to set responsibilities between many multi-level public authorities (Shekdar, 2009; Al-Khatib *et al.*, 2010).

Even though the cooperation of the private sector (*via* privatizations or PPPs) seems to be an effective way to foster public education provision (Osborne and Gaebler, 1992), economic literature recognizes the existence of two geographically distinct markets, an urban market segment (which is profitable for the private sector) and a rural market segment, which is perceived as a high cost area (Gasmi *et al.*, 2000; Chowdhury, 2002). Market based private providers might not offer the best alternative to rural areas as they might result in under-provision given that the revenue per student might not support infrastructure investment (Gasmi *et al.*, 2000; Chowdhury, 2002). Under these circumstances, one major challenge to policy makers regarding to public education provision is how to ensure this universal service to the high cost rural area without distorting the competitive market environment in the urban segment (without cross-subsidizing).

Even though economists tend to attribute the production of economic services either to the private sector or to the public sector, the past decade has witnessed a surge in non-governmental organizations (NGOs[5]) as a response to *"fill in the blanks"* where both the government and the markets have failed. This has usually been called the "third sector"[6] (Salamon, 1989; Young, 2000; Brinkerhoff, 2002). The economic contribution of NGOs as a sector is quite significant given that it offers potential as innovations sources of education provision or quality improvements, and can play supportive roles to the public services (Rose-Ackerman, 1996; Young, 2000; Brinkerhoff, 2002; Chowdhury, 2002).

NGOs are considered, particularly by donor agencies, as an effective vehicle to reach part of the target population of foreign aid in developing countries (Gore, 1993; Young, 2000; Brinkerhoff, 2002). This new global trend, in which donors look to NGOs as implementers of donor-driven development policies, fosters a new model that emphasizes efficiency in the use of the resources while consistent with the principle of subsidiarity (Brinkerhoff, 2002). NGOs are important for public education provision because they are concern for increasing the supply of public good as governments and because they have a comparative advantage over business in rural areas (information advantage) which reduces operating costs compared to business in the rural context[7] (Rose-Ackerman, 1996; Chowdhury, 2002).

In sum, the potential advantages of partnerships in the public educations provision are many. New trends (Public-Private Partnerships and Public-NGO Partnerships) have led to a search for new models of

[5] For the purpose of this study we will refer to NGOs following the definition proposed in Chowdhury, 2002: *"It is an organized sector, institutionally separate from government, and does not return any profits to its owner(s)"*.

[6] The underlying economic theories that have evolved to explain the rapid emergence of this third sector include demand-side theories, supply-side theories, partnership theory, and social origins approach.

[7] Some scholars explain that NGO might incur in less cost because they have existing operations and networks in a rural area which reduces the set- up costs (Chowdhury, 2002); however, the empirical evidence that NGOs are more efficient than business are inconclusive since some scholars argued that NGOs do not necessarily supply the same good as business (Rose-Ackerman, 1996).

inter-sectoral cooperation in the context of public service delivery (Osborne and Gaebler, 1992; Brinkerhoff, 2002). The exploration of partnerships is important in the context of the economic planning agenda regarding to education financing given that the nature and scale of public education needs and challenges are impossible to address alone by the public sector; however, the advantages in the use of partnerships (with the business or NGOs sector) requires a strategic planning and coordination leadership from the public sector in order to reach efficiency and effectiveness objectives using all the available resources (Chowdhury, 2002) See Fig. 2.

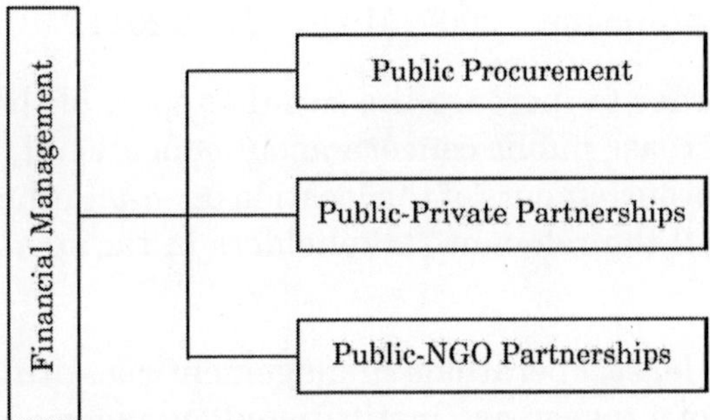

Fig. 2: Financial sources for investment

Operation Management and Public Support

From an economic planning point of view, social management faces an important challenge to achieve efficiency in the integrated system. There are some cases of resistance to public infrastructure provision. The risk of social opposition to projects must be defined as a clear task for the public authorities.

One of the main challenges to social management is the increasing difficulty in securing locations for public schools, which is known as the NIMBY (Not-In-My-Back-Yard) syndrome (Besfamille and Lozachmeur, 2010; Feinerman *et al.*, 2004; Musso *et al.*, 2011). As an economic resource, land has several alternative uses, therefore, it is important to analyze which of those uses to schools could be an expectation of residents and include it in the mitigation strategy.

To reduce the effects of this problem, there is an important role of public authorities: (i) urban planning; (ii) the use of environmental studies that certifies that the chosen areas are not sensitive to public schools; and (iii) the requirement of investment to mitigate impacts (like excessive noise or traffic jams) in areas where public schools could be developed; however, despite all these strategies aimed at promoting social acceptance by minimizing the NIMBY problem, it is impossible to fully mitigate the problem (Pellow *et al.,* 2001; Marchetti, 2004; Feinerman *et al.,* 2004).

It is important to note that in order to achieve the goals of a sustainable integrated system, all relevant stakeholders besides users should be involved. Social strategy could work together with non-governmental and community-based organizations to increase support to public schools (Jimenez, 2005; Musso *et al.,* 2011).

In sum, in order to increase the social support of the system, it is important to increase public concern about educational infrastructure benefits, the appropriateness of the location *vis-à-vis* other alternatives and to include all the relevant stakeholders in the strategic planning process.

Last but not least, operations management constitutes a keystone in the building of a responsive institutional arrangement according to the ISP. Operations management relates to two aspects: how delivery channels are integrated and how procedures are regulated in a way that makes available effective planning. In traditional public procurement systems, operation management relates to laws governing the acquisition and public works, institutional organisation and processes behind the working of the systems. Peru and Colombia show similar procurement systems, but operations management is different, given the strong process of decentralisation of Colombia, the more developed system of central purchases through *Colombia Compra*, to mention some. UK and South Africa, for instance, are not deviant cases and share similar management systems also.

III. ISP APPROACH IN POLICY PRACTICE

A balance needs to be found regarding the scope of diagnosis of infrastructure state and the institutional arrangement that is proposed in order to bridge the gaps up. ISIP is an approach that aims to improve policy practice from a practitioner's point of view. This way, infrastructure planning goes beyond spatial and architecture dimensions, and lands into the need of designing responsive institutional arrangements that allow results and effective policies.

One important tool in planning from ISP approach represents the so called "Master Plans", in which the government (local or national) sets goals to the educational policy, in which infrastructure development is a key element. If planning in a particular country has a top-down planning system, it would be the central authority the one setting the main goals, and the one setting the institutional arrangements that are needed to accomplish them. If planning systems are bottom-up, subsidiarity process will remain stronger but not necessarily more efficient and effective. Balance needs to be found between both systems.

Some of these Master Plans also set the main construction design and technology in which the choice accurate technological solutions for several geographical contexts set relevant questions to local authorities. It is important to note that sustainable systems do not only need a legal framework that sets the goals, it is also important that set clear responsibilities, activities and administrative tools among the different institutions involved in the system in order to let them work in the most efficient way (Shekdar, 2009; Al-Khatib *et al.,* 2010). A legal framework of an integrated infrastructure planning system, sets clear answers regarding the following questions:

- Which institution is responsible for the quality of the public education service? Which institution is in charge of the strategic planning in education?
- Which institution is responsible of infrastructure development? Which institutions make the choice of the best technological solution? Which institution makes the choice of the schools that should be recovered and those new schools that need to be constructed?
- Which institution has administrative obligations regarding to human resources development?
- Which institution is in charge of setting fees for operation and maintenance?
- Which institution is in charge of controlling that the system works properly?
- Which institution is responsible for those students that require specific services?

Finally, it is important to note that traditionally in academic research on educational policies it was argued that the responsibility and management should exclusively rest with the public authorities (Sawell *et al.,* 1996; Bel, 2006; Shekdar, 2009). However, in recent years, several authors have suggested that in order to get efficient results, it is important to promote cooperation between the public and private sectors by allowing the former to participate in the operation[8] of the system (Bartone *et al.,* 1991; Rotich, 2006). In this sense, legal framework should be flexible enough to promote the participation of the private sector through several PPP contracts such as concessions.

The institutional arrangement is important given that all local authorities should have a clear understanding of which are their main responsibilities in the system. Furthermore, the legal framework should also be flexible enough to promote private participation through PPP or new forms that look forward to improving the public education service, but without taking into account that role such as planning and supervising should keep as main public responsibilities in order to keep all the incentives aligned.

Taken from one of our case studies, Peru represents a case in which best practices from the United Kingdom have been adopted, and holds similar constitutional systems and economic performance indicators. In terms of education, both are overtaking the problem of infrastructure deficit with same processes: the formulation and implementation of a National Plan of Infrastructure. Different from Peru, Colombia has exploited its more developed process of fiscal decentralization to build a new institutional arrangement in which infrastructure gaps of schools will be up fronted upon formation of a National Trust with clear and bold rules for co-financed projects with territorial entities, and fully financed projects by the national government for poor fiscal performance territorial entities. This institutional arrangement suggested by the Ministry of Education and National Council for Economic and Social Policy– CONPES seem to be more responsive to national needs and context.

In contrast, Peru represents an example of how institutional arrangements are not consistent with educational infrastructure gap reduction policies. Decentralization process is still blooming and shows many failures regarding management. Fig. 3 summarizes the implicit system in Peru. As in Colombia, Peru has embarked on the task of designing a National Plan of Infrastructure that is still in process. This plan presents a diagnosis of infrastructure situation and also, aims to

[8] Planning and control activities should remain with the public authorities.

promote an institutional arrangement that allows Peru to overcome critical school facilities. Yet, the task would not be easy since Peru does not hold the same institutional solid basis in their subnational levels, in order to make that master Plan effective. Moreover, when the decentralization process obeys more to a political process rather than a fiscal one, public support is a key component of success.

IV. CONCLUSIONS

Research on infrastructure planning has gained the attention of many fields in the scientific community; however, few of them focus on the importance of economic planning to achieve sustainable investments. This chapter presents an overview of four international strategies to reduce public investment gaps in educational infrastructure. The main objective of this chapter is to highlight the challenges and practices in these countries to provide the basis for further research on the development of economic planning.

From the analysis of international experiences, it is possible to note that some special characteristics should be taken into account in economic planning regarding to public investment in educational infrastructure.

First, successful investment in educational infrastructure cannot be measured by the compliance of norms related to architectonic designs. Furthermore, even though functional environments are necessary to improve the quality of the public service, this constitutes one part of the problem and does not ensure effectiveness of infrastructure policies, especially when economic efficiency needs to be approached.

Second, there is not a unique recipe for overcoming infrastructure deficit in education. Institutional arrangements need to be responsive to political processes, local capacities and citizen accountability. Economic planning from an ISP perspective integrates aspects of institutional analysis and political economy to explain why investment planning in educational facilities needs to be understood as a task that involves complex management structures.

Third, the potential advantages of partnerships in the public educations provision are considerably important. Public-Private Partnerships, Public-NGO Partnerships and strong tools that should be part of economic planning to educational infrastructure financing.

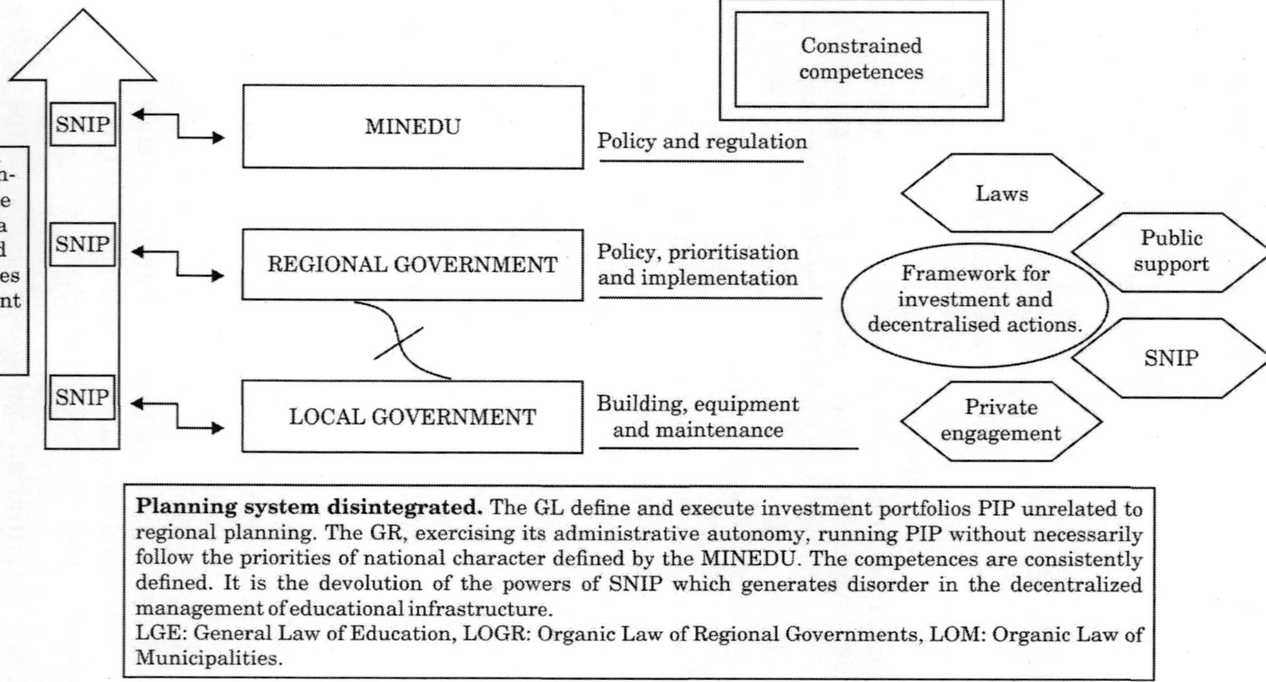

Fig. 3: Case study: Institutional arrangement organisation of investment in infrastructure in Peru

It is important to note that public education needs are impossible to address alone by traditional public procurement. However, the accurate use of the resources that come from these partnerships calls for a strong institutional setting and leadership in the public sector, as well as the engagement of distributed agents in most of the stages of institutional changes.

Finally, regarding to social acceptability, it is important to note that even when social opposition is not as strong in educational public investment as could be in other sectors, there is still the need for an accurate social management that requires resources to provide all the information that the stakeholders need and to reduce the probability of impacts on the infrastructure sustainability due to lack of social support.

REFERENCES

Alesina, A. and Perotti, R. (1996). Income distribution, political instability and investment. *European Economic Review*, 81: 1170–1189.

Alesina, A. and Rodrik, D. (1994). Distributive politics and economic growth. *Quarterly Journal of Economics*, 109: 465–490.

Andrews, M. (2013). The limits of institutional reform in development: Changing rules for realistic solutions. Cambridge University Press.

Aschauer, David A. (1989). "Is public expenditure productive"? *Journal of Monetary Economics,* 23: 177–200.

Barro, R.J. (1999). Inequality, growth and investment. NBER working paper no. 7738. Cambridge, MA: NBER.

Benabou, R. (1996). Inequality and growth. *In*: NBER macroeconomics annual. Cambridge, MA: NBER.

Besfamille, M. and Lozachmeur, J.M. (2010). NIMBY and mechanism design under different constitutional constraints. *International Tax and Public Finance*, 17(2): 114–132.

Besharati, N. (2015). "Private sector investment in South Africa's education sector: Nature, extent and incentives". JET education services. Overseas Development Institute, UK. Research Brief.

Brinkerhoff, J.M. (2002). Government–nonprofit partnership: A defining framework. *Public Administration and Development*, 22(1): 19–30.

Cadot, O., Röller, L.H. and Stephan, A. (1999). *A political economy model of infrastructure allocation: An empirical assessment* (Vol. 2336). Centre for Economic Policy Research.

Chang, M., Memon, M.A. and Imura, H. (2003). International experiences of public-private partnerships (PPP) for urban environmental infrastructure and its application to China. *International Review for Environmental Strategies (IGES)*, 4(2).

Chong, E., Huet, F., Saussier, S. and Steiner, F. (2006). Public-private partnerships and prices: Evidence from water distribution in France. *Review of Industrial Organization*, 29(1–2): 149–169.

Chowdhury, S.K. (2002). Attaining universal access: Public-private partnership and business-NGO partnership (No. 18755).

Cohen, D.K. and Bhatt, M.P. (2012). The importance of infrastructure development to high-quality literacy instruction. *The Future of Children*, 22(2): 117–138.

Dennison, G., Dodda, V. and Whelanb, B. (1996). "A socio-economic based survey of household waste characteristics in the city of Dublin, Ireland." *Resources, Conservation and Recycling*, 17: 227–244.

Department of Basic Education (2013). Regulations relating to minimum uniform norms and standards for public school infrastructure. No. 37081.

Devarajan, S., Swaroop, V. and Zou, H.F. (1996). The composition of public expenditure and economic growth. *Journal of Monetary Economics*, 37(2): 313–344.

Eckstein, Z. and Zilcha, I. (1994). The effect of compulsory schooling on growth, income distribution and welfare. *Journal of Public Economics*, 54: 339–359.

Feinerman, E., Finkelshtain, I. and Kan, I. (2004). On a political solution to the NIMBY conflict. *The American Economic Review*, 94(1): 369–381.

Fields, G. (1980). Education and income distribution in developing countries: A review of the literature. *In*: King, T. Education and income. World Bank staff working paper no. 402 Washington, DC: The World Bank, pp. 231–315.

Fobila, J., Armahb, N., Hogarhc, J. and Carboo, D. (2008). "The influence of institutions and organizations on urban waste collection systems: An analysis of waste collection system in Accra, Ghana (1985–2000)". *Journal of Environmental Management*, 86: 262–271.

Gasmi, F., Laffont, J.J. and Sharkey, WW. (2000). Competition, universal service obligation and telecommunications policy in developing countries. *Information Economics and Policy,* 12: 221–248.

Glomm, G. and Ravikumar, B. (1992). Public versus private investment in human capital: Endogenous growth and income inequality. *Journal of Political Economy*, 100: 818–834.

Gong, L. and Zou, H.F. (2002). Effects of growth and volatility in public expenditures on economic growth: Theory and evidence. *Annals of Economics and Finance*, 3(2): 379–406.

Gore A. (1993). Creating a Government that works better and costs less. US Government Printing Office: Washington, DC.

Gruening, G. (2001). Origin and theoretical basis of New Public Management. *International Public Management Journal*, 4(1): 1–25.

Hauss, C. and Haussman, M. (2012). Comparative politics: Domestic responses to global challenges. Nelson education.

Hulten, C.R. (1996). Infrastructure capital and economic growth: How well you use it may be more important than how much you have (No. w5847). National Bureau of Economic Research.

Iossa, E., Spagnolo, G. and Vellez, M. (2013). The risks and tricks in public-private partnerships (No. 64). IEFE, Center for Research on Energy and Environmental Economics and Policy, Universita'Bocconi, Milano, Italy.

Jimenez, E. (1986). The public subsidization of education and health in developing countries: A review of equity and efficiency. *Research Observer*, 1: 111–129.

Jimenez, L. (2005). From nimby to yimby: Understanding community opposition to special needs residential facilities in Vancouver (Doctoral dissertation, Simon Fraser University).

Joos, W., Carabias, V., Winistoerfer, H. and Stuecheli, A. (1999). "Social aspects of public waste management in Switzerland". *Waste Management*, 19: 417–425.

Klijn, E.H., Edelenbos, J., Kort, M. and Van Twist, M. (2008). Facing management choices: An analysis of managerial choices in 18 complex environmental public—private partnership projects. *International Review of Administrative Sciences*, 74(2): 251–282.

Marchetti, N. (2004). Face to face negotiation to overcome the nimby syndrome: Theory and experimental design (No. 2004s-53). CIRANO.

Musso, J., Weare, C., Bryer, T. and Cooper, T.L. (2011). Toward "strong democracy" in global cities? Social capital building, Theory driven reform, and the Los Angeles neighborhood council experience. *Public Administration Review*, 71(1): 102–111.

Osborne, D. and Gaebler, T. (1992). Reinventing the Government: How the entrepreneurial spirit is transforming the public sector. Addison-Wesley: Reading, MA.

Osborne, S.P. (*ed.*) (2000). Public-private partnerships; Theory and practice in international perspective, London: Routledge.

Pellow, D.N., Weinberg, A. and Schnaiberg, A. (2001). The environmental justice movement: Equitable allocation of the costs and benefits of environmental management outcomes. *Social Justice Research*, 14(4): 423–439.

Persson, T. and Tabellini, G. (1994). Is inequality harmful for growth: Theory and evidence. *American Economic Review*, 84: 600–622.

Pissourios, I.A. (2014). Top-down and bottom-up urban and regional planning: Towards a framework for the use of planning standards. *European Spatial Research and Policy*, 21(1): 83–99.

Ram, R. (1989). Can educational expansion reduce income inequality in less-developed countries. *Economics of Education Review*, 8: 185–195.

Reyes, A.M. (2010). Fundamentos de la organizaciόn y del funcionamiento del Estado colombiano. Universidad del Rosario.

Rose-Ackerman, S. (1996). Altruism, 'Nonprofits and Economic Theory.' *Journal of Economic Literature,* 34: 701–728.

Saint-Paul, G. and Verdier, T. (1992). Education, democracy and growth. Centre for Economic Policy Research, London. Discussion Paper No. 613.

Salamon, L.M. (1989). "The changing tools of government action: An overview". *In*: Beyond privatization: The tools of Government action, Salamon, L.M. (*ed.*), Urban Institute Press: Washington, DC, pp. 3–22.

Schenone, V.O.H. and Wiesner, D.E. (1994). Colombia: Descentralización y Federalismo Fiscal.

Schultz, T.W. (1963). *The economic value of education.* New York: Columbia University Press.

Shekdar, A. (2009). "Sustainable solid waste management: An integrated approach for Asian countries". *Waste Management*, 29: 1438–1448.

Sullivan, H. and Skelcher, C. (2002). "Working across boundaries; Collaboration in public services", Houndmills Basingstoke: Palgrave Macmillan.

Sylwester, K. (2002). Can education expenditures reduce income inequality? *Economics of Education Review*, 21(1): 43–52.

West, A., Allmendinger, J., Nikolai, R. and Barham, E. (2010). "Decentralisation and educational achievement in Germany and the UK". *Environment and Planning C: Government and Policy*, 28(3): 450–468.

Wilkinson, R. (2002). Monitoring and evaluation of public policies for educational infrastructure.

Young, D.R. (2000). "Alternative models of government-nonprofit sector relations: Theoretical and international perspectives". *Nonprofit and Voluntary Sector Quarterly*, 29(1): 149–172.

Zhang, J. (1996). Optimal investments in education and endogenous growth. *Scandinavian Journal of Economics*, 98: 387–404.

10

The Stimulation of Scientific Investigation in the Classroom through Didactic Unities

KENIA NAARA PARRA[1*] AND ANA CLÁUDIA KASSEBOEHMER[1]

ABSTRACT

We intend to show that didactic unit is potentially a powerful instrument for improving science teaching. The elements of a general didactic unit are shown and discussed based on an example of a Chemistry didactic unit. The students' involvement in a scientific investigation promoted by a problematic situation from pre-established content and activities articulated are key to the improvement in science teaching / learning process. Besides the daily practice we indicate the necessity of constant formation of the teachers and their contact with researches in the field of education to overcome their lack of knowledge and problematic views about the Nature of Science.

Key words: Didactic unit, Problematic situation, Chemistry

[1] Instituto de Química de São Carlos, Universidade de São Paulo, C.P. 780, CEP 13560-970, São Carlos-SP – Brasil.

* *Corresponding author*: E-mail: kenia@iqsc.usp.br; claudiaka@iqsc.usp.br

WHAT ARE DIDACTIC UNITIES?

About the didactic unities, Zabala (1998, p. 18) states that they "(...) *are a set of activities ordered, structured and articulated to the realization of certain educational goals which have a beginning and an end known both by the teachers and the students*".

WHY ARE THEY IMPORTANT?

In the analysis of the teaching practice, the identification of the interaction and coordination among the activities is more important than the determination of the activity itself. This is because the didactic unities are structured according to the educational intent of that proposal and therefore, they are characterized as differentiator element of the teaching methodologies (Zabala, 1998).

In the author's words, *"The types of activities, but especially your way to articulate, are one of the differentiators that determine the specificity of many didactic proposals"* (Zabala, 1998, p. 53).

Thus, we observe that the use of didactic unities is not unique to one particular educational approach. All approaches to teaching science have sequenced activities, but what differentiates the transmission-based approach from the research-based approach, for example, are not the activities themselves, but the articulation between them in a process that will demonstrate, finally, the educational goals of each approach.

The didactic unities developed in order to create immersion opportunities to the students in the scientific culture are aimed at overcoming the disciplinary fragmentation and the decontextualisation of education (Guimarães and Giordan, 2011). Although the contents are traditionally organized in subjects, it is also possible to establish relationship with other curriculum components and integrate concepts apparently isolated, even because the natural phenomena do not manifest second a disciplinary division.

According to Gil Perez and colleagues (2005), one of the requirements for science education is the development of skills and scientific knowledge to solve problems. Based on Studies in Sociology of Science, Machado and Mortimer (2007) state that the resolution of open issues is at the core of everyday scientific practice. Thus, it is essential that the school promotes conditions for students to analyze and seek for solutions to the conflicts of their community and also to the global problems.

In this process, the importance of the role of solving problematic situations at school is high and this is reflected in the development of didactic unities. For Guimarães and Giordan (2013, p. 2) didactic unit *"is a set of activities articulated and systematically arranged around a central problematic"*.

The goal of any didactic unit is not to teach the teachers to "give" lessons or to follow recipes. Rather, the didactic unities represent a teaching organization model in which activities are articulated so that the student can relate them to previously learned content and give meaning to these contents in a gradual process. In addition, through didactic unities, the teachers guide their students in the construction of knowledge through activities developed by them and stop transmitting ready proposals from educational materials developed by other authors, such as the textbook. In this process, besides the teachers have more autonomy, they are engaged in a constant process of research and learning.

Detailed planning of didactic unities is essential for the evaluation of the articulation between the classes and activities, as well as to make any further changes to classes in which the sequence will be applied. Didactic unities can also be adapted in different regions and contexts and discussed in manuals, workshops and conferences not only by teachers but also by other specialists.

Considering the role of the didactic unities and its relationship with a problematized structure, *how we can develop a didactic unit?* To answer this question, we first suggest the teacher could watch out for the following elements: *content, problematic situation, activities / tasks and evaluation* (Table 1).

For the didactic unities be well structured and organized, the proposal must be clear and intelligible, the activities should be coordinated in a progressive level of complexity and the time should be adequate to the proposed activities and the deepening of the content that the teacher wants to offer. Therefore, for each class of the didactic unit, the teacher also develops their lesson plan that must be articulated to the others and allow the planning in detail of the methodology used and the approximate time of each activity. Besides this the lesson plan facilitates

Table 1: Elements of the didactic unit

Content	• Conceptual, procedural and attitudinal • Organization and chaining of contents
Problematic situation	• The relationship between the problem and the Science, Technology, Society and Environment (STSE) education • Articulation between the contents and problematic situation • Coordination between the activities and the problematic situation • The problem and its resolution • The relationship between the problem and the exercise of citizenship
Activities/ Tasks	• Methodological aspects • Materials and teaching resources • Contextualization and organization of activities
Evaluation	• Integrated evaluation

making adjustments when necessary. But *in which element should we think first? Why these elements are relevant*? Next, we will discuss the aspects of Table 1, showing the function of each of these elements and their relationship with others.

Contents

According to Zabala (1998), the contents have close relationship with the educational purposes of the didactic unities. The contents assume the role of involving all dimensions of learning, from the following types of content:

- *Conceptual* - includes facts, concepts, principles (*what should we learn?*)
- *Procedural* - refers to the skills, techniques and methods (*what we should do to learn?*)
- *Attitudinal* - encompasses values, attitudes and norms (*how we should be to learn?*)

Since the contents are directly related to educational purposes, is from the different types of content you want to teach, that the teacher will propose a problematic situation able to assign meaning to such contents. In addition, each content type will require the use of different activities and learning materials, therefore, the content is the guide of didactic unit.

Zabala (1998) reinforces the importance of contextual aspect in the development of the didactic unities. For him, the didactic unities must meet the educational demands of a particular group of students in relation to various types of content. They should also contemplate the appropriate learning activities to these contents. The learning materials help to develop teaching activities proposed by teachers, according to the specific needs of a group and the educational settings.

This diversity of content and relationship with the materials, activities, methodologies and school context, requires from the teacher a repertoire of knowledge involving critical issues often ignored in discussions related to the principles for effective teaching.

After the observation of students during the training process and the beginning of the teaching profession, as well as the comparison between veteran and novice teachers, Lee Shulman (1987) proposed a new educational reform to overcome the stemmed obstacles of traditional models of teaching.

According to Shulman (1987) *knowledge base* is the repertoire or set of understandings, knowledge, skills and dispositions that a teacher needs for effective teaching and should be the basis for the development of educational programs for teachers. Such *knowledge base* can be divided into categories that include *subject knowledge matter*, *pedagogical knowledge matter* and *curricular knowledge*. Even with some modifications in later works, these three categories remained at the *knowledge base* proposed by the author.

The *subject knowledge matter* refers to cognitive organization of content, *i.e.,* facts, concepts, specific processes and procedures of the matter by a teacher, should involve the understanding of the nature of science and scientific work and important related questions, *what are the content, principles and facts? How were they built? How are they represented? How are they organized? Why can we consider them valid? What makes them valid? Are they linked to STSE education?*

In *pedagogical knowledge matter* the attention turns to the teaching process. At this point of the didactic unit development the teachers should ask themselves about: *how can I problematize it? How should I explain? Are there clear examples? Could I show pictures? Could I make comparisons? Which analogies could I use?* The teachers also can think about other possibilities of involvement, understanding and conceptualization that students may have, adding other questions: *such content would be easy or difficult? What are the possible representations that students already have about? What alternative concepts the students may have about the content? What strategies can be used to address these alternative concepts?*

The *curricular knowledge* is of great importance to the teaching practice and should also permeate the development of didactic unit, since for each students group, the teacher should be able to develop and implement educational situations taking into account the disciplinary program and the use of instructional materials. Therefore, the teacher should wonder about: *how the program is organized according to each series? For certain series and content, which materials can be used: videos, books, texts, images, games and /or laboratory experiments?*

The continuous use of didactic unities also allows the teacher to discuss the same content at different times and levels deep. So even though the teacher in a didactic unit does not follow exactly the sequence of suggested content in books or disciplinary curriculum, he/she must know it well to ensure, at some point, the approach of such content. Also in relation to curricular knowledge, as important as knowing the own discipline program is to be familiar with the programs of other disciplines, in order to be able, whenever possible, correlate them in the classroom and to develop activities of the didactic unit together with other teachers.

The approach of the same concept in different moments and depth levels (Machado and Mortimer, 2007) allows, between comings and goings, that the students have the opportunity to review or deepen the content in different situations, while the students delayed, have the opportunity to reinforce it. In this process, the teacher will not be the sole determinant of the duration of the unit, because the students will also exert influence on its duration (Espinoza, 2011).

To Zabala (1998, p. 86),

> Not everything is learned in the same manner, at the same time or with the same job. Discern what can be the object of a didactic unit, as a priority content from which requires a more complicated work, over several unities, including in diverse areas and school situations, it might be an exercise to which we are not sufficiently used, but even so it cannot be less necessary.

This spiral form of contact with the same content can pass the impression of a too long and disorganized learning process, however, beyond the time that can be estimated, teaching requires interaction between people and the world in a process influenced social, political, economic and environmentally and that consequently can escape from the naive and calculating expectations of the teacher. Marcondes and Peixoto (2007) reported the results of a project developed in 2006 that involved the use of thematic sequential modules by high school teachers and students. They showed that despite the teachers recognize the increased student motivation, they had difficulties with the time differences of learning of each student, the way the contents were organized and resistance that students offer, because they are not used to learning to learn. The overcoming of these conflicts requires constant self-reflection and engagement, including in the preparation of the didactic unities for greater familiarity with the proposal.

The excessive concern with time, space, textbook, surprises or frustration possibilities stems from problems in initial teacher education based on traditional models that fit the paradigm of Technical Rationality (Kasseboehmer and Ferreira, 2012). Praia, Cachapuz and Gil Perez (2002) discussed aspects of teaching practice in high school and showed that teachers often have distorted views about the Nature of Science, and therefore, reproduce in their class conceptions of science as socially neutral, individualist, elitist, a problematic, a historical, linear, infallible and dogmatic.

These views are a heritage of the Technical Rationality model and have been object of research in education and curriculum reform proposals, such as the proposed by Shulman (1987) previously discussed. Among other changes, such proposals seek to cause disruption of teacher formation without autonomy and open up space for the researcher and reflective teacher, based on Learning by Reflecting on Action (Kasseboehmer and ferreira, 2012).

This new paradigm goes beyond the reflective teacher theorized by Schön and criticized by many as reductionist and short-sighted, having focus on individual practices in the classroom. What is expected of this new paradigm is that the teacher's reflection extrapolates the scholar context, the students and the peers reaching the critics to the social, cultural, economic and political teaching practice in a process in which the teacher fulfills an intellectual task and not technical (Contreras, 2002).

For Contreras (2002) it is expected that the teacher has autonomy to develop their own curriculum according to the school environment and the community, the diversity of students and educational changing needs.

Faced with this new paradigm and the importance of the education cover conceptual, procedural and attitudinal content, in referring to the conceptual content more specifically, what then would be the concepts that teachers should address in the classroom?

For Espinoza (2011) the choice of content is a complex task and is closely related to the concept of didactic transposition proposed by Yves Chevallard. The scientific knowledge produced by the scientific community must be transformed so that they can circulate in the school environment. First comes the selection from the work of pedagogues, authors of books and manuals and other experts. And in a second step, this scientific knowledge is taught in fact, a process in which the teacher plays a key role, not only to make the connection between the scientific environment and the school, but to shape the content to stimulate activity science classroom (Espinoza, 2011).

For the author, the natural sciences are structured by central and decisive concepts to the knowledge of other content. So, should serve as an instrument for guidance of the teacher in his work.

> (...) The structural concepts collaborate in the construction field because this allows it constitutes a coherent body of knowledge, that can also be used as a criterion for selecting the contents and establish a sequence for them (Espinoza, 2011, p. 35).

In the natural sciences, the structural concepts are: matter, energy, transformation or change, and classification system. Because students consider them difficult, these structural concepts require several successive approaches (Espinoza, 2011).

For Chemistry Teaching in particular, Machado and Mortimer (2007) argue that the excess of chemistry concepts in traditional curricula ultimately provide evidence of the limited intentions of Chemistry Teaching, restricted to conceptual content. Overcoming the priority concern with the conceptual dimension is a challenge for the teaching intervention. The authors proposed a Chemistry book for high school which includes key concepts for the understanding of the constitution, properties and processing of materials and substances and discussed beyond the selection and organization of content, problem solving as a way to address the Chemical concepts, everyday language and science, teamwork, among others[1].

Chassot (2014) discusses the futility of chemical content that is being taught instead of the need for *"(...) Science Teaching emphasizes preparation citizen so you can handle with responsibility the social issues related to science"* (p. 141).

For the author,

> It is in the selection and definition of what and how they will teach that chemical educators need to be permanently re-educated so that they can select and define which knowledge can be built and transmitted to may lead to empowerment of all women and all men and also, and this is crucial, for women and men as a whole and as individuals (Chassot, 2014, p. 142).

So he cautiously suggests eight topics concepts in chemistry area for Secondary Education (discussed here briefly), showing that when teachers teach to the formation of citizenship, in addition to chemical knowledge they also raise issues relating to ethical and political commitment. *Topics revolve around the atmosphere*: our dependence on the atmosphere; *Water*: our dependence on water; *Energy*: the different forms of energy; *Metals*: metals in the earth's crust; carbon compounds, the chemical carbon atom; *Building materials and protection*: the syntheses; *Bromatological chemistry*: food and preservatives and chemical topics applied: fertilizers.

In addition to discussing the concepts that can be derived from each topic, the author shows that their teaching must start from the reality of the students (the community lives from crafts, work in the industry or of the rural work? What do they produce? What are the problems that face?) And accompanied by experimental classes.

Problematic situation

The problematic situation contributes to the didactic unit through social and scientific issues that may justify the issue, attribute sense to the

[1] Mortimer, E.F.; Machado, A.H. Química para o Ensino Médio. São Paulo: Scipione, 2002 (single volume).

activities and to the contents addressed and should, for these reasons, be considered in a second phase.

By stimulating scientific activity in the classroom, the teacher addresses the constructive and interpretative character of science so that the student understands the role of experiments, its relationship with the theories and function of models. Therefore, the teacher should identify the feasibility of linking certain situations and concepts in order to stimulate reflection during the scientific activities in the classroom or outside, which is possible through the problematization (Espinoza, 2011).

Although scientific research is considered a core activity in science education there is, however, differences between the issues commonly addressed by teachers and textbooks and those of unknown nature in which the means to solve them depend on a structured research process. In this regard, Torregrosa and Sifredo (2005) discuss the distance between the closed statements, that represents situations of mere training and do not require raising hypotheses, and the authentic problems, represented by problematic situations that can be resolved from the scientific work.

According to the authors above, the process of resolving these problematic situations must follow certain guidelines as:

- The problematic situation must be related to issues/topics of interest to students to be motivational and cause positive attitudes toward research. Therefore, should move among the relations of STSE;
- Initially, the problematic situation should be treated qualitatively, to allow the clear understanding of the problem and of the conditions involved to its resolution;
- Raise assumptions that focus and guide the resolution, and indicate the parameters to be taken into account;
- Develop and explain possible resolution strategies before starting the investigation taking into account the different possible ways that allow the comparison of results and consistency with the knowledge that you have;
- Search for the resolution, verbalizing at most, substantiating what is done and avoiding the operationalization without physical meaning;

- Carefully review the solutions based on the hypotheses, questioning whether they are unique, reasonable, adjustable to other situations and if they depend on qualitative parameters addressed in the beginning. It should also be considered the possibility of the resolution generate new problems;
- Consider new opportunities during the investigation, as the interest in increasing the level of complexity or to design new situations of investigation;
- Conduct a review of the resolution process with emphasis on the aspects of greatest interest in the treatment of problematic situation and reflect on the work and the content learned to incentivate the research.

Activities / tasks

As discussed above, each content type will require the use of different activities and materials.

The conceptual content requires activities that promote motivation, research, observation, generalization and synthesis and can be addressed through manipulation, dialogues, debates, texts, illustrations and videos.

The procedural contents are learned with the repetition of exercises appropriate for each student according to their degree of domain and from activities that progressively encourage students to research, design, interview, report, record, manipulate and using materials support, such as notebooks, notepads, records, laboratory records, etc.

Unlike other content, attitudinal contents are not directly related to well-defined materials and methods, but can be learned through activities that allow dialogue, debate, teamwork, visits, excursions, etc. (Zabala, 1998).

Evaluation

Seeking for the scientific education, school evaluations should be consistent with the teaching strategies to avoid the increase of the types of content, new methodologies and diversification of materials, but maintaining the same evaluative instruments of memorization, operation and conceptual reductionism.

To Zabala (1998) a didactic unit, to accommodate different learning content, should promote an evaluation that also contemplates them. From examples of general schemes of didactic unities, the author shows that the analysis of these sequences demonstrates the educational intentions of the teacher. One example is a teacher who applies a didactic unit that also contemplates the procedimental content, such as activities involving handling and attitudinal contents with encouraging participation and work together. If the evaluation of his/her didactic unit contains conceptual questions, it means that his/her goal is that the students "know" only the conceptual content, disregarding the fact that the procedimental and attitudinal contents are also goals to be taught. So contrary, when evaluating beyond the conceptual content, procedural and attitudinal contents is that the teacher seeks a more comprehensive training, since the procedures and attitudes are not only used to make the most pleasurable conceptual learning, but to be learned in fact.

Gil Perez and Torregrosa (2005) reinforce the growing debate and concern of investigators around the evaluation of science education, since the way it is disseminated is related to ideas, behaviors and attitudes of the teachers that are often erroneous and must be overcome. For the authors the evaluation functions are promote learning, contribute to the improvement of teaching and influence the curriculum itself, since the teacher is fundamental in the definition of what can be worked to arouse the interest of students.

The authors establish issues to be considered in the evaluation process, which include:

- The inclusion of open problematic situations that allow the formulation of questions and bring up issues for students.
- The request for comments on possible implications STSE, decision-making, the relationship with the rest of the program, etc.
- The request for qualitative analysis to avoid the mere operation and help to understand and limit the situations.
- The request to students to propose hypotheses: The addition of activities to know the previous knowledge.
- Encouraging the development of strategies: Attention to practical activity (experiments, mounting, measurements, etc.) and management of current technology (computers, internet ...) in

order to promote a more accurate view of contemporary techno-scientific activity.

- A request for analysis of results (physical interpretation, reliability, etc.) using the knowledge available, the hypotheses formulated and other outcomes;
- The integration effort to consider the contribution of studies to make a coherent body of knowledge and the possible implications for other areas of knowledge.
- The request for activities related to the STSE implications (possible applications, social transformations, negative impacts, etc.), decision making related to serious problems that can affect the humanity and the importance to contribute to a sustainable future: Incorporating activities involving non-formal education (museums, press, etc.); the value of products developed by students (prototypes, collections of objects, posters...).
- The focus on communication as an essential aspect of scientific activity: Encouraging the development of scientific reports; the request to read and criticize scientific texts; the contact of students with the history of science;
- Strengthening collective dimension of scientific work based on the value of teamwork.

It is observed that important aspects in the evaluation process coincide with those that must also be considered in the scientific curriculum, since the construction of knowledge should be consistent with how it is evaluated (Gil Pérez and Torregrosa, 2005).

Sanmarti (2005) agrees with Gil Perez and Torregrosa (2005) when considers that the evaluation should also be a learning tool. Therefore, the author adds that the teacher should make clear its teaching proposal, the purpose of learning and also the evaluation criteria so that students know from the start what to learn and how to achieve that goal. If they are aware of the purpose of learning, they will be able to self-regulate their own actions and transfer learning to other similar situations, without depending on someone who at all times indicates the best way. The author also discusses the importance of error in the process, as contributor to teaching and learning processes, emphasizing that teachers cannot blame the students for their mistakes in the same way that they cannot simply fix the activities just to approve or not the student. It is important to encourage students to identify their mistakes and to seek ways of overcoming them. For this, the author suggests the use of both the mutual evaluation, as the self-assessment.

An international instrument example developed to assess how students can apply the knowledge to real life situations and be prepared for full participation in society is the PISA (Programme for International Student Assessment) (Gil Perez and Vilches, 2006). PISA is applied every three years for students with 15 years old in order to assess international educational systems. Despite of the discussions about the way that the countries are compared, the program can be taken as a reference in the daily activities of teachers providing indications about the consistency between the knowledge that is taught and what actually is evaluated.

Concerning to the content, Gil Perez and Vilchez (2006) analyzing the PISA 2003 goals, have shown that the program is designed by issues related to the disciplines of physics, biology, chemistry, medicine, among others, and the content to be evaluated are selected from four important criteria:

- They must appear in common situations of everyday life and have a high degree of usefulness in daily life.
- They must relate to relevant aspects of science, selecting the most likely to maintain its scientific importance in the future.
- They must be relevant to the scientific training of students.
- They must be suitable for use in scientific processes and not only corresponding with definitions or classifications that should only be recalled.

The 13 major scientific topics used are: structure and properties of matter; atmospheric change; physical and chemical changes; energy transformations; forces and motion; function and form; physiological change; biodiversity; genetic control; ecosystems; Earth and its place in the universe; geological change.

Validation

Once elaborated the didactic unit should be validated. Guimarães and Giordan (2013) proposed elements for validation of didactic unities based on the process of elaboration, implementation and reworking. Zabala (1998) discussed the validation as eight aspects: Previous knowledge;

Significance of new content and functionality; level of development; zone of proximal development; cognitive conflict and mental activity; positive attitude; Self-esteem and self-concept and learning to learn.

To treat in detail the aspects of validation second Zabala (1998) we will use an example of didactic unit developed by students of initial training of Chemistry teachers at the University of São Paulo, USP/Brazil in 2014 and adapted by the authors of this chapter on the themes "Pesticides".

The didactic unit is presented more as an example to be analyzed and discussed in this chapter than to be followed. This observation is made, first because considering the goal of meaningful learning, the criteria we will use to analyze it can be extended to other areas of education, not just chemistry and can encourage the development, implementation and evaluation of other didactic unities in different areas. Secondly, despite having been developed for an educational context close to the authors of this chapter, such unit was not applied and can be considered as ideal intervention proposal, purposely elaborated thinking of what is valid do than what is possible to do. Therefore, if the reader judges it is interesting, he/she shall draw up a detailed plan for each class. It is helpful to become familiar with the proposal and to make the necessary adjustments according to the conditions of his/her educational context.

Title	Pesticides in food: Is it good or bad?
Characterization of students	Middle school students
Justification	Each year are used in the world approximately 2.5 million tons of pesticides. The annual consumption of pesticides in Brazil has been more than 300 thousand tons of commercial products. Expressed in amount of active ingredient, are consumed annually about 130 thousand tons in the country; representing an increase in pesticide consumption of 700% in the past 40 years, while agriculture increased 78% in this period.
Problematic situation	Quality and sustainability-Pesticides in food: good or bad?
Exercise of citizenship	Preparation and distribution of the "Book of the marketer/farmer".

Methodology

Class	*Specific goals*	*Content*	*Dynamics of activities*
1	Check the students prior knowledge about agriculture and pesticides; Present the problem ; Organize the class to investigate the problem.	Agriculture; Pesticides in foods; Elaboration of questions about a theme.	Presentation and comparison of images of fruits and vegetables grown in different ways; Discussion of the reasons for the differences in appearance, size, color and scale of production of fruits and vegetables; Presentation of the problematic situation; Division of students into groups; Analysis of the issues that need to be answered during the investigation; Proposition of hypotheses for each group; Proposition of information sources: books, teacher, visits, experiments, taking into account what they already know about the topic.
2	Guide the students to the visit to the city's agricultural products market; Prepare a script for interview to be applied with the fairground / farmers; Teach the development of visit reports.	Reflection on group; Elaboration of questions about a theme.	Elaboration in groups of an interview script to be applied to farmers in the market of agricultural products of the city;-from where they receive food? • what is the type of agriculture? • do they know the cultivation process? • how much is produced? • what are the costs and problems encountered? • do they know alternative ways of cultivation? • who are the major consumers? Explanation of the development of the report on the visit.
3	Visit the market and collect data.	Observation; Questionings; Data collect; Cooperation.	Guided tour at the market; Application of questionnaires to market traders / farmers; Observation and recording of the quality of the products, such as color, odor, appearance.
4	Analyze the data collection and the advancement of research considering the different types	Development and presentation of reports; Comparison of results; Cooperation.	Group presentation of the reports containing the answers or data provided by market traders / farmers, photos and their impressions of the production processes, as well as the advantages and disadvantages of each process, pesticide use, improvement opportuni-

Table (*Contd...*)

Table (*Contd...*)

Class	*Specific goals*	*Content*	*Dynamics of activities*
	and scales of agricultural production.		ties.
5	Prepare a pesticide for organic farming; Identify solute, solvent dilution of final solution; Analyze the advantages of home production of pesticides, their uses and the correct periods of application and harvest.	Solution; Solute; Solvent solubility; Dilution; Concentration; Natural pesticide recipe; Formulation of hypotheses; Analysis of results; Generalization; Cooperation.	Preparation in groups of a homemade fungicide; Discussion on the use of this agricultural fungicide, efficiency and implementation; Discussion on other recipe of natural pesticides.
6	Study the chemical product packaging labels.	Reading; Interpretation; Classification.	Division in pairs: General analysis of the labels of different pesticide containers: • Active ingredient, use techniques and handling; Toxicological class of pesticides, concentration of the active ingredient.
7	Extend the study of the solutions, composition of solutions, dilution; Do exercises; Develop pesticide packaging labels;	Solution; Solute; Solvent solubility; Dilution; Concentration; Reading; Interpretation.	Individually: Specific analysis of packaging labels: • Solutions: Solutes, solvents, concentration calculation, dilution, solubility; Exercises to fix the concepts; Development of the package label of the pesticide produced in class 5.
8	Extend the study of the organic compounds, active ingredient and organic functions; Do exercises; Finalize the development of pesti-	Organic compounds; Organic function; Nomenclature; Reading; Interpretation.	Individually: Specific analysis of packaging labels: • Active ingredient, organic compounds, molecular formula, structural, nomenclature, organic functions; Exercises to fix the concepts; Completion of the development of the package label of the pesticide produced in class 5.

Table (*Contd...*)

Table (*Contd...*)

Class	*Specific goals*	*Content*	*Dynamics of activities*
	cide packaging labels;		
9	Discuss the recommended concentrations for application of pesticides; Discuss the consequences of incorrect use	Limits of concentration for application; Environmental contamination; Reading and interpretation of texts, graphs, tables.	Debate about the abusive use of pesticides • Health and environment; Reading of texts on the effects of pesticides on the environment.
10	Discuss the storage and disposal of packaging of agricultural products and the use of personal protective equipment (PPE).	Environmental contamination; Personal protective equipment (PPE); Storage and disposal of the packaging of pesticides; Discussion.	Debate on the use and incorrect disposal of pesticide containers: • how these attitudes directly and indirectly affect health and the environment? Exhibition of a video about the storage and disposal of the packaging of pesticides and use of personal protective equipment (PPE);
11	Analyze the evolution of investigation and what solutions students are able to present, compare and discuss.	Reflection; Self-analysis of progress; Comparison of results with other students; Synthesis.	Discussion in groups for the resumption of the initial problem: Pesticides in food: Is it good or bad?
12	Synthesize and gather all the knowledge acquired in the "Book of the marketer / farmer".	Calculation of concentration and dilution; Natural pesticides; Dispose of packaging; Personal protective equipment (PPE);	Development in group of the book to be distributed to merchants/farmers containing the problematic situation, information about the knowledge of the food production process of the food, correct application of pesticides, possibility of utilization of natural pesticides and use of Personal protective equipment (PPE).

Table (*Contd...*)

Table (*Contd...*)

Class	*Specific goals*	*Content*	*Dynamics of activities*
		Integration of the results; Synthesis; Writing; Refl-ection; Memo-rization; Co-operation.	
13	Presenting the book to the fair-ground/farmers; Learn how to keep the school vegetable garden	Presentation; Cooperation; Socialization; Solidarity.	Meeting between students and marketers/farmers at school for reflection and exchange of information and experiences: Delivery of "Workbook marketers/farmers" and exchanges of ideas and experiences on the school vegetables garden maintenance with the marketers/farmers.

Evaluation The evaluation will be made during the lessons considering the involvement and participation in the discussions, experiments, visit and meeting with the marketers/farmers, besides the elaboration of the interview, report delivery, field diary during the visit the fair and development the "Workbook marketer/farmer".

References

Alimento orgânico: vantagens e desvantagens. [updated 2014 Nov 11; cited 2016 April 08]. Available from: http://danimedeiros nutricao.blogspot.com.br/2009/10/alimento-organico-vantagens-e.html.

Alimentos orgânicos: saúde, ambiente e viabilidade econômica. [Internet]. [updated 2014 Nov 11; cited 2016 April 12]. Available from: http://www.gentequeeduca.org.br/planos-de-aula/alimentos-organicos-saude-ambiente-e-viabilidade-economica.

Aula prática sobre fungicida. [Internet]. Santa Catarina: Universidade Federal de Santa Catarina. [updated 2014 Nov 11; cited 2016 April 10]. Available from: http://www.cca.ufsc.br/labfitop/2008-2/calda%20bordalesa.pdf.

Braibante, M.E.F. and Zappe, J.A. (2012). A Química dos agrotóxicos. Quím. Nova na Escola. 34:10-15.

Carraro G. Agrotóxicos e meio ambiente: uma proposta de ensino de ciências e Química. Universidade Federal Do Rio Grande Do Sul Instituto De Química. Porto Alegre. 1997. [updated 2014 Nov 11; cited 2016 April 10]. Available from: http://www.iq.ufrgs.br/aeq/html/publicacoes/matdid/livros/pdf/agrotoxicos.pdf.

Table (*Contd...*)

Table (*Contd...*)

	Cavalcanti, J.Á., Freitas, J.C.R., Melo, A.C.N. and Freitas Filho, J.R. (2010). Agrotóxicos: uma temática para o ensino de Química, Quím. Nova na Escola. 32:31-36 [updated 2014 Nov 11; cited 2016 April 10]. Available from: http://qnesc.sbq.org.br/online/qnesc32_1/07-RSA-0309.pdf. Destinação final de embalagens vazias de agrotóxicos. [Internet]. [updated 2014 Nov 11; cited 2016 April 12]. Available from: http://www.andav.com.br/repositorio/36.pdf. Morte de agricultor reforça questionamentos contra os agrotóxicos. Radioagência NP, Vinicius Mansur. [2014 Nov 11; cited 2016 April 08]. Available from: http://www.radioagencianp.com.br/node/5568. Receitas de defensivos naturais. [updated 2014 Nov 11; cited 2016 April 08]. Available from: http://vidaeestilo.terra.com.br/casa-e-decoracao/confira-23-receitas-de-defensivos-naturais-para-o-jardim,65e2c1bb37928310VgnVCM3000009acceb0aRCRD.html. Tecnologia de aplicação de agrotóxico. [Internet]. Embrapa. [updated 2014 Nov 11; cited 2016 April 10]. Available from: http://sistemasdeproducao.cnptia.embrapa.br/FontesHTML/Pessego/PessegodeMesaRegiaoSerraGaucha/defensi.htm.

The didactic unit was here exposed following the framework for the elaboration of didactic unit according to Guimarães and Giordan (2013). In it we can find in addition to data identifying the didactic unit, the aspects presented in Table 1, as content, questioning, activities and tasks and evaluation.

We begin the discussion of the example of didactic unit above, according to Gil- Perez and Torregrosa (2005):

By analyzing the characteristics of the problematic situation, we realize that it is open enough to allow possible questions as: *pesticides are good or bad for what? for the economy? to increase production? for health? for plants? for the environment? for the world's population?*

Such questions lead to some possible scenarios:

> *The benefit or harm of pesticides depends on the type of crop; how much is applied; how it is applied; the type of pesticide, among others.*

Taking into account how the problematic situation was elaborated and hypotheses were formulated, the teacher can ask students what strategies could contribute to the investigation, so that at this time, the qualitative analysis and the hypotheses have a guiding role for the search-solving strategies.

After that, there are student's suggestions for experiments, visits, interviews, observation, reading texts, videos, and other activities that will provide contact with different agricultural products, cultivation methods, different pesticide types, ways they are applied and market traders/farmers.

As they know the pesticide names, indications and modes of application from the visit, observations and interviews, for example, it is essential to learn conceptual content that will delve into the complexity of the problem to answer: *what differentiates a pesticide on the other? Why should be diluted? How to make the dilution? There are alternatives to pesticides found in the market? What merchants should know to be able to apply them? What precautions the public should have to consume them?*

Those questions to be answered give space for learning concepts such as solutions, solute, solvent, organic compounds, organic functions and procedures as the calculation of concentration and dilution, as well as attitudes such as cooperation, responsibility, tolerance, etc.

In the process, encouraged by dialogues, debates and exercises, students compare the values of the content in concrete cases. Using generalization they can apply the new knowledge in other different situations, such as reading, interpretation and preparation of labels of chemical containers.

At the end, the resumption of the important aspects for the development of research was carried out not only through discussion between the groups, but also in the development and distribution of "Workbook marketer/farmer" which also is realized in a social return activity and citizenship. In the workbook, we seek to show the variables that can determine the benefit or harm of pesticides, such as the type, concentration and method of use, and therefore must be known, controlled or even replaced so that the cultivation of agricultural products can contribute to the economy impacting as little as possible to society and the environment.

It is important to discuss about the design of an unique and definitive solution to the problems. Just as the ways to solve problems are varied, many are also the solutions to problems such as those expected in the didactic unities. Knowing the variables and trying to control them is possible to decide, for this moment, the best solution considering the cost and benefit, the risks and the existence of alternative routes (Machado and Mortimer, 2007). This solution is not unique and is not definitive, since both *"(...) the problems and their circumstances change in time and space, transforming and singularizing - and the solutions must be accepted as provisional approaches that try to adapt as attempt of concrete circumstances of each case (...)"* (Contreras, 2002, p. 234).

From the same theme of this didactic unit, it would still be possible to increase the level of complexity or design new situations arising from research of solutions. An example of deepening would be developed and implemented by Lopes *et al.* (2011) in a school of integrated technical training to high school. In this study, the students had to take consistent roles with their future professions and develop during the unit, divided into five major phases, the knowledge and skills necessary to solve the problem. More specifically, they were placed in the technical position of clinical and toxicological analysis so that they could find a laboratory test to confirm possible contamination of blood samples rural workers by pesticides. In this case the teaching of chemistry was applied to toxicology and among the solutions, stands out colorimetric and chromatographic analysis tests.

Also we validate the didactic unit, according to the criteria discussed by Zabala (1998).

1. ***Previous knowledge*:** This is known throughout the activities of the first class, when students are asked about the reasons for the differences in the appearance of certain agricultural products. Also when the teacher presents the problematic situation and when the students themselves formulate questions that should answer and suggest their hypotheses. The teacher must also retake them in the presentation of the report of the visit to the market and in other debates that follow to integrate them with new knowledge or overcome them if they represent misconceptions. The fact that the students are divided into groups at these meetings, in particular, enables the exchange of information between them and encourages communication groups with the teacher who should verify that everyone is participating and not only those can have more information on the subject.

2. ***Significance of new content and functionality*:** The contents will only be discussed in the appropriate moment: when they are necessary for the resolution. Thus, the contents, conceptual, procedural or attitudinal, is not merely transmitted. In teaching chemistry, to overcome the priority concern with the conceptual dimension is a challenge for the teaching intervention.
3. ***Level of development*:** To capture the difficulties of students and the ability to engage in activities, the teacher's dialogue with the students and between them should be constant. With clear communication is possible to notice the difficulties in relation to a new content, for example, when the students formulate hypotheses or when they submit possible solutions.
4. ***Proximal development zone*:** The more diversified and progressively ordered the activities are, the greater the ability of the sequence cover and encourage the participation of students, regardless of the different profiles that feature. At the same time are challenging, allow the progress of each student with the help necessary according to their rhythm and skill. The activities where there is the understanding of the contents enough to apply it in other situations are in the meetings 7 and 8. Besides solving exercises also build packaging labels for pesticides produced in the school are important to satisfy this aspect of validation.
5. ***Cognitive conflict and mental activity*:** The presentation of a problem and its contradictions promotes cognitive conflict and forces students to question their knowledge and to reconsider their own interpretations of what is observable to promote mental activity, something present in the whole unit as they establish relations between the new content and previous knowledge.
6. ***Favorable attitude*:** The ability to arouse the interest of the student to continue with the research is stimulated in the exposure of the problem, with the visit to the market and contact with people who deal daily with agricultural products from different forms of cultivation. In the case of the problematic situation, in particular, it is that the consumption of agricultural food, of which we do not know the origin and cultivation, is very close to the reality of the student. Added to this, students can submit ideas on economic, social and environmental effects of agricultural production, which at the same time that show important and beneficial can negatively, impact the quality of life. All this conflict includes the

STSE relations that will be present not only at the starting point but also in the development of the didactic unit.

Involvement is also promoted when considering various activities and strategies in order to address different profiles of students. As an example, while the more introverted students feel comfortable in conducting literature searches, make notes or take pictures, those more extroverted will have the opportunity to conduct interviews, present the data collected and distribute the "Workbook of the marketer/farmer." In this case, the teamwork allows the exchange of data and information in order to resolve the conflict that all together.

The way the evaluation will also be held influence the favorable attitude since the interest for knowledge can be transferred by the interest in the note very easily. As the whole process is evaluated, including procedural and attitudinal contents, students will appropriate the pleasure of the investigation. To evaluate, for example, the "Workbook marketer/farmer" includes not only the definitions of concepts such as calculating concentrations and dilutions of solutions, but also attitudes such as cooperation and solidarity.

In addition to these factors, the emotional climate and communication established with the teacher and among students will favor the maintenance of motivation for learning.

7. ***Self-esteem and self-concept*:** Activities that promote dialogue, analysis of the progress in each class and the teacher feedback, facilitate personnel evaluation and promotion of a positive image of yourself. These activities and strategies are presented in all the units to allow the views and contributions to solving the problem and have greater space in the meeting 11 during the analysis of the evolution of the investigation. The very "Workbook marketer/farmer" is the fruit of all the work done during the didactic unit and have both the valuation of the teacher and own fairground/farmers benefit from the production and distribution which possibly contribute positively to building self-esteem and self- concept.
8. ***Learning to learn*:** The search for information activities such as library research, interview script formulation, the interview itself, experimentation, exercises, observation of the market, notes, photographs include not only important skills in schools, as study techniques and exercises as also other skills that allow the

extension and application of the contents in other situations and thus promote learning autonomously.

It is still possible to involve other characters in the field of education in the validation process. According to Guimarães and Giordan (2013), after the development phase and before the implementation phase, the teacher must share and allow the validation of didactic unit by researchers in the field, by the peers and coordinators of the school where the didactic unit will be applied. Only then it will be applied, and after this phase begins the new elaboration phase of the didactic unit with the experience gained during the implementation.

FINAL CONSIDERATIONS

In the search for the most meaningful learning possible, the teacher should realize that among the many possible didactic unities, the most complex tend to better offer the relevant conditions for the stimulation of scientific work. Also to present conflicts close to the students' interest, give opportunity to express their views and expectations, be challenging, stimulate learning, autonomy and self-esteem, to show the functionality of content and value the results, all while contemplating the different profiles of students.

For these reasons that the careful preparation of the didactic unit is necessary. With the validation is possible to notice the need to add or strengthen some activities and the objectives of each class, the dynamics of activities and if the content to be contemplated are clear enough so that complexity does not allow the loss of purpose and/or the disarticulation of the activities along the unit.

The fact that the units are not universal is what allows their application in different cultures, conditions and structures. There is no standard method that can be followed in any situation. Thus, the effectiveness of the activities set in a didactic unit depend on the planning according to the conditions under which will be submitted, as the target audience and the social context.

It is important to note that the base knowledge, especially which focused on character investigative methodologies is not only from the initial training and daily practice, but also of research in the field of education.

REFERENCES

Contreras, J. (2002). Autonomia de professores. São Paulo: Cortez.

Gil Pérez, D., Sifredo, C., Valdés, P. and Vilches, A. (2005). ¿Cuál es la importancia de la educación científica en la sociedad actual? *In:* Gil Pérez, D. *et al.* (*eds.*), ¿Cómo promover el interés por la cultura científica? Una propuesta didáctica fundamentada para la educación científica de jóvenes de 15 a 18 años. Santiago de Chile: Oficina Regional de Educación para América Latina y el Caribe (OREALC)/UNESCO, pp. 15–28.

Gil Pérez, D. and Torregrosa, J.M. (2005). ¿Para qué y cómo evaluar? La evaluación como instrumento de regulación y mejora del proceso de enseñanza-aprendizaje, *In*: Gil Pérez, D. *et al.* (*eds.*), ¿Cómo promover el interés por la cultura científica? Una propuesta didáctica fundamentada para la educación científica de jóvenes de 15 a 18 años. Santiago de Chile: Oficina Regional de Educación para América Latina y el Caribe (OREALC)/UNESCO, pp. 159–182.

Gil Pérez, D. and Vilches, A. (2006). ¿Cómo puede contribuir el proyecto pisa a la mejora de la enseñanza de las ciencias (y de otras áreas de conocimiento)? *Rev. Educ.*, pp. 295–31.

Guimarães, Y.A.F. and Giordan, M. (2011). Instrumento para construção e validação de sequências didáticas em um curso a distância de formação continuada de professores. Proceedings of the 8th Encontro Nacional de Pesquisa em Educação em Ciências, 2011 Dec 5-9 Campinas. Anais. Campinas: ABRAPEC.

Guimarães, Y.A.F. and Giordan, M. (2013). Elementos para validação de seqüências didáticas. Proceedings of the 9th Encontro Nacional de Pesquisa em Educação em Ciências, 2013 Nov 10-14; Águas de Lindóia. Anais. Águas de Lindóia: ABRAPEC.

Kasseboehmer, A.C. and Ferreira, L. (2012). Formação inicial de professores de Química: A instituição formadora (re)pensando sua função social. São Carlos: Pedro and João (*eds.*).

Lopes, R.M., Silva Filho, M.V., Marsden, M. and Alves, N.G. (2011). Aprendizagem baseada em problemas: uma experiência no ensino de Química Toxicológica. Quim. Nova, 34: 1275-1280.

Machado, A.H. and Mortimer, E.F. (2007). Química para o ensino médio – fundamentos, pressupostos e o fazer cotidiano. In: Zanon, L.B. and Maldaner, O.A. (*eds.*), Fundamentos e Propostas de Ensino de Química para a Educação Básica no Brasil. Ijuí: Unijuí, pp. 21–41.

Marcondes, M.E.R. and Peixoto, H.R.C. (2007). Interações e Transformações - Química para o Ensino Médio: Uma contribuição para a melhoria do ensino. *In*: Zanon, L.B. and Maldaner, O.A. (*eds.*), Fundamentos e Propostas de Ensino de Química para a Educação Básica no Brasil. Ijuí: Unijuí, pp. 43–65.

Praia, J.F., Cachapuz, A.F.C. and Gil Perez, D. (2002). Problema, teoria e observação em ciência: Para uma reorientação epistemological da educação em ciência. *Ciênc. Educ.*, 8: 127–145.

Sanmartí, N. and Otras, Voces (2005). ¿Para qué y cómo evaluar? *In*: Gil Pérez, D. *et al.* (*eds.*), ¿Cómo promover el interés por la cultura científica? Una propuesta didáctica fundamentada para la educación científica de jóvenes de 15 a 18 años. Santiago de Chile: Oficina Regional de Educación para América Latina y el Caribe (OREALC)/UNESCO, pp. 419–422.

Shulman, L.S. (1987). Knowledge and teaching: Foundations of a new reform. *Harvard Educ. Ver.*, 57: 1–22.

Torregrosa, J.M. and Sifredo, C. (2005). ¿Cómo convertir los problemas de lápiz y papel en auténticos desafíos de interés? *In*: Gil Pérez, D. *et al.* (*eds.*), ¿Cómo promover el interés por la cultura científica? Una propuesta didáctica fundamentada para la educación científica de jóvenes de, 15. a 18 años. Santiago de Chile: Oficina Regional de Educación para América Latina y el Caribe (OREALC)/UNESCO, pp. 103–121.

Torregrosa, J.M., Sifredo, C. and Verdú, R. (2005). *¿ Cómo diseñar los contenidos de un tema o de un curso? In.* Gil Pérez, D. *et al.* (*eds.*), ¿Cómo promover el interés por la cultura científica? Una propuesta didáctica fundamentada para la educación científica de jóvenes de 15 a 18 años. Santiago de Chile: Oficina Regional de Educación para América Latina y el Caribe (OREALC)/UNESCO, pp. 185–196.

Zabala, A. (1998). A prática educativa: Como ensinar. Porto Alegre: Artmed

11

Understanding EFL Learners' Revision in Writing: A Comparative Study

Hafida Hamzaoui - Elachachi[1]*

ABSTRACT

Revision is an essential step for successful Writing. This study explored the revision process of 16 Algerian EFL university students when writing in English (FL2) and compared it to the one used in Arabic (L1) and French (FL1) compositions. The purpose of this work was to shed light on how operations of revision intervened during various phases of writing in FLs as well as in L1, to what extent they were effective, whether they were used similarly in the three languages and whether learner expertise affected his revision process. This was done to propose how to improve EFL learners' revision to achieve more effective writing. The results revealed students' misconception of revision and misunderstanding of its role as it was regarded as an optional final step in writing and unnecessary when one was proficient in a language. To conclude, training EFL learners to revise effectively is highly recommended.

***Key words*:** Revision, Writing process, Writing strategy, L1 and FL composition, Text modification.

[1] Department of English, Faculty of Letters and Languages, University of Tlemcen, Algeria.

* *Corresponding author*: E-mail: hamzaouihafida@yahoo.fr

INTRODUCTION

Writing is one of the four basic language skills whose social significance has become increasingly important, thus appealing for more research. To develop learner writing competence, composition researchers became more and more interested in the process he is engaged in establishing a relationship between his strategy use and successful task completion. Indeed, many studies reveal a correlation between full and proficient use of writing strategies and achievement in writing (Jacobs, 1982; Kasper, 1997; Hamzaoui, 2006) and record revision as an essential strategy for successful writing; however, the faculty in the English Department (University of Tlemcen) complains about EFL students' neglect of revision and explains that this writing process tends to receive the least amount of time and effort from learners. Then, it seems worth investigating the use of revision by these students when writing in English (FL2), and compare it to Arabic (L1) and French (FL1) writing for a better understanding of this strategy use in writing, putting forward the following research questions:

- When do Algerian EFL university students operate revision in English (FL2), Arabic (L1) and French (FL1) writing across the four years of their curriculum?
- How do these students use revision in the three languages across their four years of study?

LITERATURE REVIEW

In the nineteen sixties, cognitive psychology renewed interest in the study of human thinking in general and the mental processes of language learners in particular. Then, researchers became interested in the mental path students undertook to learn or realise a language task. Along this line, writing was one of the language skills examined as early as the nineteen seventies.

Early Models of Writing and Revision

Researchers were interested in the common steps and strategies undertaken by successful writers. They highlighted a number of them with different appellations, but generally those steps were grouped under five stages, each comprising several strategies (Frederick, 1987):

1. ***The pre-writing stage*:** It is considered to be the most important stage where students brainstorm to select a topic, generate ideas either individually or in groups, gather information, determine the most appropriate purpose and style and develop an outline or a tentative plan.
2. ***The drafting or actual writing stage*:** The student starts writing a tentative product that will require evaluation and revision later on.
3. ***The revision stage*:** This stage and the previous one begin nearly at the same time because as they write, students revise and evaluate their text in order to make changes if necessary in both form and content. Sommers (1982, p.134) sees revision as "a process of making changes throughout the writing of every draft, changes that work to make the draft congruent with a writer's changing intentions".
4. ***The editing stage*:** When the draft of a writing task is realised, students review the document in the light of decisions made during the pre-writing stage. Form and structure are given more importance than content (in the process approach, this step could be realised either in groups, or with the teacher's assistance).
5. ***The publishing or presentation stage*:** The student presents a final version of his written text to the intended audience.

Research into the writing process was motivated by the idea of developing instructional strategies that help novice writers improve their writing competence believing that gaining knowledge on which strategies are used by expert writers will help determine composing instruction, revision being recognized as one essential step in writing. Then, it is necessary to review the key writing models in order to understand the progress made to recognize the cognitive processes used in writing namely those of revision: what they consist of and how they interact with other processes.

In the beginning of the eighties, research on writing revealed that the process of writing is not linear involving the five successive stages mentioned above (see Fig. 1), but recursive in which the writer returns to various elements of his written product before going ahead to produce more text. In her studies, Perl (1980, 1981) instigated a revolution in attitudes to writing when she studied the composing processes of under-prepared college students and found that writing was a recursive process, *i.e.,* the writer returns to various elements of the text already produced before going ahead to produce more text (Fig. 2).

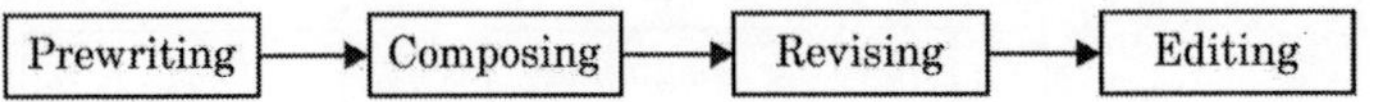

Fig. 1: Classical view of writing

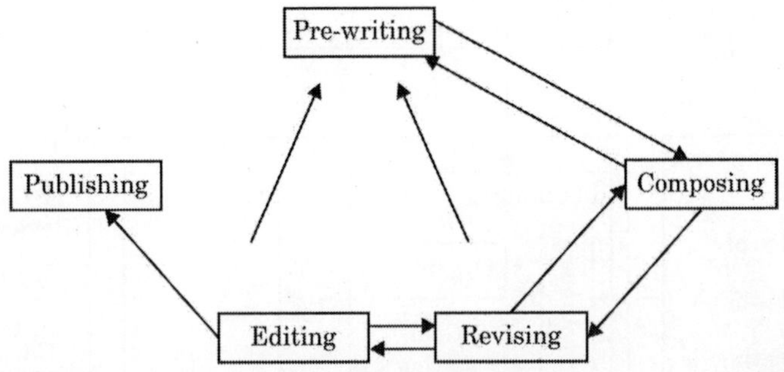

Fig. 2: The process of writing as viewed by Perl and her successors.

Using the same mentalist approach, a composition teacher, L. Flower and a cognitive psychologist, J.R. Hayes (1980) accumulated massively what they called "composing aloud protocols", *i.e.,* transcripts of writing sessions where subjects were asked to record every thought that came to mind while writing. This led them to develop a model of the writing process (see Fig. 3) which they used to explain many unclear writers' behaviors obtained from the protocols. They also rejected linearity in writing, and therefore, in teaching. According to them writers plan, translate (*i.e.,* write) and review (*i.e.,* revise). These three steps are integral parts of the writing process and are considered to be:

- Hierarchically structured, each consisting of sub-processes: planning, for example, comprises goal setting and organizing.
- Independently organized, that is each contributes to the writing process and may occur in any order with respect to the others. So, one can write without planning, and write without reviewing, but this would give a different result.
- Interacting with two other important sources of information: the task environment and the writer's long-term memory. The interaction is seen to be constant, multi-directional and rendering writing difficult.

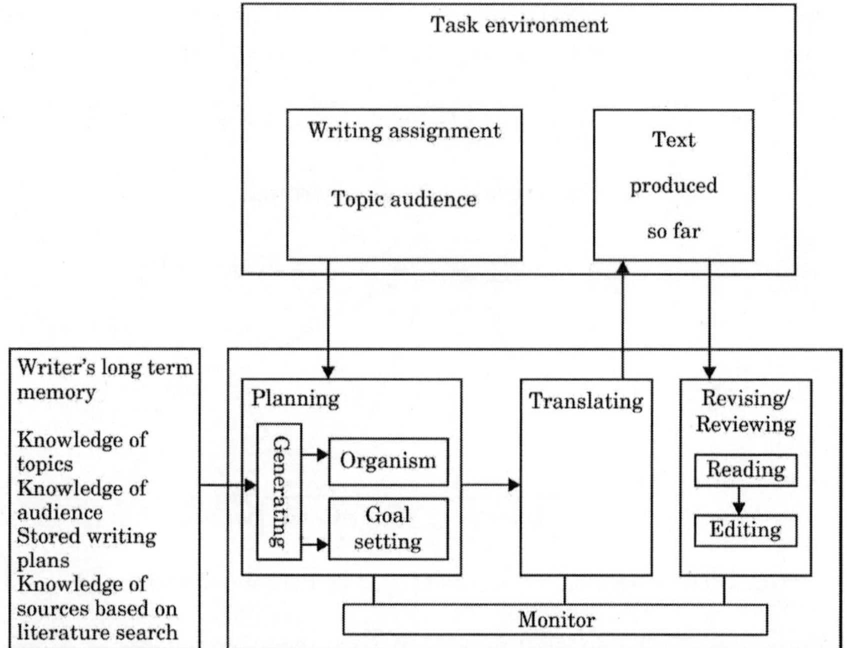

Fig. 3: Flower and Hayes' (1981, p. 370) model of cognitive processes used during revision

In this model, the process of revision is called reviewing and consists of checking and correcting. It is divided into two sub-processes: *reading*, which involves error detection and evaluation of the text as compared to the writer's goals, and *editing*, which is the actual correction of the text. The reviewing process may be recurrent and occur during writing or after the text has been produced. In 1983 Flower and Hayes continued to develop the revision process stressing the difference between reviewing as a mental process and revising resulting in physical modifications.

Evolution of Revision Models

Working on the model of Flower and Hayes, Scardamalia and Bereiter (1983, 1986) further elaborate the revision process which comprises three cyclic activities *Compare, Diagnose* and *Operate* (CDO). These activities consciously happen in the revision process during writing pauses to correct the text sentence by sentence. They occur the following way: (1) the writer compares the written text with the intended one to find out whether there are any discrepancies, if any are found, (2) the diagnose operation is launched to detect the nature of the discrepancy, this is followed by, (3) the operate activity which consists in choosing a solution to the problem and proceeding to text change accordingly, *i.e.,* to correct. After obtaining a new textual representation, the cycle of CDO continues.

Then, Flower *et al.* (1986) and Hayes *et al.* (1987) propose a more complex writing model in which revision is described as being intentional, conscious and strategic. The model consists of two sub-stages: processes and knowledge.

1. Processes include Task definition, evaluation, strategy selection and text modification
2. Knowledge includes different types of knowledge: linguistic, referential, pragmatic, etc.

In this model revision is realized thanks to the constant interaction between the different types of knowledge and the revising processes which have been identified as follows:

- *Task definition* involves specifying the revision objectives, the characteristics of the text to be examined and how to reach the goals; in sum it orients all the process of revision.
- *Text evaluation* consists in reading the written product in order to comprehend, evaluate and define problems. At this level, Hayes *et al.* (1987) speak about three types of evaluation: the writer (1) compares between his intention and text, (2) compares between the text plan and his goals, (3) evaluates his text considering grammar, spelling etc. This will lead him to diagnose the problem and to move to the third process.
- *Strategy selection, i.e.,* the writer will choose a strategy to solve the problem encountered. According to the model five revision strategies are available (1) to ignore the problem, (2) to delay its resolution, (3) to search for more information to clarify it, (4) to rewrite the text and preserve the same ideas, (5) to revise the text by changing what needs to be changed and keeping what seems appropriate.
- Finally, the writer will operate *text modification*. This will depend on the strategy chosen, *i.e.,* using his knowledge of communicative aims and different linguistic levels of the text, the writer may choose to delete, insert, replace, etc.

Yet, these processes are closely linked to some factors such as the writer's expertise, the writing task and other contextual constraints like time (Barkaoui, 2007). It should be noted that the last three processes of this model (evaluation, strategy selection and text modification) broadly correspond to the CDO procedure of Scardamalia and Bereiter (1983, 1986).

In 1996 a new writing model was drawn by Hayes stressing the importance of reading in the revision process. As explained above evaluation consists in reading and comprehending the text to detect and diagnose any problem encountered (Hayes *et al.,* 1987). Unlike a usual reader, the writer reads not only to understand the text, but also to detect problems in this text. Thus, revision is more than a writing process, it is "a composite of text interpretation, reflection and text production" (Hayes, 1996, p.15). This model consists of three components: the control structure, the fundamental processes and the resources.

- The first component being a set of knowledge for revision and defined by Hayes as *task schema,* it engenders a goal, revising activities, attentional goals, revising criteria and strategies.
- *The fundamental processes* include *text processing* (critical reading), *reflection* and *text production*.
- Finally *the resources* are compiled either in *long-term* or *working memory*. The long-term memory represents the individual's knowledge of the topic, the audience, etc. The working memory represents the various immediate task related memory functions.

According to this model, during revision the writer activates one of his fundamental processes such as critical reading or reflection, then if a problem is discovered he will choose an appropriate resource available in his long-term memory and activate it in his working memory. Hayes (2004) stresses the prominence of reading during revision focusing on three areas: content comprehension, task definition and text revision.

Several extensions to Hayes' model have been presented; Rijlaarsdam and Van Der Bergh (1996) put more emphasis on the cognitive process part of the original model. In their model four interrelated functions are at the source of cognitive activity: (1) the writing assignment, (2) reading written text, (3) translation of meaning into text, (4) generation of ideas. They found a relationship between occurrence of a specific cognitive process in the writing process and the finûnal text quality, *i.e.,* activation of any of the above mentioned activities during the writing process increases the chances for additional discovery for generating writing.

To sum up, during the 1990s research into the writing process focused on cognitive strategies and working memory capacity as prominent conditions to develop writing expertise as explained by Becker (2006, p. 34): "It became very apparent to researchers that the well-developed reading ability and extensive writing experience expert writers possess expands working memory capacity and long term memory knowledge."

The development of the various cognitive based writing models which occurred during the end of the last century encouraged further research to analyze key aspects of these models and to measure the cognitive activities that novice and expert writers use when writing or revising texts to test the validity of the writing models. Then in a series of studies (Chenoweth and Hayes, 2001, 2003; Hayes, 2009), Hayes further developed his model which consists of four components (see Fig. 4): *The proposer* is responsible for creating conceptual content (an idea package) which is sent to the translator. *The translator* produces a language string which is then evaluated by the *evaluator / reviser*. If the string is acceptable it is passed to the *transcriber* to be turned into text. If the string is not acceptable, then the *reviser* can call on the other processes to produce a revised version of the language or idea package, and this can in principle operate over a number of cycles before text is produced. The *reviser* can interrupt all other processes at any time.

Revision in L1 and L2

Research on difference in revision between L1 and L2 writers was examined by Roca De Larios, Murphy and Marin (2002) who conclude that writers revise more and pay more attention to the linguistic aspect when writing in L2 than in L1 for two reasons either they lack familiarity with the L2 material or would like "to intensify their efforts to make their texts reflect their writing goals" (p.34). Hall (1990) was also interested in comparing the revision processes of L2 advanced learners in their L1 and L2. He found that his subjects used on the one hand some similar processes such as the same type of revision (*e.g.,* substitution, deletion, addition) at the same level (*e.g.,* word, phrase etc.), the same stages (*e.g.,* planning, drafting) and with the same purposes (*e.g.,* informational, grammatical). On the other hand, his

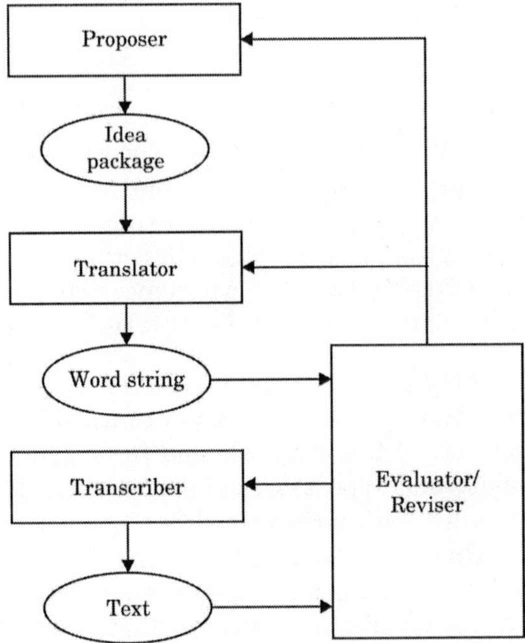

Fig. 4: Chenoweth and Hayes (2003, p. 13) model of text production

students spent more time, revised more and used more strategies in L2 revision. To conclude, Hall (1990, p. 56) highlights an important finding explaining that advanced L2 writers use "a single system of revision across languages".

Chenoweth and Hayes (2001) explored the impact of linguistic experience on burst length (bursts are parts of sentences rather than completed ones produced when writing and separated by pauses and other activities). Their subjects were American students learning French or German as L2. They compared text production of students writing in their L1 with the same students writing in L2. They also compared students with more L2 experience (5 or more semesters of study) with students who had less L2 experience (3 semesters of study). Their major finding was that the length of P-bursts (in words) was reduced when writers wrote in L2 compared to L1 and that less linguistically proficient L2 writers produced shorter bursts than more proficient L2 writers. In addition, they found that L2 writers revised a higher percentage of the sentence parts they produced.

Product- Focused Model of Revision

Faigley and Witte (1981) were less interested in the revision process and more in the revision outcomes thus presenting a taxonomy that can be used to analyze revisions made to a piece of writing. The taxonomy divides revisions into two major categories: *Surface Changes* which concern spelling, punctuation, grammar and meaning preserving changes such as additions, deletions, substitutions etc, and *Meaning Changes* which affect the text either at a macro level or a micro level as shown in The full taxonomy below:

- Surface Changes
  - Formal Changes
    - spelling
    - tense, number, and modality
    - abbreviations
    - punctuation
    - format
  - Meaning-Preserving Changes
    - additions
    - deletions
    - substitutions
    - permutations
    - distributions
    - consolidations
- Meaning Changes
  - Microstructure Changes
    - additions
    - deletions
    - substitutions
    - permutations
    - distributions
    - consolidations
  - Macrostructure Changes
    - additions
    - deletions
    - substitutions
    - permutations
    - distributions
    - consolidations

After the review of the development of cognitive models of revision processes and the taxonomy of revision activity essential to the understanding of this work, we turn to the description and presentation of the present study.

THE STUDY

Having stated the importance of revision for successful writing, the purpose of this study is to explore the use of revision processes by Algerian EFL students in the three languages Arabic (L1), French (FL1) and English (FL2) and across the four years of their curriculum. This is done in order to understand how students of different expertise operate revision in the three languages and to propose how to improve its use to achieve more effective writing.

Participants

The subjects of this study were university students enrolled in a four year English degree course (*Licence* Degree)[1] offered by the Foreign Language Department of the Faculty of Letters and Languages, at the University of Tlemcen (Algeria). The present work involved four students (two male and two female students) randomly selected from each level of instruction (*i.e.,* 1st, 2nd, 3rd and 4th year). Sixteen students in all participated in this study. These students were in the 17 to 27 years old age group. Their mother tongue (MT) is the western variety of Algerian Arabic while their first language (L1) is Standard Arabic[2]. French and English are respectively the students' first and second foreign languages (FL1 and FL2).

Before entering university, the subject students learned English in Middle and Secondary Schools for five years, whereas French was learned for nine years, *i.e.,* since the fourth year of the Primary School. Communicative Language Teaching was used for English and French instruction. At university, students used English in language and content based courses. Arabic was taught as a separate course and concerned language and literature. French was not included in their curriculum. Regarding students' proficiency level in English, it was estimated as follows:

1st year students: low intermediate

2nd year students: intermediate to high intermediate

3rd year students: high intermediate to advance

4th year students: advanced

It should be noted that in this study we will refer to students' "year of study".

---

[1] The equivalent of a BA degree obtained after a four year study.

[2] It should be pointed out that the terms MT and L1 are often used interchangeably in the literature, but the linguistic situation in Algeria compels the researcher to discriminate between these two terms. MT is the term used for the language acquired at home (a spoken form of dialectal Arabic), and L1 is used for Standard Arabic that is the national language and the first language learned at school and used as a means of formal instruction.

Research Method

The present research work was a *case study* involving sixteen EFL students at the University of Tlemcen. This research design was used because it provides a detailed study of a few cases that can help enhance our understanding of the issues raised by other cases as Nunan (1992) remarks:

> ... one can learn a great deal about one's own students in general through a detailed study of one particular student, in the same way as insights into language classrooms in general can be derived from the intensive analysis of a single classroom. (p. 89)

Moreover, case study allows a variety in sampling and triangulation of results which is an important methodological aspect of the present research.

Instruments

Except for the production tasks, the remaining tools used in this study were self-report ones. Though these instruments are criticized for providing data largely shaped by the informant perceptions and beliefs, they are valuable for unveiling learners' cognitive processes and consequent behavior.

Production tasks: Essay writing

The students were asked to write in the classroom a narrative essay every week during three successive weeks, but every time using a different language [Arabic (L_1), French (FL_1), and English (FL_2)]. The topic was the same (see appendix A). The essays were about 150 words long, and were written in a period of time of 30 minutes to one hour. Essay writing was chosen as a task because it is a free type of writing and an elaborated one which may unveil a large number of revision processes used by writers. In addition, it is typically used to answer test questions in all the courses of the degree curriculum of these students. The mode of discourse chosen for the three topics was narration because students were observed to have a great deal to say when narrating, and therefore, expected to reveal much information about their revision processes.

The think-aloud procedure

Think-aloud techniques are instances in which subjects complete a task or solve a problem while speaking about their thought processes at the same time. In other words, they let their thoughts flow verbally in a stream of consciousness fashion without trying to control, direct, or observe them. This technique is believed to reveal a great deal about mental actions because it is done simultaneously rather than thinking back on actions performed at some prior time (Nunan, 1992). In the present experiment, the subject students were assigned the writing task, then asked to verbalise all their thoughts while writing. This verbal report was recorded, and then transcribed. These protocols represented the data used by the researcher to gain insights into the learner's writing processes and more specifically revision ones (see appendix B). The investigator had to deal with 48 different protocols as the sixteen students wrote 48 essays (every student wrote three essays).

It should be noted that before the first think-aloud session took place, the investigator held a group discussion with subject students at each level of instruction. During this session she explained the objectives and the different steps of the procedure providing examples of think-aloud data and demonstrations. In addition, students were shown how to use the recorder and tried out the think-aloud technique. When the investigator felt that students understood the principles of this technique she invited them to start writing their essays isolating each student in a room with a recorder and the essay topic to be dealt with.

The interview

After treatment of think-aloud data, a second data collection instrument, the interview, was designed and administered to subject students to clarify some points, check the validity of others and complete the missing information. This self-report tool addressed the perceptions of subject students about their writing behaviour and processes because the perceptions of participants, however subjective, are a crucial means to understand their learning behaviour. In fact, the use of the interview was incited by the advantage of the interaction between the interviewee and the interviewer.

In the present study, the semi-structured interview was preferred for the benefits it offers. Unlike the structured one it is flexible allowing to obtain richer information, and unlike the unstructured interview it permits some kind of comparability and structure for analysis. The interview turned around three major points: whether students revised, when they revised and what they revised in the three languages.

RESULTS

When being interviewed, 12 students out of 16 claimed revising in the three languages, Arabic, French, and English; 2 other informants reported not revising in Arabic; and 2 students never revised in the three languages. Then, the majority of these students used *revision* across the three languages. Yet more importantly, the purpose of this study was to find out when and how these students revised their compositions in the three languages across the four years of study. Interesting findings related to each research question were reached as displayed below.

When Do Algerian EFL University Students Operate Revision in Arabic (L1), French (FL1) and English (FL2) Writing across the Four Years of Study?

The think-aloud protocols revealed that revision processes occurred in the three languages and across the four years of study at three stages:

- *On draft*: When drafting students revised their texts and edited them.
- *While transferring*: When copying down the text from the rough paper to the one to be submitted, students proceeded to text change.
- *On the paper to be submitted*: Students still edited their texts after having written them on the paper to be handed in.

The following Table 1 summarizes these results.

These figures reveal that few students revised their essays when drafting, and that the majority revised their texts while transferring them.

On the other hand, the interview data show that most students see revision as the last step of writing as revealed by their answers (see Table 2) to the question "when do you operate revision processes when writing in the three languages?"

Table 1: Stages of revision (think-aloud data)

Revision	*1st year*			*2nd year*			*3rd year*			*4th year*		
	NE AR n/4	*NE FR n/4*	*NE EN n/4*	*NE AR n/4*	*NE FR n/4*	*NE EN n/4*	*NE AR n/4*	*NE FR n/4*	*NE EN n/4*	*NE AR n/4*	*NE FR n/4*	*NE EN n/4*
On draft	1		1		1	1			1		1	1
While transferring	4	4	4	3	3	4	2	4	3	2	3	2
On the Submitted paper				1		1	1			2	1	2

NE: Narrative Essay; AR: Arabic; FR: French; EN: English

Table 2: Stages of revision (interview data)

Answers	*Students (n/16)*
At the end on the paper to be submitted	07
If there is time after each paragraph, if not at the end of drafting	03
At different times	01
At the end on the submitted paper if ever I have time	01
At the end of drafting in English and French, but not in Arabic	02
I Don't revise	02

These results show that most students considered revision as an independent final stage of writing and sometimes even optional as they linked it to availability of time. In addition, those students, who claimed not revising in Arabic, argued that it was unnecessary because they were sure they made few mistakes in their L1 as they were proficient in this language. Regarding the two other students, who never revised in the three languages, they explained that this was to avoid rewriting their essays.

The results suggest students' misunderstanding of the role of revision and therefore of when it should be operated. Three major findings confirm this idea as explained below:

- First, except for few advanced students (4) who reported revising at different times, revision was seen by most participants as a final step of writing and not as an ongoing process during the realization of the task. Moreover, the verbal protocols showed that many students revised while copying their drafts on the final paper. However, the resulting revision was not very effective: the qualitative analysis of students' products revealed some mistakes found on the submitted paper which did not appear on their drafts. The reason is that when copying on the paper to be submitted, it is difficult for the writer to pay attention to meaning, structure, word choice, grammar, and handle at the same time writing mechanics, *i.e.,* hand writing, punctuation and capitalization (overload of the working memory).

- Second, some students reported that unlike French and English their Arabic writing did not necessitate revision believing that proficiency in one language exempted from revision in writing ignoring the fact that real writing is created through revision which is a vehicle for sharpening the form, meaning, and power within their writing whichever the language.
- Finally, a third group found revision unnecessary in the three languages to avoid rewriting their essays which took too much effort. This reveals misunderstanding not only of the revision process, but of the whole writing process as well.

How do Students use Revision in the Three Languages across the Four Years of Study?

In his 1996 model, Hayes stresses the importance of reading as a fundamental process in revision. Indeed, the protocols revealed students' activation of critical reading during revision. Yet, this reading took two forms: the first one was that of a final linear reading, and the second one was reading and re-reading parts of the text.

The majority of students used a linear reading either at the end of their writing on draft and/or on the submitted paper. It should be noted that this kind of reading resulted rarely in text change, and when it occurred it was concerned with spelling or few grammatical mistakes such as verb tense, subject-verb agreement, or omission/ addition of the plural marker 's'. Few other students read and re-read parts of their written texts to comprehend them and/ or to detect problems (see Table 3).

Re-reading for revision occurred on draft during text production and/ or while transferring from draft to the submitted paper. Students activated their critical reading, and then if a problem was discovered they tried to choose the most appropriate way (*i.e.,* change, addition, deletion, substitution, or consolidation) to proceed to text modification. It should be noted that this type of reading resulted in more corrections than the preceding one. However, most of these text modifications were concerned with surface errors such as spelling, grammar, or word choice. Table 4 illustrates the different types of text change which occurred during the process of re-reading as revealed by the verbal protocols. Each type of modification was recorded only once even if the students repeated it several times.

Table 3: Re-reading for revision across the four years of study and the three languages

	1st year			*2nd year*			*3rd year*			*4th year*		
	NE AR n/4	*NE FR n/4*	*NE EN n/4*	*NE AR n/4*	*NE FR n/4*	*NE EN n/4*	*NE AR n/4*	*NE FR n/4*	*NE EN n/4*	*NE AR n/4*	*NE FR n/4*	*NE EN n/4*
Re-reading	3	2	2	1	1	2	1	2	3	2	2	2
Total (n /16)	7	4	6	6								

Table 4: Types of text modification produced by students while re-reading

Text modification	*1st year*			*2nd year*			*3rd year*			*4th year*		
	NE AR n/4	*NE FR n/4*	*NE EN n/4*	*NE AR n/4*	*NE FR n/4*	*NE EN n/4*	*NE AR n/4*	*NE FR n/4*	*NE EN n/4*	*NE AR n/4*	*NE FR n/4*	*NE EN n/4*
Vocabulary	2	1	3				1		1			
Grammar	2	1	1		1			1	2			1
Spelling/ Punctuation	1	1	3			1		1	1		1	
Style										2		

These results are further confirmed by the interview data (presented in Table 5) related to the question why do you revise your composition in Arabic, French and English?

Table 5: Students' focus on revision

Answers	*Number of students (n/16)*
To correct grammatical mistakes	11
To see again punctuation	01
To correct spelling	02
To link ideas and correct mistakes	01
To correct form and content	01

The results reveal that whichever the language revision was regarded by most students as proofreading for errors. Only two 4th year students reported that they usually paid attention to both form and content. The remaining 14 students explained that revision of form should be given priority over content because teachers paid more attention to form and penalized more grammar and spelling mistakes.

On the other hand, the verbal protocols revealed that the students who proceeded to revision in the three essays either made very few text changes or did not make any change. Yet, their corrections in Arabic were more effective than the ones done in the foreign languages. In addition, when these subjects were asked why they made few text modifications, they explained that they did not find any errors in their essays (actually their texts were full of mistakes namely in the foreign languages). In fact, poor writers in one language could not improve their texts even if they revised them many times. Indeed, when students' ability in one language was low their revision did not result in any correction or text improvement as highlighted by some researchers (Faigley and Witte, 1981; Graham, 1997; McDonough, 1995) who found that even if they revised their essays, poor writers in a language did not enhance their texts. Our results further confirm that effectiveness of revision is related to students' language proficiency. To sum up, revision tended to receive the least amount of time and effort in the students' process of writing; moreover, it was generally limited to proofreading for errors.

DISCUSSION

Revision in the Three Languages

The results suggest that the language used to write had little impact on the stage when revision occurred. Revision on draft was rarely done in the three languages; it was used by only one student out of four at each level of instruction and only in English and French writing (it was used in Arabic by one 1st year student only). On the other hand, revision while transferring was more frequently and consistently used across the three languages within each level of instruction. Likewise, revision on the submitted paper was used, though rarely, but consistently (*i.e.,* by the same students) across the three languages namely by 4th year students. These results suggest that most students operate revision processes at the same stages in the three languages.

On the other hand, the results show that the language used to write (L1, FL1 or FL2) had an impact on how students used revision. Re-reading for revision occurred slightly more in English writing than in Arabic and French (see Table 3). In the interview, participants revealed that when writing in the foreign languages they were more careful and needed to read many times for revision to correct any errors. This was not the case in Arabic writing as they were more proficient and wrote more confidently. It was also noted that linguistic competence in one language was important for effective revision. Indeed, at all levels of instruction students were more successful in detecting and diagnosing the problem, then solving it in their Arabic writing than in the foreign languages, because they had a firmer grasp of the pattern to which they were referring, and they were better able to find an appropriate substitution when changes were necessary. Moreover, revision of English essays was more effective in the hands of advanced students.

Revision Across the Four Years of Study

If we consider students' level of instruction, we noticed that it had an impact on the stage when revision occurred. Revision while transferring was used at all levels of instruction, but with different frequencies. Its use decreased from year 1 to year 4 (it was used by all 1st year students, but only half of 4th year students). Regarding revision on the final paper, it was rarely used and mainly used by 4th year students. On the other hand, revision on draft was occasionally undertaken at all levels which did not allow comparability. These results suggest that the more students were advanced the less they revised while transferring and the more they revised on the submitted paper. A finding further confirmed by the interview results which revealed that advanced students were aware of the uselessness of revision while transferring: a conclusion they achieved thanks to their writing experience. At the same time these students stressed the importance of a final revision before submission.

The level of instruction also affected how students used revision. Regarding the frequency of text modification, 1st year students were the ones who operated more text change. They seemed to be highly preoccupied by correctness when writing in the three languages. However, many of their text modifications in English writing were inappropriate. They had an incomplete linguistic knowledge of English, used inappropriate rules of grammar or spelling and thus expressed themselves poorly in their narrative writing. On the other hand, advanced learners (*i.e.*, 3rd and 4th year students) showed a more effective revision of their English essays not only at the linguistic level, but at the strategic one as well. It seems clear that during their undergraduate studies, students reinforced their linguistic knowledge in English and gained more experience in writing. This allowed them to operate revision more effectively. Then if we look at types of text modification which were undertaken, 1st year students concentrated in their revision on errors related to spelling, punctuation, grammar and word choice. They seemed to ignore those errors related to inappropriate style, cohesion or coherence. In fact, most students dealt with surface errors except for two 4th year students who operated their revision processes to correct their text style: they made global changes in their texts and rewrote major parts. It should be noted that revision of style requires language mastery and writing experience. This is why it appeared only with advanced students.

CONCLUSION

The analysis of revision across the three languages revealed that most students used it at the same stages thus revealing a misconception of this writing stage. Yet, students operated revision processes in the FLs namely English more frequently than in L1 as they felt lack of linguistic competence and seemed more preoccupied by error detection and correction. Nevertheless, they focused on surface errors. On the other hand, comparison of revision at the four years of study showed that revision was more effective in the hands of advanced students not only in English writing, but in Arabic as well, as these writers gained more English proficiency and above all more writing expertise. These results further confirm the importance of language proficiency and writing experience for successful revision.

In sum, this study shows that most subject students ignore the importance of revision in writing whether be it in the FLs or in L1. They do not realize the importance of this process in the construction of their text, the cohesion of their sentences and the coherence of their ideas. They consider revision as mere correction of surface errors which can be avoided because of either proficiency in the language they write in or unwillingness to change what has been already written. Moreover, they hold a mistaken thought of when to operate revision considering it as a final stage in writing and not an ongoing process during writing.

To conclude, Revision, which is an essential strategy in the writing process, encompasses two basic elements: rewriting the content to assure clarity, and editing the draft to eliminate mechanical and grammatical errors. It is important for teachers to plan lessons to train students to use effectively this strategy helping them to make more sense of their messages. This training will focus on four main stages: (1) demonstrate to learners the need for content revision, (2) help learners clarify the content of their writing, (3) demonstrate to learners the need for editing changes, and (4) assist learners in their editing efforts.

Yet, it should be noted that though the learner may receive good training in revision still other factors may affect the effectiveness of this strategy such as learner language proficiency, the time allowed for the writing task and content knowledge.

REFERENCES

Barkaoui, K. (2007). Revision in second language writing: What teachers need to know. *TESL Canada Journal*, 25(1): 81–92.

Becker, A. (2006). A review of writing model research based on cognitive processes. *In*: Horning, A.S. and Becker, A. (*eds.*), Revision: History, theory and practice Indiana (USA): Parlor Press, pp. 25–49.

Chenoweth, A. and Hayes, J. (2001). Fluency in writing: Generating text in L1 and L2. *Written Communication*, 18: 80–98.

Chenoweth, A. and Hayes, J. (2003). The inner voice in writing. *Written Communication*, 20: 99–118.

Faigley, L. and Witte, S. (1981) Analysing revision. *College Composition and Communication*, 32(4): 400–414.

Flower, L. and Hayes, J.R. (1980). The cognition of discovery: Defining a rhetorical problem. *College Composition and Communication*, 31(1): 21–32.

Flower, L. and Hayes, J. (1981). A cognitive process theory of writing. *College Composition and Communication*, 32(4): 365–87. Retrieved from http://faculty.goucher.edu/eng221/Flower_and_Hayes_Cognitive_Process_Model_article-version.htm.

Flower, L., Hayes, J.R., Carey, L., Schriver, K. and Stratman, J. (1986). Detection, diagnosis, and the strategies of revision. *College Composition and Communication,* 37(1): 16–55.

Frederick, R.C. (1987). Improving writing skills through social studies. *ERIC Digests,* 40. Retrieved from http://www.ed.gov/databases/ERIC_Digests.

Graham, S. (1997). *Effective language learning*. Clevedon: Multilingual Matters.

Hall, C. (1990). Managing the complexity of revising across languages. *TESOL Quarterly*, 24: 43–60.

Hayes, J.R. (1996). A new framework for understanding cognition and affect in writing. *In*: Levy, M. and Ransdell, S. (*eds.*), The science of writing: Theories, methods, individual differences and applications, Mahwah, NJ: Lawrence Erlbaum, pp. 1–27.

.... (2004). What triggers revision? *In*: Allal, L.K., Chanquoy, L. and Largy, P. (*eds.*), Revision: Cognitive and instructional processes Mass (USA): Kluer Academic Publishers, pp. 9–21.

.... (2009). From idea to text. *In*: Beard, R. Myhill, D., Riley, J. and Nystrand, M. (*eds.*). *The SAGE handbook of writing development*, London: Sage Publications, pp. 65–79.

Hayes, J.R. and Flower, L. (1983). A cognitive model of the writing process in adults. National Inst. of Education (ED), Washington, DC.

Hayes, J.R., Flower, L., Schriver, K.A., Stratman, J.F. and Carey, L. (1987). Cognitive processes in revision. *In*: Rosenberg, S. (*ed.*), *Advances in applied psycholinguistics Reading, Writing and Language Learning,* 2: 176–240. Cambridge (UK): Cambridge University Press.

Jacobs, S. (1982). Composing and coherence: The writing of eleven pre-medical students. *Linguistics and Literacy* (Series 3). Center for Applied Linguistics, Washington D.C.

Jones, S. (1982) Attention to rhetorical form while composing in a second language. *In*: Campbell, C., Flashner, V., Hudson, T. and Lubin, J. (*eds.*). *Proceedings of the Los Angeles Second Language Research Forum*, (2: 130–143). Los Angeles. University of California.

Kasper, L.F. (1997). Assessing the metacognitive growth of ESL student writers. *TESL-EJ*, 3(1): A–1. Retrieved from http://www.zait.uni-bremen.de/wwwgast/tesl_ej

McDonough, S.H. (1995). *Strategy and skill in learning a foreign language*. London: Edward Arnold.

Perl, S. (1980). Understanding composing. *In*: *College Composition and Communication,* 31(4): 363–69.

.... (1981). Coding the composing process: A guide for teachers and researchers. Manuscript written for the National Institute of Education. Washington DC. ED 240609.

Rijlaarsdam, G. and Van den Bergh, H. (1996). The dynamics of composing - An agenda for research into an interactive compensatory model of writing: Many questions, some answers. *In*: Levy, C.M. and Ransdell, S. (*eds.*), *The Science of writing theories, methods, individual differences and applications*, Mahwah, NJ: Lawrence Erlbaum Associates, pp. 107–125.

Roca De Larios, J., Murphy, L. and Marin, J. (2002). A critical examination of L2 writing process research. *In*: Ransdell, S. and Barbier, M.L. (*eds.*), New directions for research in L2 writing, Dordrecht, Netherlands: Kluwer Academic Publishers, pp. 11–47.

Scardamalia, M. and Bereiter, C. (1983). The development of evaluative, diagnostic and remedial capabilities in children's composing. *In*: Martlew, M. (*ed.*), *The psychology of written language: Developmental and educational perspectives,* London: John Wiley & Sons, pp. 67–95.

………… (1986). Research on written composition. *In*: Wittrock, M.C. (*ed*.), *Handbook of research on teaching* 3rd ed, New York: Macmillan, pp. 778–803.

Sommers, N. (1982). Revision. *Journal of Teaching Writing,* 1(2): 133–148

Zamel, V. (1982). Writing: The process of discovering meaning. *TESOL Quarterly*, 16: 195–209.

APPENDIX A: ESSAYS TOPIC

This topic was used for the three narrative essays. The same topic has been translated into French and Arabic.

> Your grandfather/ grandmother was a mujahid / mujahida who took part in the Algerian War of Independence. Narrate one of his/ her exploits during the war.

APPENDIX B: SAMPLE VERBAL PROTOCOL

The student made use of English and French (FL1) to generate ideas while writing in English. The words in italics indicate French words, non-underlined ones were spoken only, whereas those underlined indicate when the writer was speaking and writing or self-dictating (on the model provided by McDonough, 1995).

N.E. ENGLISH

The 3rd topic which speaks about my grandfather in the Algerian war of independence. *So since I was young, I was always listening to my father and mother, when they were telling me the story of my grandfather when he was a moudjahid and they also* they also tell me *told me that my grandfather was a courageous moudjahid and he was also a man which* has *had a* ...a patriot or a *nationalism* .....or if you want a nationalism *ame or character* and *it was a very bad life in that epoch but since they loved* they loved *their country they were very happy* and they were very happy *and quiet in their life*. Ok so what I want to say *is my grandfather look a part of the Algerian in* the Algerian in the Algerian *war of independence* yes independence, *and had many or did many exploits or courageous ach during this war. As I know my grandfather was very young* was very young *when he left school and join the moudjahidin in the mountain.* And they …eh…eh… *ils ont fait des pieds et des mains* … they made … hands and feets to *they made hands and feets to …quitter* to *leave away the French army* and my father, *my father said that my …… his father was a specialist in,* was a specialist in … faire des commissions… *in sending and writing commissions but he was very young he was also…*so we put since he was very young he was also ….. *comment dirai-je ….eh…..ils lui ont confié…il lui ont confié des missions de…..* he was also *specialised to do all the* all the *comment dirai je ..il etait spécilisé, on lui confié de faire tous les achats* to do all the shopping yes *shopping….*so*….these acts of courage were simply done by* by *our grand father and mother because they loved their country and they paid* they paid *….all their life to make out the French,* the French *army.*

Finally I think that I'm very *fier, la fierete I am very satisfied … satisfait* also ….only this I'm very satisfied by *…by the things* my father *my grandfather did and we can say that* we can say that *if they were not like this* that is to say if they were not *courageous,* courageous *and nationalist* we are? we will be? if they were, we are … *quel est le temps qu'il faut utiliser?…* if they were not like this, courageous and nationalists, we are… *quest-ce que je veux dire?* if they were not like this, courageous and nationalists *so we are still,* we can still yes *we can be still* colonised colonised yes.

Now we move to the proper sheet: *since I was young, I was listening to my father and mother when they were telling me the story witch became a history* yes… *of my grandfather when he was a moudjahid and they also told me that my grandfather was a courageous moudjahid and he was also a man with a …*no *who had a patriot and nationalist character.*

It was a very bad..eh… *hard life in that epoch since they lived they country they were very happy and quiet in their life. My grandfather took a part as I said in the Algerian war of independence and had many or did many exploits or courageous acts during this war… and join the moudjahidin in the montain they made hands and feets to leave away the French army and father said his father was a specialist in sending and writing commissions but since he was very young he was also specialized to do all the shopping …je dois expliquer… it means that he bought* he bought *food and all what the moudjahidin needed. these acts of courage were simply done by* by *our grand father and mother because they loved their country and they paid ….all their life* to make out no *to leave away the French,* the French *army.*

Finally I think that I am very satisfied by the things my grandfather did....and we can say *that if they were not like that courageous and nationalist co we* can no could *be still colonized.*

C'est bon

12

Organizational Culture as a Basis for Implementing Innovation Leading to Improved Business Results

YOEL SULLAM[1]*

ABSTRACT

Innovation has become a key value in the contemporary business environment, yet many still see it as no more than a slogan, and are unsuccessful in their attempts to implement and employ it correctly for achieving desired business results. If innovation is to fulfil expectations, it must be ingrained in the organizational DNA and culture, and become an integral part of a process of a well-executed organizational change. Organizational culture is a significant differentiating factor among companies within the same field and possessing the same technologies. A strong organizational culture is the basis for implementing the kind of innovation that will create surplus value in a dynamic and competitive business environment.

Key words: Organizational culture, Innovation, Organizational change, Organizational performance.

[1] Eliyhu Hanavi 16, KiryatAta, Israel.
* *Corresponding author*: E-mail: yoel@yayacon.com

INTRODUCTION

Organizational culture is a key to successfully confronting the challenges of our contemporary business environment, where employees are paradoxically confronting increased demands coupled with diminished job security (Mohrman and Cohen, 2005). Specifically, an organizational culture that fosters innovation is necessary in the face of mounting work pressures and the difficulties involved in creating and maintaining a lasting competitive advantage. Innovation is crucial for manufacturing, for process management, and for handling changes in the business model.

Where for many years, innovation was merely a slogan bandied about by corporate managers, today we increasingly appreciate how it must truly be adopted and integrated correctly into organizational culture, even when allowing for the potential difficulties and obstacles faced by businesses experiencing transformation. Only an organizational culture contributing to innovation, and to increased employee motivation, can generate results and returns on investment that pave the way to a sustainable, lasting competitive advantage.

ORGANIZATIONAL CULTURE

The term *culture* typically refers to the beliefs, value systems, and behaviors attributed to a specific group. *Culture* also influences the manner by which we interpret reality and define success. *Organizational culture* can be seen therefore as an agent of social cohesion, uniting the different entities of an organization, and guiding employees towards pursuing the most appropriate solution for a given business problem, even when that solution is not the easiest one (Alvasson, 2002; Riad, 2007).

A complementary definition for organizational culture sees it as a major and influential component affecting the capacity of organizations to function properly and achieve their aims (Ashkanasy *et al.,* 2001). Since all organizations are composed of the individuals employed in them, organizations must engineer the common basis to unite their employees. This, therefore, is one of the central roles of organizational culture: to transform a group of diverse individuals into a team that functions well together–a crucial factor influencing the capability of organizations to operate successfully in an ever-changing business environment.

The origins of the term organizational culture can be attributed to the work of Blake and Mouton (1969) in the 1960's, which first explored the relationship between organizational cultures with excellence. Heskett (2012) distinguishes between four inter-organizational factors contributing to success: organizational culture (the how), goals (the why) strategy (what, where and when) and performance (the who).

Within such framework, it can be said that organizational culture provides the environment for members of an organization to create, acquire, share, and manage knowledge. Organizational culture includes behavioral patterns, dress codes, symbols, and communication patterns within the organization (John, 2006). Different studies have pointed towards how organizations that base their culture on *leading by example* can improve their productivity and results (Krug and Henrischke, 2008). It has also been shown that culture can influence the entirety of organizational behaviors- and therefore also directly affect results (House *et al.,* 2004).

The approach developed by Schein (1992) is central to the study of organizational culture. According to this approach, culture is composed of three layers–the first of these reflecting the daily routine within the organization, and includes organizational symbols, dress code and common language. The second layer includes the values that unite the members of an organization, and the third layer is comprised of the main assumptions within the organization about its business outlook and how work is executed. Among these factors, the importance of shared values is the most important, since these values in effect shape the workplace environment, contribute to worker commitment, and form the overall behavior of the organization. For example, studies show that organizations that promote values of openness, trust, teamwork, creativity, and empowerment, benefit from better business results (Becker *et al.,* 2001; Huang and Dastmalachin, 2006).

Clearly therefore, organizational culture is immensely influential on the functioning of the organization, including employee interaction, performance, decision making capacities, and the ways employees cope with the challenges they face at work. Additionally, organizational culture can create successful communication channels that will aid innovation, increased business results, and maintaining competition in the business environment (Lopez *et al.*, 2006; Graham and Nafunko, 2007). The organizational environment within which we are operating today is undergoing rapid transformation, leading to changes in policy and in how different processes are undertaken in the organization to maintain competitiveness. There is great importance therefore to shaping the ways employees respond to changes, and organizational culture has the capacity to influence the attitudes of employees towards change and win their support towards its implementation and success (Ahmed, 1998; Lorenzo, 1998).

Organizational culture leads to behavioral patterns that can directly influence employee attitudes and the quality of their output. From this, we can infer that culture can directly influence employee motivation through rewards, workplace atmosphere, and satisfaction (Green and Zhu, 2010). Motivation is in fact derived from organizational innovation which encourages engagement in day-to-day activities in the workplace, as well as a feeling of belonging and connection to the organization itself.

Employee motivation is one of the most significant aspects managers must address and develop when they are aiming to improve results and profitability. Not only are employees ultimately responsible for producing goods and services, they also hold the most important asset in any organization–knowledge.

Though motivation has been defined in a multitude of ways, it can be best described as the various factors that influence how employees perform. Lange's definition of motivation–which I tend to accept–sees it as an operative force which is the result of psychological needs–on the one hand survival needs such as rewards and benefits; and on the other hand employee aspirations to advance in the organization and maximize capabilities.

Fresko *et al.* (1997) identify two approaches with respect to motivation: the first is negative, where individuals are characterized as disliking the workplace and therefore the role of managers is to encourage them through reward and punishment. The second, positive, approach sees employees as striving to fulfill their desires, goals, and potential through displaying responsibility, self-control, and commitment to organizational objectives. The second approach is certainly more widely accepted, and has been used to account for how employee performance is related to factors such as work advancement and promotion, challenge, honors, and compensation. We can therefore determine that motivation is ultimately the product of fulfilling employee needs, and that organizational culture can be a substantive influencing factor.

An additional approach suggests that employee motivation is derived from three conditions that must be fulfilled by the organization: personal responsibility for work output, viewing the work as important, and recognizing the contribution of the employee to the final product (Ramlall, 2004). Yet another approach emphasizes the importance of employees' feelings of belonging to an organization (Pellissier, 2011).

Adams (1965) and Herzberg (1996) suggested two ways to understand employee needs: Adams developed the theory of organizational justice at the workplace, wherein employees are constantly attempting to create an equilibrium between the degree of their contributions and efforts at the workplace and the compensation they receive. If they feel that the rewards are equal or greater than the contribution, this result in a feeling of justice, directly increasing motivation. A feeling of injustice on the other hand will result in motivation being considerably diminished.

Herzberg sees employee motivation as influenced by two main factors, internal and external. Internal factors motivate employees by providing a feeling of growth, positivity, and productivity, whereas external factors are related to feelings of security and comfort in the workplace. Herzberg claims that the presence of external factors will not positively influence motivation, but their absence could have a negative effect–and therefore the organization must ensure their presence; whereas internal factors will have a directly positive influence on motivation.

INNOVATION

Organizations are constantly seeking ways to improve and increase productivity, and are therefore pursuing novel means to produce and market their goods. They integrate new technologies while at the same time pursuing internal changes, out of a need to improve competitiveness. Innovation contributes to increased employee motivation and can solidify common efforts to achieve aims (Somech and Drach-Zahavy,

2011). In the current business environment, there is little doubt that one of the only ways to create growth and maintain a competitive edge is to foster innovation, as simply imitating other business actors is no longer sufficient, and therefore we must continue to develop new capabilities in order to move ahead (Desmond, 2009).

Innovation can be defined in different ways, but is perhaps best understood - within the framework of a business environment - as the harnessing of new ideas for the purpose of creating value. This does not just include new products or technologies, which often naturally lead to the creation of a market advantage – since once these products or technologies enter the market they are subject to rapid imitation and the loss of the competitive advantage (Keeley, 2002). If we examine the business environment, some of the most significant recent breakthroughs in terms of innovation – customer experience at Starbucks, the growth of Amazon.com, low cost flights – all of these were related more to providing value to the customer than to technological invention.

Innovation is a process whereby employees take part in the improvement of their workplace, therefore creating improved ways to sell goods or to identify customer needs–and thus to improve business results (Mayfield, 2009).

One of the central business challenges is related to the manner of internalizing innovation in the organization and the organizational culture. A study conducted by Cottam *et al.* (2001) showed that many companies understand the importance of innovation, but face difficulties in their efforts to integrate it into an organizational strategy. This argument is supported by a survey conducted among 750 senior managers at 150 organizations across the US (Ceswarani and Greetwood, 1999) which pointed out that 80% of the respondents acknowledged the importance of innovation, but only 14% felt they are able to integrate it effectively into their workplace.

We can demonstrate the importance of innovation by imagining a scenario where every employee at an organization is motivated by the fact that their ideas are respected and could potentially influence the future course of the organization. In such a setting, every employee has been taught to utilize the principles, techniques and tools of innovation, so that they are able to uncover new insights, opportunities and business models.

When the former CEO of Whirlpool, Dave Whitman, redefined his company's global strategy in 1999 he crucially stressed the importance of innovation, and that it was expected anywhere and for each employee at the company. This was met with skepticism, as Whirlpool at the time employed 68,000 workers in 170 countries. Today, Whirlpool is a symbol of success and a role model for implementing innovation at a global company. The rationale behind Whitman's stressing of the importance of innovation was to encourage every employee to think outside the 'big box of home electronic appliances' and to create new and revolutionary solutions for its customers – that will also provide value for the company. The results were a company-wide wave of new ideas for products and processes, and an increase in profits. The revenue from new products grew from 78 million USD in 2003 to 1.6 billion USD in 2006. In 2008, the company was working on 500 new projects, expected to bring in future revenues of 3.5 billion USD.

As we have noted, one of the main concerns related to innovation is how to internalize and implement it within an organization. Over the past two decades, the appeal of innovation has waned, as many organizations have invested large sums without an understanding of how innovation should be a part of a continuous process taking place at every level of the organizational structure. A global study conducted in 2007 among 250 senior managers in 58 countries showed that most of them are not satisfied with the return on investment in innovation (Andrew *et al.,* 2007). For many years therefore innovation has been a slogan not truly acted on, an ostensible organizational value that is not a part of the real process of growing a business. This was mainly the result of a failure to appreciate how a change in organizational culture takes time, money and above all commitment – that it is not enough to award an annual prize for innovation, to finance a one-time project or to hold a single brain storming session.

Whirlpool's decision to set out on the path towards implementing innovation into the core of its business operations was highly criticized at first. The successful process was ignited however when 75 employees from the different branches of the company around the world were reassigned for a period of nine months, and grouped into teams charged with implementing innovation. During this time, they examined the best ways to promote new ideas, to determine which ones may or may not work, and to shape opportunities for growth within an organization. At the end of the nine-month period, a third of the participants in this team were returned to their former roles in the organization–to proselytize innovation within the entire company.

Another organization that found an original way to incorporate innovation is 3M, which allowed employees to set aside 15–20% of their time at work for personal projects using company resources. Google adopted the 70/20/10 formula whereby employees work on their main role in the company 70% of the time, 20% is devoted to strategic company projects and 10% for 'pet projects' where each employee is allowed to devote their time to any project that interests them personally.

Innovation could be brought about in another way–the transformation of a company's business model. The rapid pace of product distribution shortens the life span of many business models. New competitors emerge globally, seemingly every day, and jobs and resources are diverted towards countries with lower wages. All of these factors lead to increased business-related risks, and therefore are pushing organizations towards choosing the path of innovation. Business model innovation is even more valuable in such periods of uncertainty, since during these periods this type of innovation has the potential to transcend the limits of the normal competitive environment.

Two examples of such innovation can demonstrate its importance. The first is in the Australian air carrier market. Virgin Australia, which in 2001 broke into the airline business with the Virgin Blue brand, began offering low cost flights. This has led to 30% market share and a severe blow to existing players. Qantas, the market leader, realized it could not compete with Virgin directly and decided to launch its own low cost brand–Jetstar–operated as a separate division in the company. Jetstar launched in 2004 with new plane models and lower fares and, following its success in the domestic market, in 2006 it became the first low cost airline to operate international flights, offering new solutions for its customers such as upgrading the in-flight meal, seat location, and other options.

A second example of business model innovation is from Swedish furniture maker Ikea. After learning that every new location it opens in Russia leads to a significant bump in the real estate prices in the surrounding areas, Ikea decided to open shopping centers, called Mega Malls, near its branches. Today these malls are seeing higher revenues than Ikea's traditional stores.

ORGANIZATIONAL CHANGE

To realize innovation, organizations often must go through a process of effective organizational change. Such change is a crucial factor for achieving organizational aims, and is usually implemented through a concentrated effort led by management when attempting to improve business operations. For an organization to stay competitive and compete in the dynamic business environment it must be flexible and implement necessary changes (Cohen, 1999). However, such changes often involve risk, and aren't always successful. Different studies have shown how between one and two thirds of initiatives for organizational transformation fail (Beer and Nohria, 2000). A study conducted by Mackenzie & Company found that, over a period of 5 years, of the 1536 companies that initiated processes of organizational change only 38% actually were successful in improving business results.

The main motivating factors influencing organizational transformation are vision, strategy, organizational culture, structure, technology and managerial style (Yang *et al.*, 2009). The importance of initiating organizational changes in many business situations is clear, yet it is one of the most difficult to implement - and the question therefore must be what factors make this process so challenging?

A survey conducted by Deloitte among 400 companies pointed towards one main reason–internal opposition to change (Erwin and Garman, 2010). Individuals are often opposed to change when they are invested in maintaining the status quo, yet the success of organizational transformation is predicated on employees being fully committed to this process. Failure is usually the result of a lack of motivation among employees, impeding their desire to act towards its success. Though most employees may support organizational change if they see the future benefits in it, some do require other forms of motivations to implement it.

Employees fear changes in the workplace since such changes force them out of their known comfort zone, and requires of them a change in their own workplace habits. They are threatened by the economic implications of the change, and by the unknown future it brings with it. Management must learn how to react to these fears and act to change such attitudes in the workplace, in order to implement the course of organizational change with fewer objections.

Studies point towards four necessary steps for implementing change successfully–the acknowledgement that such change is necessary (Burke, 2002); building a strategy that includes specific goals and plans; engaging employees in the process; and the support and commitment of management for this process (Burke, 2002; Yukul, 2002).

There are two main models for the successful implementation of organizational transformation: the first is by Kurt Lewin (Evison, 2014), who suggested three stages to be undertaken by management:

1. *Unfreeze* – Where the organization is being primed to accept change – management should be setting the stage for the change through education, guidance, inclusiveness and involvement.
2. *Change* – Implementation of the change through the cooperation of employees and of management.
3. *Refreeze* – Promoting stability once change has been implemented, through providing a framework of structures, processes, norms, regulations, and defined roles that will offer guidance on how to act within the new environment.

A second central model for organizational change is that of the eight stages suggested by John Kotter. Kotter believed that the successful implementation of change could be achieved through:

1. *Understanding the necessity of the change* – This phase is carried out by examining the business environment and locating opportunities and threats. To communicate the urgency of change, the organization must provide clear information pointing towards the reasons for it.
2. *Forming a coalition for change within the organization* – When the need for change is acknowledged, the right people to lead it through this entire process must be selected.
3. *Creating vision for change* – By determining central values and creating an appropriate strategy, the team leading this process must introduce its vision for how the organization will be shaped in the period following the implementation of the change.
4. *Communicating the vision* – Opening channels of communication that will aid in driving the strategy and vision, and providing a model for what is required of the employees.

5. *Empowering the change* – Contending with all of the obstacles for the change and taking action to remove any organizational activity preventing its implementation.
6. *Creating short-term wins* – To help employees gain confidence in the path towards change, short term goals must be created and the necessary steps to achieve them must be taken. Many such short-term wins will allow the entire organization to gain confidence in the process of change.
7. *Evaluating the process* – Throughout the process of change, it is pertinent to examine what worked according to the plan, and what difficulties arose on the way to its implementation – and perform the necessary adjustments to help the process along.
8. *Anchoring the change in corporate culture* – Ensuring that the change will be sustained, by anchoring it within the organization and by stressing the correlation between desired behaviors and success.

Examining the two models leads to a common conclusion– for a process of organizational change to succeed, be it the implementation of new values or a change in the business model, management must win the support of the employees for it, lay out the reasons for its necessity, and work together to remove any possible obstacles. Only a change that is undertaken through cooperation, and that involves open communication among the entire units of the organization, can lead to successful results for the organization.

ORGANIZATIONAL CULTURE AND INNOVATION

As we have noted, Schein (1992) sees organizational culture as a social force that is mostly hidden from view, yet is highly powerful. Organizational culture strongly influences employee behavior beyond formal procedures and authority structures, and therefore is highly influential for achieving the aims of an organization.

Academic studies have shown how organizational culture and its social context influence the development of values (Dose, 1997; Rokech, 1973). Values in an organizational environment are tied to standards in the workplace and to employee understanding of what is or is not acceptable. When an organization is facing threats and opportunities, organizational culture is especially influential on decision making, attitudes, and employee behavior (Ozigbo, 2010). Employees today have a significant role in the effort to achieve a competitive advantage, in the ability of an organization to recognize customer needs, to acquire and localize external knowledge, and to utilize it for introducing improved products. Innovation will only be successful within an organizational culture that supports these efforts (Kantsperger and Kunz, 2005).

Effective management within the organization promotes open and active dialogue among team members, and leads to improved understanding of market conditions, and the ability to build appropriate models from implementing innovation (Akugan *et al.,* 2010). Numerous studies emphasize how innovation improves results by encouraging corporate members to develop new goods and services, in order to successfully face changes in the marketplace (Mas Tsou, 2006). Organizational culture influences innovation in two main ways: through processes of socialization, where employees learn what behavior is expected of them, and the necessity to adopt innovation as part of their job description; and through spreading values and perceptions that form the basis for the corporate structure, policy, and processes. Together, these factors promote an understanding among employees that innovation is desirable, and encourage them to contribute to fostering it (Tusman and Orielly, 1997).

Increasingly, we are seeing how organizational culture is the key to success in nurturing innovation, with companies that are adept at developing and manufacturing new technologies emphasizing their unique culture. Apple is a notable example - in that it offers its employees a chance to work at a company that develops groundbreaking technology. M3 and Google are also noteworthy examples for emphasizing that their products are based on significant research, and for highlighting the freedom and individuality of its employees.

Why is it crucial for organizational culture to promote innovation? In an age where technology is more easily copied, and thus may not prove to be the competitive advantage it once, was human capital cannot be as easily imitated by the competition (Macy *et al.,* 2009). When organizations can achieve successful outcomes through emphasizing organizational culture, they gain stability and robustness, with competitors finding it harder to imitate such results (Haskett, 2010). Employee behavior will determine the long term success of an organization, and desired results are only achieved through the entirety of the actions of all of the employees across all units of an organization. Every employee in turn is influenced by the organizational culture–structure, decision making processes, and motivation (Baron, 2006). In conclusion, we may say that a strategy and culture of fostering innovation may lead to a significant increase in the organization's value, as well as in profit oriented business results (Ajarozelski *et al.*, 2011).

CONCLUSION

Innovation is not to be thought of as simply another slogan found on the wall of a given organization. Over the past decade, innovation has become the most significant tool for achieving organizational success in a tumultuous, dynamic, ever-changing business environment. Organizations and companies must implement innovation within their daily business operations, and provide motivation for its employees, who are the holders of organizational knowledge - knowledge that could be the basis for developing new ideas that provide greater value for clients and increase profits.

As we have seen, it is challenging to initiate organizational change within a framework of organizational culture, but if this process is conducted properly it can be the basis for securing a competitive advantage which will be difficult to imitate. When the business environment poses difficult challenges, the prudent attitude is to avoid delaying our response, and to act in order to implement innovation within the organizational culture by providing employees with the motivation to release their creativity for the success of the organization, and for improved business results.

REFERENCES

Adams, J.S. (1965). Inequity in social exchange. *In:* Berkowitz, L. (*ed.*), *Advances in Experimental Social Psychology.* New York: Academic Press, 2: 267–299.

Ahmed, P.K. (1998). Culture and climate for innovation. *European Journal of Innovation Management*, 1(1): 30–43.

Akgün, A.E., Keskin, H. and Byrne, J.C. (2010). Procedural justice climate in new product development teams: Antecedents and consequences. *Product Development & Management Association*, 27: 1096–1111.

Alvesson, M. (2002). Understanding organizational culture, Sage, London.

Andrew, J., Sirkin, H., Haanaes, K. and Michel, D. (2007). Innovation, Boston Consulting Group.

Ashkanasy, N.M., Wilderom, C.P.M. and Peterson, M.F. (2011). *Recent Developments in Organizational Culture and Climate Research. In*: 71st Annual Meetings of the Academy of Management, San Antonio, pp. 12–16.

Becker, B.E., Huslid, M.A. and Ulrich, D. (2001). The HR scorecard, Harvard business school press, Boston, MA.

Beer, A. and Nohria, N. (2000). Cracking the code of change, Harvard business review, pp. 133–141.

Blake, R.R. and Mouton, J.S. (1969). Building a dynamic corporation through grid organization development, Addison-Wesley.

Burke, W. (2002). Organizational change theory and practice, Sage Publication.

Censerani, C. and Greatwood, P. (1999). Innovation and Creativity, Price Waterhouse, London.

Cottam, A., Ensor, J. and Band, C. (2001). A benchmark study of strategic commitment to innovation. *European Journal of Innovation Management*, 4(2): 88–94.

Desmond, V. (2009). How a systematic approach to innovation can bring radical improvement to organizations by liberating the staff. *Industrial and Commercial Training*, 41(6): 321–325.

Dose, J. (1997). Work value: An integrative framework and illustrative application to organizational socialization. *Journal of Occupational and Organizational Psychology*, 70(3): 219–240.

Erwin, D.G. and Garman, A. (2010). Resistance to organizational change linking research and practice. *Leadership and Organizational Development Journal*, 31: 39–56.

Evison, Anne (2014). Understanding the three stages of change. Mindtools. N.p., n.d.

Fresko, B., Kfir, D. and Nassar, F. (1997). Predicting teacher commitment. *Teaching Teacher Education*, 13(4): 429–38.

Graham, C.M. and Nafuko, F.M. (2007). Employee's perception toward the dimension of culture in enhancing organizational learning. *The Learning Organization*, 14(3): 281–292.

Green, F. and Zhu, Y. (2010). Over qualification, job dissatisfaction and increasing dispersion in the returns to graduate education. *Oxford Economic Papers*, 62(4): 740–763.

Herzberg, F. (1966). Motivation-hygiene theory, *In*: Pugh, D. (*ed.*), Organization Theory (Harmond-sworth, Penguin, 1971).

Heskett, J.L. (2012). The culture cycle. How to shape the unseen force that transforms performance, New Jersey: FT Press.

Huang, H.J. and Dastmalchian, A. (2006). Implications of trust and distrust for organizations: Role of customer orientation in a four nation study. *Personal Review*, 34(4): 361–371.

Isern, J. and Pung, A. (2007). Harnessing energy to drive organizational change. *McKinsey Quarterly*, 1: 16–19.

Jaruzelsky, B., Loher, J. and Holman, R. (2011). The global innovation 1000-why culture is key, strategy and business, p. 65.

Kantsperger, R. and Kunz, W.H. (2005). Managing overall service quality in customer care centers: Empirical findings of a multi-perspective approach. *International Journal of Service Industry Management,* 16(2): 135–151.

Keeley, L. (2002). Inspiring innovation: Abandon the crowd. *Harvard Business Review*, 80(8): 39–49.

Kotter, John (1995). "Leading change: Why transformation efforts fail." Harvard business review. N.p., Web. 23 Feb. 2014.

Krug, B. and Hendrischke, H. (2008). "Framing China: Transformation and institutional change through Co-evolution". *Management and Organization Review*, 4(1): 81–108.

Lange, P.J. (2011). Emotion and motivation: Toward consensus definitions and a common research purpose. *Emotion Review,* 3: 8–16.

Lopez, S.P., Peon, J.M.M. and Ordas, C.J.V. (2006). Organizational learning as a determining factor in business performance. *The Learning Organization,* 12(3): 227–245.

Lorenzo, A.L. (1998). A framework for fundamental change: Context, criteria and culture. *Journal of Research and Practice*, 22(4): 335–348.

Macey, W.H., Schneider, B., Barbera, K.M. and Young, S.A. (2009). Employee engagement: Tools for analysis, practice and competitive advantage, West Sussex: John Wiley-Blackwell.

Matsuo, M. (2006). Customer orientation, conflict and innovativeness in Japanese sales departments. *Journal of Business Research*, 59(2): 242–250.

Mayfield, M. (2009). Sparking worker creativity: Culture where garden variety creativity can flourish. *Development and Learning in Organizations*, 23(5): 10–14.

Mohrman, S.A. and Cohen, S.G. (1995). When people get out of the box: New relationships, new systems. *In*: Howard, A. (*ed*.), the changing nature of work, San Francisco, Jossey-Bass.

O'Reilly, M.S., Holmgren, L., Shing, Y., Chen, C., Rosenthal, R.A., Moses, M. and Folkman, J. (1994). Angiostatin: A novel angiogenesis inhibitor that mediates the suppression of metastases by a Lewis lung carcinoma. *Cell,* 79(2): 315–328.

Ozigbo, N.C. (2012). The implications of human resources management and organizational culture adoption on knowledge management practices in Nigerian oil and gas industry. *Communications of the IIMA,* 12(1): 91–104.

Pellissier, R. (2011). The implementation of resilience engineering to enhance organizational innovation in a complex environment. *International Journal of Business and Management,* 6(1): 145–164.

Ramlall, S. (2004). A review of employee motivation theories and their implications for employee retention within organizations. *The Journal of American Academy of Business, Cambridge.*

Riad, S. (2007). Of mergers and *cultures*: What happened to shared values and joint assumptions? *Journal of Organizational Change Management*, 20(1): 26–43.

Rokeach, M. (1973). *The Nature of Human Values.* Vol. 438. New York: Free press.

Schein, E.H. (1992). Organizational culture and leadership. New Jersey: John Wiley & Sons.

Somech, A. and Drach Zahavy, A. (2011). Translating team creativity to innovation implementation. *Journal of Management,* 39: 684–708.

Tushman, Michael L. and O'Reilly, Charles A. (1997). Winning through innovation: A practical guide to leading organizational change and renewal. Boston, MA: Harvard University Press. Web. 19 Feb. 2014. *<http://www.mindtools.com/pages/article/newPPM_94.htm>.*

Yang, R.S., Zhuo, X.Z. and Yu, H.Y. (2009). Organization theory and management: Cases, measurements and industrial applications. Taipei Yeh-Yeh.

Yukul, G.A. (2002). Leadership in organizations, Prentice Hall.

13

The Need for Facilities Managers in Adopting Energy Consumption Behavioural Assessment for Malaysian Universities

Mohd Hafizal B. Ishak[1]*

ABSTRACT

Towards sustainable universities, energy consumption behaviour is one of the several matters that require attention by the facilities manager. Information on energy consumption behaviour helps on developing a good strategy for energy management. Therefore, this chapter proposes an energy consumption behavioural assessment of Malaysian universities students through an 'energy culture' framework. It is an approach that behaviour seen as an amalgam of 'material culture', 'cognitive norms', and 'energy practice'. The components interact together to produce a self-reinforcing system that becomes characterized by strong habits. The objective is to recognize the potential of the framework for assessing energy consumption behaviour. It recommended that energy culture framework to be practices as basis for assessing the energy consumption behaviour. Furthermore, the assessment requires further exploration in

[1] Department of Real Estate Management, Faculty of Technology Management and Business, Universiti Tun Hussein Onn Malaysia, 86400 Parit Raja, Batu Pahat, Johor Darul Takzim, Malaysia.

* *Corresponding author*: E-mail: mhafizal@uthm.edu.my

the future where several issues were emerged other than theoretical mainframe issue.

***Key words*:** Energy consumption, Behaviour, Assessment, Energy culture, Universities.

---

1. INTRODUCTION

Electricity is a form of energy which is very important and very useful in everyday life, even in the smallest and most simple. It is fast, quiet, inexpensive and easily converted, divided or combined. High dependence on electricity has created a range of issues such as global warming problem[1]. Control use is an option to create a more livable community[2]. However, this is very difficult to implement in practice. Two energy-saving options have been studied in the literature: physical installation of energy-efficient appliances and approach behavior[3]. The cheapest option is to understand and change individual behavior regarding energy consumption. This approach has many advantages; However, the complexity of the variables have left many gaps and needs further exploration[4].

In universities, students are the main group responsible for wasting energy[5]. Use of energy (electricity) and lifestyle are key factors contributing to the increase in energy consumption. Towards sustainable campus, one option is to assess the students' perspective through their behaviour. However, lack of knowledge about behaviours related to energy consumption has become an obstacle to this goal. It leads to the unspecified behavioural pattern and uncertainty of potential energy savings that can obtain through behavioural aspects. Therefore, the assessment of energy consumption behaviour is necessary.

'Energy consumption behaviour' studies have not typically focused on universities but have instead tended to focus on the housing sector and industry[6]. This is supported by the previous studies, that lack of discussion about energy consumption behaviour in large organisations[7]. Knowledge about energy consumption behaviour is particularly important for facilities managers in the universities. It enables the university to have the correct approach on developing strategies and programs towards energy saving.

1.1 Issues in Relation to Energy Consumption Behaviour Studies

Lutzenhiser[8] suggested that energy consumption embedded in cultural processes. In order to assess the lifestyle aspect and its relation to energy consumption, the cultural dimension must be the mainframe. Therefore, this study suggests an energy consumption behavioural assessment for Malaysian public universities students through an 'energy culture' framework.

It is an approach; that behaviour is seen as an amalgam of 'material culture', 'cognitive norms', and 'energy practice'. The components interact together to produce a self-reinforcing system that becomes characterized by strong habits[4]. However, before this discussion is extended to the main aspects of the use of 'energy culture', study key issues need to be understood first.

Previous researchers have concentrated on 'direct' data (energy consumption data) (*e.g.,* electricity bills, growth rate). It is used to analyse the pattern of energy consumption[9–12]. These types of data describe only the general pattern of energy consumption without taking into consideration the 'indirect' aspect (internal behaviour of individuals). It supported by earlier studies in which the end-use data is not fully exploited by the other researchers, creating an obstacle to the analysis of individual energy consumption[13].

There are several advantages to consolidating the direct and indirect aspect of individual energy consumption. This approach is not only able to explain the relevant energy consumption pattern, but also the factors that affect energy consumption. This has been done by some researchers that include 'indirect' aspect in their assessment of the energy consumption behaviour pattern[14–19]. Although it is a good method, previous researchers rarely test a range of behavioural factors together but tend to focus on a few factors only, such as demographics and energy practice. Despite this focus on demographic factors and energy practice, there are still no consistent analytical results. Other factors that influence energy consumption behaviour, such as building regulations, comfort, education, environmental concerns and social aspirations, and cannot be best explained by previous studies. It is difficult to find researchers who can produce results that replicate those of previous researchers. It resulted in weaknesses in the knowledge and information on the energy consumption behaviour and the factors influencing it.

Another particular aspect of the research on energy consumption behaviour is found to be less emphasized. Researchers who use billing data or index tend to present patterns of energy consumption in the form of trends and charts (*e.g.*, the cumulative percentage compared to the level of energy consumption)[10–12]. On the other hand, researchers using individual data tend to segregate energy consumption behaviour patterns either by using percentage/ cumulative consumption (kWh) presented in the form of charts[14–19]. However, the approach cannot segregate the energy consumption pattern in the exact number. It has never been reported before the actual minimum and maximum amount of energy consumption for each behaviour pattern. Furthermore, the current method cannot explain the normal energy consumption.

Exact figures or numbers are important for facilities manager, especially when outlining potential energy savings. It is important in developing a good energy management strategy in the higher education sector. Thus, the econometric model is suitable for implementation. Previous studies have shown econometric model can combine aspects of direct and indirect energy consumption behaviour in a single model. However, as mentioned, the factors that influence energy consumption behaviour are not as well tested. Previous researchers have focused less on certain aspects of econometric models, especially in terms of a combination of direct and indirect factors. Furthermore, it has focused on the conceptual model, which describes the behavioural intentions [20–24]. The models tend to suggest behavioural change as a strategy for saving energy. However, it is difficult for this model to show the cumulative amount (kWh/$) of potential savings expected to result from behavioural change. The econometric models not only help to predict energy consumption and behaviour patterns, but can be used as a tool to assess the potential for energy savings.

Issues on 'direct' and 'indirect' data; factors that influence energy consumption behaviour; pattern segregation and modeling subsequently leads to a knowledge gap of the energy consumption behaviour assessment. For facilities manager, the information on the types of behavioural pattern, factors influencing the patterns, energy consumption prediction, normal energy consumption and potential energy saving are valuable. The information helps on energy management process in the universities.

2. ENERGY CONSUMPTION BEHAVIOUR

Economic psychology is part of human life. It combines the two major disciplines of psychology and economics. Psychologists tend to use a "synthetic science" approach rather than "scientific analysis". They listen to what people say and describe their behaviour. Psychologists believe that choice is determined not only by economic factors but by attitudes, values and beliefs. Therefore, another discipline was developed and is known as social psychology. This is the beginning of economic psychology.

Social psychology deals with how the thoughts, beliefs, attitudes and emotions of an individual are influenced or determined by behaviour or specific characters[25]. This discipline uses techniques and ideas from sociology and philosophy. It holds that at every level, the laws governing behaviour are orderly and able to be understood. There are three main concepts in social psychology; attitude; people's explanation of their own behaviour; and the comparisons they make between themselves and other people[26]. These concepts have been widely discussed and have generated several famous theories within social psychology including social facilitation theory, consistency theory, equity theory and attribution theory. However, these are not fully-fledged theories but serve as guiding ideas[25].

There are several reasons highlighted by Lea *et al.*[26] for the establishment economic psychology. They include: personality may be crucial to economic behaviour; motivation or previous learning may affect how we spend or save; social context may determine the extent to which we gamble or give; cognition and perception may influence our susceptibility to advertising; and our biological and genetic state may influence our spending priorities. These are the important reasons that social psychology is so important for understanding economic behaviour.

Through behavioural economics, consumers have been conditioned through the media to act in a certain way, or associate certain aspects or emotions with a product. According to the Behavioural Perspective model, consumer choice will be influenced by various stimuli, for example, with regard to information. Information may suffice to persuade a consumer to act in a certain way; or 'aversive' stimuli may persuade a consumer to act to avoid a negative outcome[27,28]. Cultural and societal influences will help determine the behaviour[28,29]. Cultural compatibility has been proven to affect the adoption process[30]. This research takes the advice of the Behavioural Economic and Behavioural Perspective Models in order to assess energy consumption behaviour.

Cottrell[31] cited that, energy must be defined in terms of the ways in which it manifests itself. It is variously classified as heat, light, sound, radio, radar, TV, electricity, magnetism, mechanical energy, growth, and even "matter". It has been difficult for the layman to accept that this range represents different manifestations of the same thing. Hence, to do justice to the concept of energy, it requires treating each of its manifestations as it is treated by experts in that particular field.

Energy consumption behaviour can be defined as the total energy use of the occupant from both human and physical characteristics. The statement is aligned with Hitchcock's[21] explanation from Stafford[32] and Cramer *et al.*[33] who stated that:

> *"Buildings per se do not consume energy; rather people living and working in building use energy"* – Stafford[32]

> *"Human attitudes, income and intentions do not directly consume electricity. Rather they influence how the physical devices are operated"* – Cramer *et al.*[33]

These early statements strongly agreed that user behaviour is the key to explaining energy consumption. It has to combine the physical elements (*e.g.*, the building's characteristics, appliances, etc.) and the human variables (*e.g.*, beliefs, demographic, lifestyle, etc.) in order to measure the energy consumption behaviour. Other researchers also view energy consumption behaviour as demand which serves to explain the needs and preferences of individuals in terms of their energy use[20,22,34,35].

The remains need to explain energy consumption behaviour. Although it has been studied since 70s, when the popularity of the topic was rising, many unexplained elements still exist. Lately, the trend in energy studies has shifted towards a conservation focus. A high level of awareness among researchers regarding global warming problem means that energy consumption behaviour research is again taking place, where an assessment of the micro aspects of behaviour is required in order to develop strategic policy and programs for reducing energy demand. However, as reported in the literature, model development was found to be lacking, especially in terms of determining exact figures, which are not provided by the conceptual model which is generally used in relation to this topic.

2.1. Lifestyle as the Main Frame

People's lifestyle affects energy consumption in a significant way, due to both cultural and social variables[36]. 'Lifestyle' is originally a sociological term that has developed many meanings. Lifestyle is defined as "distinctive modes of existence that are accomplished by persons and groups through socially sanctioned and culturally intelligible pattern of action" [8,37]. The concept is famous in marketing studies and has long been used in consumer research and advertising. In energy research, it refers to the combination of culture, social class, consumer choices, behaviour, historical trends, and marketing that determines energy end-use[38]. The relevance of lifestyle to energy consumption is illustrated by findings that similarly structured households with identical physical shells are associated with widely varying energy usage[37].

Lifestyle is usually conceptualized as a consumption pattern influenced by decisions at various points across the lifespan, such as what profession to engage in, where to live, when (or whether) to marry and have kids, and more proximal choices regarding what types of electrical appliances to buy, and how and when to consume the energy[37,39]. Thus, this concept suggested that that analysis of lifestyle and energy consumption needs to encompass not only the traditional demographic segmentation elements, but also the information about types of appliances the individual owns and how they use them[37]. Furthermore, through understanding lifestyles, better public policy can be designed in relation to energy[40].

The energy aspect of lifestyle has generated much attention from researchers. One of the intentions is the greater number of research of the integrating models. Aims of the integrating models are to seek the driver of behaviour, and show relationship between drivers. Early studies have examined household energy use in term of their energy behaviour related. The aims were to model the energy use from the residential towards energy conservation[20]. These include their socio-demographic factors, family life-style; energy prices; energy related behaviour; cost benefit trade-offs; effectives and responsibility; feedback;

information and home characteristic discussed in term of ventilation and temperature perspective.

The focus is 'energy-related behaviour' which consists of three main factors including purchase related, usage related and maintenance related behaviour[20]. Purchase related behaviour focuses on the purchase of household appliances, heating equipment and ventilation equipment and is related to the choice process when buying. Usage related behaviour refers to the day to day usage of appliances in the home including frequency, duration and intensity of the use. Maintenance related behaviour refers to activities dedicated to maintaining the in-home heating system and appliances, and includes servicing, small repairs and home improvements. The present study is interested in educating people through feedback about their energy use and an evaluation of their behaviour. The study offers a deeper understanding of household behaviour related to energy usage.

Dholakia *et al.*[34] develop a theoretical framework for a macro-micro energy consumption behaviour model. The framework was based on household energy behaviour. In the framework, the important factor in determining energy consumption behaviour is choice. The theoretical framework shows how the macro level such as socialization, psycho-economic factors and policy interact and affect people's behaviour towards the available alternatives. Based on this framework, household energy consumption pattern can be explained by three dimensions: the social relations of consumption (individual *vs.* collective consumption denote the polarities of this dimension); the domain of availability (private *vs.* goods); and human involvement (passive *vs.* active types of consumption).

In the same article, Dholakia *et al.*[34] also highlight that the micro level of energy consumption is important for capturing the "per capita" not only because it has strong relationship with consumption but also with conservation. Conservation programs have an impact on consumer awareness of energy problems, but only small effects on actual energy use behaviour. Hence, the best conservation method will work best if it provides an economic incentive. The assessment of individual energy consumption will provide strong benefits not only at a household level but also for large organizations such as universities, especially on strategic policy. Again Dholakia *et al.*[34] suggest that by focusing on the levels of energy use behaviour, a comprehensive energy policy can be developed which includes:

a) Familiar strategies that are more relevant in terms of communication, persuasion and behaviour;
b) Re-socialization and cost benefit policy that will be made more relevant by giving more attention to economic considerations and reducing psychological inconvenience; and
c) Structural changes by which multiple consumption patterns become socially and politically viable and available to the consumer to choose.

There are some other models that provide an integrated approach from other disciplines. Hitchcock[21] proposes an integrated descriptive framework for energy use and behaviour based on system theory. The framework integrates the engineering and social science of energy use. The discuss highlight question from a household perspective where the physical and the human are correlated to produce a pattern of energy use. In the framework, the physical is the driver of technical change while the human is driven by social change.

The physical system involves parameters and variables. The parameters are defined as the static characteristic of a building such as size, materials, heating system and stock of appliances. The variables are defined as dynamic characteristics such as internal temperatures, ventilation rates, amount of hot water consumed and the use of appliances. The system is the set of characteristics of the physical dwelling and can be calculated as total energy used. The human system consists of the demographic, biophysical and psychological variables. Biophysical variables are the physical characteristics of the body which determine physical comfort: metabolic rate, respiration, clothing etc. Demographics relate to income, social status, number of occupants etc. Psychological variables relate to the individual and include beliefs, attitudes, knowledge and personalities.

Through the systems, Hitchcock[21] also highlighted that there are other variables that comprise the household environment. Three major elements are the climate system, the economic system and the cultural system. The climate system includes the external temperatures, insulation, wind, shelter and the demands of heating and lighting. The economic system includes the price, tax structure and other economic regulations. The culture system consists of general beliefs held by society and environmental issues, comfort, consumption habits etc.

Two main perspectives highlighted are the engineering perspective and social perspective[21]. From the engineering perspective, the model was to give an understanding of the physical processes carried out in a dwelling and how energy was consumed. It gives an understanding of the household's physical and mechanical systems. For example, how in flow and output in the building's heat system have reached equilibrium? The engineering model predominantly deals with physical subsystem of the household and the climate system of the environment, but fails to describe human elements of the household system. On the other hand, the social perspective is based on human phenomena and very focused on the human sub-system within the economic and cultural systems.

Three main types of model which come from a social perspective: cultural and social models, demographic and economic models, and psychological models[21]. Cultural and social needs models relate to the relationship between the fundamentals of energy use and social behaviour. They determine patterns of behaviour and the needs generated by those patterns. Demographic and economic models describe the demographic character of households and the economic system of the environment. They use the economic factors to explain the energy demand. Psychological models explain the cultural system in the environment in order to understand behaviour, attitudes and the effect of information. There continue to be discussions about the social perspective model especially in terms of its lack of attention to direct energy use. It found that only model to head somewhat in this direction was the cultural and social need model. However like the other two, it did not attempt to deal with energy use directly.

Wilk[22] promotes the 'multigenic' model of energy consumption. The multigenic model incorporates three main theories, first is the individual choice theories, second is social theories and finally a cultural theory with the goal of developing effective policymaking, and knowing what determines and change energy consumption levels. The major obstacle highlighted for changing consumption was the existence of social rules, that is, social desires and needs. Hence, Wilk[22] proposed three approaches to consumption including habits, naturalization and cultivation. The 'multigenic' model of analysis explored connects energy consumption behaviour to gender relations within the family, community governance institutions, health and nutrition and property development regulations. Other researchers have also combined several energy consumption models such as Keirstead[41] who introduced the

'Actor-Network Theory'. Keirstead[41] reviewed five models of energy consumption behaviour: the behavioural model[20]; the political economic model[34]; the cultural model[42]; the system approach[21]; and the global consumption model[22] as examples of the domestic energy consumption field. In the paper, Keirstead[41] introduced an integrated framework of domestic energy consumption that acknowledges the expertise of disciplinary approaches (*e.g.,* social and behavioural factors).

Barr and Gilg[23] developed the 'multi-factorial model'. The model was constructed based on social and environmental variables, situational variables and psychological variables, and focused on filling the gap between behaviour and behavioural intention. The major focus of this model is the attitudes toward environmental behaviour. The model shows correlation between variables on behaviour and behavioural intention from purchase, habitual and recycling behaviour. Wilson and Dowlatabadi[43] proposed a different model of behavioural drivers in residential energy use, focusing on decision making in relation to social and technological influences. They highlighted the unexplored potential of reconciling the theoretical preferences of different research traditions, adding to other integrative approaches that have been proposed in the past. It appears from the studies discussed here that the most challenging task is to combine the economic and sociological bases for behaviour.

The impetus for this research came from the studies of Lutzenhiser[42,44]. The idea of an 'Energy Culture' was first introduced by Lutzenhiser[42,44] for household energy consumption. Lutzenhiser[42] discussed the cultural model of energy consumption. The cultural model was based on four dimensions of energy consumption: engineering, economic, psychology and anthropology.

Engineering models focus on the physical aspect of human action, such as "normal" or everyday behaviour and routine. Measurements within engineering models tend to be based on simulation and real-world systems[44]. These were able to create the concept of "energy service" which imputes self-conscious rationality to energy use. However, Lutzenhiser's review reveals that the explanation of this concept is still unclear. The nature of the engineering model is that it relates to planning and management[45]. It seeks to provide an optimum allocation rule for a particular objective function and set of inequality constraints. It tends to function better as an allocation and accounting tool for the purpose of setting allocation rules to achieve a given optimum energy usage, under given constraints.

Another aspect of the engineering model, and one of its strengths, is its ability to provide demand forecasting. The assumption is that the "normal consumer also directs attention away from variations in current consumption, and weakens their capacities to predict long-term changes in behaviour, lifestyle and energy demand"[44].

There are several deficits in the engineering model in terms of its inability to explain energy consumption behaviour. Engineering models deal with the hardware of energy consumption and its efficiencies. This type of focus gives an accurate prediction of energy consumption and an understanding of closely defined parameters. However, it does not offer an understanding of fully human action or motivation.

Next is the economic model. Economic modelling underpins economic theory. In relation to economic or econometric modelling that a regression equation is not necessarily an econometric model[46]. The results of an econometric estimation–which may in fact be a simple regression equation–are interpreted in light of the theory. For example, an equation estimates energy-GDP electricity, and correlates analyses of one variable with another. The econometric model provides an input-output framework which is not based on a traditional fixed coefficient but is functionally related to relative input price change specifications. Projections of final demand elements such as consumption investment activities are provided from long-term macro-economic growth which is also econometrically estimated.

With regard to energy use the economic model basically discusses rationality among users. It considers how people act according to a set of reasoned actions designed to maximize some utility function[42]. It can be seen in the link between price and behaviour, for example, response to price and the notion of a discount rate in personal investment decisions[47]. The economist seeks a measure of price elasticity to understand the relationship between price and demand but this does not say much about the underlying behavioural process. Policy action which addresses information issues may be more effective in changing consumption behaviour than adjustments to price[47].

Psychological models relate to attitudes. Attitude is not a good predictor of energy efficiency behaviour[42]. In Bell *et al.*[47] who cited

Stanley *et al.*[48] works, it is argued that an understanding of attitudes and norms plays an important part in explaining energy efficiency behaviour. The psychological model is concerned with the provision of information and the way in which users understand their energy use, and suggests closer links with actual behaviour[47]. However, this model is not well developed in the literature and it lacks supporting information.

Finally, the sociological model of behaviour considers the behaviour of individuals in making decisions, for example whether to insulate or turn down the thermostat or to accept their lot and be cold. It is concerned with the dynamic behaviour of human groups. Compared to the psychological models, the sociological model raises difficult questions about the sharing of energy between groups in society in an equitable way. Much of the concern with fuel poverty is of this nature. The existences of fuel poverty, when there are obvious technical solutions which would make many people better off while not making others worse off, requires an understanding of the social forces which operate either to bring about change or to prevent it. It is a combination of these types of model which was proposed by Lutzenhiser[42] who argues that material culture such as buildings, furnishings, technology etc. interweaves with "roles, relationships, conventional understandings, rules and beliefs into the cultural practices of groups", in other words that "lifestyle" can

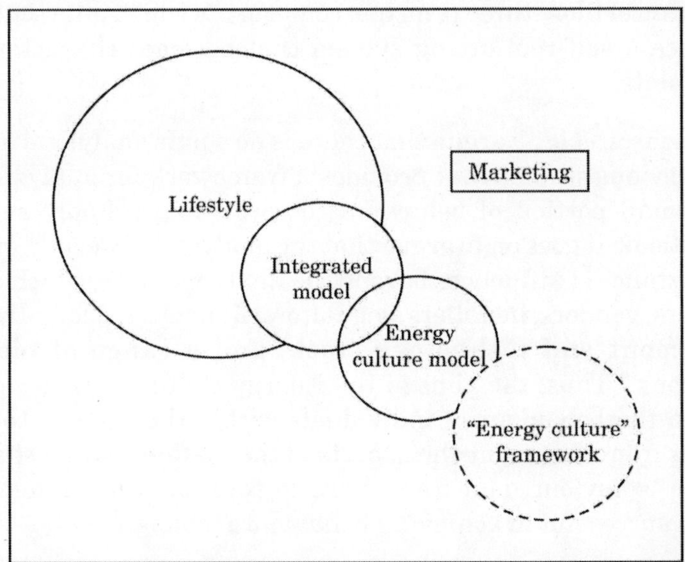

Fig. 1: Flow of energy culture development. *Source*: Ishak[2]

explain the energy consumption within an organization. The promising part of the cultural model is that it can be beneficially applied for descriptive, explanatory and predictive purposes. By assessing these three applications, a systematic understanding of how the group behaves can be captured.

3. ENERGY CULTURE FRAMEWORK

Energy culture as drawn by Lutzenhiser[44] is only a concept. Stephenson *et al.*[4] draws on a wide range of literature on energy behaviour and attempts to use a systems perspective. While the approach acknowledges an important sociological influence from practice theory it also has strong links to lifestyle research in marketing. Research by Stephenson *et al.*[4] is the first that attempt to realize the idea of energy culture empirically.

"Culture" here refers to the diversity of values, beliefs, knowledge, practice, technology and other cultural determinants that exist within any given society[4]. The 'Energy Cultures' approach developed has some interesting parallels to all these approaches[4]. They proposed that different integrated patterns of behaviour–similar to 'lifestyles'–should be identifiable based on the differences in material culture, cognitive norms and everyday practices. In this approach, behaviour is seen as an amalgam of those three principal components which interact together to produce a self-reinforcing system that becomes characterized by strong habits.

Stephenson *et al.*[4] argue that there is no single analytical approach in the previous studies that provides a framework for analyzing more than a small portion of behaviour, or providing reliably successful interventions. It goes on to argue that the analysis by Stern[49] overlooks the importance of influences beyond the final consumer, which includes "producers, vendors, installers, regulators, financiers, a long-lived built environment and technology stock, and a range of ideas and motivations." Thus, the aims of the Energy Cultures framework is to centre on the behaviour of individuals within the system, to explore outwards from that point the aspects of the system that most strongly influence behaviour, and from there to consider what interventions might be successful in achieving behavioural change.

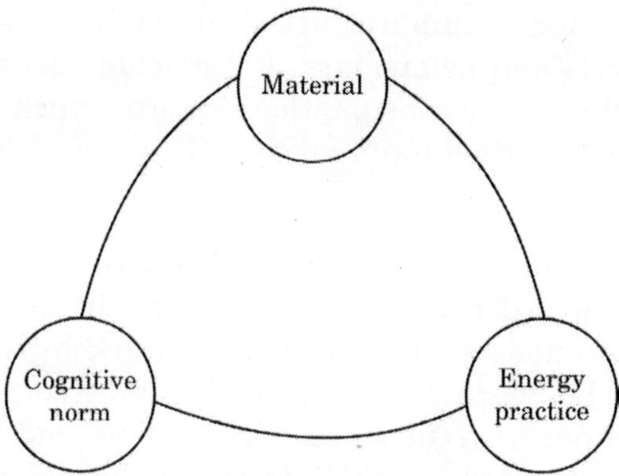

Fig. 2: Energy cultures framework by Stephenson *et al.*[4]

The framework in Fig. 2 suggests that consumer energy behaviour can be understood at its fundamental level by examining the interactions between cognitive norms, material culture and energy practice[4].

Basically, Energy cultures are in turn interwoven with roles, relationships, conventional understanding, rules and beliefs into the cultural practices of groups living in particular natural environments[44]. Stephenson *et al.*[4] proposed that material culture has a significant role in shaping outcomes. Gathered from Actor–Network theory, the material world and its objects create a network of dynamic interactions which drive both stability and change[50,51]. Thus, the material culture of a household or an industry can be understood as a technical system in its own right. Cognitive norms strongly influence people's choice of technologies and the practices that they undertake. Cognitive norms can be understood as an attitude/value/belief system[4]. Energy practices determine how technologies are used, and also partly shape people's belief and understandings. Energy practices can be systematically understood as the interactions between individual, social and institutional behaviour[4].

3.1. Behavioural Pattern

'Lifestyle' was introduced to marketing research as system concept. One of its aims in the system was to profile the lifestyles of consumers[52]. In marketing studies people/buyers were categorised into different groups in order to seek buyer capability in relation to the product, and identify the target market of a product[53,54]. The same concept is used in this study, where students are divided into several energy consumption levels and behaviours. A particular behaviour pattern indicates a certain energy consumption pattern, which can be used in program and policy development in HEIs for reducing energy consumption.

Three recommended users are proposed here: high, medium and low energy users. In order to capture the patterns of student behaviour, several key references such as the early work by Van Raaij and Verhallen[35] and Louviere and Hensher[55] that introduced the concept of 'lifestyle', together with the recent work of Paço and Varejão[56] and Yohanis[57] have provided insight into energy behaviour studies and are helpful for this stage of development.

Behavioural patterns are groups of related behaviours which describe how people behave[58]. With energy consumption behaviour, these patterns were difficult to describe compared to other energy behaviours such as conservation and energy saving. In energy behaviour studies, there are many researchers who have determined behavioural patterns particularly from a household perspective. These studies also have different point of views and different approaches in accessing and categorizing these patterns.

3.1.1. *Temperature and ventilation perspective*

This perspective has been widely discussed and was given great attention by researchers within engineering and economic modelling studies. Van Raaij and Verhallen[35] studied the residential energy behaviour patterns of home temperature and ventilation. Five clusters of behaviour patterns have been examined: conservers, spenders, cool, warm and average. Conservers use less energy, while spenders use more energy than the average group. The cool and warm clusters use less energy than the average group. This clustering approach is arrived at by looking at the socio-demographic and attitudinal variables: home temperature while at home, home temperature during absence from home, airing rooms, and the use of hall door. Andersen *et al.*[59] used standard behaviour patterns to predict indoor environment responses such as window opening behaviour and heating. It found that ventilation and heating behaviour is influenced by perception, gender and ownership. The result could be interpreted as behavioural differences between the summer and winter periods.

Santin[58] discussed energy consumption for heating and ventilation as the main concerns of the paper. His examination of behaviour categories showed that: 'spenders' used more space, more electronics, more hours of heating, more hours of ventilation, and had no energy saving concern; 'affluent cool' used more space, more hours of ventilation; 'conscious warm' used more space, more electronics, more hours of heating, fewer hours of ventilation, and showed concern for energy saving; 'comfort' used more electronics, more hours of heating, more hours of ventilation; and 'convenience cool' used more electronics and more hours of ventilation. The patterns were similar to the earlier findings in terms of climate perspective, indicating consistent findings within this area[35].

3.1.2. *The appliances and devices perspective*

In explaining resource consumption researchers have generally used the activity of the building occupant to measure their behaviour. The activity measured includes general activities at home such as cooking, sleeping, watching TV. Duration and frequency was measured to give a full understanding of the occupant's interaction with their environment. For example, Papakostas and Sotiropoulos[14] used the occupancy approach for determining energy behaviour patterns. They found that the use of electrical appliances and occupant activities influenced the generation of heat in the residence. Al-Mumin *et al.*[16] studied the activity patterns of occupants in Kuwait residences with regard to electrical appliances such as lights, television sets, personal computers and vacuum cleaners. Their study used the occupancy pattern approach, in which an individual's hourly use of appliances is recorded. In the study, patterns are shown by a timeline in every zone of the house such as the living room, bedroom, kitchen and bathrooms.

Tso and Yau[15] studied domestic energy use patterns in Hong Kong. A two phase self-administered diary survey was used in this study. The patterns were separated into summer months and winter months, and a large difference in energy consumption was found between the two. Paauw *et al.*[60] developed an Energy Pattern Generator (EPG) using occupancy patterns. In the study, Paauw *et al.*[60] combined the technical and architectural characteristics (heating, lighting, etc.) with household behaviour (household characteristics). Four types of profile were proposed as drivers for energy demand: convenience–based on the need for comfort, with no interest in energy use, money, or the environment;

conscious–choices were made based on comfort, but with awareness of the consequences for the environment and personal finances; costs–this group was aware of the energy costs and consumed as little energy as possible to save money; and climate–choices were made entirely out of concern for the environment. Yohanis[57] studied household energy behaviour and domestic energy use. Household demographic characteristics were recorded together with numbers of appliance with frequency and duration of use. On the other hand, the paper added the variable of 'energy saving.' It was found that the general awareness of energy issues was high within the observed households. However, the implementation of energy efficiency measures did not match the claims of awareness.

3.1.3. *The environmental perspective*

The environmental perspective was much discussed in relation to 'green segmentation' by the marketing field. The purpose of segmentation is to identify who are 'green consumers' based on their attitude and environmental concerns[61–63]. Furthermore, these type of study use psychological variables (*e.g.*, belief, awareness, habit, etc.) combined with demographic variables (*e.g.*, age, gender, education, etc.)[64]. Eleni[65] cited that environmental information feedback and consciousness of energy problems are characteristics of the energy-saver. Such environmental variables are environment-friendly buying behaviour, activism, knowledge and concern[66]. Paço and Varejão[56] outline the theme of saving energy resources (relationship with conservation of the environment) and the important role played by the consumer market in the adoption of environmentally-friendly behaviour at the level of energy resource saving. In the study, two categories of people are determined: the "saver", or environmentally friendly consumer and "non-cares" or less environmentally friendly consumers. Based on demographic variables, it was found that females contribute more as "savers" than males in terms of household energy use behaviour.

3.1.4. *The value perspective*

Vringer *et al.*[67] determine the values pattern from household energy requirements based on the WIN-model. Based on the analysis, consumers with more individualistic value patterns, such as 'hedonists', 'conservatives' and 'materialists' are less focused on social problems like climate change than consumers with more collective value patterns such as the broad-minded and socially minded. They found no significant difference in the energy consumption of groups of households with different value patterns. However, they also found that families that were least motivated to save energy and used 4% more energy. Poortinga *et al.*[68] studied household preferences for energy saving measures. It found that different socio-demographic groups and people with different environmental concerns preferred different types of energy saving measures. Average acceptability of energy saving measures varied among people with different environmental concerns (*e.g.*, single, senior and low-income households were less willing to apply energy saving measure at home).

Gilg and Barr[69] found four types of environmentalists in relation to water and energy saving in the home: committed, mainstream, occasional and non-environmentalist. They argued that all of these groups were related to levels of perceived comfort, commitment and sacrifice. Again, the differences reflected their lifestyle choice. Eleni[65] who developed an empirical model to investigate the main determinants of household energy conservation patterns in Greece by employing cross-section data, explains that socio-economic variables (*e.g.*, consumer income and family size) are suitable for explaining differences in energy conservation preferences.

3.1.5. *The energy consumption behaviour perspective*

In terms of individual behavioural patterns, discussion mainly focuses on the characteristics of the patterns. There are two types of pattern that are frequently discussed in the literature: the "high" energy user and the "low" energy user. The differences can be explained by the factors present in their particular energy culture. Overall differences in the energy consumption behaviour pattern are explained in Fig. 3.

The building regulations factor explains that "high" energy users were less supportive of the law compliance within a society[70]. In relation to the environmental concern factor, the "high" energy user lacked energy awareness and was less environmental friendly[56,58], compared to "low" energy user, who was highly motivated around environmental concerns and energy issues.

Social aspiration factors show that the "high" energy user demonstrates no interest in practising energy saving behaviour[71], with personal wealth also playing a significant role here[70]. On the other

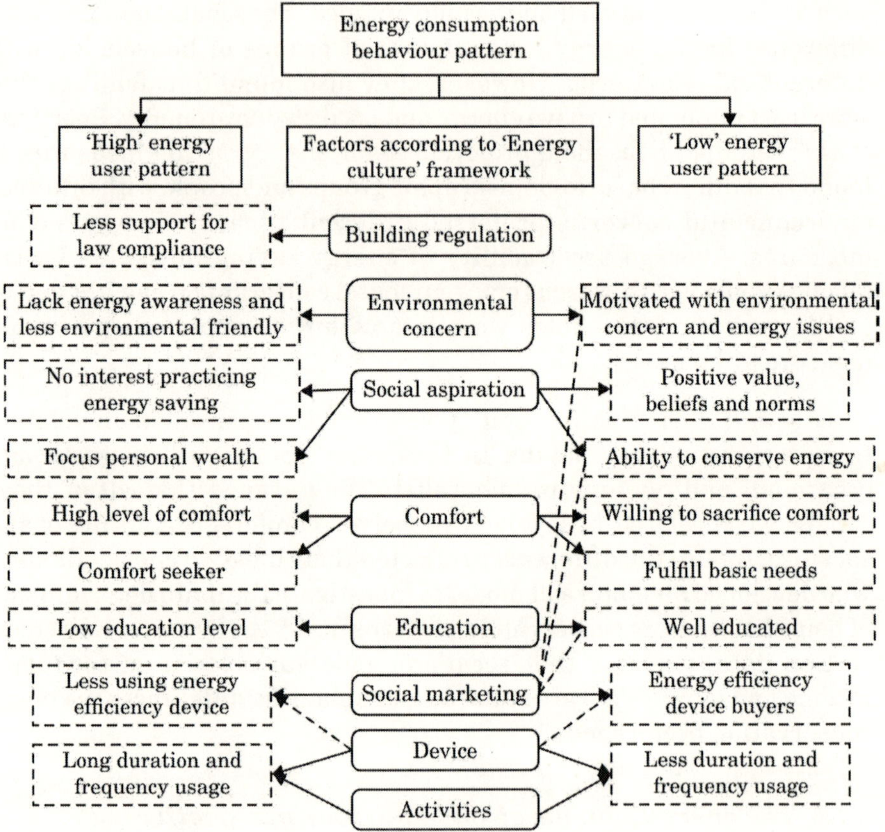

Fig. 3: Energy consumption behaviour pattern based on literature

hand, "low" energy users, have a positive attitude to energy usage[63,72–76]. This type of user has the ability to conserve energy[77] and basically has positive internal values, beliefs and norms[49]. In general, the individual in this group has a sense of obligation or duty to take measures against environmental deterioration[78,79]. These positive beliefs translated into behaviour such as energy saving practices[80].

"High" and "low" energy users also can be differentiated by comfort factors. The "high" energy user seeks high levels of comfort in the comfort hierarchy pyramid such described by[22,35]. Compared to the "low" energy user, who has the ability to sacrifice their level of comfort and fulfil only their basic needs[81].

There is no detailed examination of the way users sacrifice comfort levels, however, from the energy conservation studies; fulfilling basic needs can be interpreted to mean the use of natural energy such as daylight, window opening. The studies explained that, without operating installed light, or air-conditioning, the users found their environment already comfortable enough for their daily activities[68,82–86].

Education level differences also differentiate the “high” and “low” energy user. “High” energy users tended to demonstrate a low level of education about environmental issues. They lacked clear information and knowledge about energy saving[81]. This was distinct from “low” energy users, who tended to be well educated people with a high level of energy saving awareness and a well developed knowledge of environment issues[28,30,64,68,87,88].

Social marketing has never been specifically interpreted in the literature. However, it can be explained through the level of acceptance of energy marketing. For example, the “high” energy user appeared in the “no-cares” behaviour patterns of consumers who had no conscious intention related to environmental issues and used non energy-efficient devices. The opposite was the case for “low” energy users[56]. This is discussed in the context of consumer studies, where researchers have found that the buying process as it relates to energy efficient products and processes has a strong correlation with high environmental concern in the consumer[81,89–91].

Devices and activities have a direct relationship with energy consumption and are the most discussed factor in the literature. Van Raaij and Verhallen[35] and Azar and Menassa[92] determined that the “high” energy user is the one who use more electronics, and more hours of heating and ventilation. The same question was also tested by Santin[58] and the result was found to be the same. In terms of devices, “high” energy users use less energy efficient devices, frequently and for a long duration[58,93]. “Low” energy users used their devices infrequently and for a short duration[58,92,93].

Based on discussion above, there are several perspectives on behaviour pattern determination which have been developed in relation to energy use. In this research, focus was given to the general pattern and influencing factors. In accessing these patterns, a combination of engineering (physical) and social variables were found to be the best options discussed in the literature. This combined concept has never been attempted in universities for assessing student energy behaviour patterns. However, since the assessment have in the past been based on households, and not all the variables (*e.g.*, demographic variables) can be used for determining the energy consumption behaviour patterns (*e.g.*, income) from the university's student. Other variables such as heating systems were also not suitable variables to be studied in tropical regions like Malaysia. For this reason only selected and relevant variables can be used for assessing energy consumption behaviour among Malaysian universities.

4. ADOPTING THE CONCEPT TO FACILITIES MANAGEMENT

Facilities management (FM) is defined as covering business organization, people, premises, service's working environment and resources[94]. The objective of FM departments is to coordinate the physical environment and people in order to create an overall environment that strongly supports the aims of the organization[95–97].

FM is the department within a university which has responsibility for implementing any Energy Management strategy. Elmualim *et al.*[98] cited that the FM industry was found to lack relevant knowledge and skills. FM has not yet been fully recognised as profession within the UK and the role of the FM is both diverse and inconsistent, so that the experiences of managers across sectors are not readily comparable.

In FM, energy management is one of the building operations and maintenance aspect[99,100]. Energy management was define as a technical and management function the remit of which is to monitor, record, analysis, critically examine, alter and control energy flows through systems so that energy is utilized with maximum efficiency. It embraced the disciples of engineering, science, mathematics, economic, accountancy, design and operational research, computation and information technology[101].

Energy management is not a one off exercise, but needs to be an on-going process in order to be effective[102]. There are five steps to effective energy management: commitment (*e.g.*, policy to promote energy efficiency and keep carbon dioxide emissions to a minimum); understanding, or establishing the facts (*e.g.*, data related to the high cost of fuel should be analysed); planning and organizing, (target setting and encouragement of the staff to participate); action – such as conducting an energy walk-round to feel the assessment process; and control, monitoring and reviewing which promotes continual improvement[102].

The most important part of energy management is the evaluation of consumption patterns and identification of specific energy saving measures[10]. One of the energy management tools used to help building owner/manager to manage the energy usage efficiently is the energy audit[10]. O'Callaghan[101] argued that the energy audit is a fundamental part of energy management of any organization that wishes to control energy costs.

The aim of an energy audit is to obtain a simple but comprehensive 'photograph' of the overall energy flow within a declared system boundary, which may be, for example, a building, or group of buildings[101]. The energy audit can provide important guidelines and insight for energy managers into major areas of energy use, if properly performed. An audit can even lead to immediate savings in some cases, simply by making people aware of how energy is being used. This information is important and can be used by energy managers to guide the formulation of a program, and to establish where the priorities should be placed[103].

The focus of an energy audit in FM is to assess energy consumption patterns and the potential for energy saving within the organisation. Although this method of assessing energy consumption patterns is practical and within the scope of FM, there are limited studies that address the topic. For example, Botsaris and Prebezanos[9] present a technique that can be used to design an energy audit. The method uses energy indices such as the Index of Thermal Charge or Index of Energy Disposition to simulate the heat losses of the building. Haji-Sapar and Lee[10] focus on the benchmarking of energy management in an office building in Singapore. They use 24 monthly electricity bills to evaluate consumption patterns and specific energy saving measures. Stuart *et al.*[11] study the electricity consumption pattern in a secondary school. The research uses billing data which was monitored to identify any changes in patterns. Jamaludin *et al.*[12] present an assessment of the efficiency of electricity usage and potential electricity reduction within the University Malaya, Malaysia. Using annual energy consumption data and the information on the building floor area, they develop baseline data for current electricity usage and potential energy conservation in residential buildings. These researchers used macro energy consumption data through assessing bills, without considering the micro level data of, or individual analysis. Compared to the other fields of studies on energy consumption patterns, the scope of individual analysis has become a major source of discussion.

This has been demonstrated by Papakostas and Sotiropoulos[14], who use individual occupancy data to determine energy behaviour patterns in Greek residences. Furthermore, Tso and Yau[15] assess energy usage patterns using individual daily data regarding energy use and report that local weather and cooking styles have a great influence on energy consumption in Hong Kong. Al-Mumin *et al.*[16] study occupants' behaviour and activity patterns that influence energy consumption in Kuwait. Armstrong *et al.*[17] explore the daily electric load of Canadian housing to generate an electrical demand profile which includes detailed information on appliances, annual consumption targets and occupancy patterns. Almeida *et al.*[18] and Verma *et al.*[19] study consumption patterns based on household activities and potential energy saving. These studies show that individual analysis is the best way to understand energy consumption patterns. They are supported by Fleming[104] who suggested that facilities manager should take advantage of the behavioural approach. This concept could be adopted by an energy audit conducted in HEIs to determine student's energy consumption patterns and the potential for energy saving. Through the audit combination, the team can develop a holistic view of facilities and a strategy for continuous improvement.

Rowley[105] explained that there are six main purposes of higher education including civilization and values, developing and transmitting knowledge, meeting the needs of the economy and industry, meeting the aspirations and needs of the students, serving local and regional governments and performing higher education as tradable activity (international). He pointed out that there are four main elements for developing higher education namely students, academic development, resources/quality and research. In the higher educational environment, facilities refer to the site, buildings, furniture and equipment that contribute to a learning environment[106]. According to Housley[107], it is important for facilities managers to understand the link between the institution's aims and objectives and the various groups in the institution.

For facilities manager, energy is a cost that needs to be managed properly without wasting the organization's resources. As discussed in Chapter One, students are the chief group of energy wasters[5]. Students' lifestyle is a main cause of energy wastage which is mainly a result of their socio-material practices. To reduce energy waste, one of the options is to assess the behavioural perspective of students on their own energy usage. This is the cheapest method when compared to the physical approach (*e.g.*, installing energy efficiency equipment).

Studying energy consumption behaviour at an individual level should be the first step. Yen *et al.*[108] highlight that Malaysian universities' inefficient use of energy and lack of awareness among students have contributed to energy wastage. They suggest that the non-structural method can contribute to energy conservation in Malaysian universities. This viewpoint is also supported by Ting *et al.*[109] and results from the studies of Muhieldeen *et al.*[110]. The findings again demonstrate that university students' behaviour contributes to energy waste although they have a high level understanding of the energy problem[111].

There is little to be found in the literature about individual energy consumption behavioural patterns within the university environment. Lack of analysis on individual energy consumption behavioural patterns has meant a lack of detailed explanation of the factors that affect total energy consumption. Without consideration of these issues, there will be uncertainties in measuring individual energy use and this will lead to the lack of information on potential energy saving.

Facilities manager must investigate energy consumption behaviour patterns within their organization. A similar strategy has occurred in marketing practice where market scanning has been given high priority to ensure the success of product development[54]. In terms of energy consumption behaviour, categorizing the occupant behavioural pattern will help to develop energy saving strategies and programs in the university. The energy consumption pattern of the consumer group will reveal the current conservation landscape.

5. SUMMARY

Based on the prior discussion, the main concern of this chapter is to employ the sequence concept of integrated method and 'energy culture' framework to establish data and consistency issues in energy consumption behaviour. The concept was discussed and tested from a household and industrial perspective, but has never been assessed or applied to student accommodation. For facilities manager, the adoption of this concept is expected to reveal valuable information on energy consumption from a behavioural perspective. Facilities managers in public universities are bound to ensure energy that be managed effectively without hurting the organisation's budget. Thus, the manager must develop a strategy to reduce energy consumption that fits the universities idea of sustainability. Behavioural assessment is one of the possible solutions which can be adopted by universities to save energy.

Policies or programmes can be used as platforms to educate students on energy saving. Researchers has highlight that Malaysian universities' inefficient use of energy and lack of awareness among students have contributed to energy wastage; thus, the suggested behavioural approach is the best solution for energy saving. However, before formulating policy and strategy, fundamental knowledge of the students' behaviour must be acquired and understood.

As stated, the importance of this concept with regard to public universities is how it will reflect and help the facilities management department to manage their energy. The energy consumption behaviour assessment as proposed, in addition to explaining current energy usage, would be able to illustrate the existing patterns of energy consumption behaviour and the characteristics of energy users. The behavioural patterns have the ability of categorising groups of related behaviours which will eventually indicate how people behave[58]. Early research has discovered that pattern categorisation is important in understanding individual behaviour towards energy usage. Hence, with the proposed concept, current energy consumption behaviour patterns and corresponding users' (students) characteristics can be disclosed.

The concept of the integrated approach and the 'energy culture' framework to the best of our knowledge–has never been tested against the Malaysian public universities student accommodation. As discussed above, this concept can be adopted by facilities managers to assess the fundamental of energy consumption behaviour among public universities' students. The assessment will contribute to enhancing essential knowledge pertinent to students' behaviour towards energy usage in order to determine the most effective energy saving strategy that can be adopted by the facilities managers.

REFERENCES

[1] Ishak, M.H., Sipan, I., Sapri, M., Mar Iman, A.H. and Martin, D. (2016). Estimating potential saving with energy consumption behaviour model in

higher education institutions. *Sustain Environ. Res*. Available from: *http://www.sciencedirect.com/science/article/pii/S2468203916300528*

[2] Ishak, M.H. (2015). Energy consumption behaviour assessment model for student accommodations in Malaysian Public Universities. Universiti Teknologi Malaysia.

[3] Wai, C.W. (2014). The conceptual model of energy awareness development process: The transferor segment. In IEEE; 2009, pp. 306–13. Available from: *http://ieeexplore.ieee.org/lpdocs/epic03/wrapper.htm?arnumber=5398630*

[4] Stephenson, J., Barton, B., Carrington, G., Gnoth, D., Lawson, R. and Thorsnes, P. (2010). Energy cultures: A framework for understanding energy behaviours. *Energy Policy,* 38(10): 6120–9.

[5] Galis, V. and Gyberg, P. (2011). Energy behaviour as a collectif. *Energy Effic.*, 4(2): 303.

[6] Ishak, M.H., Sipan, I.A., Iman, A.H.M. and Sapri M. (2015). A preliminary assessment of energy consumption behaviour pattern and factors influence among Malaysian higher education institutions students. *J. Teknol.*, 74(2). [cited 2016 Apr 23]. Available from: *https://pure.utm.my/en/publications/a-preliminary-assessment-of-energy-consumption-behaviour-pattern-*

[7] Gaol, F.L., Ishak, M.H., Iman, A.H.M. and Sapri, M. (2012). International Congress on Interdisciplinary Business and Social Sciences (ICIBSoS 2012) theoretical postulation of energy consumption behaviour assessment in Malaysian higher education institutions. *Procedia- Soc. Behav. Sci.*, 65: 891–6.

[8] Lutzenhiser, L. and Gossard, M.H. (2000). Lifestyle, status and energy consumption. *Proc. Am. Counc. Energy Effic. Econ. Wash. DC.*, pp. 207–22.

[9] Botsaris, P.N. and Prebezanos, S. (2004). A methodology for a thermal energy building audit. *Build. Environ.*, 39(2): 195–9.

[10] Haji-Sapar, M. and Lee, S.E. (2005). Establishment of energy management tools for facilities managers in the tropical region. *Facilities,* 23(9/10): 416–25.

[11] Stuart, G., Fleming, P., Ferreira, V. and Harris, P. (2007). Rapid analysis of time series data to identify changes in electricity consumption patterns in UK secondary schools. *Build. Environ.*, 42(4): 1568–80.

[12] Jamaludin, A.A., Mahmood, N.Z., Keumala, N., Ariffin, A.R.M. and Hussein, H. (2013). Energy audit and prospective energy conservation: Studies at residential college buildings in a tropical region. *Facilities*, 31(3/4): 158–73.

[13] Sheinbaum, C. and Dutt, G.S. (1996). The structure of residential energy consumption in the Mexico City Metropolitan Area. *Energy Sustain. Dev.*, 3(1): 43–8.

[14] Papakostas, K.T. and Sotiropoulos, B.A. (1997). Occupational and energy behaviour patterns in Greek residences. *Energy Build.*, 26(2): 207–13.

[15] Tso, G.K. and Yau, K.K. (2003). A study of domestic energy usage patterns in Hong Kong. *Energy*, 28(15): 1671–82.

[16] Al-Mumin, A., Khattab, O. and Sridhar, G. (2003). Occupants' behavior and activity patterns influencing the energy consumption in the Kuwaiti residences. *Energy Build.,* 35(6): 549–59.

[17] Armstrong, M.M., Swinton, M.C., Ribberink, H., Beausoleil-Morrison, I. and Millette, J. (2009). Synthetically derived profiles for representing occupant-driven electric loads in Canadian housing. *J. Build. Perform. Simul.*, 2(1): 15–30.

[18] de Almeida, A., Fonseca, P., Schlomann, B. and Feilberg, N. (2011). Characterization of the household electricity consumption in the EU, potential energy savings and specific policy recommendations. *Energy Build.*, 43(8): 1884–94.

[19] Verma, A., Jaiswal, Y.K. and Wani, K.A. (2012). Energy consumption behaviour of an urban residential sector in the northern province of Madhya Pradesh (India). *Indoor Built Environ.*, 21(5): 703–9.

[20] Van Raaij, W.F. and Verhallen, T.M.M. (1983). A behavioural model of residential energy use. *J. Econ. Psychol.*, 3(1): 39–63.

[21] Hitchcock, G. (1993). An integrated framework for energy use and behaviour in the domestic sector. *Energy Build.*, 20(2): 151–7.

[22] Wilk, R. (2002). Consumption, human needs and global environmental change. *Glob. Environ. Change*, 12(1): 5–13.

[23] Barr, S. and Gilg, A.W. (2007). A conceptual framework for understanding and analyzing attitudes towards environmental behaviour. *Geogr. Ann. Ser. B Hum. Geogr.*, 89(4): 361–79.

[24] Wilson, R.E. and Maxwell, C.D. (2007). Research in geographic profiling: Remarks from the guest editors. *Police Pract. Res.*, 8(4): 313–9.

[25] Adrian, Furnham A.L. (1986). The economic mind. The social psychology of economic behaviour. *J. Econ. Psychol.*, 7(3): 389–91.

[26] Lea, S.E.G., Tarpy, R.M. and Webley, P. (1987). The individual in the economy: *A Textbook of Economic Psychology*. CUP Archive, p. 660.

[27] DiClemente, D.F. and Hantula, D.A. (2003). Applied behavioural economics and consumer choice. *J. Econ. Psychol.*, 24(5): 589–602.

[28] Faiers, A., Cook, M. and Neame, C. (2007). Towards a contemporary approach for understanding consumer behaviour in the context of domestic energy use. *Energy Policy,* 35(8): 4381–90.

[29] Dunphy, S. and Herbig, P.A. (1995). Acceptance of innovations: The customer is the key. *J. High Technol. Manag. Res.*, 6(2): 193–209.

[30] Pedersen, L.H. (2000). The dynamics of green consumption: A matter of visibility? *J. Environ. Policy Plan.*, 2(3): 193–210.

[31] Cottrell, F. (2009). Energy and society (revised): The relation between energy, social change and economic development. Revised edition. Bloomington: Author House, p. 484.

[32] Stafford, B. (1985). Energy consumption in dwellings: Some findings of the before and after study. Work Pap Cent Urban Reg Stud Univ Birm.

[33] Cramer, J.C., Hackett, B., Craig, P.P., Vine, E., Levine, M., Dietz, T.M. *et al.* (1984). Structural-behavioural determinants of residential energy use: Summer electricity use in Davis. *Energy,* 9(3): 207–16.

[34] Dholakia, R.R., Dholakia, N. and Firat, A.F. (1983). From social psychology to political economy: A model of energy use behavior. *J. Econ. Psychol.,* 3(3–4): 231–47.

[35] Van Raaij, W.F. and Verhallen, T.M.M. (1983). Patterns of residential energy behavior. *J. Econ. Psychol.,* 4(1–2): 85–106.

[36] Eyre, N., Anable, J., Brand, C., Layberry, R. and Strachan, N. (2011). The way we live from now on: Lifestyle and energy consumption. *Energy*, 2050: 258–93.

[37] Sanquist, T.F., Orr, H., Shui, B. and Bittner, A.C. (2012). Lifestyle factors in U.S. residential electricity consumption. *Energy Policy*, 42: 354–64.

[38] Kempton, W. (1993). Will public environmental concern lead to action on global warming? *Annu. Rev. Energy Environ.*, 18(1): 217–45.

[39] Weber, C. and Perrels, A. (2000). Modelling lifestyle effects on energy demand and related emissions. *Energy Policy,* 28(8): 549–66.

[40] Bin, S. and Dowlatabadi, H. (2005). Consumer lifestyle approach to US energy use and the related CO_2 emissions. *Energy Policy*, 33(2): 197–208.

[41] Keirstead, J. (2006). Evaluating the applicability of integrated domestic energy consumption frameworks in the UK. *Energy Policy,* 34(17): 3065–77.

[42] Lutzenhiser, L. (1993). Social and behavioural aspects of energy use. *Annu. Rev. Energy Environ.*, 18: 247–89.

[43] Wilson, C. and Dowlatabadi, H. (2007). Models of decision making and residential energy use. *Annu. Rev. Environ. Resour.*, 32(1): 169.

[44] Lutzenhiser, L. (1992). A cultural model of household energy consumption. *Energy,* 17(1): 47–60.

[45] Europe UNEC for. Energy modelling studies and conservation: Proceedings of a Seminar of the United Nations Economic Commission for Europe, Washington D.C., 24-28 March 1980. Published for the United Nations by Pergamon Press 1982, p. 732.

[46] Agnew, M., Ali, T., Barcella, Mary L., Basile, Paul S. *et al.* (1982). Energy modelling studies and conservation: Proceedings of a Seminar of the United Nations Economics Commission for Europe, Washington D.C., 24-28 March 1980 1st, Yong Zhou - Amazon.com [Internet] [cited 2016 Apr 24].

[47] Bell, M., Lowe, R. and Roberts, P. (1996). Energy efficiency in housing. Avebury, p. 200.

[48] Stanley, J., Stern, P.C. and Elworth, J.T. (1985). Personal and contextual influences on househould energy adaptations. *J. Appl. Psychol.*, 70(1): 3–21.

[49] Stern, P.C. (2000). New environmental theories: Toward a coherent theory of environmentally significant behavior. *J. Soc. Issues*, 56(3): 407–24.

[50] Law, J. and Hassard, J. (1999). Actor network theory and after [cited 2014 Apr 6]. Available from: *http://cat.inist.fr/?aModele=afficheN&cpsidt=110466.*

[51] Latour, B. (2012). We have never been modern [Internet]. Harvard University Press. [cited 2014 Apr 6].

[52] Lawson, R. and Williams, J. (2012). Understanding energy culture. *Present Annu. Conf. Aust. N Z Acad. Mark ANZMAC Univ. New South Wales Adel* [Internet]. Available from: *http://www.otago.ac.nz/csafe/research/otago055641.pdf*

[53] Kotler, P. and Zaltman, G. (1971). Social marketing: An approach to planned social change. *J. Mark.*, 35(3): 3–12.

[54] Kotler, P. (2003). Marketing management. Prentice hall, p. 706.

[55] Louviere, J.J. and Hensher, D.A. (1983). Using discrete choice models with experimental design data to forecast consumer demand for a unique cultural event. *J. Consum. Res.,* 10(3): 348–61.

[56] Paço, A do and Varejão, L. (2010). Factors affecting energy saving behaviour: A prospective research. *J. Environ. Plan. Manag.*, 53(8): 963–76.

[57] Yohanis, Y.G. (2011). Domestic energy use and householders' energy behaviour. Energy Policy.

[58] Santin, O.G.S. (2011). Behavioural patterns and user profiles related to energy consumption for heating. *Energy Build.*, 43(10): 2662–72.

[59] Andersen, R.V., Toftum, J., Andersen, K.K. and Olesen, B.W. (2009). Survey of occupant behaviour and control of indoor environment in Danish dwellings. *Energy Build.,* 41(1): 11–6.

[60] Paauw, J., Roossien, B., Aries, M. and Santin, O.G. (2009). Energy pattern generator; Understanding the effect of user behaviour on energy systems. pp. 9–10.

[61] James, A.R. (1996). Green consumers in the 1990s: Profile and implications for advertising. *J. Bus. Res.*, 36(3):217–31.

[62] Minton, A.P. and Rose, R.L. (1997). The effects of environmental concern on environmentally friendly consumer behavior: An exploratory study. *J. Bus. Res.,* 40(1): 37–48.

[63] Peattie, K. (2001). Golden goose or wild goose? The hunt for the green consumer. *Bus. Strategy Environ.*, 10(4): 187–99.

[64] Straughan, R.D. and Roberts, J.A. (1999). Environmental segmentation alternatives: A look at green consumer behavior in the new millennium. *J. Consum. Mark,* 16(6): 558–75.

[65] Eleni, S. (2007). Estimating energy conservation patterns of Greek households. *Energy Policy*, 35(7): 3778–91.

[66] Paço, A do and Raposo, M. (2009). "Green" segmentation: An application to the Portuguese consumer market. *Mark. Intell. Plan.*, 27(3): 364–79.

[67] Vringer, K., Aalbers, T. and Blok, K. (2007). Household energy requirement and value patterns. *Energy Policy*, 35(1): 553–66.

[68] Poortinga, W., Steg, L., Vlek, C. and Wiersma, G. (2003). Household preferences for energy-saving measures: A conjoint analysis. *J. Econ. Psychol.*, 24(1): 49–64.

[69] Gilg, A. and Barr, S. (2006). Behavioural attitudes towards water saving? Evidence from a study of environmental actions. *Ecol. Econ.*, 57(3): 400–14.

[70] Martinsson, J., Lundqvist, L.J. and Sundström, A. (2011). Energy saving in Swedish households. The (relative) importance of environmental attitudes. *Energy Policy,* 39(9): 5182–91.

[71] Masoso, O.T. and Grobler, L.J. (2010). The dark side of occupants' behaviour on building energy use. *Energy Build.,* 42(2): 173–7.

[72] Kaiser, F.G. and Shimoda, T.A. (1999). Responsibility as a predictor of ecological behaviour. *J. Environ. Psychol.*, 19(3): 243–53.

[73] Gatersleben, B., Steg, L. and Vlek, C. (2002). Measurement and determinants of environmentally significant consumer behavior. *Environ. Behav.*, 34(3): 335–62.

[74] Haron, S.A., Paim, L. and Yahaya, N. (2005). Towards sustainable consumption: An examination of environmental knowledge among Malaysians. *Int. J. Consum. Stud.*, 29(5): 426–36.

[75] Ek, K. and Söderholm, P. (2010). The devil is in the details: Household electricity saving behavior and the role of information. *Energy Policy*, 38(3): 1578–87.

[76] Manan, Z.A., Shiun, L.J., Alwi, S.R.W., Hashim, H., Kannan, K.S., Mokhtar, N. *et al.* (2010). Energy efficiency award system in Malaysia for energy sustainability. *Renew. Sustain. Energy Rev.*, 14(8): 2279–89.

[77] Abrahamse, W. and Steg, L. (2009). How do socio-demographic and psychological factors relate to households' direct and indirect energy use and savings? *J. Econ. Psychol.*, 30(5): 711–20.

[78] Fransson, N. and Garling, T. (1999). Environmental concern: Conceptual definitions, measurement methods and research findings. *J. Environ. Psychol.,* 19(4): 369–82.

[79] Wenshun, W., Xiaohua, L. and Hualong, L. (2011). Empirical research of the environmental responsibility affected on the urban residential housing energy saving investment behavior. *Energy Procedia*, 5(0): 991–7.

[80] Chirarattananon, S. and Taweekun, J. (2003). A technical review of energy conservation programs for commercial and government buildings in Thailand. *Energy Convers. Manag.,* 44(5): 743–62.

[81] Ma, G., Andrews-Speed, P. and Zhang, J.D. (2011). Study on Chinese consumer attitudes on energy-saving household appliances and Government policies: Based on a questionnaire survey of residents in Chongqing, China. *Energy Procedia*, 5(0): 445–51.

[82] Brian, A.R. (1997). Impact of daylight saving time on residential energy consumption and cost. *Energy Build.,* 25(1): 63–8.

[83] Rijal, H.B., Tuohy, P., Humphreys, M.A., Nicol, J.F., Samuel, A. and Clarke, J. (2007). Using results from field surveys to predict the effect of open windows on thermal comfort and energy use in buildings. *Energy Build.*, 39(7): 823–36.

[84] Kotchen, M.J., Grant, L.E. (2008). Does daylight saving time save energy? Evidence from a natural experiment in Indiana. Natl Bur Econ Res Work

Pap Ser [Internet]. No. 14429. Available from: *http://www.nber.org/papers/w14429*

[85] Aries, M.B.C. and Newsham, G.R. (2008). Effect of daylight saving time on lighting energy use: A literature review. *Energy Policy*, 36(6): 1858–66.

[86] Rosenberg, M. and Wood, L. (2010). The power of policy to influence behaviour change: Daylight saving and its effect on physical activity. *Aust. N. Z. J. Public Health,* 34(1): 83–8.

[87] Vlosky, R.P., Ozanne, L.K. and Fontenot, R.J. (1999). A conceptual model of US consumer willingness-to-pay for environmentally certified wood products. *J. Consum. Mark.,* 16(2): 122–40.

[88] Tudor, T.L., Barr, S.W. and Gilg, A.W. (2008). A novel conceptual framework for examining environmental behaviour in large organizations. *Environ. Behav.*, 40(3): 426–50.

[89] Follows, S.B. and Jobber, D. (2000). Environmentally responsible purchase behaviour: A test of a consumer model. *Eur. J. Mark.*, 34(5/6): 723–46.

[90] Sütterlin, B., Brunner, T.A. and Siegrist, M. (2011). Who puts the most energy into energy conservation? A segmentation of energy consumers based on energy-related behavioural characteristics. *Energy Policy*, 39(12): 8137–52.

[91] Gadenne, D., Sharma, B., Kerr, D. and Smith, T. (2011). The influence of consumers' environmental beliefs and attitudes on energy saving behaviours. *Energy Policy,* 39(12): 7684–94.

[92] Azar, E. and Menassa, C. (2010). A conceptual framework to energy estimation in buildings using agent based modeling. *In*: Simulation Conference (WSC), Proceedings of the 2010 winter, pp. 3145–56.

[93] Santin, O.G. and Itard, L. (2010). Occupants' behaviour: Determinants and effects on residential heating consumption. *Build. Res. Inf.*, 38(3): 318–38.

[94] Amaratunga, D., Sarshar, M. and Baldry, D. (2002). Process improvement in facilities management: The SPICE approach. *Bus. Process Manag. J.,* 8(4): 318–37.

[95] Cairns, G. (2003). Seeking a facilities management philosophy for the changing workplace. *Facilities*, 21(5/6): 95–105.

[96] Mohammed, A.H., Sapri, M. and Baba, M. (2006). Pengurusan fasiliti [Internet]. Skudai, Johor Bahru: Penerbit UTM; [cited 2014 Apr 8], p. 289. Available from: *http://www.penerbit.utm.my/cgi-bin/katalog/buku.cgi?id=395*

[97] Pathirage, C., Haigh, R., Amaratunga, D. and Baldry, D. (2008). Knowledge management practices in facilities organisations: A case study. *J. Facil. Manag.*, 6(1): 5–22.

[98] Elmualim, A., Shockley, D., Valle, R., Ludlow, G. and Shah, S. (2010). Barriers and commitment of facilities management profession to the sustainability agenda. *Build. Environ.*, 45(1): 58–64.

[99] Williams, B. (1986). The premises audit —facilities management structures. *Facilities*, 4(8): 4–7.

[100] Thomson, T. (1990). The essence of facilities management. *Facilities*, 8(8): 8–12.

[101] O'Callaghan, P.W. (1993). Energy management [Internet]. McGraw-Hill Book Company; [cited 2014 Apr 8]. Available from: *http://www.getcited.org/pub/102987164*

[102] Geethanjali, B., Hansa, L.M. and Daniel, M. (2007). An optimization of effective energy management as a tool to facilitate managers. In WIT Press, [cited 2012 Jun 14]. pp. 61–70. Available from: *http://library.witpress.com/pages/PaperInfo.asp?PaperID=17813*

[103] Smith, C.B. (1981). Energy-management principles: Applications, benefits, savings. [cited 2014 Apr 8]; Available from: *http://www.osti.gov/scitech/biblio/5684129*

[104] Fleming, D. (2004). Facilities management: A behavioural approach. *Facilities*, 22: 1–2. [Internet]. 2004 [cited 2016 Sep 25]. Available from: *http://www.emeraldinsight.com/doi/abs/10.1108/02632770410517933*

[105] Rowley, Jennifer (1995). Contextual issues for education in library and information studies in England for the year 2000. *Libr. Rev.*, 44(8): 49–55.

[106] Abdul, Moied M. (2004). Assessment of automating facilities management current practices: Potential framework models for Saudi Arabian Universities [Internet] [Thesis] [cited 2014 Apr 20]. Available from: *http://core.kmi.open.ac.uk/display/12099756*

[107] Housley, J. (1997). Managing the estate in higher education establishments. *Facilities*, 15(3/4): 72–83.

[108] Yen, N.S., Abdul Shakur, E.S. and Wai, C.W. (2010). Energy conservation opportunities in Malaysian universities. *Malays. J. Real Estate,* 5(1): 26–35.

[109] Ting, L.S., Mohammed, A.H.B. and Wai, C.W. (2011). Promoting energy conservation behaviour: A plausible solution to energy sustainability threats. *Int. Conf. Soc. Sci. Humanity (IPEDR),* p. 5.

[110] Muhieldeen, M., Adam, N.M., Salleh, E., Tang, S.G. and Kwong, Q.J. (2009). Student behavior that leads to energy abuse: Case study at a teaching institution in Malaysia [Internet]. Scribd. [cited 2016 Sep 25]. Available from: *https://www.scribd.com/document/13455165/Student-Behavior-That-Leads-To-Energy-Abuse-Case-Study-At-A-Teaching-Institution-In-Malaysia*

[111] Kagawa, F. (2007). Dissonance in students' perceptions of sustainable development and sustainability: Implications for curriculum change. *Int. J. Sustain. High Educ.,* 8(3): 317–38.

14

Third World Production Development in the Millennium: The Role of Researchers and Academics

Kifordu Anyibuofu Anthony[1*],
Muhammad Abubakar Abdullahi[1] and Chinedu Onueizugbe[1]

ABSTRACT

Even though the millennium development goals have the target years of 2015 and 2020, A Millennium in itself has duration of 1000 years. This means that this millennium will end in 2999. Development is the process of increasing the socio-economic condition of society from a particular state to a more desirable state. It is a multi-faceted concept but Economic Development is a prototype. Production is that function of management that establishes the relationship between the input of factors and the outputs. The production system has raw materials as the inputs, the production process as the transform and products and services as the outputs. Production development is the process of increasing the socio-economic condition of the production system of a society. Third world countries need production development so as to increase the wealth of their countries. They have to choose the appropriate type of technology since with different combinations of inputs, different combinations of outputs, would be produced depending on the type of technology used.

[1] Business Administration Department, Edo University Iyambo, Edo State, Nigeria.
* *Corresponding author*: E-mail: anthony.kifordu@yahoo.com

Unfortunately, many third world countries which are those developing Countries located in Africa, Asia and Latin America does not have indigenous technology. The developed countries do not agree to transfer technology. So the per capital gross National products of most of the third world countries are low when compared with the average of the G7 industrialized Nations. The research design is a combination of the use of secondary data, content analysis and model modification.

Key words: Millennium, Socio-economic, Development, Researchers, Academics, Multi-faceted, Inputes, Outputs Gross National Products (GNP) G7.

INTRODUCTION

It is difficult to ignore the contribution of production to a society's well-being. It is what creates national wealth, the common material basis without which no country can exist. Wealth is considered to be the aggregate amount of goods and services created during a given period. Goods include such things as automobiles, clothing, houses, food, furniture, roads, ships, books, radio and television sets, airplanes, etc. Services would be represented by the activities where there are no tangible products like in consultancy, banking, insurance, education, transportation, administration etc.

It is also difficult to ignore the contribution and importance of production to the individual organization. This is because every organization, no matter its form, whether it is housed in the private or public sector of the economy, is engaged in the production of either a physical good or a service. Regardless of the form of the organization, its continued existence depends on its ability to create a good or service for which there is a demand. So, production can be looked at as the foundation on which every organization rests. Let us now make up some concepts and definitions relevant to product management. The Bendavieds (1974) have observed that development is the movement of the socio-economic condition of a society from a particular state to a more desirable state. Most economists agree to this definition. However, there is a lot of disagreement of what consists the particular and more desirable States.

There are lots of aspects of development such as economic development, management development, business development and production development. However, the interest in this paper is on production development. This has to do with the increase from a particular to a more desirable socio-economic condition of the relationship between the input of factors and outputs of those factors.

The objectives of the study are:

1. To explain the 3M's of production management.
2. To solve quantitative examples.
3. To determine the 7 areas that layout planning provides space for.
4. To ascertain the 3 stages of systematic layout planning procedure.
5. To modify the system's cybernetic model of the transform of the process of production development.

PRODUCTION MANAGEMENT

These are the areas that manage the sections of the company. They include marketing, finance, production and personnel. Functional managers adopt a specialist view. Most of the policies implemented by functional managers require knowledge of how a functional policy relates to corporate policy to enhance the functional manager's contribution to the corporate goal achievement. At times, it is beneficial for the functional specialist to forgo the interest of his department in order to achieve global optimality (Unyimadu and Ugwu, 2008).

Production

This is the management function that establishes the relationship between the input of factors and the output achieved by factors. Every business organization has a circuit of activities which starts front the financing phase to production in which the goods and services are, followed by marketing through which goods created are sold. It is in the marketing phase of the circuit that the goods and services are transformed back into money. The money derived is often used to replace the resources that have been consumed and to enhance the organization's output capacity. The new resources are used to create additional goods and services which are transformed back into money. The entire process repeats itself over and, over in a revolving cycle. The financing phase starts before the production phase because both working and fixed capitals are needed to finance the establishment's initial operations (Uiyimadu, 2007).

Production System

This is an integrated whole that creates useful products and services. Traditionally, the creation of services has not been managed to the level which the production of goods has been. However, this state of affairs is changing because of the growing awareness that the principles of production/operations management can be applied to products and services alike (Banjoko, 2006).

Production / Operations Management

This is the management of the productive system. The creation of goods and services in our society is achieved through productive systems. As late as 1965, the field concerned with the management of these productive systems was thought of in terms of manufacturing management. Manufacturing is a type of industry where a lot of labour has to be put in to get the end-product. The steel plant and foundry works are models of manufacturing system. However, the importance of service and non-manufacturing systems has grown rapidly and today, "modern" production management must include both kinds of system– products and services, and integrate them into a common conceptual framework (Banjoko, 2006).

ADMINISTRATION

This is the aspect of management concerned with the interpretation of policy and implementation of procedures to effect it. Policy is a decision regarding the course of action an organization wants to take. The first step in policy formulation is to lay down the goals or objectives of an organization; and then identify alternative courses of action. In policy formulation and implementation, the major emphasis is on goals. Policy is sometimes defined as a recognized pattern of action, but in reality, however, policy is the laying of goals, identification of alternative course of action and the formulation strategies (Unyimadu and Ugwu, 2008).

DECISION-MAKING IN PRODUCTION/OPERATIONS MANAGEMENT

The obvious implication of a decision is that alternatives exist. In the process of decision-making a course of action is selected to be carried out from a set of alternatives. The problem of judging desirability immediately points to the need for a purpose and criterion for measuring or comparing the desirability of the alternatives in relation to the purpose. The decision process increases in complexity when it is realized that future values are being considered and unfortunately these future values, often conflict and it is not possible to predict the future with certainty. The problem becomes that of ability of obtaining exact values since the results expected exist in the future. There is also a problem of knowing the possibility of obtaining the results for each alternative or knowing the risk of not getting the forecasted result (Myer, 2000).

DECISION-MAKING IN THE PRODUCTION FUNCTION

Production is the process by which goods and services' are created. Production abounds in factories, officers, hospitals, supermarkets and even polytechnics. Production/operation management handles decision making as it relates to productive systems so that the resulting goods or services are produced according to specifications in the amounts and by the scheduled demands and at minimum cost. In accomplishing its objectives' production/operation management is associated with two broad areas of activity—the strategic or longer run decisions focused in the design of the system and the day-to-day or tactical decision of operations, (Chase and Aquilano, 2000).

STRATEGIC DECISIONS RELATED TO DESIGN OF THE PRODUCTIVE SYSTEM

The long run or strategic decisions related to the design of the productive systems are:

1. ***Selection and design of product*:** There are strong interactions between product selection and design with productive capability and vice versa.
2. ***Selection of equipment and processes*:** Usually alternative equipment and processes are available for any given need. Management must take decisions that commit capital of the enterprises and establish its basic approach to production in the facility design.
3. ***Production design of items processed*:** Cost interacts strongly with the design of parts, products, paper work, forms etc, for the design of services offered. Design decision often set the limiting characteristics of cost and processing for the system.

4. ***Job design***: Job design is an integral part of the total system design involving the basic organization of work, as well as the integration of human engineering data, to produce optimally designed jobs. Job design differs from work study in that in job design we plan how to do the work but in work study, we study the technique.
5. ***Location of the system***: Decision have to be made on where to locate the future building and handling requirements to house the raw materials, purchased parts; etc. it is important to examine both the primary and secondary factor affecting plant location, in service system, location in- relation to decision may be of significance.
6. ***Facility layout***: Facility layout decisions are important because space is required for operating equipment, materials movement, operating personnel movements and safety, storage, indirect material and labour, other support services and for future expansion. Decisions related to design capacity, basic modes of production, shifts, use of overtime, and subcontracting must be made. In addition operations and equipment must be located in relation to each other in a pattern that minimizes overall interaction cost or meets the requirements of more complex criterion. Such factors like heating, lighting and other utility requires the allocation of storage space, etc and design of the buildings to house the layout must be taken care of (Buffa, 2000).

SHORT RUN OR TACTICAL DECISIONS RELATED TO THE DAY-TO-DAY OPERATION AND CONTROL

1. ***Inventory and production control***: Decisions must be made concerning the allocation of productive capacity consistence with demand and such things like inventory demand, ordering and holding costs to yield the economic order quantity, number of orders/year recorder level, and whether or not there should be safety stock. Feasible schedules must be worked out, and the loan on workers and machines and flow of production will be worked out, and also the load on workers and machines and the flow of production must be controlled.
2. ***Maintenance and reliability of the system***: Decision must be made regarding maintenance effort, the random nature of equipment breakdown and the possibility that machine down time may itself be associated with important costs or loss, of sales.

3. ***Quality control:*** In order' to ensure customer satisfaction and avoid customer complaints, to guarantee good quality products instead of defective products, decisions must be made to set the permissible levels of risk. Sometimes bad parts are produced and shipped, errors are made or good parts are scrapped. Acceptance sampling plans are used instead of 100% inspection because of problems of cost and time. Inspection costs must be balanced against probable losses resulting from passing defective materials or services.
4. ***Labour control:*** Labour is still the major element in most products and services. Production planning requires an appraisal of the labour components, thus much effort must go into developing work measurement and wage payment systems.

THEORIES OF ECONOMIC GROWTH AND DEVELOPMENT

The dependency theory states that the dependence of less developed countries (LDCs) on developed countries (DCs) is the main cause for the underdevelopment of the former. This theory of underdevelopment originated in the writings of a new Latin American Economist whose translations began to appear in English in the mid-I960s and early 1970s. The explanations of dependencies given by the various writers differ in degree only. Each tries to pinpoint and specify certain factors which have been responsible for the undevelopment of LDCs by DCs, So "there is a plurality of dependency views; different in leanings are accorded the concept of dependence, and different analyses are offered to explain underdevelopment as a result of the interplay between internal and external structures". As there are varieties of dependency theory, we shall briefly discuss the views of the main writers in the form of certain characteristics (Jihingan, 2008).

MEANING OF DEPENDENCY

According to the dependency economist, the whole world is divided between two sets of countries; DCs (developed countries) and LDCs (less developed countries). The former are in the centre (Western Europe, Britain and the United States) and the later are in the periphery (backward countries of Asia, Africa, and Latin American) Frank calls the DCs as metropolis and LDCs are satellite countries. Others call the former as dominant and the last as dependent countries. There are unequal centre-periphery relationship whereby LOCs are dependent on trade, investment, technology, etc. this dependence results in underdevelopment of the periphery because the centre is dominated by the powerful capitalist countries that exploit the former for their benefit (Anyanwu and Oaikhenan, 2000).

There is only one specific definition of dependency to be found in the literature on dependencies. This is by Dos Sanros. According to him dependency is "a situation in which the economy of certain countries is conditioned by the development and expansion of another economy to which the former is subjected" A dependent relationship between two or more economies is one when some countries (the dominant ones) can expand and be self-sustaining, while other countries (the dependent ones) can do this only as reflection of that expansion, which can have either a positive or a negative effect on their immediate development (lyoha, 2006).

But there is no unanimity among economists about the meaning of dependencies because of difference among them about the relative role of various features of dependence which have caused underdevelopment of LDCs. Sanjay Lack points out in this context: "one sometimes goes the impression on reading the literature that 'dependence' is defined in a circular manner. LDCs are poor because they are dependent, and any characteristics that they display signify' dependence." Thus, according to Lall, "in the usage of the dependencies school, 'dependence' is meant to describe certain characteristics (economic as well as social and political) of the economy as a whole and is intended to trace certain processes which are causally linked o its underdevelopment and which are expected to adversely affect its development in the future (Anyanwu and Oaikhenan, 2000).

THE DEPENDENCY THEORY

Dependency economists belong to different schools of thought and are classified as marxists, neo-marxists and structuralism. Todaro classified them under the neo-colonial dependence model, the false-paradigm model and dualistic-development thesis. But Todaro's categorization of dependency streams of though does not include all that is contained in writings of the dependency theorists. Bath and James identify and four unifying elements in the views of dependency economists: "(I) identification of underdevelopment with the expansion of industrial capitalist countries; (2) the view that development and underdevelopment are parts of a unified system; (3) the view that underdevelopment Is a persistent natural condition, not a temporary, precapitalists, stage; and (4) agreement that dependency affects internal politics, society and culture." Economists have, therefore, tired to explain a single dependency theory, which contains the main views for all the dependency economists in the form of the features or characteristics. As such, the dependency theory is explained below in terms of the following characteristics.

DEPENDENCY: A HISTORICAL INTERNATIONAL PROCESS

Dependency theorists Like Frank, Santos, SunkeL, Amin and Furtardo hold that the present economic and socio-political conditions prevailing in the periphery are the result of a historical international process. According to Dos Santos, development emerged as a global historical phenomenon as a consequence of the formation, expansion and consolidation of the capitalist system, known as dependent capitalism. Both the DCs (developed countries and LDCs (less developed countries) are integral parts of the capitalist system. But the global system is such that the development of the centre occurs at the expenses of underdevelopment of the periphery. Meier, therefore, characterizes underdevelopment of the periphery as the "Siamese twin" of development at the center. According to Frank, it is the world capitalist system which produced under-development in the past and generates underdevelopment in the present. This has led to what Frank calls "the development of underdevelopment at three levels" (Jhingan, 2008).

At the first level, many countries in the periphery have been incorporated into the world economy since the early days of colonialism. At the second level, such peripheral countries have become capitalist economies through incorporation into the world economy. At the third level, the incorporation of the peripheral countries in the world economy has led to "metropolis-satellite chain" in which the surplus generated at each level in the periphery is successively drawn off the centre. As a result, the periphery is impoverished and the centre is enriched. According to Sanjay Lall, "The development of underdevelopment" may be viewed as leading to immiseration *i.e.,* the growing poverty of the mass of the population on the periphery (Jhingan, 2008).

According to Amin, capitalist relations are introduced in the periphery by the centre. It leads to dependent development which is an inappropriate pattern of development imposed upon the periphery by the centre. In such a system the peripheral economies are without nay internal dynamism of their own and are dominated by absentee capitalists of the periphery. The peripheral country is a mere appendage of the central economy. The development of the centre causes underdevelopment of the periphery and its dependence on the centre (lyoha, 2006).

The peripheral LDCs are heavily dependent on the center for foreign capital. Foreign capital leads to "external orientation" of LDCs by exporting primary commodities, importing manufactures and making them dependent for industrialization of their economies. According to Sunkel, it is the stagnation of agriculture, high concentration of primary commodities for exports, high foreign exchange content of industrialization and growing fiscal deficit in the peripheral countries which necessitate foreign financing for them. In Sunkel's words, "it is this aspect which finally sums up the situation of dependence; this is the crucial point in the mechanism of dependence." The foreign investors that exploit LDCs by insisting on the choice of projects, making decision on pricing, supply of equipment, known and personnel, etc. In fact, they impose a development pattern that is not compatible with local needs further, the dependence on foreign capital leads to a much higher outflow in the form of declared profits, royalties, transfer pricing, payment of principal and interest to foreign investors of the centre. Debt service and repayments drain third world wealth; foreign aid stunts agriculture, encourages trade and investment dependencies and reinforces the dominance of exploitative elites of LDCs. Thus, foreign investment and aid signify dependence and as a means of exploitation of the periphery by the center (Jhingan, 2008).

TECHNOLOGICAL DEPENDENCE

The peripheral countries use excessively capital-intensive technologies imported from the developed countries of the centre. These technologies are inappropriate to the production and consumption needs of LDCs and are sold by multinational corporations (MNCs) of developed countries. The technological dependence of LDCs on DCs arises because of the urgency of importing technologies as they cannot innovate them. They lack information about the availability of appropriate technologies which, leads to exploitation of LDCs due to their weak bargaining power. MNCs lead to economic and political distortions in LDCs (Anyanwu and Oaikhenan, 2000).

Some of the economic distortions created by multinational companies (MNCs) are transfer of technologies to LDCs by restricting their right to use or change or transfer according to their discretion or requirements. This leads to their total technological dependence on MNCs. Capital-intensive technologies have limited labour absorption capacity and thus ad to unemployment in LDCs. They create social tensions by worsening the distribution of income. There are large wage differentials between workers employed in the branches of MNCs and those engaged in local firms in LDCs. Such wage differentials increase income inequalities and create social tensions which retard the development of LDCs (Anyanwu and Oaikhenan, 2000).

TRADE AND UNEQUAL EXCHANGE V

Dependency economists contend that DCs at the centre exploit LDCs of the periphery by forcing them to specialize in the export of primary products with inelastic demand with respect to both price and income. So LDCs, "continue to face stagnant export earnings often coupled disruptive short-term fluctuations in prices".

This has created shortage of foreign exchange and BOP deficit in LDCs.

Santos gives two reasons for BOP deficit

(a) Foreign capital from DCs controls major sectors of LDCs with the result that there are large outflows of profit, interest and principal.

RESEARCH AND METHODOLOGY

The Research Design chosen in the study is the use of secondary data, content analysis and model modification. For a research work of this nature, there are two sources of data namely: Sources of secondary data and sources of primary data.

Data is a representation of facts, Observations and Occurrences (O'brien, 2000). Data is the unprocessed data which could be in the form of figures, words or even computer codes. But in this research work, the data is in the form of words, if the data is properly processed, it becomes information that is used in managerial decision making. In the third world because of the peculiar nature of the challenges which are problems, barriers, threats that militate against the strategic managers and administrators who are either intellectuals or researchers or need to use their services as advisers, contractors, suppliers and designers, the one way of systematically activate the millennium goals and moving forward not just as third world countries in dire need of development but as third world countries with perspective strategies that make them to plan and go ahead to design and implement long term strategies of moving from the third world to the first world (Uyimadu, 2008).

However, even when the secondary data to be analyzed are secondary or existing in nature, these could be content analysis used and evaluated. These will ensure internal consistency. This makes them reliable especially as their sources are published.

A model is a representation of reality and not reality itself. A system is an integrated whole with parts or elements. If the elements have an interaction with the environment, they' are said to be open as is the situation in the social and management sciences. In the Leontief's model, applicable to all Systems, the elements are three in number, namely inputs, transform and output.

However, in the system's cybernetic model, two additional elements are these namely, feedback and control (O'brien, 2008).

QUANTITATIVE PROBLEMS

Example 1

Find two clinics that serve all communities at the lowest weighted level cost for the information given

From community	*Two clinics (Distance)*				*Population of community*	*Relative weight*
	A	*B*	*C*	*D*		
1	0	11	8	12	10,000	1.1
2	11	0	10	7	8,000	1.4
3	8	10	0	9	20.000	0.7
4	9.5	7	9	0	12,00	1.10

Solution to Example I

Step 1: Involves constructing a weighted population distance (entry) times population (in thousands) times weight.

From	*To clinics*			
community	*A*	*B*	*C*	*D*
1.	0	121	88	132
2.	123.2	0	121	78.4
3.	112	1400	125	
4.	114	84	108	0

Step 2: Involves circling the smallest win-zero number in each row, drawing an arrow to zero in each row and eliminating the clinic with the lowest distance pointing to it.

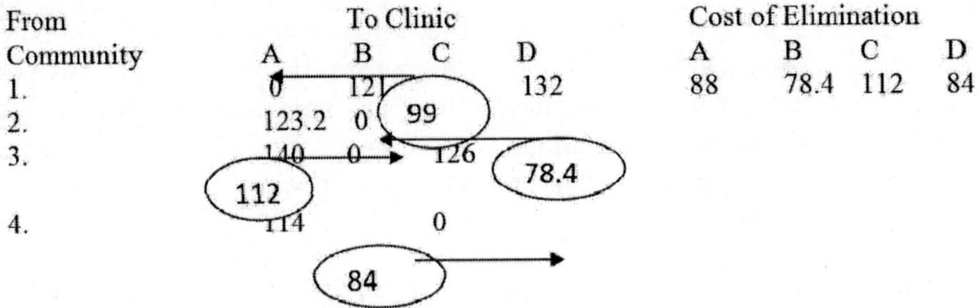

Step 3: Involves subtracting the smallest circled number from itself and remaining numbers as in row and constructing a matrix reflecting the subtracting and the eliminating of the clinic.

From	*To Clinic*			*Cost of Elimination*		
Community	*A*	*B*	*D*	*A*	*C*	*D*
1.	0	88	123	88	112	33.6
2.	44.8	33.6	0			
3.	112	0	126			
4.	114	108	0			

In Step 4: Clinic A has been eliminated as 88 is the next lowest entry and the column that is pointing to under A is eliminated.

From Community	*To Clinic* C	D	*Cost of Elimination* C	D
1.	0	44		
2.	33.6	0	44	33.6
3.	0	126	126	108
4.	108	0	170	141.6

Clinic C serves communities I and 3 while clinic D services community 2 and 4.

Example 2

Five different markets are stationed at A (0.0), B (3,6), C (10,2) D (920,2). The unit costs of transport are related in the ratios 5:22:41; 60:34. Assuming a rectangular problem, determine the optimal location of the plant.

Solution to Example 2

X	*Coordinate*	*Weight*	*Cumulative weight*
A	0	5	5
B	3	33	27 less than 162/2 81
C	8	60	87 more than 81
D	10	41	
B	20	34	
		162	

So the X coordinate of the optimum location is 3 or 8

X	*Coordinate*	*Weight*	*Cumulative weight*
A	0	5	5
C.E	2	41.34	80 less than 81
B	6	22	102 more than 81
D	12	60	162

So the Y coordinate of the optimum location is 2,6

Also the X and Y coordinates are (3,2),(3,6)(8,2) and (8,6).

Example 3

A new airline company is to transport Cargo the under mentioned cities. The transport cost is assumed to be square of the Euclidean Distance. For every trip to one of the cities, the cargo comes back to the central terminal, for intra city transport, the cargo has to stop over at the central terminal. The expected numbers of trips per say on individual basis from the central terminal to the respective cities are 20, 14, 12, I0, 8, 4, 24 and 12, respectively. The coordinates of the nine cities are Lagos (50, 75), Ibadan (150, 200), Kano (400, 1030), Kaduna (600, 110), 108 (900, 1230), Maiduguri (990, 1350), Ife (500, 250) Benin (500, 150), and Port Harcourt (1050, 50). Determine the coordinate of the new central terminal.

Solution to Example 3

S.no.	*X coordinate*	*Weight*	*Y coordinate*	*Weight*	*XW*	*XY*
1	50	20	75	20	1000	1500
	150	14	200	14	2100	2800
	400	12	1030	12	4800	12360
	600	10	110	10	600	1100
	900	8	1230	8	7200	9840
	990	4	1350	4	3960	5400
	500	4	250	4	3600	1000
	500	24	150	24	12600	600
	1050	12	50	12	12600	600
	Total	**108**	**108**	**51660**	**38200**	

$$X = \frac{51699}{108} = 478.33$$

$$Y = \frac{38200}{108} = 353.70$$

DATA ANALYSIS AND MODEL SOLUTION

Table 1 shows the 8M's of Production Management.

Table 1: The 8Ms of production management

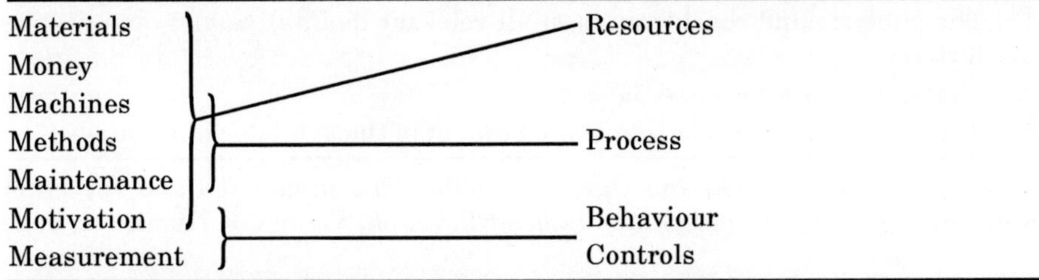

Source: Uyimadu S.O., and Ugwu (2008). The production and operations function. *Nigerian Journal of Management Research*, Volume 3, Number 1, page 5.

From Table 1, it is shown that the 8Ms are men, materials, money, that are the resources, machines, methods and maintenance that make up the process, motivation is needed for behaviour and measurement needed for control.

Table 2 shows the 7 areas Layout Planning provides space for.

Table 2: The 7 Areas layout planning provides space for

1.	Operating equipment
2.	Material equipment
3.	Operating personnel movement
4.	Storage
5.	Indirect material and labour
6.	Other operating service
7.	Future expansion

Source: Unyimadu, S.C., and Ugwu. J. (2008). The production and operations function. *Nigerian Journal of Management Research*, Volume 3, Number I, page I4.

From Table 2, the 7 areas that layout planning provides space for are operating equipment, material equipment, operating personnel movement, storage, indirect material and labour. Other operating service is for future expansion.

Table 3 shows the 3 stages of Systematic Layout Planning Procedure.

Table 3: The 3 stages of systematic layout planning procedures

1.	The analysis and consideration of all relevant qualitative and quantitative factors.
2.	The search for alternative layouts.
3.	The evaluation and selection of the best out of the available alternatives.

Source: Unyirnadu, S.O., and Ugwu, J. (2008). The production and operation function. *Nigerian Journal of Management Research*, Volume 3, Number 1, page 15.

From Table 3, it is shown that the 3 systematic layout planning procedures are the analysis and consideration of all relevant qualitative and quantitative factors, the search for alternative layouts and the evaluation and selection of the best out of the available alternatives.

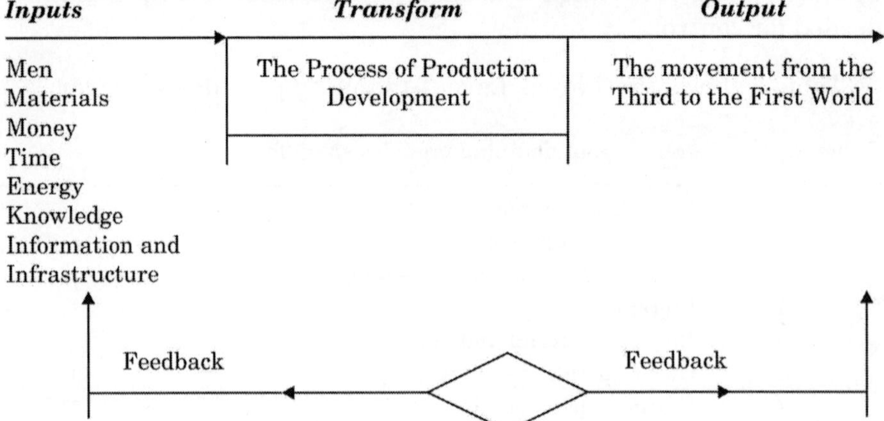

Source: Q'brien J.A. (2000). Computers in Business Management: An Introduction Homewood, Illinois: Richard D. Irwin Incorporated, Page 100.

Fig. 1.1: The system's cybernetic model of the transform of the process of production development.

From Fig. 1.1, it is shown that the system's cybernetic model has five elements namely inputs: men, materials. Money, time, energy, knowledge, information and infrastructure, transform of the process of production development, output of the movement from the third to the first world, control and feedback.

SUMMARY OF MAJOR FINDINGS, CONCLUSION AND RECOMMENDATIONS SUMMARY OF MAJOR FINDINGS

The Objectives of the Study Were

1. To explain the 3M's of production management.
2. To solve quantitative examples.
3. To determine the 7 areas that layout planning provides space for.
4. To ascertain the 3 stages of systematic layout planning procedure.
5. To modify-the system's cybernetic model of the transform of the process of production development.

1. The 8Ms of production management were men, materials, money that were the resources, machines, methods and maintenance that make up the process, motivation needed for behaviour and measurement needed for control.
2. The 7 quantitative procedures were fully solved. Areas layout planning provided for were operating equipment, material equipment, operating personnel movement, storage, indirect material and labour. Other operating services are for future expansion.
3. The three stages of systematic layout planning procedures were the analysis and consideration of all relevant quantities and qualitative factors, the search for alternative layouts and the evaluation and selection of the best out of the available alternatives.
4. The system's cybernetic model has five elements namely inputs, men, materials, money, time, energy, knowledge, information and infrastructure, transform of the process of production development, output of the movement from the third to the first-world, control and feedback.

CONCLUSION

The finding that the 8Ms of production management had men, machines and money that were the resources implied that they were very important achieving third world country objectives. The finding that 3 quantitative problems were fully solved implied that production management was quantitative in nature. The finding that operating equipment was the first area, that layout planning provided space for implied that, this area was very important. The finding that the first stage in systematic layout planning procedure was the analysis of the relevant quantitative factors implied that both were necessary for adequate systematic layout planning. The finding that the systematic cybernetic model had five elements implied that it was more sophisticated than the Leontief's model that had three elements.

RECOMMENDATIONS

It is recommended that to meet the millennium challenges needed to move from the third world to the first world, the third world researchers and intellectuals that were the strategic managers and administration needed to put together the 8Ms of production, management, solve quantitative production problems, examine the 7 areas of layout planning, examine the stages of systematic layout planning and use the system's cybernetic model of transform of the process of productive development.

REFERENCES

Anyanwu, J.C. and Oikhenan, H. (2000). Modern macroeconomic theory. Onitsha: Joannee Educational Publishers Limited.

Banjoko, S.A. (2006). Production and operations management. Yaba, Lagos: Saban Publishers.

Bendavied, A. and Bendavied, C. (1974).

Buffa, E.S. (2000). Modern production management. New York: John Wiley & Sons.

Chase, A. and Aquilano, B. (2000). Production management: A life cycle approach, New York: McGraw-Hill.

Iyoha, M.A. (2006). Macroeconomic theory: Benin City: Mindex Publishers Limited.

Jhingan, M.L. (2008). The economics of development and planning, New Delhi: Vrinda Publishing (P) Limited.

Meyer, R.R. (2000). Production and operations management. New York: McGraw-Hill.

O'brien, J.A. (2000). Computers in business management: An Introduction Homewood, Illinois: Richard D. Irwin Incorporated.

Unyimadu, S.O. and Ugwu, J. (2008). "The production and operations functions: A theoretical review with solutions to 3 quantitative problems" in *Nigerian Journal Management Research*, 3(1): 3–26.

Unyimadu, S.O. (2007). Production and operations management. Benin City: Harmony books.

Unyimadu, S.O. (2008). Business policy, strategy and management, Benin City: Harmony books.

15

Reflection of the Kazakh Culture in Language

S.S. Issakova[1]*, A.T. Taganova[1] and B.Sh. Baimukhanov[1]

ABSTRACT

The characteristics of the concept "father" which is one of the major national concepts reflecting the culture of the Kazakh people is introduced for your consideration in the research work called "Reflection of the Kazakh Culture in Language".

In the article the following issues are considered:

1. *The concept "father" was formed in the result of modeling the Kazakh concepts.*
2. *The linear system is founded on the social roles carried out by the father and is presented in the block form.*
3. *The frame structure is presented step by step.*
4. *The concept "father" is a complicated dynamic structure connected with non-material manifestation of culture whose features are closely connected with historical changes of social roles of men (fathers), differences of public systems of the compared cultures, and also not only with the change of systems of values of one historical cycle in comparison with another, but also with the development of social relationship. The concept "father" is considered within the frames of age-related changes of the man (father).*

[1] Zhubanov Aktobe Regional State University, Aktobe-city (Kazakhstan)
* *Corresponding author*: E-mail: sabira-i@yandex.ru

5. *The system of the values, rules, ethical standards of behavior, various stereotypic representations accepted in the civilized society and reflected in the frames of the conceptual image is analyzed.*

***Key words*:** Man-language-culture, National mentality, Cognitive linguistics, Concept, National concept, Conceptual system

---

INTRODUCTION

Relationship between culture and language in linguistics was investigated by the following linguists: W. von Humboldt, Potebnya, L. Vaysgerber, E. Sepir, B.L. Worf, Yu. Stepanov, V.N. Teliya, A.D. Arutyunova, V.V. Vorobyov, V. Shakleyn, V.A. Maslova, etc.

In the Kazakh linguistics this topic can be found in the works of A. Kaydar, E. Zhanpeisov, Zh. Mankeeva, M. Kopylenko, G. Smagulova, K. Zhamanbayeva, N. Zhanpeisova, S. Isakova, M. Kushtayeva, etc.

The given work presents the characteristics of the fundamental national concept "father" reflecting the culture of the Kazakh people in language.

Special value is determined by the role, activity, national indicators defining the culture and traditions, customs, mentality of the Kazakh consciousness peculiar to the father through a prism of the developing cognitive theory.

In general, the relevance of this research is determined in the trichotomy "man–language–culture" which can be revealed through the language data presented by culture, everyday life, the Kazakh national spirit.

The following methods and approaches were used in the work: linguo-cognitive, cultural and informative, research, lexicographic, comparative-historical methods and method of explanation and grouping.

THE MAIN PART

In the last decade special attention in cognitive linguistics is paid to the problems of "doctrines of the worldview", to the ratio "man - language - culture". In order to explain these combinations we rely on wider concepts of cognitive psychology such as "scene", "prototypical scene", "scenario", "scheme", "frame", etc.

According to scientists, in order to fully understand and characterize lexical unities it is necessary to consider them linked with the frame system[3,85].

From the point of view of language-specific and cultural aspect the following items are offered: the term of the conceptual scheme understood as "conceptual system or structure", "the text model block tool" (Fillmore); as stereotypic representation in the form of the frame designated by a language sign of a component of a certain condition or a structure (Minskiy); the modeling of the text based on the theory of frames and presented by a system of schemes; the scene based on individual memoirs and perception of real activity of objects of surrounding reality (Fillmore)[3,85].

According to Fillmore, activity of people in reality (their experience) results in the conceptual scheme: in a person's consciousness the word frame gives rise to a frame and connects it with the scheme by means of association; schemes are tools of blocks of text models, appropriate models of the worldview.

This terminological review was necessary in connection with consideration of the peculiarities of the concept "father" as the object of our research. It is possible that while studying concepts of material cultural values, artifacts cognitive linguistics will need new concepts. The totality of "it's a biological components" peculiar to an individual and objective and biological factors forming it as a national concept, regulating social and historical conditions of its activity can be considered to be the characteristic property of the concept "father".

It is also to be noted that in the analysis of the concept "father" within the frames of cognitive science it is necessary to take into account the following phenomena:

1. In order to consider the concept "father" in respect of the aspect of the Kazakh conceptual system and for wider review we use the modeling method.
2. Creation of the system of schemes in the form of blocks is based on the social activity of the father.
3. The frames are subdivided into several stages.

4. The concept "father" is a complex dynamic structure connected with non-material demonstration of culture whose features are closely connected with historical changes of social roles of men (fathers), distinctions of social systems of the compared cultures, and also not only with the change of systems of values of one historical cycle in comparison with another, but also the development of social relationship. The concept "father' is considered within the frames of age-specific changes of the man (father).

   Thus, each block was considered separately: ("Young father", "Father of middle age", "Father of advanced age").

5. The system of the values, rules, ethical standards of behavior, various stereotypic ideas accepted in the civilized society, reflected in the frames of the conceptual image is exposed to the analysis.

Thus, let us consider the content of the concept "father' within the frames of the Kazakh conceptual system. The totality of the duties carried out by the man (father) from the point of view of cultural and language-specific understanding is based on the models consisting of three blocks: [2]. "The young father", [22]. "The father of middle age", [222]. "The father of advanced age". Information about the social role, culturally filled stereotypic image was taken into account in each block respectively.

As a result, in Block I the father can be at the same time the parent, the husband, the son-in-law, the sister's husband, the head of the family and workman (worker);

In Block II he can be the parent, the husband, the son-in-law, the sister's husband, the head of the family, the father-in-law, the co-father-in-law, workman (worker);

In Block III the father is the parent, the husband, the son-in-law, the sister's husband, the head of the family, the father-in-law, the co-father-in-law, the grandfather, the great-grandfather.

We used stereotypic blocks of manifestation of the known social roles of the father. In the conventional national combination the abstract scheme of the concept "father" looks approximately as follows:

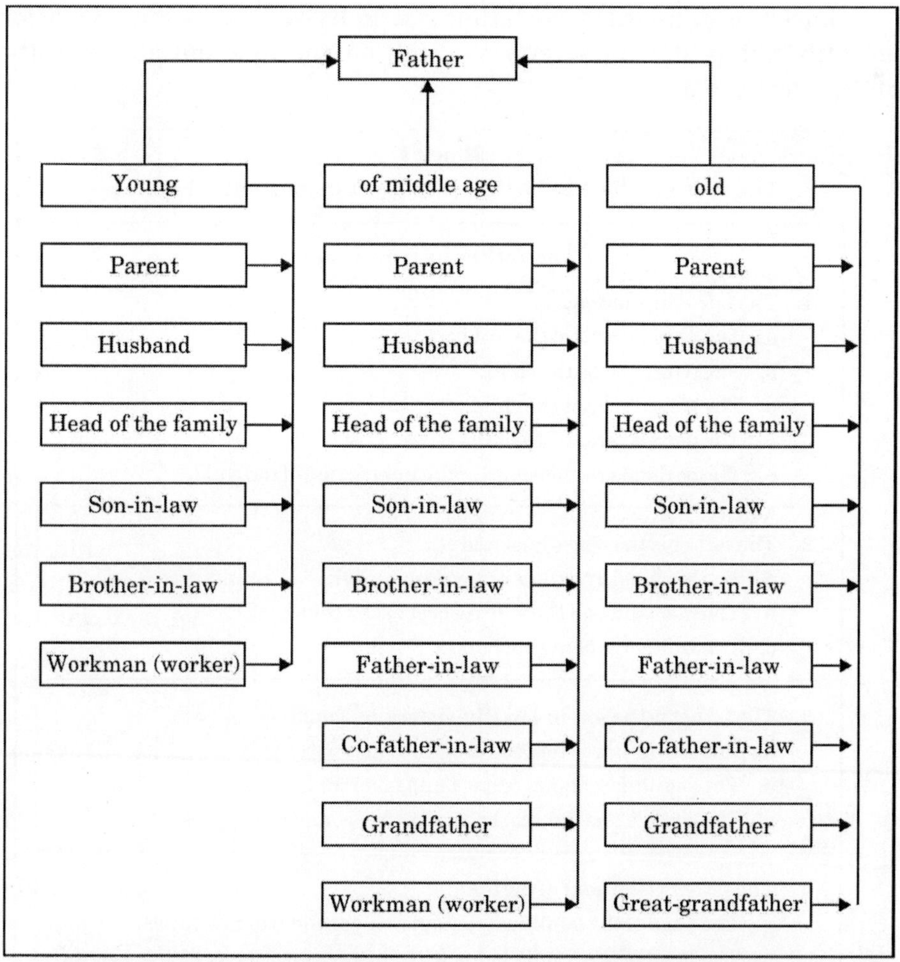

In modern times the perception of mental knowledge of the people speaking the same language in respect of a definite concept depends on the level which is assigned to the father in the family, and is also connected with various forming factors of social and cultural types and their relationship.

In our work we try to consider the stereotype "What kind of person should a good father be?"

In general, in the middle age (Block II) the social role of the son-in-law, the sister's husband becomes somewhat irrelevant, and strengthens closer to advanced age, *i.e.,* (Block III) when the standard of upbringing is defined, there is respect, favor from the wife's relatives to the older son-in-law, the sister's husband.

Since the standard of the father is usually defined by manifestation of father-ship, it is necessary to dwell on the role and duties of the father as parent.

Block I

The concept "father" within the Kazakh conceptual system

The father of young age

1. The father is a parent
   a. Tha parent cares of the child.
   b. The parent loves the child.
   c. The parent names the child.
   d. The parent cares of his child.
   e. The parent is responsible for the upbringing of the child.

2. The father is the wife's husband
   a. The husband and the wife love each other.
   b. The husband and the wife respect each other.
   c. The wife cares of the husband.

3. The father is the son-in-law (the sister's husband)
   a. The son-in-law is respectful of the wife's parents.
   b. The son-in-law shows respect and favor for his wife's elder relatives.
   c. The sister's husband cares of his wife's younger relatives.

4. The father is the hear of the family.
   a. The head of the family carries out all household man's duties.
   b. The head of the family helps with the organization of festive events of his wife's relatives.
   c. The head of the family welcomes guests.
   d. The head of the family is its supporter.

5. The father is a workman (worker)
   a. The workman (worker) carries out his duty regulations.
   b. The workman (worker) receives his salary.
   c. The workman (worker) cares of the financial situation of the family.
   d. The workman (worker) deserves rest.

CHARACTERISTICS, EXPLANATIONS

If we consider in the first block the role of the man as parent, we cannot fail to dwell on the customs, traditions, festive events of the Kazakh people connected with the ceremony of the birth of a child. After the wedding ceremony any nation dreams about the the birth of the first child. And the Kazakh people are not an exception. Having married off the daughter and the son, they wish the fastest birth of the child[1,67]. Thus, if the mother is personally responsible for the birth of the child, the role of the father involves the father-husband's care of of the wife and the unborn baby (certainly after care of his mother).

In spite of the fact that traditions and customs are usually kept in the territory of all Republic of Kazakhstan, it should be noted that nowadays they have undergone changes. In general, some families preserve customs in pure form in spite of the fact that in the majority of customs magic, symbolical signs began to be forgotten, and religious and other features ceased to be considered.

Conservation of welfare of all the family members is considered to be the object of family traditions and customs. It is certainly connected with the health of the unborn child and the woman bearing the child.

Pregnant women have to keep up a number of beliefs (not to have their hair cut, not to go out alone at night, not to spend the night at home alone during the absence of her husband).

In modern society the birth of the child is not only the problem of parents, but of the whole society, being a state demographic problem. If in former times the mother-in-law carried out a controlling role and ensured that the pregnant woman gave birth to the child in a circle of pregnant neigbours, now the position of mother and child is under control of the state. Only in some cases, especially in rural areas, a woman can deliver a child at home. In that case the person who was taking part in childbirth, maintaining all hygienic rules is considered the godfather.

Earlier Kazakh women gave birth to children at home. The mother-in-law, the husband or the woman herself chose the child's godparent in advance. The person who cut the belly stalk at the child's birth was considered the godparent. There was a peculiar custom: people appointed by godparents cut the belly stalk with an axe when a child was born from people who had not been able to have children for a long time. It was also considered that the man cutting the belly stalk was the godfather, and his wife was the godmother. There are a lot of ceremonies connected with the birth of the child and cutting the belly stalk

Among others it would be desirable to mention the ceremony of buying out the child from the godmother by his father. “In families where newborns died very often and pregnancy did not come for a long time, the main charge was laid down on a black giant bird. In order to save the newborn from dark forces of a giant bird he was wrapped in baby linen and tied with ropes and carried through shanyraks of seven yurtas and through a horse-cloth of an elderly person. It was considered that by such ceremony they will be able to hide from what house the child was and who his parents were, and besides, according to beliefs such newborn was to do great in life. After such ceremony the godmother took the newborn home, and the father of the child donated her with a sheep, a bag of coal[1,74]. Even though such ceremonies are already not held nowadays, nevertheless, the tradition to choose the godfather and the godmother still remains. Family members and dear ones, friends of the child’s mother can be godparents. The husband of the godmother is considered the godfather. Sometimes the doctor-obstetrician, a woman or a man, was considered the godparent. Godparents have to carry out all necessary ceremonies, from birth to forty days of age. Also it should be noted that in the future Godparents care of their fosterling until he has his own family.

Giving the name to the newborn is one of the exciting problems of the Kazakh society. Notably, giving the name to the boy was considered to be a more responsible ritual, than to the girl (parents can give the name to the girl themselves). Most often “the grandfather or a chance comer who visited the house at the time of the child’s birth gives the name to the boy, the successor, the heritor[1,83].

Now the child is named already in maternity hospital. By tradition options of names for the baby can be offered by grandfathers and grandmothers, some respectable relatives, however, the main decision remains with the newborn’s parents. As before children are named after famous public figures, historic figures, and reputable people of their family or settlements. Girls can be named by foreign names or in honor of somebody. But names of the father, mother, and close relatives of the father of the child are not given to the child. Perhaps due to this the majority of Kazakh names have their direct meaning (the Successor, the Companion). For this reason there are no cognate words among names of the Kazakh people.

Earlier the celebration in honor of the newborn was arranged in villages on the day of the child's birth, now it is organized on the day of leaving the maternity hospital.

In villages the custom of laying the child in a children's bed-besik is still kept. Many ceremonies are also connected with it.

In city conditions the child is put into the baby cot, the baby carriage. Ceremonies from evil eye are carried out. There still remains the tradition of celebrating the child's forty days of age. After the child is forty days old, the husband is allowed to kiss, embrace, and caress his wife.

If the son and the daughter-in-law live together with parents, the care of children, their upbringing mostly falls on the mother-in-law's shoulders. In cases if husband and wife live separately from parents, the husband helps his wife with the household and children. The ceremony of cutting "fetters" of the child who takes the first steps is still popular. Usually a reputable female person, light on her feet, is entrusted with this procedure as the parents want their child to be akin to her. Recently men also began to be involved in this ceremony[3,95].

The custom of circumcision of boys of 5-7-9 years old is widespread among the Kazakh people. In such cases the father assumes a role of the head of the family, *i.e.,* senior after the grandfather as usually all power in the family belongs to the senior generation.

The birth of children and carrying out the events connected with it, religious practices, various bans concern young married couples only indirectly as usually in the Kazakh upbringing system the first-born is considered to be the child of the grandmother and the grandfather who in turn consider him their child.

Only the mother-in-law can usually introduce amendments in relationship of the newly-weds. Until the next son creates his family the newly-weds are obliged to live with the husband's parents. Younger or only sons are obliged to care of their parents until their old age. Another role of the father is the relationship with the wife's relatives.

The head of the family will be always respected in his community if he keeps the bowls of scales in balance, impartially treats his wife's relatives as his own, is in good relationship with people, treats them with respect and attention, does not offend his daughters and treats them correctly. The wife's relatives always keep the sacred brisket for the son-in-law. The son-in-law will ridicule the daughter-in-law if there is no minced brisket in the dish given to him. The son-in-law has to personally divide the brisket between the women present. There is a custom in which the son-in-law puts money in a dish with brisket. It is also necessary for him to be on good terms with women and younger daughters-in-law on the part of his wife, which will not look indecent for others. There is a popular saying "You can carry ashes on the son-in-law's horse." When the groom goes to the wife's relatives, he behaves modestly. He does not sit in the place of honor, he is not given the head of a sacred animal, and he does not say a prayer at the table[4,60]. The son-in-law's duties are to help about the house, to meet and see off guests, to slaughter cattle, to work hard in the yard. Respect for the the daughter-in-law's relatives is seen in his manner, politeness, dexterity and sense of duty[5,22-23].

Let us pass to the father's duties. Certainly, the father is the main earner and supporter in the family. And what is to be done if there are two supporters in the family - the father and the son? This situation depends on the individual attitude of each supporter to the family. The supporter whose contribution to the family income is larger has the right to control it. Therefore, if the real head of the family receives more notable earnings in a public place, he will be in power.

If the greater part of the family treasury is made up by parents who are still strong enough, they will make provision for the son and the daughter-in-law. And, if the main earnings are the share of the son and the daughter-in-law, and parents do not work any longer, being pensioners, and are engaged in the household, reins of power pass officially to the son. Certainly, traditionally respecting the senior generation, most of young sons do not demonstrate an official standing of the family power, and remain in the shadow in public. Under such circumstances parents do not make any crucial decisions without an agreement with their sons[1,258].

DESCRIPTION, EXPLANATIONS

The role of the father during this period is closely connected with upbringing of their adult children, their marriage, becoming the father-in-law, and then the grandfather. The role of the father in upbringing of his son has always been special. The father always tried to teach his

Block II

Father of middle age

1. The father is a parent
   i. The parent loves his children.
   ii. The boy is brought up by the parent (father).
   iii. Children loves their children

1a. Children respect their parents.

2. The father is the defender of his wife.
   a. The husband and the wife love each other.
   b. The husband and the wife respect each other.
   c. The wife cares of the husband.

3. The father is the son-in-law (the sister's husband)
   a. The son-in-law is respects senior relatives of the wife.
   b. The son-in-law cares of the sisters-in-law and brothers-in-law
   c. The son-in-law is respected by his wife's relatives.

4. The father is the hear of the family.
   a. The head of the family carries out all man's duties connected with household.
   b. The head of the family is responsible for the financial condition of the family.
   c. The head of the family welcomes guests.
   d. The head of the family is responsible for the organization of festive and funeral events.

5. The father is the father-in-law
   a. The father-in-law in the house of his son and daughter-in-law
   b. The father-in-law does not live in the house of the daughter and son-in-law.
   c. The son-in-law and the father-in-law respect each other.

6. The father is a co-father-in-law
   a. The co-parents-in-law honor and respect each other.

7. The father is a grandfather.
   a. The grandfather loves his grandchildren.
   b. The grandfather brings up his grandchildren.
   c. The grandfather considers grandchildren from the son closer, than grandchildren from the daughter.

8. The father is a workman (worker)
   a. The workman (worker) carries out his duty regulations.
   b. The workman (worker) receives a salary.
   c. The workman (worker) deserves rest.

son the skills he possessed himself. And each son, in turn, learnt, imitating the brother, the father. Kazakh proverbs perfectly characterize upbringing and family values: "Having been taught by the father, the son will be able to build the tool ..." or "What you saw in the family, you will do, having left it". So, till the age of 13-15 years old the Kazakh people prepared the sons and daughters for life. Girls were married off at the age of 13 and became housewives, sons married after they were 15[1,82].

Another popular expression is: "The father is the child's critic". Each father early revealed the features of his son, that is, he saw what abilities he had. He did his best to develop natural abilities of the sons. For example, if the child had a potential mind, they tried to make him a public figure; if the son possessed creative abilities, he was taught by singers and akyns; and, if the teenager had the desire to manage the household, the father put his matter into his son's hands. A thoughtful father propagates to his children actions of ancestors, their skill, and respect of all relatives to each other so that it served as a model for the future generation[1,83].

The son-in-law of middle age shows respect for the senior relatives of his wife. It can be seen on the following example: grown-up sons-in-law joke: "I am not the son-in-law, but the nephew in this house". Though this phrase is playful, it has its own sense. A quick-witted man will understand these words as: "As the son-in-law I have been working hard for the household. And therefore I am respected among my wife's relatives. I am already a member of this family. That is why I am a son-in-law with the nephew's whims. As the nephew I am free and I am beloved of all". Sometimes the wife's relatives also pamper the son-in-law calling him "nephew". Such special attention is shown to a bosom son-in-law who lives with their daughter for many years and raises children.

In the book called "Aynalayyn" D. Mataykyzy speaks about men as follows: "The man in a Kazakh family is a family man, the host. However, household routines, hardships, life, upbringing of children, the spiritual relations, cultural vigilance have always been in their life. Here the woman plays a special role. Her character combines wisdom, patience, endurance. In the house the woman should not argue or contradict her husband. The family man has to control everybody, to be authoritative; the role of the father has to be above all. Even khans depend on the mood of the wife. But a good wife will never show it, on the contrary she will be always proud, respectful and supportive of the authority of her husband among others. Seeing that, children will begin to respect the father even more. If the family man is in anger, it is neither shameful nor humiliating for a Kazakh woman "to fit into a peel of one millet". After all, the man in the house is the family support, the defender of the relatives, the patron of the family, and the woman is a symbol of peace and fertility. Their children grow between them; they are their pleasure, continuation of life. Authority of mother has been always considered the highest, the father-in-law and the mother-in-law are also honored. After all they are the roots of home, decoration of the village, mentors and advisers of all settlement. If the husband and the wife live in peace and quiet, the son thinks soundly, the daughter is happy, the old men are respected and live long; peace and unity always reign in such country. Unity of the home depends on the stability and unanimity of family members."

The family is considered solid and happy, if the man is the head of the family, and the woman is his adherent[4,50-51].

In some traditions, as farewell to the girl and acceptance of the daughter-in-law, the role of the father is especially significant. In such cases the father takes a place of honor. In modern conditions of the development of the Kazakh society holding a wedding, the question of living conditions of newlyweds and other problems are solved by the groom's parents as well as the main stages of the wedding: matchmaking, delivery of gifts of two parties, registration in the Civil Registry Office and holding the solemn party. As soon as the question of marriage is settled, both parties begin preparation for matchmaking. 3-4 People participate in this ceremony: the groom, the main matchmaker, the relative of the groom's father who is given credence to, and close relatives. Here they decide on the date of the wedding, the number of the people invited, the gifts to the parties. In token of the fact that the matchmakers came to become related with the daughter-in-law's relatives, they are given "kuyryk-bauyr" (liver with a fat tail). This tradition is called "kuyryk bauyr zhegizu" (trying liver with a fat tail). At the time of matchmaking relatives of the groom bring gifts and money to the bride's parents. They are called "chest" or "opening of a suitcase".

Sometimes, the groom steals the bride and then they arrange the wedding. After the wedding ceremony, relatives of both parties become co-parents-in-law. In the system of kin relations co-parents-in-law were highly valued. Perhaps that is why there is a proverb confirming the wisdom of the people: "The son-in-law is for one century, and the co-father-in-law is for the millennium".

For the daughter-in-law the father of the husband is the father-in-law. The daughter-in-law always greets him bowing, trying to show her politeness, courtesy, modesty, and manner. The daughter-in-law never shakes hands with the father-in-law and the brother-in-law as it is considered bad manners[4,60].

All this is the evidence of the special position of the father, father-in-law and father-in-law in the Kazakh mentality.

The father-in-law and the mother-in-law do not interfere with affairs of their daughter and son-in-law. The proof of that are the proverbs: "Be heated yourself at your fire ", "The flesh is yours, the body is mine"[3,104].

In the Kazakh understanding the daughter and the son-in-law cannot live together with the wife's parents. The guy living at the father-in-law's is called "kushik kuieu" (literally–a dog son-in-law)[1,43].

The father as the grandfather is engaged generally in upbringing of grandchildren, teaching them wisdom and prudence. The first grandson is considered the child of the grandfather and the grandmother. In this connection the child calls the grandfather father, the grandmother mother, and he treats his father as the elder brother.

CHARACTERISTICS, EXPLANATIONS

Today the position of parents and senior generation sometimes undergo changes. In an old age elderly parents live with their sons and the daughters-in-law. If they have no sons, they live with daughters (seldom). If the mother and the father are rather energetic and healthy, their grandchildren living in city conditions can shelter them despite their advanced age.

In general the parents living with the children are given great honor and respect. In a word, "In each house the most respectable family members are parents", "You understand respect for parents when you become the parent", "The house without a grandfather is a shelter", proverbs say[2,41].

Block III

Father of advanced age

1. The father is a parent
   a. The parent loves his children.
   b. The boy is brought up by the parent (father).
   c. Children love their children.
   d. Children respect their parents.

2. The father is the defender of his wife (woman)
   a. The husband and the wife love each other.
   b. The husband and the wife respect each other.
   c. The wife cares of the husband.

3. The father is the son-in-law (the sister's husband)
   a. The son-in-law carries out his duties.
   b. The son-in-law is respected by younger relatives of his wife.

4. The father is the hear of the family.
   a. The head of the family carries out all man's duties connected with household.
   b. The head of the family welcomes guests.

5. The father is the father-in-law
   a. The father-in-law lives in the house of the son and daughter-in-law
   b. The father-in-law does not live in the house of the daughter and son-in-law.
   c. The son-in-law respects his father-in-law

6. The father is a co-father-in-law
   a. The co-parents-in-law honor and respect each other.

7. The father is a grandfather.
   a. The grandfather loves his grandchildren.
   b. The grandfather brings up his grandchildren (mostly the grandchildren from the daughter).
   c. The grandfather considers grandchildren from the son closer, than grandchildren from the daughter.
   d. Grandchildren love their grandfather.
   e. Grandchildren consider him a role model.

8. The father is a great-grandfather
   a. The great-grandfather loves his great-grandchildren.
   b. Great-grandchildren love the great-grandfather and consider him a role model.

From time immemorial the Kazakh people honor and respect adult and elderly people. Favorable and respectable attitude for the elderly is seen in proverbs and sayings of the Kazakh people. Any event begins with words of the elderly and finishes with their blessing.

The parental house is a house where a person grows, and "having matured and having built his own house, he starts calling it "a yurta of the head of a big family", "the big house".

If parents die, the youngest of all sons stays in the parental house. For the youngest son the parental house becomes a special place in which he continues his life and life of the subsequent generations proceeds. All family members, daughters, daughters-in-law come and bring gifts to this house. It is considered that manifestation of respect for the yurta of the head of a big family is the respect for all ancestors. By tradition the father spares no care in relation to his wife's relatives. The main care of parents is to marry off the daughters and successfully marry off the sons.

Today, if the father is strong enough, he does household chores and teaches it to his sons and grandsons. In the village, certainly, they graze cattle and look after a kitchen garden. And if he is not very healthy, children help parents. An elderly father takes a place of honor, gives blessing and says a prayer at various events, celebrations, commemoration of the relatives.

Traditions of a funeral and commemoration of the Kazakh people at the end of the 20th century are described in ethnographic materials of E. Zh. Ernazarov, A.B. Kalyshev, K.A. Bekbolat.

It should be noted that the traditions of a funeral and commemoration forgotten in the period of the Soviet Union now began to renew. The deceased person is carried out on the right side; he is dressed and wrapped in fabric, a carpet. By traditions of the Kazakh people it is necessary to bury no later than in three days, the elder looks after the deceased. On this day everyone who comes to the funeral is given food. On the day of the funeral people come to say goodbye to the deceased. If it is a woman, there are women near her, if it is a man, only men are near him. After ablutions, the body is wrapped in grave clothes. Also traditions of commemoration, mourning of the deceased remain. In the south of Kazakhstan men also mourn the deceased. Then the deceased is wrapped in a carpet, tied up with threads three times and taken outside, put on a clean place; a prayer is said. The fabrics put on the carpet with which the deceased was wrapped up are taken by the mullah and representatives of the kozha family. After the prayer the representatives of the kozha family and the mullah take the redemptive sacrifice. Then the body of the deceased is taken to the grave. When the body of the woman is carried out an essential condition is loud mourning of the deceased. Only men go to the grave. The people who come to the commemoration are given pieces of cloth.

There are several types of commemoration: day of death, 3 days, 7 days, 40 days, 100 days, a year. Among them the day of death, 3 days, 40 days and year are the most important. The next year a monument is erected on the grave. If there is an opportunity, it is better to put up a monument after 40 days, *i.e.*, before a year has passed.

On the monument the name, the surname, the middle name, the family, the date of birth and date of death are written. Also the moon, stars or the photo of the deceased are placed on it.

Thus, if the logical model of the concept "father" is presented by the following mental representations: *paternalism, kindness, superiority, domination, management, arrogance, etc.*, in language models the above concepts are presented as: *daddy, the father– top of mountains, the father– the defender, a good father for the child is the supporter for forty years, etc*. In language representations the image of the father is expressed in the following frames: *the man, the father, the grandfather, resolute,* in public aspect: *superiority, domination, management, etc.*

The concept finds such expression in the physiological aspect: the child (6-7 years of age), the childhood (8-12 years of age), the teenager (13-15 years of age), the young man (16-19 years of age), the young guy (20-30 years of age), the man in the pride of years (30-40 years of age), the man successor (in an interval between 40-50 years of age), the man of middle age (in an interval between 50-60 years of age), black-bearded (in an interval between 60-70 years of age), a white-bearded aksakal (in an interval between 70-80 years of age), the old man, the aged man (over 80 years of age). From the point of view of the psychological aspect an affective feeling of perception is given through steady language frames: careful father, paternal kindness, good grandfather, beloved daddy.

CONCLUSION

So, in the light of cognitive linguistics language and culture, continuity between people is the result of understanding of reality created in human consciousness. Due to the language all mankind develops and prospers. Therefore, the tool of relationship between people is language in which customs and traditions, moral values, mentality and religion, history and culture are preserved. In a word, each word, each value implies the national motive, the national core, the past and the future. At the heart of the concept considered by us the image of the father understood by the Kazakh people, the role which is carried out by him in a family, his social position, authority among people is implied.

Throughout centuries the Kazakh people perceive the father as a valorous, honest man who always keeps his word. Modern society was divided into two categories of men and women welcoming polygamy. Early marriages for bride wealth became a norm of comparison of the type: "the daughter is someone else's", or "a woman has long hair but no mind". The Kazakh people listen to the man, respect and obey him. There are authoritative men sent by god. Generally people say "the man is the head, the woman is the neck, the father is the branch, the child is the leaf" or "a good wife will make a bad husband good". It shows conditions of everyday life of people.

Each nation is rich with the language, eloquent words, and popular wisdom. For example, people say, "Even if you are hungry for six days, respect your parents" "Respect the father at home, the mother all over the country." These proverbs of the Kazakh people express their attitude towards parents. Therefore, such concepts as "father", "mother", "child", "family" are highly valued and find expression in simple words. The role of the father among the Kazakh people is great, as basically the Kazakh families are patriarchal. Such words as *the father's order, the father's power, the father's blessing, and the father's reputation* found reflection in the national literature. The concept "father" is "not only an embodiment of courage, strictness, force, but also of kindness, care, favor.

In summary it would be desirable to note that the concept "father" can be considered not only from the point of view of language, but also as a cognitive model, which finds language representation through lexical and grammatical groups, proverbs and sayings, phraseological units and aphorisms.

LITERATURE

[1] Argynbaev, Kh. (1996). Kazakh otbassy: Kazakh otbassynyn keshegessi men bygingissi zhaiyndagygylymi-zerteu enbek. - Almaty: Kainar, p. 288.

[2] Adambayev, B. (1996). Khalyk danalygy. Almaty: Rauan, p. 160.

[3] Zhanpeisova, N.M. (2003). Representation of national spheres of concept in the worldview of the Kazakh-Russian bilinguals: Theoretical aspects. – Almaty: DOIVA – Bratstvo, p. 195.

[4] Aynalayyn, Mataikyzy D. (2004). Zhobanyn avtory M. Kemel. Astana: Audarma, p. 104.

[5] Niyazbekov, M. (1992). Biz kalai tuysamyz? – Almaty: Oner, p. 48.

Subjet Index

A

Active learning 25, 58, 60, 68
Active participation 59, 63
Activities/Tasks 199, 207
Adolescents 145, 146, 155, 156
Anti-national event 50
Assessment tools 59, 64
Attitude 145, 146, 147, 150
Awareness 71, 72, 73, 74
Axiology 147, 148, 155

B

Behavior 148, 149, 150, 151
Behavioural assessment 265, 267, 290
Behavioural model 275
Behavioural pattern 266, 268, 279, 280
Brainstorming 82
Business 249, 250, 251, 252
Business model 2502, 254, 256, 259

C

Case studies 172, 183, 190
Chemistry teaching 204
Chile and Peru 172
Clippings from movie and excerpts from novels 82
Coca-Cola issue in Kerala 81
Co-existence 87, 104, 109
Cognitive linguistics 318, 319, 334
Cognitive processes 226, 235
Collaborative learning 62, 63, 67
Collaborative learning technologies 81
Colombia 172, 180, 181, 183
Communication skills 71, 75, 81
Communicative language teaching 71, 72, 75, 83
Competitive advantage 27, 35, 41, 43, 250, 254, 260, 261
Composition 224, 225, 227, 237
Content 197, 198, 199, 200
Contents of didactic unities 198, 200
  Attitudinal 200, 204, 207, 208
  Conceptual 200, 204, 207, 208
  Procedural 200, 204, 207, 208
Critical cultural 74
Culturally Responsive Pedagogy (CRP) framework 83
Cultural barriers 73
Cultural insensitivity 81
Culturally Responsive Pedagogy (CRP) 77
Culturally-grounded learning 78
Curricular knowledge 201, 202
Customs and traditions 334

D

Data analysis 312
Decision-making 301, 302
Definition 74
Dependency 304, 305, 306, 308

Didactic unit 197, 199, 200, 201
Differences of perceptions 80
Discourse competence 71

E

Economic development 298, 299
Economic growth 304
Ecuadorian companies 41
Editing 226, 228, 244
Education 46, 48, 49, 50, 86, 87, 101, 103, 114, 115, 118, 120, 145, 146, 154, 161, 171, 172, 173, 174
Education foreign direct investment 5
Employee motivation 2502, 252, 253
Employment 114, 117, 118, 121
Energy consumption 265, 266, 267, 268
Energy culture framework 265, 278
Energy saving 266, 268, 280, 281
Engaged learner 58
Ethics of values 147
Euro disney failure 81
Evaluation 199, 200, 207, 208
Existential harmony 87, 88, 90, 93
Existential orders/systems 88, 89, 92, 103

F

Facilities management 286, 290
Facilities manager 265, 266, 268, 288
Faculty recruitment 22
Family 145, 146, 151, 152
Family relations 151, 152, 154, 155
Father of advanced age 320
Father of middle age 320
Feedback 58, 59, 60, 62
Firm performance 28, 31, 33, 37
Foreign directinvestment 1, 4, 5, 6
Forming 66

G

Global citizenship education 82
Grey areas 123
Group dynamics 66, 69
Group processes 59, 69

H

Harmonious education 86, 87, 108, 111
Harmony 86, 87, 88, 89
Holistic 86, 89

I

Impact 27, 28, 32, 37
Infrastructure planning 171, 173, 175
Innovation 1, 3, 4, 11, 27, 28, 29, 31, 249, 250, 252, 253
Innovation activities 27, 28
Innovation types 27, 28, 37
Institutional arrangements 172, 174, 175, 180
Integral sustainable infrastructure planning 172
Integrated model 271
Interconnected 92, 96, 99, 100
Intercultural communication 71
Intercultural sensitivity 82
International business 75
Intrinsic motivation 79
Invention and Innovation 17, 18
Investment 27, 29, 31, 35, 172, 174, 175

K

Kazakh conceptual system 319, 320
Kazakh national spirit 318
Kazakh people 317, 318, 323, 324
Knowledge base 201
Knowledge transfer 78

L

L2 teaching 71
Language pedagogy 74
Language proficiency 241, 243, 244
Language skills 75
Learning by reflecting on action 203
Learning strategies 60
Lifestyle 266, 267, 270, 271

M

Madhyasthdarshan 89, 91
Malaysian universities 265, 286, 290

Man language culture 318
Management 250, 2547, 258, 259
Managing multiplicity 72
Market performance 35, 42
Maternity hospital 324, 325
Meaning changes 233
Meaning-making 78
Mentality 318, 330, 334
Mercedes benz conflict 81
Misunderstandings 73
Model solution 312
Mother-in-law 323, 325, 329, 330
Movie and excerpts from novels 82

N

National concept 317, 318, 319
Nature of education 48
Norming 66

O

Observable 81
Online video conference 82
Organizational innovations 28
Organizational culture 249, 250, 251, 252
Organizational change 249, 257, 258, 259
Organizational effectiveness 46, 52, 55, 56
Organizational performance 27, 35, 41, 43, 249
Organizational success 261

P

Parents 152, 153, 155, 156
Peace 86, 87, 98, 101
Pedagogic innovation 58
Pedagogical knowledge matter 201
Performing 66, 67
Personality development 23
Philosophy of peace 103
Pragmatic 73, 75
Pragmatic competence 73, 75
Problematic situation 197, 199, 200, 205
Production management 300, 301, 315
Program 146, 161, 163, 165
Public investment 172, 173, 180, 183
Public management 172, 178, 182

Q

Quality Management Systems (QMS) concept 54
Quality education 50, 51
Quality in higher education 1, 2, 4, 6

R

Readiness to the future family life 154
Reading 228, 229, 230, 231
Recursive 226
Reflection 59, 61, 69
Reflection of the Kazakh Culture in Language317
Reflections and language production 81
Research and Development (R&D) 31, 34,43
Reviewing 227, 228
Revision 224, 225, 226, 228
Revision models 228
Rhetorical analysis 81
Role model 63, 67
Rural family 161, 162
Rural school 145, 146, 159, 160
Rural schoolchildren 145, 146

S

Sanatana dharma 106, 107, 108
Science, Technology, situation Society and Environment (STSE) Education 200, 201, 206, 208
Self-actualization 149
Self-directed learning 62
Silver-linings 114, 119
Skill 114, 115, 116, 117
Skill training 114, 116, 117, 118
Small group 57, 58, 59, 60
South Africa 172, 178, 179, 180
Stages of revision 238
Storming 62, 66

Strategies 225, 226, 229, 230
Strategy 251, 254, 255, 257
Subject knowledge matter 201
Supportive environment 58, 65
Supportive learning environment 62, 63, 67
Surface changes 233
Syllabi development 24
Synchronous 82

T

Teacher 147, 160, 162, 164
Teacher-facilitator 58
Teaching methodology 25
Technical rationality model 203
Text modification 224, 229, 230, 239
The concept "father" 317, 319, 320, 333
The father's blessing 334
The father's order 334
The father's power 334
The father's reputation 334
Think-aloud 236, 237
Types of innovation 27, 28, 32, 38
- Marketing innovation 32, 33, 36
- Process innovation 28, 32, 33, 36
- Product innovation 32, 33, 37, 38

U

United Kingdom 172, 174, 175, 180
Universality 107, 108

V

Valuable relation to the family 146, 153, 155, 158
Value 145, 146, 147, 148
Value attitude 147
Value attitude to the family 145, 152, 153, 166
Value orientation 147, 150, 151, 166
Value relation 145, 151, 153, 155
Value-conscious attitude 145, 146
Values 251, 258, 259, 260
Values education 87, 103
Verbal protocols 238, 240, 241
Village 146, 159, 160, 161

W

Walmart debacle 81
Writing models 226, 231
Writing process 224, 225, 226, 227

Y

Young father 320
YouTube 82